JOHN DEWEY'S ETHICS

JOHN DEWEY'S
ETHICS

DEMOCRACY AS EXPERIENCE

Gregory Fernando Pappas

Indiana University Press

BLOOMINGTON AND INDIANAPOLIS

This book is a publication of

Indiana University Press
601 North Morton Street
Bloomington, IN 47404-3797 USA

http://iupress.indiana.edu

Telephone orders   800-842-6796
Fax orders   812-855-7931
Orders by e-mail   iuporder@indiana.edu

MANUFACTURED IN THE UNITED STATES OF AMERICA

Library of Congress Cataloging-in-Publication Data

Pappas, Gregory Fernando, date
    John Dewey's ethics : democracy as experience / Gregory Fernando Pappas.
       p. cm. — (American philosophy)
    Includes bibliographical references (p.   ) and index.
    ISBN-13: 978-0-253-35140-1 (cloth : alk. paper)
    ISBN-13: 978-0-253-21979-4 (pbk. : alk. paper) 1. Dewey, John, 1859–1952—Ethics. I. Title.
B945.D44P37 2008
171'.2—dc22

                                                                        2007046929

            1 2 3 4 5   13 12 11 10 09 08

Para Beatriz, John, y Fema

CONTENTS

PART TWO
DEWEY'S VIEW OF MORAL EXPERIENCE

PART THREE
THE IDEAL MORAL LIFE

PREFACE

It is one of the delights of authorship that one can publicly express one's gratitude to those who helped along the way. And this book is to a large extent the product of my very fortunate interaction with many people at different stages of my inquiry. I am grateful to my dear colleague John J. McDermott for his advice and support throughout the years, and for stressing the importance of living aesthetically. I learned how to approach pragmatism from my friend and mentor, Douglas Browning, to whom I owe my deepest gratitude. As a teacher, Browning's radical approach to the classical American pragmatists is to try to read them as openly, honestly, and empathetically as possible; in other words, we must try to understand their philosophies on their own terms. A text is, of course, subject to a plurality of reasonable interpretations, but too many philosophers cannot help but read their own theoretical commitments into the text. In doing so, many have missed Dewey's radical reconstruction of philosophy. In particular, Browning tirelessly insists that we must pay attention to what Dewey himself tells us in regard to the proper way of engaging in philosophical inquiry.

The message from Dewey is clear. The practical stance of everyday life has been neglected in philosophy when it should be the primary focal point for philosophical inquiry. The legitimate starting and ending point for any philosophical investigation is our own everyday, concrete experience, that is, nothing more or less than that which appears, rough-and-tumble as it usually does, in our lives from day to day. This book grew as a project to make sense of what Dewey wrote about moral life, keeping in mind his commitment to starting with everyday experience. But I also wanted to make explicit Dewey's most fundamental moral commitments or ideals and explore whether they cohere with and are supported by his philosophy. I quickly realized that given the organic character of Dewey's thought, and the centrality of his moral commitments throughout his life, that it would be difficult to write a book on Dewey's ethics without also writing a book about his entire philosophy. I dealt with this tension by aiming at a comprehensive interpretation of John Dewey's moral philosophy that also provides further support for a particular interpretation of his entire philosophy. Dewey's philosophy is an effort to establish the reasonableness of a certain vision about how to live. For Dewey, democracy is part of a general moral outlook about how to engage in life. These were my working assumptions throughout this inquiry.

In my efforts to provide a full-blown exposition of Dewey's moral philosophy I benefited from reading the important work of Jim Gouinlock, Todd Lekan, Jennifer Welchman, and Steven Fesmire on different aspects of Dewey's ethics. I am also grateful to them for their criticisms, suggestions, and encouragement to complete my project. Many people kindly agreed to read parts or early versions of the evolving manuscript and provided useful suggestions. David Hildebrand read an early draft of the manuscript; Todd Lekan, Bill Myers, and Shannon Sullivan wrote detailed comments about the entire manuscript; Steven Fesmire helped me formulate what distinguished Dewey's ethics from that of others; and Derrick Darby and Vincent Colapietro helped me think through revisions of some key points of the final manuscript. Thanks to them all.

Thanks to Colin Koopman, Robert Kane, and Robert Talisse for their comments and help on the chapters about democracy. Everyone at Indiana University Press has been splendid, especially Dee Mortensen, Robert A. Crouch, and John Stuhr. I appreciated their many suggestions throughout the process of bringing the book to press. The conferences of the Society for the Advancement of American Philosophy and my graduate seminars at Texas A&M have been great opportunities to try out my ideas. Thanks to Jim Garrison, Raymond Boisvert, James Campbell, Doug Anderson, John Shook, John Capps, Tom Burke, Judith Green, Bill Gavin, Patrick Dooley, and my graduate philosophy students (too many to mention) for asking such good questions. Special thanks are owed to the late Ralph Sleeper, Tom Alexander, my former dear colleague Larry Hickman, Michael Eldridge, Peter Hare, Jorge Gracia, and Charlene Seigfried for their encouragement over a long period and the example they set. I am indebted to Ronald Chichester, who painstakingly worked through many chapters to improve the prose. I am extremely grateful to my parents, John and Fema, and my wife, Beatriz, for being unending sources of patience, support, care, and advice. What good fortune to have them in my life!

I am also happy to acknowledge institutional support I received. A Ford Foundation Postdoctoral Fellowship from the National Research Council (Sept 1991–May 1992) allowed me to conduct the initial research for this book. Research at the Dewey Center at Southern Illinois University was kindly facilitated by Larry Hickman and his staff. And a 1998–1999 Faculty Development Leave from Texas A&M University let me devote myself fully to writing this book.

Portions of part 1 are drawn from my "Dewey's Ethics: Morality as Experience," in *Reading Dewey: Interpretive Essays for a Postmodern Generation*, ed. Larry A. Hickman (Bloomington: Indiana University Press, 1998), 100–123; "New Directions and Uses in the Reconstruction of John Dewey's Ethics," in *In Dewey's Wake: Unfinished Work of Pragmatic Reconstruction*, ed. William J. Gavin (Albany, N.Y.: State University of New York Press, 2002), 41–62; and "Dewey's Moral Theory: Experience as Method," *Transactions of the Charles S. Peirce Society* 33, no. 3 (1997): 520–556. Portions of part 2 are drawn from my "To Be or To Do: John Dewey and the Great Divide in Ethics," *History of Philosophy Quarterly* 14, no. 4 (1997): 447–468; and "Dewey and Feminism: The Affective and Relationships in Dewey's Ethics," *Hypatia* 8, no. 2 (1993): 78–95. And portions of part 3 are drawn from my "Open-mindedness and Courage: Complementary Virtues of Pragmatism," *Transactions of the Charles S. Peirce Society* 32, no. 2 (1996): 316–335. I am grateful to the editors and publishers of these books and journals for permission to reprint material here. I also gratefully acknowledge the Banco de Mexico for permission to use Diego Rivera's "Retrato de John Dewey" on the book cover.

ABBREVIATIONS

Citations of John Dewey's works are to the thirty-seven volume critical edition published by Southern Illinois University Press under the editorship of Jo Ann Boydston. Citations give text abbreviation, series abbreviation, followed by volume number and page number.

Series abbreviations for *The Collected Works:*
EW   The Early Works (1882–1898)
MW   The Middle Works (1899–1924)
LW   The Later Works (1925–1953)

JOHN DEWEY'S ETHICS

Introduction

In this book, I present the first comprehensive interpretation of John Dewey's original and revolutionary moral philosophy.[1] Dewey had a cohesive and coherent ethics developed in many writings that spanned his long career. It is a moral philosophy that provides answers to questions raised by moral agents in the midst of living, such as: How should we live? How should we approach moral problems and reach moral judgments? And: How should we settle moral disagreement? Dewey wanted to provide better answers to these moral questions than had traditional ethical theory. Achieving this goal required that he critically engage tradition at a fundamental level by examining common starting assumptions about moral experience and how to do ethics. This is one reason why it is impossible to place Dewey's ethics in traditional pigeonholes.[2] The upshot, as I will argue, is an alternative normative and positive view, one that is both plausible and compelling. Dewey's moral philosophy is also the key to understanding the rest of his philosophy, in particular, his conception and defense of democracy.

Dewey's Reconstruction of Moral Philosophy

In the second half of the twentieth century, modern moral theory came under attack. Many consider G. E. M. Anscombe's 1958 essay "Modern Moral Philosophy" as marking the beginning of this critique. Before then, however, Dewey had already embarked on a criticism of the philosophical assumptions that had characterized ethical theory since Kant and Mill. The linguistic turn at the beginning of the twentieth century was hardly a radical turn from these assumptions. Dewey's reconstructive proposal for ethical theory is not, however, that we must stop doing moral philosophy "until we have an adequate philosophy of psychology"[3] or that we need to return exclusively to the concerns that today define virtue ethics. Dewey proposes instead that philosophers must make an honest effort to take, as a proper starting point, moral experience *as it is experienced*. Hence, my task is first to make explicit what this starting point amounts to (part 1), and then to show its consequences and implications for ethics. Dewey's view of moral life (part 2) and his normative ethics (part 3) are the upshot of this new starting point.

Dewey proposes that in moral life, duty, virtue, and the good have their irreducible and proper place. We need not choose between deontology, virtue ethics, and consequentialism. Dewey includes and reconciles ideas about moral life that, from the point of view of these other theories, may seem incompatible. Dewey's insights are attractive in light of today's growing awareness of the reductionistic and myopic character of modern ethics. However, the challenge today is to present an inclusive and pluralistic account of moral life that is both unified and coherent. Dewey's ethics is not the result of ad hoc moves, nor is it a matter of adding together the insights of others. Instead, it is an ethics that is the result of a reconstruction that abandons the assumptions that have forced us to take sides, and it is one that reveals a moral life that is rich and complex.

Dewey once explained that the radical empiricism he shared with William James yielded two kinds of contributions for philosophy. One contribution is to provide answers to old problems, while the other advances philosophy by undercutting the genuineness of certain problems.[4] Dewey felt that there are questions insufficiently grounded in everyday moral experience that continue to be divisive among philosophers. There are also other questions, he thought, whose legitimacy is based on the assumption that there are no alternatives to extreme options. Dewey undercuts these kinds of questions in order to clear the way for his own answers to legitimate traditional questions, and he proposes and defends new tasks for ethical theory.

In presenting Dewey's rich account of moral experience, I will highlight both the differences and the continuities between Dewey's thought and the assumptions of mainstream ethical theory. If there is more emphasis on the differences, it is only because I believe that we have yet to appreciate the distinctiveness of Dewey's ethical thought, and how it departs from traditional alternatives. Dewey reconstructs traditional conceptions of the moral self, of deliberation and of moral problems. He points to dimensions of moral life that tend to be overlooked and undervalued in much modern ethical thought, but that are increasingly of interest in contemporary ethical theory. Moreover, a growing body of research in social psychology and cognitive science has begun to offer an alternate picture of moral judgment and of moral deliberation that is very much like Dewey's. For example, Mark Johnson claims that: "The issue of the role of feelings in thought is one area in which cooperative cognitive science is perhaps only recently catching up with the early arguments of James and Dewey."[5] A comprehensive reconstruction of Dewey's ethics is needed so that it can be used to revitalize ethical theory.

A full engagement of Dewey in mainstream moral debates is beyond the scope of this book. I weigh in on some of the most important contemporary debates, but I limit such discussions in order to maintain the focus and unity of the whole. I hope that my comments about contemporary debates will be sufficiently provocative to encourage those who are familiar with mainstream ethics to engage Dewey and to take his ethics seriously. I also hope that what I have done in this regard is enough to assist or to inspire other Deweyans to pursue this line of inquiry further than I have. There needs to be a more detailed consideration of the arguments and views in current moral theory from a Deweyan perspective. My present project, however, issues a warning: we must not become so eager to become part of the mainstream philosophical dialogue that we compromise Dewey's unique and most worthwhile contributions. The Dewey who is worth reconstructing is often the one who calls into question the basic assumptions that ground present debates. A selective reconsideration of Dewey's ethics fails to represent the more radical Dewey and may amount to a failure to use his approach in the most productive way.

In many cases, to understand Dewey's ethics requires that we divest ourselves of traditional pictures and look at things from a new angle. This is not easy. I will try to help the reader by explicitly contrasting Dewey to philosophers who take more traditional approaches. Sometimes, however, contrast is not enough. One has to count on the reader to consult his or her own experience. In fact, as a philosopher Dewey did not just appeal to arguments; his denotative method often implied an invitation of the following sort: "If you want to understand and verify what I am talking about, please try to put aside for the moment all of the theories of moral life that you know, and instead consult your everyday, gross, and crude experience of moral decisions and problems."

Three Facets of Dewey's Ethics

Providing a unifying account of Dewey's moral philosophy requires that I show how his contributions to ethics are interrelated. His contributions result from a larger inquiry grounded on the same core commitments, and are not just a collection of disparate philosophical insights about morality. Dewey's ethics cannot be understood in isolation from the larger fabric of the whole of his philosophy, and his ethics cannot be judged or appreciated from the standpoint of assumptions that are foreign to his wider philosophy. The holistic character of his philosophy should not be considered a weakness; on the contrary, it is something that Dewey shares with great ethical thinkers like Kant and Aristotle.

Moreover, Dewey's ethics is the key to understanding his wider philosophy. He had a lifelong preoccupation with democracy, which for him was a *moral* ideal. Dewey also wrote that his

> choice of intelligence as the preferred method of action implies, like every choice, a definitive moral outlook. The scope of this choice is so inclusive that the implication outlines, when followed out, an entire ethical and social philosophy. (LW 8:101)

Dewey, however, did not consolidate his ideas about moral philosophy in any single work. The few books in which Dewey focused explicitly on ethics were textbooks and syllabi, written primarily for classroom work and not intended to be systematic theoretical formulations. It would have been fitting for him to write one more revision of his 1932 edition of *Ethics* (with James Hayden Tufts), not as a textbook, but as a more comprehensive and definitive rendition of his moral thought in light of the philosophical commitments that distinguished his philosophical outlook. The present book is the one that Dewey should have written on his moral philosophy.

In my effort to bring Dewey's scattered contributions to moral philosophy into a cohesive moral vision, I borrow from all phases of his work to find the best formulations of his theses. My presentation of Dewey's ethics will not be chronological. Dewey's ideas about ethics, just as his ideas about other subjects, underwent gradual but continual reconstruction during the seventy-one years that constituted his public career.[6] Although these modifications are important, they are not substantial or drastic enough to support a sharp distinction between an early and a late Dewey. It is more accurate to say that Dewey developed his views about moral experience early in his career, and that he then tended to revise his thinking as the implications of his views became apparent and as he felt the need to present his case in deeper detail or broader scope.[7] There is a gradual shift from an ethics of self-realization to a mature pluralistic ethics that came as a result of acquiring a better phenomenological sensitivity to moral experience.[8] In his ethics and his more general philosophy, Dewey was increasingly faithful to his early commitment to a radical empiricism, that is, to a description of how experience is experienced in all of its complexity and details.[9] His later ethical writings reveal a more acute awareness of the pluralism in moral experience, of the indeterminacies and elements of novelty in situations, of the importance of the affective or qualitative, and of the social and instrumental nature of our character.[10] The works that best represent Dewey's mature treatment of ethics are: *Democracy and Education* (1916); *Reconstruction in Philosophy* (1920); *Human Nature and Conduct* (1922); "Three Independent Factors in Morals" (1930); and *Ethics* (1932).

Unlike many contemporary approaches to ethics, Dewey's moral thought does not rest on a set of postulates and arguments that constitute a formal ethical system. Instead, he criticizes the tradition while simultaneously offering the reader a hypothetical account of moral experience and proposing commitments that he sometimes left unstated. Nevertheless, in presenting Dewey's ethics, one must have a focus and a principle of organization, and this book is so organized.

I explain Dewey's views in three parts. Each of the book's three parts corresponds to a different area of moral philosophy and a corresponding aspect of Dewey's ethics:

1) Meta-theory or Method of Inquiry: a critical stand on the limits, nature, problems, and function of the type of inquiry that takes our moral experience as its subject matter;
2) Descriptive Ethics or Metaphysics of Morals: a treatment of the generic traits and components of moral experience; and
3) Normative Ethics: a constructive, though not explicitly articulated, proposal regarding how we should live, that is, how to interact in morally problematic situations.

These facets of Dewey's ethics are found intertwined throughout his writings. His philosophical investigations into each of these areas led him to continuously develop, modify, and refine the others. Should each part be read in the order presented? I think one will find it easier to understand, or even embrace, Dewey's normative proposals (part 3) once one has dispelled the kind of theoretical skepticism that is encountered at the meta-ethical level (part 1), and once one appreciates Dewey's view of our moral experience (part 2). The lessons learned from the first two parts strike me as fundamental to avoid misunderstandings about the nature and the limitation of Dewey's proposals outlined in part 3. Nevertheless, each part is sufficiently independent that readers can start with the material about the aspects of Dewey's ethics they find most interesting, and only then return to the book's other parts. For example, those more interested in moral education and democracy, and who are already familiar with Dewey's most basic methodological and philosophical assumptions, may want to begin with part 3.

Although all the parts of this book are important to my overarching aim, there is an obvious emphasis on the normative in Dewey's thought. Dewey's philosophy is an effort to establish the reasonableness of a certain vision about how to live. This normative emphasis is in accord with the same reconstructive spirit of Dewey's ethics, and with his view that philosophies embody "not colorless intellectual readings of reality, but men's most passionate desires and hopes, their basic beliefs about *the sort of life to be lived*" (MW 11:44, my emphasis). Skepticism in regard to normative ethical theory is common in the contemporary intellectual climate. Many believe that recent global events, such as 9/11, have made us more aware of "the ineliminable diversity of moral convictions among the people's of the earth."[11] Joseph Margolis claims that these events "lend an unexpected legitimacy to questioning whether what we call ethics or moral philosophy may not, after all, be deeply and terribly wrongheaded."[12] Normative ethics is also not something that most people associate with pragmatism. Instead, pragmatism is associated with ethical skepticism and ethical relativism. For example, Richard Posner thinks that pragmatism's skepticism about moral ideals is worth reconstructing. For Posner, pragmatism means "practical and business-like, 'no-nonsense,' disdainful of abstract theory and intellectual pretension, [and] contemptuous of moralizers and utopian dreamers."[13] On the other hand, pragmatic arguments against moral absolutes, or against fixed and final ends, have led many to be concerned about the moral consequences of pragmatism. In the words of Jeffrey Stout,

> [P]ragmatism, so its critics say, leads to unwelcome consequences in ethics and may even contribute to the collapse of all we hold dear. . . . Is not pragmatism itself an expression of modernist decadence, what a MacIntyre might call emotivism American style? Doesn't it induce in its

6

adherents a kind of moral aphasia, an inability to talk back in the face of generalized tyranny? Can any moral language worthy of use survive for more than a moment if defended primarily in pragmatic terms?[14]

Although Louis Menand's thesis that "pragmatism arose out of disillusionment with postures of moral certitude"[15] is true, pragmatists also had a disgust for postures of moral skepticism, moral relativism, and the evils of moral anarchy. In fact, the more I read Dewey's ethics, the more I became convinced that his ethics arose out of disillusionment with extremist postures and the inability to appreciate any possibility of moving beyond them in moral life. Is the only alternative to the moral certainty provided by absolutism the absence of any basis to come to reasonable and objective moral judgments in a situation? If there is no ultimate criterion of right and wrong, then is anything at all allowed? If one is committed to a pluralistic democratic society, then must one embrace complete neutrality or relativism in regard to moral issues? In the end, I was convinced that a careful consideration of Dewey's ethics and his views on moral experience would serve to debunk the assumptions that have led many to extremism in morality and the conclusion that "as a general philosophy, pragmatism does not seem to offer a guide to life's perplexity."[16] Such a consideration requires nothing less than a full-blown exposition of Dewey's moral philosophy and this is what prompted my inquiry into Dewey's moral thought.

The tarnished reputation of pragmatism in ethics is, in part, a consequence of the selective overuse of the critical tools of pragmatism without adoption or acknowledgment of the positive commitments that grounded them. I not only unearth and reconstruct these positive normative proposals, but I also show that they are compatible with Dewey's contextualism and with his severe criticism of traditional normative ethical theories. The challenge for a pragmatist ethical theory today, as I see it, is not just to be critical and edifying, but to provide an ethics sufficiently robust to be taken seriously as something that may assist us in moral life.

Dewey's Ethics and His Philosophy of Experience and Democracy

Dewey's ethics is the key to his entire philosophy. It is essential for understanding how his empiricism led him to a radical turn in philosophy, one that recognizes the importance of the present, context, and the qualitative. Dewey stood traditional ethics—which takes reasoning, justification, and judgments as matters of working downward from rules to situations—

on its head. In contrast to traditional ethics, Dewey took what is local, unique, qualitative, and ineffable as starting points and as the basis of what is universal and cognitive. At the very least, a fuller appreciation of Dewey's ethics may serve to correct interpretations of Dewey that overemphasize pragmatism's concern for instruments, the cognitive, and the future. Indeed, a comprehensive treatment of Dewey's moral theory reveals a more balanced picture of Dewey's overall thought than is often assumed. For example, there is a common tension today among Deweyans who locate the center of gravity of Dewey's corpus in *Art as Experience* (and who thus downplay the role of science), and those who locate it in his *Logic* and instrumentalism. From the standpoint of Dewey's ethics, these two views seem one-sided and reinforce the contemporary polarization between science and art that Dewey considered detrimental to the lessons that can be learned from each for a balanced moral life. He wrote,

> Surely there is no more significant question before the world than this question of the possibility and method of reconciliation of the attitudes of practical science and contemplative aesthetic appreciation. Without the former, man will be the sport and victim of natural forces which he cannot use or control. Without the latter, mankind might become a race of economic monsters, restlessly driving hard bargains with nature and with one another, bored with leisure or capable of putting it to use only in ostentatious display and extravagant dissipation. Like other moral questions, this matter is social and even political. (MW 12:152–153)

In this book, I argue that the intelligent and aesthetic are mutually dependent aspects or qualifications of a single normative moral vision. They are integral aspects of Dewey's ideal self and democratic community.

Dewey's ethics is crucial for understanding his socio-political thought. In spite of the fact that Dewey referred to democracy as a *moral* ideal, commentators and critics often segregate Dewey's views on democracy from his moral thought on the assumption that his views on politics and social thought can be understood on their own. What would happen if instead we treated Dewey's view of democracy as an extension of his ethics? This is my venture in part 3. I will consider Dewey's democratic ideal from the standpoint of his ethics rather than from the context of the history of American Liberalism or socio-political theory. This approach yields definite benefits worth mentioning in this introduction.

It is common today to find extensive criticisms of formalistic and procedural visions of democracy. Cornel West, for example, has recently argued that "to focus solely on electoral politics as the site of democratic life is myopic. Such a focus fails to appreciate the crucial role of the underlying moral commitments and visions and fortifications of the soul that empower and inspire a democratic way of living in the world."[17] Scholars have recently recognized how much more substantive Dewey's view of democracy is than the prevalent political notions of democracy. As Robert Westbrook says, "Whereas Dewey called for the shaping of a democratic character and the creation of a democratic culture . . . other liberals have moved to strip democracy of its positive, substantive claims in order to render it a purely negative, procedural doctrine."[18] But the most difficult and necessary task for Deweyans is to provide some convincing substance and depth to the notion that democracy is a way of life. I believe that the required resources are found in Dewey's ethics. It is in Dewey's ethics that we find the particular virtues, relationships, and experiences that make his view of democracy substantive. In fact, understanding Dewey's views of democracy from the standpoint of his ethics reveals a much more radical view of democracy than often assumed.

Dewey's ethics is also a resource for answering the recent skeptical challenges regarding the justification of democracy, especially if we surrender belief in natural rights and a fixed human nature. This challenge has even been posed by pragmatists such as Richard Rorty who argues that we must abandon, once and for all, the notion that we can provide a philosophical justification for democracy. The character of justification available to a pragmatist for her democratic hopes and inspirations cannot be discussed independently of her view of moral experience, ideals, and judgments. It is, however, amazing and disturbing how many of Dewey's critics and sympathizers continue to presuppose that, though his politics is grounded in his ethics, his ethics contains an ultimate criterion for all value judgments. Furthermore, they presuppose that self-realization, human fulfillment, or growth is the good that is provided by democracy; they maintain, in other words, that Dewey is committed to some form of consequentialism or a teleological view.[19] Yet I intend to show how Dewey's criticism of these views is unequivocal, and that his ethics has the resources to provide a very different way of establishing the reasonableness of democracy.

Perhaps the most important benefit that comes from reassessing Dewey's ethics is its capacity to shed light on our contemporary situation. As Hilary Putnam has recently written,

> I believe that Dewey's perceptive and realistic refusal to reduce ethics to a single biological trait (such as sympathy) or to any single concern or to any one rule or system of rules, coupled, as it was, with his insistence that nonetheless intelligence—*situated* intelligence—is both possible and

necessary in the resolution of political and ethical problems, makes him particularly relevant to our time.[20]

The continued relevance of Dewey's ethics may be because the conditions that we are today unhappy with are very similar to the conditions with which Dewey was himself discontent. It is remarkable how our moral practice today suffers from the same types of problems that Dewey experienced and that grounded his inquiries in ethics. Moral anarchy and the moral rigidity of absolutism are for many the only viable options. Today, morality is still conceived and practiced as an area of our experience that is somewhat remote or separated from our daily affairs. Moral values and concerns are not organically integrated in the decisions and operations of our business transactions and institutions. We still suffer from the same dualisms that lead to extremism and polarization. Dewey's notion of an ideal self and community continues to be appealing as a source of direction and hope in our fragmented and pluralistic society.

Dewey seems prophetic at times about the problems that a world like ours would have to face, especially if we care about democracy. We have found new situations in which the values implicit in democracy seem in conflict. How do we reconcile freedom and tolerance with equality, fraternity, and order? The struggle for a more democratic world is far from over. Even in societies with a political democracy there is a growing concern about the deterioration of public discourse and of communal bonds, and the transformation of citizens into apathetic consumers. We are learning, as Dewey once told us, that conditions for genuine democracy are not just political. As Mark Malloch Brown, administrator of the United Nations Development Programme, concluded after the launch of their report, "the international cheerleaders for democracy have underestimated what it takes to build a functioning, properly rooted democracy."[21] We are also learning that a democratic way of life is not something that can be forced, exported, or implanted. As journalist Steven Erlanger says, reflecting on recent efforts at democratization around the world,

> Democracy, in other words, grows out of a nation's history and experiences. It can't be inserted like a silicone implant or put on like a new hat. Nor can it be imposed, even by the most well meaning or well armed. Democracy can be nurtured, even fertilized. But one need only read a few pages of Churchill's "History of English-Speaking Peoples" to realize how tender a plant it is, and how aberrant.[22]

With this, history has validated a central tenet of Dewey's ethics: moral amelioration or democratization must grow from within, and, while it is not altogether under anyone's control, we can inquire about the indirect conditions by which a better moral life may grow. In this book, I present the philosophical underpinnings of this humble but positive tenet.

The Centrality of Experience in Dewey's Philosophy

This book is informed by, and intends to provide further support for, a particular interpretation of Dewey's entire philosophy. The notion of lived experience goes to the heart of Dewey's philosophy, where this implies both: A) a method of doing philosophy; and B) a commitment or faith that grounded his philosophical project and ideals. I agree with Thomas Alexander that Dewey's 1905 essay, "The Postulate of Immediate Empiricism," "is one of the most radical and revolutionary pieces Dewey wrote."[23] In that essay, Dewey explicitly and firmly allies himself with the radical empiricism of William James, or with what he later characterized in *Experience and Nature* as the "empirical denotative method." To be empirical in philosophy, however, is not to be scientific but instead to take experience as the starting point. If this notion is difficult to understand, it is only because of problems with the word 'experience'. To take experience as the starting point is simply to begin where we are, not with a theory, but with what is pre-theoretically given in the midst of our lives. To be empirical in Dewey's sense is to be a contextualist, but the ultimate context is the stream of unique and qualitative situations that make up our lives. Dewey's experience-centric approach runs counter to the neopragmatist disregard for experience[24] and to the narrow interpretation of pragmatism as an instrumentalist method to determine the meaning of concepts, such as truth.[25] My interpretation of Dewey also goes against attempts to get at the heart of Dewey's philosophy by looking for some first thesis that he is trying to prove or to build upon. As Douglas Browning explains, the starting point of everyday experience has not received in Deweyan scholarship the attention it deserves.

> Understanding John Dewey's comprehensive and, in its details, dauntingly complex philosophy requires taking account of his view of the three essential phases of experience, namely, (1) the starting point in everyday experience of all of our attempts to enhance the meaning of our lives, (2) the process of the experiential transformation of such experience, and (3) the experience of consummatory achievement. Though much has been written about the last two phases and many scholars have centered their interpretations of Dewey on one or both of them, the first phase has been too often neglected. This is unfortunate, since Dewey's notion of experience, which is the key to grasping the

11

import of each of these phases, is initially shaped at the starting point and carried forward from it.[26]

Centering one's interpretation of Dewey on the starting point is not only justified by a careful reading of Dewey's texts, but it also has virtues for us today. First, it provides the basis by which we may criticize or revise Dewey's account and conclusions. We must be open to the possibility that some of his views may not fit experience as we find it today. Second, it allows us to construct a more inclusive or comprehensive understanding of Dewey. Scholars have disagreed in their formulation of the core project that drove Dewey's philosophical efforts. Is it, as Michael Eldridge has claimed, to "intelligize practice"? Is it, as suggested by Larry Hickman, to expand our understanding and appropriate use of technology? Is it, as Robert Westbrook has proposed, to re-define democracy? Or is it to recognize the aesthetic dimension of experience, as claimed by Thomas Alexander?[27] I would argue that these characterizations point to capacities of the starting point of everyday experience. All of them are correct about Dewey's ideal, but they are only parts of one cohesive vision that is grounded on a concern and commitment to experience. Dewey's ideal self and community are important in his answer to the question of how to live in light of a certain view of experience and under certain problematic conditions that characterize present existence.

Dewey was troubled by philosophers' disregard for experience, not only as a method of investigation or starting point, but for much deeper reasons. Experience, as a source of meaning and guidance, has been disregarded in philosophy. However, the problem extends beyond philosophy. There are complex and perhaps different historical reasons why, during Dewey's time and still today, people have failed to rely on and explore the possibilities for meaning and amelioration present in concrete, everyday life. But insofar as philosophy helps perpetuate this problem, criticism is needed to remove the obstacles, such as dualism, that keep us from trying Dewey's more promising direction. Of particular importance for Dewey is the fact that philosophy has continued to oscillate between extremes.

If there is one general concern that pervades Dewey's philosophy, it is one of ameliorating the quality of present experience by its own resources. It is true that Dewey wanted to inquire into the deeper possibilities of democracy, to find an alternative to moral absolutism and subjectivism, to procure a more organic relation between art, technology, business, and the sciences, and to extend the method of intelligence to all aspects of life. But these are all tasks promulgated by Dewey's underlying but very personal faith in experience. That is, for me, the ultimate glue of Dewey's vision. This insight highlights the importance of the mystical experience in Dewey's personal life where he felt suddenly that "everything that's here is here, and you can just lie back on it."[28] As Robert Westbrook correctly points out, Dewey "would never lose touch with this feeling, though his interpretation of its meaning and implications would change dramatically."[29]

Dewey's philosophy is committed to finding, articulating, and testing the better and worse ways in which we can lie back on life. His philosophy is saturated with hypotheses about those interactions and ways of participating in situational, everyday life that are key to its capacity to regulate, ameliorate, educate, and enrich itself with meaning without the need for something antecedent, supernatural, or external to itself. Intelligent inquiry and the creation and appreciation of art are, for instance, two modes in which we can find the way to guide the course of experience to greater depth of meaning by its own resources.

I will argue that to lie back on lived experience in a way that makes the process self-regulative requires the cultivation of a balance between virtues typically associated with experimentation, intelligence, and democracy. I will emphasize the importance of a pre-reflective, qualitatively felt present situation as not only the starting point but the ultimate source of guidance in moral life.[30] The pre-reflective is not only the background, but also the normative basis of our inquiries. To dismiss the qualitative is to dismiss context, which is for Dewey the root of all philosophical evils.

PART ONE

MORAL THEORY AND EXPERIENCE

Experience as Method

It is commonly claimed that Dewey, like other theorists in the twentieth century, sought an empirical grounding for ethics. This is true, but it is not illuminating unless Dewey's own brand of empiricism and his views about experience as method are made clear.

Although Dewey published the second edition of his *Ethics* in 1932, there is not in this text an explicit recognition or explanation of how the philosophical empiricism that he was committed to and that received its final articulation in the first chapters of *Experience and Nature* bears upon his philosophical inquiries and conclusions about morality. Dewey's criticism of traditional ethical theory presupposed a methodology, and it was informed by the systematic mistakes that he detected in other areas of philosophy.

We must first ask what one could mean by the claim that an ethical theory or inquiry, such as Dewey's, is empirical. A survey of the literature on this issue suggests the following possible tenets:

1) It is an ethics that adopts the subject matter, concepts, results, and judgments of the natural sciences (i.e., a science of morality);
2) It is an ethics that has as its starting point social psychology and

evolutionary naturalism (i.e., one based on scientific truths or standpoints);

3) It is an ethics that is like science in certain methodological respects (i.e., one modeled upon science);

4) It is an ethics that is informed by the natural sciences; and

5) It is an ethics that, like other empirical inquiries in philosophy, relies on experience as method. It takes moral experience as its starting point.

Many of the misdirected criticisms of Dewey's ethics have assumed that he held tenet (1). Dewey's defenders rightly point out that this is a caricature of his view.[1] One cannot take Dewey's remarks about a "science of ethics" at face value. Dewey cannot be identified with a naturalistic reduction of moral judgments to scientific statements or with any scientistic approach to morality. I suspect that many of the scientistic interpretations of Dewey's ethics originate from confusing Dewey's suggestions that we must apply the methods of science to the problems of morality with applying the methods of science to ethical theory. These are entirely different maneuvers and Dewey did not endorse the latter.

Tenet (2) is a more recent interpretation.[2] Dewey had a tendency to describe everyday experience by using biological and psychological terms. This successfully sidelined the modern view of the self as a subject or spectator of an antecedent reality, but it misleadingly suggests that Dewey is a philosopher who adopts a scientific outlook upon things or who starts with theoretical truths given by the sciences. The pragmatists certainly were influenced by Darwin and evolutionary naturalism, and they saw these and other developments in the sciences (at the turn of the twentieth century) as providing an indirect validation of their philosophical views. But this is different than claiming that pragmatism, in particular, their view of moral experience, is based on or presupposes the truth of Darwinism or any other evolutionary theory.

There is also no doubt that Dewey had a social psychology that influenced his ethics, but its conclusions were not the starting point of his ethics. Psychology is a type of inquiry that, however useful and important, is limited by the purposes, methods, and selectivity particular to the sciences.[3] Dewey spent many years reading and criticizing extant psychological theories because he thought they were based on problematic dualisms. This was important to Dewey because educational practices in his day were based on these psychologies, and he thus had to engage them for his criticisms to be effective. Dewey was, however, clear on the differences between philosophy and psychology as inquiries.

Instead of the narrow view assumed by tenets (1) and (2), commentators and defenders of Dewey's ethics point out that tenets (3) and (4) better convey the sense in which Dewey's ethics is empirical. Tenet (4) postulates an ethics that is constantly nurtured and informed by the results of scientific inquiries. The moral philosopher is accordingly more interdisciplinary than is typical. Compared to tenet (4), tenet (3) seems to make a stronger claim about the relation between science and ethics. An empirical ethics is one that adopts the general method of inquiry of the sciences. For example, Dewey did not see why the conclusions of moral philosophy could not be as hypothesis-driven as those of the sciences. Recent scholars have insisted that to appreciate that this was Dewey's view we must first understand what he meant by science or the scientific method. Jennifer Welchman, for example, claims that if one carefully studies Dewey's conception of the nature of science, one finds that he thought that "every scientist acts in accordance with procedural rules"[4] that can be experimentally confirmed. This indicates at least one respect in which ethics can be like science. "Commitment to such rules, Dewey holds, is the essence of science. It is in this respect that he believes ethical theory ought to become scientific."[5] If ethics is to advance it should "construct procedures for inquiries analogous to those used in the physical sciences."[6] For James Campbell, it is the "scientific attitude" and the communal ("public") aspect of science that attracted Dewey to the notion of "ethics as a moral science."[7]

I do not wish to question tenets (3) and (4) as Deweyan theses, or the above claims by Dewey scholars. However, I think there are limitations to this way of proceeding if one wants to understand both Dewey and the notion of an empirical ethics. Although the association of empiricism with science is not totally unwarranted, I question the fruitfulness of ascribing tenet (3) to Dewey for a full understanding of his radical reconstruction of moral philosophy. Dewey scholars should not assume that we must demonstrate the respects in which ethics can be like science on the assumption that a failure to do so will scuttle our claims to have articulated an empirical ethics. This is especially so if ethics is a subject within philosophy. Dewey had a well-developed view of what it means for an area of philosophy to be empirical, and it is this that is appealed to in tenet (5), a view compatible with, but not reducible to, tenet (3). Indeed, Dewey's thoughts about empirical philosophy are independent of how he conceived the relation between philosophy and science.[8]

Dewey used science as an analogy or as a paradigm, and advocated in ethics a method analogous to scientific inquiry. At the time, the analogy with science was important for Dewey because it served the function of emphasizing "the continuity of ethical with other forms of experience" (MW 8:35). Unfortunately, analogies have their limits and can outlive their usefulness. In fact, some have recently argued that art or aesthetic experience is a better analogy for understanding Dewey's ethics. This is the approach of Steven Fesmire in *John Dewey and Moral Imagination: Pragmatism in Ethics,* and it is a welcome corrective to the scientistic views of Dewey's ethics. In the process of emphasizing what has been wrongly ignored by scientistic views of Dewey's ethics, however, Fesmire may have overstated the case on behalf of an aesthetic reading of Dewey's ethics.[9] For one does not need to choose between an aesthetic and scientific view of Dewey's ethics, nor indeed for his overall philosophy. Dewey used science and art as metaphors by which to understand moral experience without committing himself to a reduction of morality to art or science. This is not a widely appreciated point.

Instead of deciding whether the science or art analogy is better, I want to move beyond them (in some sense, before them) to focus on Dewey's commitments to an empirical *philosophical* method and how this yields the kind of ethics it did. It was his commitment to a different starting point in philosophical inquiry that led him to provide one of the most devastating and systematic critiques of modern moral theory, and a radically new account of moral experience.

Experience as the Starting Point

Dewey's early insistence in making ethics scientific is part of his more general and lifelong aim to base philosophy in lived experience or to take experience as the starting point. Early on he characterized the empiricist's way of philosophizing in terms of a postulate, that is, the "postulate of immediate empiricism." This is the hypothesis that "things—anything, everything, in the ordinary or non-technical use of the term 'thing'—are what they are experienced as" (MW 3:158). A genuine empiricism in philosophy entails that, no matter how abstract and remote our philosophical speculations might turn out, we need to start and end with directly experienced subject matter. For Dewey, then, experience is a "*starting point* and *terminal point,* as setting problems and as testing proposed solutions" (LW 1:14, my emphasis). This turn toward everyday lived experienced is the most important philosophical inheritance we have received from Dewey.

This method would not be so important to Dewey if most philosophizing had been done from this empirical postulate and attitude. For the most part, however, the starting point in philosophy has been theoretical abstractions (or as Dewey says, "reflective products"), rather than primary experience, that is, everyday experience as it is found, present and given. Even modern empiricism has not been radical (or empirical) enough to distinguish a theory about experience from experience *as* it is experienced. In general, experience in modern philosophy has been understood as the content of consciousness, that is, of a knowing subject who is a spectator to an antecedent world or object. But this is a picture that we may employ when we adopt a theoretical point of view; it is not, however, how we experience our everyday life from a pre-theoretical and engaged point of view. Modern philosophers tend to start their inquiries with the feature of events *qua* known and not as they are experienced in their robust and raw character. We cannot ignore the crudities of life just because they are crude.

Dewey's moral philosophy is revolutionary because he tries to avoid all the mistaken theoretical starting points and begins with moral experience as it is lived. However, before considering what this means, we must first address some possible misunderstandings and questions about the sort of empirical method Dewey proposed.

Does not the above postulate assume the very naïve philosophical view that there are givens independent of theories that we can appeal to as a neutral court of appeal? Alasdair MacIntyre has recently claimed that "we need to avoid the error of supposing that there are facts of the moral life completely independent of and apart from theory-laden characterization of those facts."[10] If all facts of experience are theory-laden (and the given is a myth), then it seems that Dewey's empiricism, particularly his appeal to a primary experience—that is, to things as they are present and given in our everyday practical life—is at best problematic.

But Dewey recognizes that there are no hard or neutral givens. A central tenet of his philosophy is that "selective emphasis, with accompanying omission and rejection, is the heart-beat of mental life" (LW 1:31). We can distinguish two possible ways in which selectivity (or interpretation) is part of experiencing—pre-theoretically and theoretically—but for Dewey neither one renders futile the effort to be empirical.

Experience can be theory-laden. This means that either a theory we hold determines what counts as a fact or our selection of facts from the total field of experience is determined by our interest in confirming or disconfirming a theory we already hold. A recognition of this kind of selectivity lets us question the naïve idea that empirical theories are mere transcripts of independent and brute matters of fact. Although Dewey recognizes this kind of selectivity, he hardly thinks it follows that *all* experience is theory-laden and that, therefore, any appeal to primary experience is problematic. Contemporary philosophers who think otherwise must hold an extended sense of what counts as a theory or believe that in the course of everyday life we all look at the world through a theory. To begin philosophy *in the midstream of our lives* is not even to begin within a body of beliefs, as is sometimes assumed by epistemologists. Theories and beliefs are *in* our lives.

Primary experience is not, however, pure experience in the sense of something that we could access if we were able to divest ourselves of our conceptual and cultural baggage.[11] There is pre-theoretical selectivity because as social and cultural organisms we always confront a situation with a character (set of habits, emotions, beliefs) that to a certain extent determines the content of what is non-reflectively given and present. We grow up in a certain society with a certain language and in the process we acquire conceptual and perceptual habits that may determine what we directly experience. Nevertheless, we do experience things in their gross qualitative givenness in a situation. We must be faithful to this lived experience regardless of how this given might be conditioned by one's character and one's historical cultural context. The extent of this conditioning is an open question and not critical to the use of the method.

The empirical method, hence, provides a basis for continuous criticism and evaluation of theories. A philosopher proceeds empirically when her theoretical selectivity is guided by what is pre-theoretically given. If we can appeal to our description of what is directly experienced, then we can appeal to something outside of our theories. To be clear, that which is immediately or directly experienced is not, for Dewey, just sense perception, as is presupposed by some modern theories of knowledge. Instead, we immediately experience things, others, anticipations, relations, novelty, location, flow, qualities, and so on in the midstream of our everyday engagements. For Dewey, the pre-theoretical (i.e., primary experience) is the more primitive level because it encompasses the theoretical and because it is where things are present in their brute and direct qualitative givenness and thereness. We need to begin and end experientially guided inquiries on this level.

There is a sense, then, in which there are moral facts independent of theory. For there is no reason to think that everything that is experienced as moral in our everyday lives is determined by a theory. This is not to deny that it is difficult to be empirically minded in philosophy. There is, for example, the problem of designating the experiential subject matter to be studied without using or assuming a theory. This is a difficult task because one often comes to a subject matter with pre-conceived theoretical assumptions and with certain theoretical demands and interests. Yet the fact that many or most philosophers become trapped in their theories does not mean that this is inevitable, and it is not sufficient to demonstrate that the philosophical effort to be truthful to experience is futile.

Dewey's form of empiricism is not the kind that many would like. One cannot object that although the method offers a way of evaluating and testing theoretical hypothesis it cannot guarantee that they will correspond to the nature of things, or in the case of moral theory to a moral reality outside of experience. For this objection assumes a mysterious ontological gap between experience and reality that is ruled out by Dewey's postulate. On the other hand, the complaint might be that while it gives us an extra-theoretical check on our theories it does not provide us with freedom from our historical circumstances. The extent to which our primary experience is conditioned by our culture or place in history is a source of anxiety to those who would like to have the assurance that what they experience is unspoiled by their circumstances. Dewey did not experience this anxiety because he did not even understand what this last sense of freedom could mean.

However, Dewey's denial of pure experience does not mean that he held the *theory* that our starting point is always inside a language, a culture, or a socioeconomic system. He would be skeptical of any theory that claimed that our primary experience is determined (or conditioned) by one single cohesive factor such as one's historical period, culture, race, class, or biological makeup. These are all reductionistic and, as such, non-empirical theories that overlook the complexity and heterogeneity of factors and interactions that are the conditions for human experience. We do not experience ourselves *as* inside (or as trapped in) our subjectivity, language, or anything else. The notion, for example, that one's culture or social class solely determines moral experience is itself a theory, rather than what we experience when we have moral experiences.

Dewey's appeal to primary experience is not a disguised appeal to the status quo. On the contrary, the purpose is to encourage criticism. Philosophy as criticism relies on subjecting the more refined reflective products of our inquiry to the test of primary experience. But philosophy can also subject to criticism what, at any time, is taken as primary experience. This is done either by arguing that it is not really primary or by unveiling factors (e.g., historical-cultural beliefs) that condition our experience in an unwanted way. We start where we are, in the midst of our pre-reflective and immediate qualitative experiences. These experiences change and are transformed by inquiry but we must return to them as our guide. If we have prejudices or stereotypes that distort our immediate experience, then we should find this out through inquiry, the criticism of others, and further experiences. There is no privileged theoretical or objective stand-point—the God's-eye view—for us to take.

In other words, experience as method relies on what is experienced; and what is experienced not only changes but can be modified and improved by the same method. Nevertheless, effective criticism and modification of what we experience needs to begin with what we do in fact experience in our ordinary practical situations. What we cannot do, however, is *simultaneously* subject *all* our primary experience to criticism. Reflective criticism always takes place in the non-cognitive context of a situation that cannot be transcended.

Neither is the appeal to experience a disguised form of foundationalism. Experience as method is not experience as a foundation. Since Descartes, the latter has been understood as a fixed and particular subject matter that we can (as subjects or spectators) gaze at and provide the unshakable grounds of our philosophies. Yet for Dewey, this is a theoretical conception of experience. Experience cannot be a foundation because we are *in* experience as agents in situations. As Douglas Browning explains,

> Day after day we find ourselves within an integral part of those ever-changing and always unique situations that constitute our lives and mark out their shifting horizons. Each of us is bound within this situational stream, a stream which is never at rest, always in transit. We cannot stop it or freeze it even for a second; we cannot view it from without or find some external point of leverage from which we might alter the direction of its flow. We are not mere subjects for whom our situations are objects to be observed; we are agents in our situations, in our arenas of action, and part of what transpires there is our own doing. Now, this stream of situations in our lives is precisely that to which Dewey refers by the term 'experience'.[12]

Hence, in a certain sense, experience is always our starting point (and for that matter middle and end point) for we cannot get away from it. The choice is not between starting in or outside of experience but between ways of proceeding within it. The difference between adopting an empirical method of inquiry or not is ultimately the choice between affirming or denying the character of things as they are presented to us in our everyday lives. To be an empiricist is to live by the naïve and crude sort of realism that affirms that what is real is whatever is denotatively found. It is to go by how things present themselves and not by how we want them to be. It is "accepting what is found in good faith and without discount" (LW 1:372), and to settle issues by "finding and pointing to the things in the concrete contexts in which they present themselves" (LW 1:377).

Dewey's empirical method has significant implications about the resources and limits of philosophical inquiry and criticism. Argumentation and logical rigor continue to be important, but there is also the requirement of adequacy to experience, a requirement that introduces a way of evaluating philosophical hypotheses that can be both a strength and liability of pragmatism. Dewey rejects commonplace assumptions in ethics because they are not based in his everyday primary experience, and he doubts that they are a part of the primary experience of other ethical theorists. This is a good reason for Dewey to reject entire views, even when they are impeccably well argued and meet all possible objections. This, however, is a liability because it opens the pragmatist to the charge of seeming to be shallow, dismissive, and begging questions in her confrontation with alternative views.

How can anyone be certain that one is beginning with things as they are experienced and not with reflective products or theoretical presuppositions? There is no certainty here and Dewey provides no infallible method by which one can guarantee success in the empirical method he proposes. All one can do is be alert to purposes that might distort or mislead, such as holding on to a theory too zealously. Others might also keep us on alert. This is why the empiricist method requires that one's results be tested by the results and lived experience of others. One can guide others to circumstances that would let them test one's own results; but suggesting that others have certain experiences is not the same as providing a reason or an argument in their defense. It does, however, open our hypothesis to the criticism of others.

Dewey also suggests that it would help if we keep the term 'experience' in philosophy as a reminder of our method. This will remind one to run a never-ending check of one's philosophy both with one's day-to-day experiences and with the results of other philosophers. Even more helpful is the suggestion that we learn from the experience of other philosophers. To study other philosophers' mistakes might prevent one from making those same mistakes and avoid false starts of a particular, that is, non-empirical, kind. Dewey very helpfully summarizes the general and systematic kinds of mistakes made by non-empirical philosophers, and it will be helpful to consider them before continuing to disclose the proper starting point for ethical theory.

The Philosophical Fallacy

Dewey thought that the general failure to be empirical in philosophy amounted to a failure to acknowledge primary experience as the non-cognitive context of philosophical inquiry. Philosophers often denied the practical experiential context of their own investigations and took the products of their inquiries to replace experience as it is lived. Philosophers have not only failed to let their own inquiries be guided by and returned to context but they have also defended notions of thinking as devoid of all context. Hence, Dewey concludes that "the most pervasive fallacy of philosophic thinking goes back to neglect of context" (LW 6:5). This general failure was so common in philosophy that he calls it "the philosophical fallacy" (LW 1:51).

The philosophical fallacy became Dewey's main tool of criticism in different areas of philosophy, and he discovered many different ways that philosophers made the same fundamental mistake. But he never clearly set forth in a systematic way the various formulations and versions of the fallacy. I will sort out four different versions of the fallacy and show how they generate the truncated view of experience inherited by non-empirical ethics.

THE ANALYTIC FALLACY

Analysis is a process where we discriminate some particulars or elements within a context. Of course, what gives the particulars their connection and continuity is the context itself. Philosophers commit the analytic fallacy when the results of an analysis are interpreted as complete in themselves apart from any context. "It is found whenever the distinctions or elements that are discriminated are treated as if they where final and self-sufficient" (LW 6:7).

Though Dewey refers to this fallacy as one of analysis, it is not limited in its application to a specific phase of inquiry. The key to this fallacy is that the rich and concrete context from which distinctions are abstracted is forgotten and the results of inquiry are given a status that they do not and should not have. The conclusions of inquiry are not only treated as final and self-sufficient, but they are sometimes elevated, ontologized, or, as Dewey said, given "antecedent existence."[13]

As result of their analyses, philosophers have dissected the world in many ways: mind and body, reason and passion, subject and object. There is nothing wrong with these dissections per se, but the concrete non-cognitive integral contexts from which things were dissected are often forgotten. With these dissections in hand, philosophical problems are then invented that center on how to reconcile features that are actually experienced as part of a unified and integral whole. This fallacy is responsible for the atomistic, dualistic, and subjective view of experience. Instead of starting with the integrated unity and unanalyzed totality found in a situation, modern philosophy begins with ontological gaps (dualisms), and functional distinctions that regulate primary experience are taken as the starting point of philosophical inquiry, that is, as primary.

THE FALLACY OF UNLIMITED UNIVERSALIZATION

Another common way for philosophers to ignore context and elevate the conclusions of their inquiries is to give them unlimited application. This occurs when they ignore the fact that conclusions arise out of limiting conditions set by the contextual situation of particular inquiries. Philosophers are prone to this fallacy because they often try to formulate theories about truth, good, reality, or the absolute writ large. In many instances, one "converts abstraction from specific context into abstraction from all contexts whatsoever" (LW 6:16). Philosophers tend to absolutize or universalize their conclusions because they ignore the fact that philosophical inquiry always occurs against a temporal and spatial background that is not subject as a whole to reflection.

THE FALLACY OF SELECTIVE EMPHASIS

The fallacy of selective emphasis occurs when the philosopher forgets or overlooks selectivity and the purposes of selection that are part of the context of a particular inquiry. The most common consequence and sign of this is that non-empirical philosophers do not ascribe reality to whatever is left out of, or not selected in, their inquiries. Hence, whatever has value in some specific context and for some particular purpose determines what is real. But this is to confuse good or useful traits with "fixed traits of real being" (LW 1:33). Because philosophers cherish simplicity, certainty, and permanence, they convert these traits into real features of the world; meanwhile, uncertainty, change, and ambiguity are taken as phenomenal, subjective, or as lacking reality. According to Dewey, however, all that happens is equally real though perhaps not of equal worth. If one is empirical one recognizes that primary experience has precarious elements as well as stable ones.

INTELLECTUALISM

Intellectualism might be thought of as a combination of the aforementioned fallacies. But it is so pervasive in the history of non-empirical philosophy that it should be considered a separate fallacy. Philosophers have always favored cognitive objects. The problem arises when, as a consequence of her cognitive bias, the philosopher deems unimportant or unreal whatever is non-cognitive or pre-cognitive. The consequence of intellectualism in philosophy has been a certain narrow view of experience, namely, that all experience is a mode of knowing. The concept of experience that is at the heart of traditional epistemology assumes something like an intellectualist postulate: things really are what they are known to be. Therefore, we have to possess knowledge in order to reveal reality, and whatever is ultimately real has to have the characteristics of an object of knowledge.

If things are what they are experienced as, then there are many other ways in which we experience things than as objects of knowledge. In fact, we have a qualitative appreciation of our surroundings that precedes, underlies, and cannot be reduced to knowledge. Our intellectual activities always operate within the more general context of the world as encountered, lived, enjoyed, and suffered by humans. In primary experience "things are objects to be treated, used, acted upon and with, enjoyed and endured, even more than things to be known. They are things *had* before they are things cognized" (LW 1:27–28). The qualitative character of experience is not something merely subjective, but rather a trait of existence. "The world in which we immediately live, that in which we strive, succeed, and are defeated is preeminently a qualitative world" (LW 5:243).

Intellectualism is so predominant in moral theory that it operates in subtle ways in accounts and debates about moral realism, moral problems, moral relationships, and moral deliberation. For Dewey, even if the outcome of moral deliberation might be called moral knowledge, it nonetheless arises out of a context of non-cognitively experienced moral subject matter. As I will argue, even the process of moral deliberation itself is not purely cognitive; moreover, I will even claim that for Dewey the most important instrumentalities of moral life are not the usual cognitive powers associated with moral knowledge. This is not to deny the importance of knowledge, for knowledge is one mode of experience that can make a significant difference in primary moral experience. However, a pragmatist is ready to argue against a reductionism of moral life to the cognitive.

Dewey knew that his philosophical views would not be understood by philosophers who are "wedded to the idea that there is no experienced material outside the field of discourse" (LW 14:33). He became, for instance, frustrated with Bertrand Russell for "not been able to follow the distinction I make between the immediately had material of non-cognitively experienced situations and the material of cognition—a distinction without which my view cannot be understood" (LW 14:32–33). Against the common tendency by philosophers to assume the ubiquity of theory and knowledge in experience, Dewey insisted that "the universe of experience surrounds and regulates the universe of discourse" (LW 12:74). Today this intellectualist tendency continues by those who assume that everything in our everyday experience is mediated by language. This totalizing picture of language all the way down is assumed even by neo-pragmatists. I will argue that this linguistic bias is a costly one in ethical theory.

In sum, Dewey's reconstruction in ethics is a diagnosis of how these fallacies are endemic to non-empirical approaches to morality. They became his tools of criticism. The consequences of the philosophical fallacy are philosophical theories that, though simple, coherent, and cohesive, are far from being adequate to the complexity and richness of everyday experience. This is probably more true in morality than in any other area of philosophy. In ethical theory the temptation is to provide a self-serving characterization of moral life, one that gives theory the apparent power to resolve moral problems. This is done by reducing our moral experience to one or a few categories or elements. "Whatever may be the differences which separate moral theories, all postulate one single principle as an explanation of moral life" (LW 5:280). This continues today to be the basis for distinguishing among ethical theories. Dale Jamieson explains.

> Different theories take different categories as primary. For example, utilitarianism takes the goodness of outcomes as primary, and from this derives accounts of the rightness of actions and the virtuousness of agents. Deontology, on the other hand, takes the rightness of actions as primary and either derives from this accounts of other categories that it takes to be morally relevant, or supplements it with accounts of other categories.[14]

Theorists who debate each other tend to ignore the fact that in concrete moral experience neither the good nor the right is reducible to the other. Ethical theorists have neglected the non-cognitive, pluralistic, and incommensurable aspects of moral life because they are of no use in constructing a theoretically coherent system that can presumably provide solutions to moral problems. The results are reductionism and simplification. These might be considered virtues in academic circles but they are usually vices when it comes to making decisions in our moral lives. Indeed, the most elegant, coherent, simple, and philosophically puzzle-solving theory might be the most unhelpful theory for assisting anyone in his or her moral life. Dewey observed that "one cause for the inefficacy of moral philosophies has been that in their zeal for a unitary view they have oversimplified the moral life" (LW: 5:288). Moral theory will continue to be inept in throwing light upon the actual predicaments of moral conduct as long as it continues to ignore "the elements of uncertainty and of conflict in any situation which can properly be called moral" (LW 5:279).

Dewey was critical of the formalism and abstraction of Hegelian and Kantian ethical theories, whose reductionism and oversimplification is driven by the desire to construct a moral theory as a rational system, that is, a self-contained system of ideas.[15] Jim Gouinlock has recently shown how John Rawls is also part of the tradition of constructing ethical theories that are concerned with internal consistency and coherence at the expense of offering robust accounts of our complex moral lives. Gouinlock says, "Rawls is the most famous and influential exemplar of this reductive and prejudicial mode of thought. The many tributes paid to him are testimony to the weakness of philosophers for seemingly self-sufficient system of ideas."[16]

The empirically inclined ethicist wants her theory to be in accord with concrete moral experience, a desire that does not by itself guarantee success. Dewey praised utilitarians for their empirical spirit and insistence "upon getting away from vague generalities, and down to the specific and concrete" (MW 12:183). Yet utilitarians, too, never questioned the idea of a fixed end and assumed a view of moral deliberation that does not conform to anyone's experience. It is almost as if they thought they were being empirical simply because they were suspicious of reason and appealed instead to quantifiable moral subject matter (units of pleasure and pain). There are undoubtedly misconceptions about signs of concreteness and about what counts as an empirical methodology in ethics; however, the fact that contemporary ethics is more linguistic, historical, or scientific is no guarantee that it is empirical.

I have, so far, considered what Dewey meant by an empirical method in philosophy. But what does this method entail for philosophical inquiries that take morality as their subject matter? What does it mean to begin with *moral* experience? How should an empirical account of moral life proceed? The first task is designation.

Designating the Subject Matter:
Moral Situations as the Starting Point

In *Experience and Nature* Dewey calls the empirical way of doing philosophy the "denotative method," where denotation is the phase of an empirical inquiry where we are concerned to designate (as free from theoretical presuppositions as possible) the experiential (had) subject matter for which we can provide different and even competing descriptions and theories. Thus, our empirical inquiry about morality must begin by a rough and tentative designation or denotation of moral experience from within the broader context of our everyday life and activities. Once we designate the subject matter, we then engage in inquiry proper which may include constructing theories and developing concepts. That, of course, is not the end of inquiry, for we must then take the results of that inquiry "as a path pointing and leading back to something in primary experience" (LW1:17). This looping back is essential and it never ends as long as there are new experiences that may require a revision of our theories.

Notice how different this is from an ethical theory that starts with a definition of morality, or aims to arrive at one, that clearly demarcates moral from non-moral domains. Definitions can be useful, but in philosophy they are often expected to articulate an essence or some definitive criteria of relevance to the issue at hand. The attempt to pre-theoretically designate the subject matter, that is, to point in a certain direction, may be more successful if some general, even vague or crude, description of moral experience is part of the task. But this is not easy. One must be careful to designate the subject matter in a way that does not beg the question in favor of one's ethical theory or theoretical preconceptions. A philosopher must make an honest effort to designate what is moral based on that which is experienced as moral. If we are truthful to concrete experiences, moral experiences are *had* and they are experiences just as distinctive as friendly conversations or the enjoyment of music.

To individuals in their everyday pre-theoretical interactions, many things are experienced as having a predominantly moral cast, quality, or character. We need to start by pointing out and describing the experiences that we have in such situations instead of starting with theoretical definitions of morality. It is also important in ethics not to confuse this empirical task with designating correct moral conduct. To be able to designate and describe moral experience, one must have the minimal sensitivity to experience the difference between, for example, moral and aesthetic qualities, rather than to be in the possession of knowledge of what is right and wrong. Dewey's descriptions of moral experience are thus totally meaningless to individuals who are devoid of moral sensitivity. This entails a methodological commitment to take seriously how things are presented within moral life rather than from an external theoretical standpoint. I will say more on this later.

Can we be certain that everyone engaged in this sort of philosophical inquiry will be pointing to the same experiences? No, but this is not a good reason to portray moral experience as subjective or to prefer some other method. How much agreement there will be among philosophers in the tasks of designation and description is an open and empirical issue.

In locating moral experience (as a distinctive mode of experience) one is faced with the difficulty that the term 'experience' has been associated in philosophy with consciousness or subjective phenomena. For Dewey, however, experience is simply a person's practical life, that is, "the life he has led and undergone in a world of persons and things" (LW 1:369). As inclusive as this is, we always experience the world in a situational context. What is truly given at any time in experience is the context of a unique situation. In fact, to say that we are *in* experience or that "individuals live in a world means, in the concrete, that they live in a series of situations" (LW 13:25).

Although the notion of a situation is crucial to locate moral experience, it is not sufficient to distinguish moral experience from other modes of experience. Is there a way to distinguish moral experience from the rest of experience without committing oneself to its absolute separation from other modes of experience? Although for Dewey there is no area of our experience that is exclusively or essentially moral, he designates situations as predominantly moral when they have the pervasive quality of demanding of the agent that she discover what she morally ought to do among conflicting moral forces or demands. As philosophers we might step back from, and reflect on, the unique situations that are experienced as having a moral component and design theories about our moral life. Those unique moral situations, however, remain the primitive contexts of moral experience, that is, of our moral practices and activities. This is the experiential subject matter to be studied, described, and appealed to in order to test our theoretical accounts. The basis for distinguishing morality from other dimensions or modes of experience is the subject matter, problems, and pervasive quality of certain situations. There is no criterion that is antecedent to the sheer givenness of these experiences.

Moral problems are, of course, not all there is to moral life. Most situations are fairly well settled, and we plod along in our daily lives, trusting our habits (rightly so, for the most part) to get us through.

Occasionally, though, we find ourselves in a problematic situation, only some of which are morally problematic. Dewey's hypothesis in "Three Independent Factors in Morals" is that they are morally problematic because we are troubled either about what is the good, the dutiful, or the virtuous thing to do. Often, however, the problem is that each of these moral demands points in irreconcilable directions. If we find the right thing to do through inquiry, it is that which reconstructs a situation from being morally problematic to being determinate or solved.

In part 2 I will consider in much greater detail Dewey's view of moral life, but from this initial description it is already clear how different is Dewey's starting point from that of most ethical theorists. Moral theories have been classified according to whether they take good (teleological-consequentialist), virtue (virtue ethics), or duty (deontological theories) as their central category or source of moral justification. However, to abstract one factor or feature of situations which are experienced as morally problematic, and then to make that factor supreme or exclusive to morality is to commit what Dewey called the philosophical fallacy. To be empirical requires that we come to terms with the fact that good, virtue, and duty are all irreducible features without a common denominator or a set hierarchy among them. Simply put, living morally is a messier and more complicated affair than moral theorists are willing to recognize.

Ethical Theory and the Theoretical Starting Point

Debates among opposing schools in modern philosophy share a view of experience which is the result of starting philosophical inquiry by adopting a theoretical standpoint instead of with how life is experienced by engaged agents in the midst of life. Dewey calls this standpoint the "spectator view," and more recently Douglas Browning has called it the "theoretical point of view." Here is how Browning describes it,

> taking the theoretical point of view is something you and I often do. As agents, i.e., as engaged, interactive participants within an immediately experienced arena of practical, daily affairs, we frequently find it helpful to assume the role, take on the guise, of a disengaged and disinterested observer who is no longer caught up in the rough and tumble of that arena, but withdrawn from it and merely observes it or some area of interest within it from an objectifying distance.[17]

The theoretical standpoint is sometimes difficult to detect, since it is not a matter of assuming certain theoretical propositions but of implicitly adopting a certain outlook from which we construct our moral theories.

R. M. Hare, for example, is very explicit about adopting the theoretical standpoint as his starting point. He says,

> Let us imagine a society that has as yet done no moral philosophy. . . . And then let us suppose that someone does start such an inquiry. What sort of theory is he likely to come up with? The facts about moral thinking which will most obviously confront him are facts about intuitive moral thinking. He will observe that people do react in consistent ways, in their verbal and other behaviour, to certain actions in certain situations.[18]

Notice how Hare is inviting us to take a theoretical-detached-external standpoint on morality as the subject matter of philosophical investigation. For Hare, the philosopher must start by noticing that there are people in the world who use moral terms in a certain way. The philosopher must start from the same standpoint of the sciences, that is, of the anthropologist or sociologist. The situations in which the philosopher has had moral experiences or has used moral language are relevant, but a description of them *as they are experienced* seems irrelevant or distracting from the broader theoretical standpoint we need to take. Why should we favor the detached theoretical standpoint? This is important because observing and studying how people use moral terms from this standpoint looks different than when we are ourselves in the midst of living these situations. When I am in a morally problematic situation moral terms are employed but there is a lot more going on than the use of moral language. In fact, awareness of my moral language as language is usually the last thing in my mind, unless it is somehow relevant to the moral problems that I am experiencing. For the most part, I am not initially confronted with moral terms or questions, but rather find myself in the midst of what I am immediately experiencing as a moral problem or as a situation where I am experiencing that something, however vague, is morally wrong.

If from the involved participant's standpoint an action in a particular situation strikes us as immediately right or wrong (i.e., as having some moral character), from a detached-theoretical one a philosopher simply sees human beings having an experience that requires some theoretical explanation. Some philosophers have called the engaged-standpoint internal or subjective, and the theoretical one objective. This not only begs the question but it assumes a dualism. For Dewey and José Ortega y Gasset, the primacy of the engaged standpoint is based on the fact that any inquiry and its theoretical point of view is *experienced as* embedded in the more everyday, practical point of view. Here is how Douglas Browning explains why the practical is primary for Dewey,

Theorizing and indeed linguisticizing are, for him, critically important phases in inquiry. But, of course, he also insists that the starting point for inquiry, its motivating context throughout its course, and its consummation are found in the lived experience of being in a situation in which I, as agent, participate and interact. It is a consequent of this that the theoretical point of view is parasitical upon the more everyday, practical point of view; it derives its focus, its motivation, and its very significance from that down-home, flesh-and-bones course of daily affairs that Dewey had the temerity to label experience.[19]

In what way has the theoretical standpoint been favored in ethics? What are some of the most common versions of this starting point and what are its consequences? The theoretical standpoint is what led modern philosophers to start with dualisms. Dewey appreciated how in ethics the modern dualisms between the mind/body, inner/outer, subject/object, and so on had their counterpart in the assumed dichotomies between self/act, doer/deed, character/conduct, fact/value. The counterpart to the Cartesian starting point in ethics is to begin with the isolated subject who has a purely cognitive apprehension of moral truths. These modern dichotomies have in turn generated a number of false dilemmas and debates that I will discuss in this book, such as subjectivism vs. objectivism, egoism vs. altruism, and an ethics of character or virtue vs. an ethics of act (duty and rules). Dualistic starting points do not do justice to the integral character of our concrete moral experience as it is experienced. In a pragmatist ethics the distinctions that can be made within moral life are features of an irreducible whole (of the ongoing unanalyzed unity of a situation) distinguished by reflection rather than existential dichotomies.

For those philosophers who favor the theoretical standpoint of science, their starting point in ethics is a natural world with natural properties but without values. From this standpoint, the only moral facts with which she is confronted is that humans are animals that claim to have moral and aesthetic experiences. These facts must be explained in ways that square both with our scientific starting point and the goals of scientific inquiry. Dewey would have no problem with this approach so long as it is recognized for what it is, namely, an inquiry restricted by the methods and goals of science. The problem comes when the philosopher goes a step further and privileges the results of such inquiries in a way that simultaneously denigrates the moral experiences we have in the midst of moral life. This is precisely what scientistic philosophers do when, for instance, they conclude that moral behavior is nothing but action guided by the evolutionary goal of spreading one's genes, that is, this is the real reason why we behave morally.

In his well-known paper, "The Schizophrenia of Modern Ethical Theories," Michael Stocker argues that modern ethical theories recommend a kind of disharmony between reasons and motives.[20] The theoretical reasons proffered for why right acts are right (e.g., because they maximize utility or are in accord with a universal duty) are at odds with the actual motives of moral agents when they do what is right. With some of these theories it is best if reasons and motives are kept separate, for it is sometimes desirable for an agent to be motivated by thoughts that have little to do with the truth about why her acts are the right ones to perform. Stocker finds this disturbing, but he fails to provide an adequate or full diagnosis of the root of the problem.[21] The problem is methodological. The gap between reasons and motives is a consequence of the more fundamental gap in these theories between the theoretical standpoint and the practical-engaged one. Modern ethical theorists have assumed that we must determine what makes right act right by stepping outside how things appear from the motivating situational context in which we act. It is only because theorists have favored the detached theoretical standpoint that their descriptions of moral life are at odds with how we experience moral life. For Dewey, the consequences of this starting point are more severe than just schizophrenia.

What is most problematic about the theoretical starting point in ethical theory is that it has ended up "rendering the things in ordinary experience more opaque than they were before, . . . depriving them of having in 'reality' even the significance they had previously seemed to have" (LW 1:18). J. L. Mackie has, for example, claimed that although most people (in their primary moral experience) claim to be pointing to something objective when making moral judgments, they are in error.[22] From a theoretical standpoint the objectivity of moral qualities we experience seems false, or as Mackie puts it, "queer." According to R. M. Hare, those who are unable to rise above the everyday habitual engagement (what he calls the "intuitive level") may never be able to ascertain the naïveté of their realism about colors and all moral qualities.[23] Hare thinks we are fortunate animals because in spite of our limitations (we cannot be the ideal observer-prescribers) we are able to take the reflective distance of the theoretical standpoint at the "critical level." This is fortuitous because at this level we realize that our immediate partiality or moral concern for friends is actually nothing more than a habitual but useful emotional disposition that pays off from a rational consequentialist standpoint. For Hare, it is a good thing that people have the immediate experience (or should I say "appearance"?) of feeling a special obligation to particular others; but it is only when they take the critical standpoint that they become aware of the real reasons why they should care or take their experienced obligations seriously. For instance, here is what Hare says about the experienced moral bond (partiality) in the mother-child relation, "If we ascend to the critical level and ask why it ought to be, the answer is fairly obvious. If mothers had the propensity to care equally for all the people in the world, it is unlikely that children would be as well provided for even as they are."[24] So, we are all lucky that mothers are duped into feeling they have a special obligation to their children because they are their children! It is only a small step from this view to the view that all of our moral experiences are nothing but a useful fiction to propagate our genes. Whether it is Platonism, cultural relativism, or scientism, a theoretical standpoint that explains away the reality of our immediate moral experiences is often present.

The abstraction of a thinking rational subject in a value-less world is a common theoretical starting point implicit in a variety of ethical theories. It is discernible in those positions that assume that our moral principles or our desires are the sources of our moral experiences and, therefore, that morality is a human projection upon nature. It is in views that assume that ethical theory must provide rational reasons that would convince an imaginary skeptic to be moral or to take morality seriously.[25] In such views, it is as if to be rational (usually defined as pursuing one's self-interest or following the rules of logic) is primary, while all else (especially moral value) is questionable and must be derived from this imaginary standpoint. For Dewey, this is not to start with moral experience as it is had because we start in a morally value-laden world. Morality is no more in need of justification or legitimacy than the existence of the external world. Morality is just as basic, natural, and given as rationality (in any of its possible meanings). There is no more need to show that morality is rational than a need to show that rationality is moral.

Another common theoretical starting point in ethical theory is to locate morality in moral norms that are prior to, or exist across, situations. Moral theory, according to this view, must start with the fact that agents and communities inherit general moral principles and standards. This is the reason why we experience moral demands and the possession of such principles and standards determines right from wrong in a particular situation. Moral problems are in effect a matter of deciding what follows from a general criterion of right and wrong, or it is the conflict between different standards or criteria. Moral disagreement among individuals is thus a disagreement about moral norms. The task of ethical theory is to bring to our conscious attention the norms at work in our actions and judgments. It must validate (i.e., seek a rational basis for) the moral standards that ordinary moral agents take for granted. This is the theoretical view of moral experience that is assumed in debates between different forms of objectivism and relativism.

The relativist holds that moral judgments are justified only relative to standards accepted by a person or the social group to which she belongs.[26] Objectivists take this as a challenge. Morality is not just a matter of our upbringing, group mores, or desires; there must be some basic criterion of right and wrong. There are a variety of objectivist views in ethics according to what is proposed as the criterion. For example, what is right is determined by:

a) what any rational person has good reason to accept or what would be agreed upon by hypothetical contractors under ideal conditions;

b) what is self-evident according to one's moral sense;

c) what can be expected to produce more good than bad consequences;

d) what is deducible from the commands of divine authority, a categorical imperative, the concept of the rational agent, or human nature (or flourishing).

These are all objective standards insofar as they presuppose an objective standpoint, that is, a standpoint outside of the historically contingent standards of any particular individual, society, or culture. And they are proposed as the rational basis to evaluate or criticize these relative standards. Relativism, of course, denies the existence of such a God's-eye view of things. Instead, we find ourselves in life with inherited and historically contingent moral standards, and no external perspective from which we can subject them to criticism.

From Dewey's standpoint this debate goes on without questioning the notion that moral norms are the locus and source of morality, and that their application is what accounts for moral problems, deliberation, and judgment. This is, at best, a theoretical explanation of moral life, one that leaves out the concrete context where standards are found (an instance of the analytic fallacy). It is only when standards are examined, imagined, and discussed *in abstracto,* that is, apart from their role in morally problematic situations, that they seem to be in need of some philosophical justification. This, Dewey would claim, is an example of how philosophers with an a priori commitment to a particular view about our relation to general norms are concerned with problems of their own creation. As I will argue later, moral judgments are not derivable by applying a criterion of right conduct; in fact, if there are general moral standards they receive their normative force from particular judgments in situations.

Because of the linguistic turn in twentieth-century philosophy, the theoretical starting point became linguistic. It is common in ethical theory to take discrete moral terms, predicates, judgments, and propositions as the starting point of philosophical investigations. Starting with moral language seems more concrete and empirical than beginning with meta-physics, understood as the postulation of the existence of mysterious and supersensible moral values. This starting point commits the philosopher to an attempt to derive or explain the rest of our moral experience by "expos[ing] the logic of moral concepts"[27] or by discerning the meaning of moral words. Ethical theories are tested by checking whether they square "with the facts of linguistic behaviour" or with (predictions of) "what the ordinary man would treat as self-contradictory."[28]

Moral theories that begin with an analysis of moral terms or the moral properties of particular actions suffer from the same problem that the modern view of experience as a composite of atomistic simples does, namely, that it cannot adequately account for relations. Indeed, our moral lives seem like a disconnected series of atomistically isolated acts, and two propositions in moral reasoning seem disconnected when the results of ethical analysis are taken as self-sufficient. In part 2, I will claim that these and other problems do not arise when one takes the lived context of our moral problems and deliberations seriously. One commits the philosophical fallacy when one abstracts moral terms and moral judg-ments out of their contexts and tries to acontextually set their meaning, or when one begins with the assumption that there are some propositions that are inherently moral.[29] An analysis of our ordinary moral language is not sufficient to account for the richness and complexity of our moral experience.

The legalistic character of modern ethics goes hand in hand with its linguistic bias. This bias colors or determines the descriptions of every aspect of moral life. Moral problems are nothing but the conflict between principles or rules that can be stated, revised or re-written. Moral judg-ments are treated as statements or propositions that are the result of the process of moral deliberation which has the same linear character as reading a text. In other words, it is assumed that we ought to reach justified moral judgments by following the same logical order of reading.

The linguistic starting point in ethics is usually accompanied by the same intellectualist starting point of traditional epistemology. It is as-sumed that to start with moral experience is to start with moral language in the form of propositions about right and wrong (i.e., the beliefs of common morality). As W. D. Ross says,

> My starting point [is] the existence of what is commonly called the moral consciousness; and by this I mean the existence of a large body of beliefs and convictions to the effect that there are certain kinds of acts that ought to be done.[30]

Similarly, as Bernard Williams claims, "Ethical theories, with their concern for tests, tend to start from just one aspect of ethical experience, beliefs."[31] Ethics must therefore start with epistemology. Moral disagreement is the conflict between beliefs and moral judgments that are themselves propositions standing somewhere between a subject and the world. Hence, the key philosophical problems in ethics are: how do we know that moral claims and judgments are true of false? Are they capable of being derived from our knowledge of facts about the world or are they just mere exclamations or commands? These two questions are the key issues in the meta-ethical debates between cognitivists, emotivists, naturalists, and intuitionists.[32] Dewey questions the theoretical starting point that usually gives legitimacy to these questions. As I will discuss in more detail, moral judgments are not propositions. They are experienced as acts or assertions that emerge in the context of (and as the result of) a particular qualitative inquiry. The question of their warrant and evaluation cannot be discussed independently of a situation.

The linguistic outlook or bias is so taken for granted in philosophy that even a neopragmatist like Hilary Putnam, who criticizes traditional ethics (from a Deweyan perspective), still seems caught up in it. He claims, for instance, that the traditional metaphysical sources of objectivity in ethics need to be replaced by "the objectivity of *discourse.*"[33] His Deweyan criticism of traditional ethics amounts to the charge that they have a narrow and monistic "*vocabulary.*"[34] Putnam is in favor of a more pluralistic ethics but he may be inadvertently endorsing the same reduction of moral experience to moral language that is endemic to the tradition.

From Dewey's standpoint, the problem with the linguistic starting point, or starting with moral beliefs in ethics, is that it leaves too much out. If all there is to our moral lives is moral discourse, what ultimately guides our moral deliberations other than yet more discourse or some absolute external standard? The failure to recognize the non-cognitive situational context of moral discourse has impeded understanding of Dewey's views about the ultimate source of guidance in moral life. Even Deweyans often leave this out of their presentation of his view. Dewey, however, is clear: leaving out the non-cognitive situational context is to leave out "that which is the controlling factor in my entire view, namely the function of a problematic situation in regulating as well as evoking inquiry" (LW 14:44).

I have been assuming that empiricism in ethics entails contextualism, but not every contextualist position is thereby concrete and empirical. Moral philosophers like Alasdair MacIntyre have suggested that the relevant contexts for the understanding of moral terms are the moral vocabularies operative in large social and historical structures and practices. But an inquiry about moral life that begins with and comes back to shared and cohesive "moral languages" or a "network of shared moral laws"[35] is not committed to an experiential starting point. For even if these refined theoretical products explain why people experience what they experience, they are not what agents experience in primitive experiential situations. Cultural, historical, and sociological explanations of morality are perhaps better theories than universalist or Platonic ones, but they remain theories nonetheless.

For Dewey, radical empiricism in ethics entails a radical contextualism, by which he meant that each situation constitutes a unique context and while it is lived (as a process), that is all there is to moral life. Accounts of our moral life that ignore this, and begin with the assumption of absolutes across time and history, are adopting a God's-eye point of view that neglects the situational context of both our investigation and our morality. There is no standing outside where we are.

The starting point of inquiry is the most important issue in ethical theory because one's understanding of moral notions and of moral experience is conditioned by one's starting point. Dewey thought that moral experience included virtues, rules, obligations, ends and all other notions posited by moral theorists as exclusively moral. This inclusiveness was a result of taking moral situations as the primary context and discerning which notions were operative there, rather than making the moral notions themselves primary.

Dewey wondered about "how much of distraction and dissipation in life, and how much of its hard and narrow rigidity is the outcome of man's failure to realize that each situation has its own unique end and that the whole personality should be concerned with it?" (MW 12:176). And he hoped that attention to moral experience as it is experienced would lead to a shift in ethical thought toward situations as the center of gravity of moral endeavor. He insisted that moral philosophy must quit seeking ends or standards that were over and above unique morally problematic situations. The resolution of each morally problematic situation was, he believed, the goal of morality. The tendency to absolutize or universalize in ethics by providing theories of the good was a failure to see that any meaningful quest for the good is tied to a particular inquiry within the unique context of a morally problematic situation. He said, "while there is no single end, there also are not as many as there are specific situations that require amelioration" (MW 12:174–175). In other words, each concrete morally problematic situation has its own immanent end and meaning, and should not be thought of as a mere means to other, even contingent or historically situated, overarching ends.

In sum, any adequate examination of Dewey's ethical vision needs to begin and take as central the notion of a situation. The situation's importance has to be understood as a consequence of Dewey's commitment to a philosophical empiricism. Moral experience is experienced as something that is neither subjective nor merely inter-subjective. We begin where we are, in a situation as participants, rather than as inhabitants of a culture, conceptual scheme, or our society's norms. Moral situations became the most inclusive category or concept in Dewey's ethics. The categories and elements that are part of moral experience (such as character, conduct, principles, relationships, and habits) are features or traits of lived situations, not antecedent to them. Ideals are part of the means available *in* the process of ameliorating a situation. Virtues are habits operative in and integral to situations, not means to abstract notions of human flourishing. Even Dewey's philosophical speculations about how to live (the subject of part 3) were nothing more than proposals about how to engage in present situations.

Does the radical character of Dewey's contextualism preclude the possibility of theorizing about moral life? If philosophical inquiry is itself embedded in situations as unique, complex, and changing pre-reflective contexts, can moral theory perform the functions it has traditionally performed? What is left of moral theory after all the methodological mistakes are avoided? The acknowledgment of context and the abandonment of a God's-eye view have led contemporary skeptics to consider futile the ambitions of traditional ethical theory. In the next chapter, I turn to the claim that Dewey's skepticism about moral theory is based on a situation ethics and on an alternative conception of the proper function of moral theory.

TWO

Moral Theory and Moral Practice

What passes for "ethics" oscillates between sermonizing, moralizing of an edifying emotional type, and somewhat remote dialectics on abstract theoretical points. . . . It must be admitted that those who have worked it [morality] most successfully have done so indirectly. They have approached the mine not as moralists but as novelists, dramatists, poets, or as reformers, philanthropists, and statesmen. The contributions which they have made have found their way, however, into common life rather than into moral theory. (LW 2:398–399)

Moral Theory and the Quest for Rules

Dewey would agree with contemporary anti-theorists about the shallowness and sterility of most normative ethics. For centuries, philosophers have tried to formulate theories to assist and illuminate moral practice. What is seldom questioned is the notion that this is best achieved by seeking the underlying criteria, decision procedure, or antecedent moral rules by which individuals distinguish right from wrong. Dewey thought this theoretical approach to the task wrongheaded because of its flawed assumptions about morality and the role of theoretical intelligence. The subject matter of ethics is moral practice, that is, conduct in a situation where one has to decide what one ought to do. Dewey saw early on that conduct is "absolutely individualized . . . there is no such thing as conduct in general; conduct is what and where and when and how to the last inch" (EW 3:98). This raises the following issue for the moral philosopher: can there be ethical theory if theory is by its very nature general and abstract, while moral conduct and what one ought to do in a situation are always unique, concrete, and individual? Philosophers can avoid or resolve the tension expressed within this question in a variety of ways.

One could bring moral practice closer to theory by denying that practice is as concrete and individual as it seems. Hence, the belief that moral actions are unique and contextually particular, although not illusory, is nonetheless the result of ignorance or of remaining at the level of appearances. On such a view, moral reality is ultimately constituted by general or universal laws that can be represented within our theories. This rationalistic view resolves the tension, but only by reducing actions to laws in a way that denies that there is a real tension. A more empirically minded response to the disconnect between moral theory and practice would be to claim that our theories must do a better job of representing the individual character of our moral practice; in other words, we should work toward ethical theories that reflect the concreteness and particularity of moral practice. On this view, the tension is the result of the inadequacy of our current theories. This should not discourage the effort to find a theory that, for example, has a sufficiently large set of rules that covers and exhausts the particularity of our moral lives. But it is doubtful that the uniqueness of each situation can be captured by a set of rules, no matter how exhaustive. If rules are always general how can they be faithful to or fully capture the uniqueness and novelty of every situation? One might reply that a rule-based view need not capture uniqueness, but rather that it have enough particularity to be able to make particular moral decisions. The assumption here is that whatever residuum of uniqueness is not captured by our rules is not important or irrelevant. But this is precisely what needs to be proven.

The view that ethical theories can determine *the* right action prior to and across situations is an overestimation due in part to an oversimplified view of moral experience proffered by those in the grips of the philosophical fallacy. No one could raise any serious doubts about the feasibility and importance of constructing ethical theories for moral decision if, for example, any of the following were true of our concrete moral life:

1) Morality is a set of self-sufficient universal values or rules. Moral judgments are things deduced from a hierarchy of universal principles or fixed criteria.

2) All moral values are commensurable with respect to a single standard. There is a hidden unity behind the apparent conflicting kinds of moral ends and demands. There is one right answer to every moral conflict or dilemma.

3) Features that contribute to making an action right in one situation necessarily contribute to making action right in any situation in which this feature appears.

But neither Dewey's moral experience nor mine accords with (1), (2), or (3). This is not to imply that moral experience is chaotic. There are stabilities and uniformities in moral life, but they are not of the kind or degree assumed by many. Moral theorists have the tendency to forget the non-cognitive complexity, plurality, incommensurability, raggedness, changeability, and uniqueness that characterize our primary moral experience. These are the features of moral life that almost make them recalcitrant to any kind of theoretical formulation. One might even claim that in virtue of its (lack of?) structure, moral life is anti-theoretical.

Dewey's avoidance of intellectualism led him to the view that rules or any propositional knowledge are only a part of the actual material of individual moral deliberation. In fact, the qualitative, emotional, and non-cognitive aspects are more important to moral life than any propositional object of knowledge. Moral judgments are not deduced from rules but are derived from an imaginative-affective exploration of one's situation. Moral agents do not distinguish right from wrong by reference to a fixed or evolving criterion. Aside from these views about moral deliberation (which will be considered in part 2), Dewey had serious doubts that a morality based on a set of comprehensive and fixed rules was a workable possibility.

Even if we could somehow come up with a substantial number of sound moral rules, it is questionable to what extent they would be sufficient to guide our lives given that it assumes that we have secured ourselves from the flexibility of individual intelligence and sensitivity to context. For how would we know which individual situations are cases where a particular rule applies? In discussing the rule of honesty, for example, Dewey asks "what bell would ring, what signal would be given, to indicate that just *this* case is the appropriate case for the application of the rule of honest dealing?" (LW 7:276). And even if we could answer this question, we would legitimately wonder "what course in detail the rule calls for?"

(LW 7:276). The notion that an ethical theory can provide a set of rules (or even a set of virtues) by which we can automatically make the right moral decisions is naïve. Even if we could come up with such a set, Dewey thought that the kind of moral life that would follow or that is suggested by this kind of ethical inquiry would be a good enough reason to reject such a project. Instead, he thinks there are at least three dangers of this way of conceiving our moral life,

1) "It tends to magnify the letter of morality at the expense of its spirit" (LW 7:277). When what matters is mere conformity with a rule, the moral experts are those who are able to describe a situation so that it fits under a rule. Hence, for some, morals can become a device to sanction their amoral pursuits.
2) It is a formalistic and legalistic view of conduct that usually centers on avoiding the punishment that comes from a failure to follow rules; and, as Dewey observed, "any scheme of morals is defective which puts the question of avoiding punishment in the foreground of attention" (LW 7:278).
3) It "tends to deprive moral life of freedom and spontaneity and to reduce it to a more or less anxious and servile conformity to externally imposed rules" (LW 7:278). It "puts the center of moral gravity outside the concrete processes of living" (LW 7:278).

It should be evident from these concerns that the spirit, tone, and general quality of our moral activities are just as important to Dewey as the content of morality. Morality is not just a matter of determining what is right or wrong, but of how we appreciate and engage ourselves in the moral tasks presented to us. This is a distinctive feature of his ethics that I will stress in the remainder of this work. He was concerned that a rule-bound morality would result in casuistries that would "destroy the grace and play of life by making conduct mechanical" (EW 3:155). A rule ethics encourages a non-aesthetic way of life; but central to Dewey's vision is a concern for an aesthetic moral life, a claim that I will explore at a later point.

Dewey's Situation Ethics

Dewey's criticisms of ethical theory had a reconstructive aim, one designed to reorient moral theory in a more concrete and contextual direction. He advocated a contextual approach to moral decision making that may be termed situational.[1] This contextualism can be expressed in a negative or positive way according to what it denies or affirms. It denies that moral judgments that do not follow rules are thereby arbitrary; and it affirms that reasonable moral judgments come from intelligently exploring and assessing the situation in its qualitative uniqueness. In order to evaluate an action or to adjudicate conflicts among possible actions or obligations in concrete circumstances we must rely on the qualitative context rather than on some meta-rule, criteria, or fixed procedure. Although we make moral judgments and decisions on the basis of the concrete and unique situations that are experienced, this approach is not usually embraced as a method, that is, as a general approach to moral decision making. It does not have the order, definiteness and security provided by following prefabricated rules or adopting a universal decision procedure or criteria. Yet Dewey embraced it as a method. Instead of trying to come up with comprehensive theories that provide answers or decision-making procedures, he believed that we should attend to the particular, the qualitative, and the unique equipped with the best habits of reflection, imagination, and sensitivity available, that is, with what he sometimes called moral intelligence. What we morally ought to do in a situation should be determined by being true to the situation as it is experienced. A moral judgment is a decision about what action the present situation morally calls for, and this can only be determined by immersion in the situation. He thought that this would carry into the moral sphere the experiential way of doing philosophy more generally, that is, by being guided by what is qualitatively found in experience. Any theory that pretends to provide theoretical answers to moral quandaries prior to actual situations cannot be empirical, for it simply overlooks the experienced uniqueness of each situation and how the moral relevance of any feature can vary depending on the situation.

To claim that a certain sort of action is always right, or to establish rules about what is or is not right under all conditions, is to neglect context; for whether a feature of an action counts as a moral reason to do it is dependent on the context. The adoption of this kind of contextualism in morality is the same as that operative in artistic production and appreciation. For instance, whether a stroke of green in a painting contributes to the beauty of a painting depends on what other colors and lines are present; indeed, a brushstroke of green that beautifies one painting may be what ruins another.

Dewey's contextualism thus entails that there is something wrong-headed about the abortion debate if that debate is only about which value or principle is always overriding. In other words, a moral contextualist is neither pro-life nor pro-choice insofar as both entail a commitment to a value, obligation, or principle that is absolute. A contextualist could make an empirical claim that, in most situations, the life of the fetus trumps the woman's choice, but this is irrelevant to determining the rightness or wrongness of each case.[2]

The notion that deliberation and judgment should ultimately be guided by context is not new. Aristotle and W. D. Ross held a similar kind of contextualism.[3] However, the contextualism of those thinkers is only operative at the level of making particular moral judgments since their ethical views assume, at some other level, fixed moral truths. Dewey's contextualism is more radical for it is a thoroughgoing contextualism, one where no general rule or principle can escape its relativity to context. Dewey does not cling to any moral absolute; nor does he guarantee that with the most able use of intelligent reflection on the facts at hand we will succeed or be certain that we are doing the right thing. There is no right answer that fits every situation, but neither should we assume that every situation has one right answer. Many morally problematic situations are experienced as having several possible good or better answers. The idea that actions such as promise-keeping, killing, lying, and adultery are sometimes right and sometimes wrong depending on the situation and independent of a priori criteria or rules is uncomfortable for those who seek a fixed ethical standard. Can an ethics be so flexible without losing its credibility? Before considering this issue, we should guard Dewey against some misinterpretations of his position.

Dewey's situation ethics is not the narrowly individualistic view that one must decide for oneself according to one's own standards or feelings of right and wrong. Communal inquiry about shared moral problems is important, but it, too, should be sensitive to each particular context. Even for individual decision makers, Dewey is prescribing a way of interacting in a situation, rather than leaving decision making up to subjective moral introspection or some faculty of moral intuition. Moreover, Dewey is not endorsing an absolute particularism, where there is a radical discontinuity between situations and nothing of decision making importance is carried forward to new situations. On the contrary, lessons from previous experiences are part of one's present situational resources because we inherit and learn the appropriate response to situations from the evolving practices and institutions in which we participate.[4] We do this from habit and without much conscious effort. Dewey, therefore, does not hold the view that one should abandon all precedent, that we should come to a situation empty-handed and with a neutral or impartial attitude toward what is right or wrong. The abandonment of ready-made standards is consistent with a strong presumption against actions such as killing and lying. For

Dewey there is a choice between "throwing away rules previously developed and sticking obstinately by them" (MW 14:165). What is needed is to take rules as principles.

Principles

Dewey's distinction between principles and rules is not based on a difference in their contents but in the way we appropriate our inherited moral knowledge. Principles, as he uses the term, are not fixed or universal maxims that prescribe and determine what an agent ought to do. They are instead inherited instrumentalities for analyzing individual and unique situations. Dewey is willing to accept and adopt, say, the golden rule, but only as part of the tools of analysis that one might draw upon to consider what is morally relevant and to make a decision in a particular situation. Dewey explains:

> The Golden Rule gives me absolutely no knowledge, of itself, of what should I do. The question of what in this case I should do in order to do as I would has still to be resolved, though the Golden Rule be a thousand times my maxim. . . . [The Golden Rule] is a most marvelous tool of analysis; it helps me hew straight and fine in clearing out this jungle of relations of practice. (EW 3:100–101)

Similarly, he takes Kant's moral imperative as a useful device for moral deliberation, as a safeguard against intrusive tendencies in a situation, but not as an absolute test or indicator of what is morally correct.[5]

There are principles because there are stabilities in experience. Although situations are unique, they can be similar in many respects. This makes it possible for experience to be intellectually cumulative, that is, for general ideas to develop. Principles are general moral ideas in the sense of proposing generic conditions and relations to be met under circumstances of a certain kind. They are general and frequently valid maxims, but their validity ultimately depends upon their applicability to a situation; they alone have no normative force.

We can rely on principles because we can learn, and we can learn because there is continuity in experience. "Principles are empirical generalizations from the ways in which previous judgments of conduct have practically worked out" (MW 14:165). Without principles we lack the background knowledge that could help us in particular situations. They are part of the stable resources needed to confront the more precarious and novel elements of experience.

What is the appeal of a morality based on a fixed antecedent standard? Dewey diagnosed the quest for fixed rules and ideals in morality as a counterpart to the general quest for certainty that characterizes modern epistemology. Just as it has been assumed that without certainty there is no knowledge, in ethics it has been assumed that "absence of immutably fixed and universally applicable ready-made principles is equivalent to moral chaos" (MW 14:164). This is what I will henceforward refer to as the either/or dilemma: Either there is an absolute standard of value or we cannot judge or measure any value. The choice between the fixity of moral rules and moral chaos assumes that experience is either a fixed-block or a spontaneous flux. This ignores the fact that an alternative to fixity in habits or principles is change and continuity of growth. Principles can provide continuity, yet nonetheless evolve. It is possible to take seriously the moral knowledge we have inherited from our families, culture, and personal history, yet refuse to give up the kind of flexibility entailed by Dewey's situation ethics. Again, flexibility in our moral lives is needed not because of human limitations with respect to an antecedent moral truth, but because of the reality of change and novelty, that is, because "life is a moving affair in which old moral truth ceases to apply" (MW 14:164). Dewey thought it was possible and commendable to educate children to become committed to some valuable traditional moral principles, but at the same time to prepare them to be able to modify and apply these principles to complex and changing conditions. The burden of proof is on those who believe the either/or dilemma to show why this is not possible.

Principles are not independent entities capable of generating and sustaining their own status as principles. Their vitality and ability to be of use across situations depend in part on whether agents make a mechanical or an artistic use of them. We can preserve the life and spirit of a moral idea (to use a neutral term between principle and rule) as much as we can convert it into a petrification that is experienced merely as an external command or rule. When moral ideas degenerate into external rules they lose their capacity to assist us in our moral lives, for they become obstacles to a fresh exploration of a morally problematic situation. Dewey thinks we can avoid this if in our use of moral ideas we take as our model the way an artist uses her tools. "In the supreme art of life the tools must be less mechanical; more depends upon the skill of the artist in their manipulation, but they are none the less useful" (EW 3:101). We can avoid the mechanical (non-artistic) use of moral ideas if we continuously reflect upon them in light of present experience. That is, to ensure that rules are used as principles suffused with life and spirit, they have to be affected by intelligence. In reference to the golden rule, Dewey writes:

> That it, or any other rule, may be a workable tool, that it may really give
> aid in a specific case, it must have life and spirit. We cannot give it life
> and spirit necessary to make it other than a cramped and cramping
> petrification except through the continued free play of intelligence upon
> it. (EW 3:101–102)

In short, Dewey does not deny the importance of having, using, and carrying forward our inherited moral knowledge in the form of principles, ideals, and habits. But he believes that principles, etc., will lose their vitality and instrumental capacity the more they are absolutized, that is, when one does not continue to reexamine them in light of present conditions. Thus, the best way to show respect for a moral idea is to subject it to continuous reflective criticism.

> What truth-telling, what honesty, what patience, what self-respect are
> changes with every added insight into the relations of men and things. It
> is only the breath of intelligence blowing through such rules that keeps
> them from the petrification which awaits all barren idealities. (EW 3:103)

From this brief consideration of Dewey's view about the status and role of principles we have unveiled assumptions of central importance to his moral philosophy, ones that I will further explore in this study. They are assumptions about how we should engage ourselves as agents in moral experience and deliberation. The notion that the non-artistic use of moral ideas is what transforms them into useless and powerless tools in our moral life suggests important postulates of Dewey's moral philosophy. To anticipate a bit, Dewey's situational approach is inspired by, and assumes, the possibility of a moral life that is aesthetic in its mode of engagement. Furthermore, Dewey's thoughts about principles give us a clue about one important function of intelligence in his moral philosophy, namely, that intelligence constitutes the set of habits that can keep morality from degenerating into an unaesthetic activity that is externally imposed upon us. This is the way in which "moral life is protected from falling into formalism and rigid repetition. It is rendered flexible, vital, growing" (MW 12:180).

Dewey and Moral Particularism

Is Dewey's commitment to contextualism compatible with his emphasis on the importance of principles? There are philosophers today who would argue that a commitment to principles and contextualism generates an uneasy and problematic tension. Moral particularists have argued that contextualism in ethics entails that the search for moral principles in moral theory is misguided. The most radical versions hold that there is no need for moral principles; more moderate versions of contextualism claim that, although there are some principles, they are insufficient to guide moral deliberation and judgment. A brief comparison between Dewey and recent moral particularists will help clarify how distinctive Dewey's contextualism is and how he would answer common objections.

The moral particularist understands principles to be rules that establish some necessary connection between features of an action and their moral value. W. D. Ross may have been a contextualist in moral verdict (i.e., in deciding between competing principles) but his reliance on principles assumed that "if a feature counts in favor of action in one case, then necessarily it counts in favor in any case in which it appears."[6] Does the fact than an act is illegal, unjust, or a lie always count as a reason against doing it? Are there universal right-making features of an act? Is the valence of promise-breaking negative across all possible cases? The strongest possible case against the generalist (that is, those who defend this last assumption) holds instead that every reason is somehow altered with every change of context. This seems too strong a thesis, even for Jonathan Dancy, a moral particularist who sees no need for principles in ethics. Dancy prefers instead to state his position as the view that "all reasons are *capable* of being altered by changes in context."[7] Dancy allows for the possibility of a few invariant reasons across cases but he does not take this to be enough to validate generalism. He says,

> perhaps I will have to admit that not all reasons are sensitive to context in this way—that there are a privileged few, including probably the intentional inflicting of undeserved pain, which necessarily constitute the same sort of reason wherever they occur. If so, I will have lost a battle but won the war. For the main aim of my particularist position is to break the stranglehold of a certain conception of how moral reasons function—the *generalist* conception under which what is a moral reason in one situation is necessarily the same reason wherever it occurs.

Generalism, he concludes, is false as a view about what are the "rational constraints on moral thought and action."[8]

There is much about this recent moral particularist scholarship that resembles and provides further support to Dewey's ethics. Moral particularists seem to be committed to the sort of attention to the particularity of moral situations that Dewey stressed. There are, however, important differences between Dewey and the moral particularists.

First, although Dewey would agree with Dancy that "all reasons are capable of being altered by changes in context," this follows not only from Dewey's contextualism but also from his metaphysical stance that nothing in the universe is immune to change. The denial of this sort of necessity (invariance) does not mean, however, that there are no stable and persistent correlations between features of an action and their valence or rightness. Dewey would be suspicious of the options (*absolute* invariance and variance) assumed in this debate. The more interesting issue is whether ethical theory is capable of formulating, or should even try to formulate, what these stable correlations (between actions and their valence) are at any particular time. Dewey did not rule this out as a possible task of ethical theory in terms of principles, but he believed that principles were things that already function, and that perhaps function best, in the deliberations of particular agents who have inherited a moral tradition. This raises another noteworthy difference.

Principles are, for Dewey, something broader and more embedded in our ordinary moral affairs than the sort of intellectual or theoretical rule that concern particularists. Their rejection or dislike of principles is based on an overly theoretical conception of principles as propositions in a theory that specify how non-moral features are tied to moral ones in a situation. Since principles are, as Dewey believes, tools of analysis of an engaged moral agent, they need not have the sort of restricted propositional form assumed by the particularist. In other words, particularists are able to undermine the function and importance of principles simply because what they have in mind by principle is not part of anyone's moral experience.

The most important difference between Dewey and recent particularists is the ultimate context that is appealed to in the grounding of moral judgments. Dewey's particularism starts with and takes particular situations as the ultimate contexts of our moral deliberations, rather than as a holism of reasons. Dancy joins the ethical tradition he attacks in assuming that ethical theory must start with the abstraction of reasons in relation to each other in someone's moral deliberation. His concern is with "the nature of rationality" and with "holistic logic."[9] For Dewey, this way of proceeding in ethics assumes a theoretical starting point that leaves out the lived situational context that ultimately guides inquiry and in which people's reasons for action are found. In this Dancy is no different from traditional logicians who concern themselves with reasoning (the universe of discourse), as if this is all there is to inquiry, and as if the context in which reasoning occurs (universe of experience) is irrelevant to what guides the process of reasoning. For Dewey, as I will later discuss, there is a direct qualitative appreciation (judgment) of the situation as a whole that precedes and guides the survey of how reasons relate to each other in inquiry.

In the introduction to his new book, *Ethics without Principles,* Dancy acknowledges that there is more to moral life than moral thought when he says, "The book I have written is about how to understand the way in which reasons work, and deals largely with theories about reasons rather than life. As you can see, I would like to have been able to write the other book, the one about life, but this one is all I could manage."[10] This philosophical bracketing of moral thinking from moral life (experience) is the sort of starting point that Dewey was against. One cannot understand the way in which reasons work in moral deliberation without an account of moral experience. In isolating moral deliberation from moral experience, Dancy leaves out the context that was so important for Dewey and that set constraints that could help Dancy confront the charge of moral laxity raised by generalists.

For the generalist, the particularist's morality is lax because it fails to propose an account of how guidance in moral deliberation is possible without the guidance provided by principles. The particularist does well to respond that "there can be fully particular constraints on action, and the judgment that this action would be wrong is surely just such a thing. Constraints do not need to be general constraints, any more than reasons need to be general reasons."[11] From Dewey's point of view, there is no need to choose between the general constraints (i.e., the regulative function provided by principles) and the more particular constraints found in a situation. In most situations, it is precisely the interplay between principles (that represent funded experience) and the new and unique particulars that makes serious thinking difficult. More importantly, both the general and the particular are ultimately *within* and *guided by* something that is more particular than the reasons appealed to by the particularist, namely, a problematic situation. There are situations in which the weight of precedent or the need to be consistent is such that to insist on the particulars reflects a serious lack of sensitivity to the situation. In the end, it is the particular situation that demands a certain response from me, rather than the particular moral reasons or generalizations (i.e., rules). Sometimes, morality requires that we make a similar choice in a similar situation; but when this is so, it is because of what the particular situation requires, not because of what morality in general requires.

Dancy questions the assumption (of generalists) that without the moral stiffening provided by a principle-based ethics there is a serious danger of backsliding in ethics or of making exceptions in our own favor. Dewey is aware of the dangers of moral laxity and moral stiffening; and both are best guarded against by the cultivation of our characters. It is not clear, however, how the particularist can integrate virtues, as general habits, into their view. They criticize generalists in assuming the notion of the principled person as the model of a moral agent. Dancy claims, for example, that if the principled person is one merely driven by principle then this "will distort the relevance of relevant features by insisting on filtering them through principles."[12] He is silent, however, about the sort of character needed to attend with firm conviction case by case and without distorting things in one's own favor. Dewey, on the other hand, presents an alternative model to the generalist's man of principle. This is the model of the moral person that is aesthetically engaged in moral reconstruction. The sort of character that is genuinely engaged in moral experience attends wholeheartedly to what each particular situation requires but with the help, in part, of principles. I will have more to say about this later.

The most common objection against moral particularists is that, in their zeal to reject generalism, they tend to go overboard in making the particularities of a case wholly dominant. Dancy, for example, concludes that "morality can get along perfectly well without principles."[13] Even if one agrees with the particularist about the dangers of moral principles, "the particularist's response of jettisoning such principles introduces dangers that are far deeper."[14] Particularists are correct in suggesting that, with moral wisdom, as with other aspects of our practical life, it is a matter of directly exercising one's ability to judge rather than simply following rules (guidebooks, cookbooks, and primers). Yet, as Margaret Olivia Little has recently warned, "In issuing this crucial corrective, though, particularists must beware of committing the opposing sin."[15] Dewey would see this as one more instance of the "common occurrence in the histories of theories that an error at one extreme calls out a complementary error at the other extreme" (LW 13:240). Particularists defend contextualism by opposing themselves to what they call generalists and by rejecting principles. In contrast, Dewey called for a reconstruction in our understanding of moral generality and its function. Principles are part of the particular resources found in a particular situation. The alternative to the traditional view of morality that puts principles right at the center is one that puts situations at the center (which includes principles). There is no need to advocate the overthrow of generalities, abstractions, or theories. Even the most morally wise among us needs from time to time to depend on judgments about what tends to be morally relevant. What makes someone morally wise or unwise is *how* they rely on generalities. What must be dethroned are not moral generalizations per se but a way of using them that discourages moral sensitivity and precludes the genuine exercise of moral judgment.

Contextualism and the "Thinness" Challenge

Is Dewey's appeal to principles a satisfactory response to those concerned that his ethics is too flexible? Is taking certain rules as principles the way to avoid both moral absolutism and its opposite extreme? I suspect that those philosophers who lie at both sides of the either/or dilemma are likely to see in Dewey a position diametrically opposed to their own. The moral anarchist, who thinks that morality is a matter of arbitrary taste, would think of Dewey as a disguised absolutist, someone who is unwilling to accept the consequences of change and of the historical-cultural origin of our principles and morality. On the other hand, the absolutist would probably consider Dewey's way of taking moral precepts seriously as being insufficiently serious and as leading sooner or later to taking morality as something disposable. Dewey is aware that for many, "the hypothesis that each moral situation is unique and that consequently general moral principles are instrumental to developing the individualized meaning of situations is declared to be anarchic. It is said to be ethical atomism" (MW 14:167). The absolutist would argue, for example, that undesirable consequences follow if one takes the rule "you should not kill" as something that is only applicable and valid if the situation demands it (i.e., as a principle). For how can one be said to honor a rule when one is ready to break it if this is what the situation calls for? How on Dewey's view do we avoid countenancing the person who rationalizes an act of wrongdoing, such as killing, by claiming that for her "you should not kill" is merely a principle?

There is no need to be an absolutist or a moral anarchist to raise some serious challenges to Dewey's contextualism. One need not hold such extreme views to raise the following two objections. It seems to be an ethics that (1) cannot rule as morally impermissible actions that are re-garded as evidently wrong by most morally sensitive people, and (2) it is so thin that it is no help, that is, there is little substantial recommendation in terms of how to live, and how to steer in between the extremes that he criticizes (absolutism and relativism). Let's consider each one of these objections.

It is now customary in philosophy to test ethical theories by the use of counterexamples. If properly applying a proposed criterion of right con-duct in a situation leads to prescribing what is obviously morally wrong then so much the worse for the ethical theory. We cannot, however, apply this test to Dewey's ethics since his assumes no criterion. In fact, it is precisely the denial of the need for such a criterion that defines his view. Nevertheless, can his ethics rule that actions such as torturing children for fun are anything but wrong? If it cannot, then one may argue that there is something wrong with his view.

It does follow, according to Dewey's view, that it is possible for there to be a situation where torturing children for fun is morally permissible. Openness to this possibility, however, does not mean that in a concrete situation this action stands somehow on an equal basis with others, and Dewey would not have condoned the torture of children. Is there any genuine doubt that the presumption against torturing children for fun is so strong that it is hardly ever the subject of conscious deliberation? That does not make it immune to criticism, nor does it suggest that its stability and validity are independent of particular situations. It can be subject to evaluation and doubt in a situation, no matter how unlikely this may seem. Although it is hard to imagine a situation where torturing children for fun is morally permissible, it is clear that a Deweyan, fully committed to the openness entailed by contextualism, must bite the bullet and take this as evidence of the limits of our imagination.[16] There could be unique factors in a situation that may well change the moral quality of an act that has always been wrong. Does biting the bullet undermine the credibility or validity of Dewey's ethics? This would be to assume that an ethics without any absolute prohibitions couldn't be valid or helpful to moral life. Why?

This brings us to the second possible objection. If his ethics cannot rule out certain actions as wrong (by providing a fixed criterion of right or wrong) then one may question what good it is. If all that Dewey can tell us is that we should take certain purported rules as principles, then this does not help us avoid the dangers of moral absolutism and moral licentiousness that much. One hopes that Dewey's moral thought proposes something more substantial than the advice to stay away from standard moral theories and theorists. This in effect points to a challenge to any reconstruction of Dewey's ethics. The challenge is to present an ethics thin enough not to fall into another absolutist ethical system but thick enough to be taken seriously as an ethics that, in some indirect way, can at least illuminate moral practice. It is difficult for a contextualist who abandons the traditional pretensions of theory, as did Dewey, to make normative suggestions without compromising its openness to context.

The apparent thinness of Dewey's ethics has troubled both critics and sympathizers. C. I. Lewis, Sidney Hook, and more recently, Robert Westbrook and Hilary Putnam agree with Dewey that we must abandon the quest for some ultimate external, fixed, and absolute standard or criteria. But they all agree that there must be some other type of standard, otherwise Dewey's philosophy would be in trouble.

C. I. Lewis found Dewey's remarks that experience can regulate itself vague and problematic. He asked,

> But is it not the case that we must ourselves bring to experience the ultimate criterion and touchstone of the good; that otherwise experience could no more teach us what is good than it can teach the blind man what things are red?[17]

Pragmatism fails to give an adequate answer to the question about what guides us in experience. Lewis continues,

> Before one embarks upon the practical and empirical problem of realizing the valuable or constructing the good, is it not essential that one should be able to recognize it when disclosed . . . ? . . . [C]an experience determine the nature, essence, criteria of goodness?[18]

Sidney Hook and Robert Westbrook are concerned that Dewey did not say enough to meet this sort of challenge. Even if there are no fixed ends for Dewey, what criteria do we use to evaluate the success of our ends in view?[19] Even if there is no foundationalist-type of justification for democracy, Dewey must have assumed a criterion that made this way of life better than others.[20] Many scholars have tried to reconstruct Dewey's thought on the subject of criteria. These attempts strike me as either too thin or too thick because they miss something fundamental in Dewey's philosophy. Those that are too thick attribute to Dewey some criterion of goodness, even if it is not a fixed and external one. The usual candidates here are some goal or consequence, like growth or flourishing. They are too thick in the sense that they attribute to Dewey the sort of normative substance that goes against the contextualist and pluralistic character of his ethics. As I will argue, there is no criterion or standard of the good of any kind in Dewey's ethics.

Other efforts have been too thin; in particular, those that have acknowledged that even if there is no single standard in his philosophy, Dewey trusted that the plural standards that we have inherited from our previous experience and community will provide us with enough guidance. In other words, the past, in the form of principles and the lessons of previous inquiries, set present constraints. Putnam, for example, thinks that Dewey's answer to the question "By what criteria do we decide that some valuations are warranted?" is that "we always bring a large stock of valuations and descriptions" that we can rely on and "there are some good things that we have learned from inquiry in general"[21] that can be applied.

These last efforts are in the right direction. Yet they are too thin because there is for Dewey more to say about the moral guidance that he thinks we can discern in present experience. Even if some constraints are set by our previous experiences, it does not help us determine how we should guide ourselves in the use of these resources or in their criticism. Dewey's advice has to be more than that we follow the best principles available. And there is more to intelligence than applying standards of inquiry learned from experience.

Both of these interpretations or defenses of Dewey miss one of the most important, radical, and unique aspects of his philosophy. The notion that moral discourse depends only on its own evolving criteria or standards to guide itself misses the point that there is more to morality than moral discourse. In particular, there is the qualitative situational context; and far from being a mere background consideration, the context is what ultimately guides morality. Dewey has much to say regarding how we can best equip ourselves to rely on this guidance.

To adequately answer the charge of thinness requires that we take into consideration how thick Dewey's account is. As I will argue later, Dewey offers normative prescriptions; there are, in other words, better and worse ways of approaching moral problems and our moral relationships. In moral deliberation there is more to rely on than principles in coming to judgments about right and wrong; in particular, there is a qualitative context that, if we are equipped with the proper dispositions, can guide us. I will present Dewey's ethics as committed to certain dispositions, a certain character and community. One must not, however, expect to find in Dewey instructions that if followed will guarantee moral conduct or that will determine who is or is not acting morally or immorally. He does not offer any guarantee that even if we follow his advice we will stay within the bounds of moral decency or avoid relativism. This is not the function of an ethical theory. What, then, is the function of an ethical theory once one has abandoned the traditional expectations about ethical theory? Is there any legitimate role left for an ethical theory? Let's now consider these questions as a prologue to my presentation of the more substantive aspects of Dewey's ethical theory.

The Function of Moral Theory

Skepticism in regard to ethical theory is common in the contemporary intellectual climate. Bernard Williams, for example, has argued that "philosophy should not try to produce ethical theory."[22] For him the speculative kind of reflection involved in moral theory is harmful to moral practice because it tends to destroy knowledge at the practical level of specific moral decisions. On the other hand, there are philosophers who have tried to save ethics by claiming that the mistake lies in thinking that ethical theory has anything to do with aiding moral conduct. Ethical theory should be done exclusively for the sake of theoretical understanding or to solve the theoretical problems of philosophers. In other words, only meta-ethics or general and abstract theoretical speculations for theoretical purposes are possible. Dewey was sensitive to both of these extreme views but never thought we had to choose between them. For Dewey, there is an alternative which lies between divorcing ethical theory completely from moral practice and the pretensions of some normative ethical theories to dictate our moral conduct. The key to seeing this alternative lies in having an adequate empirical conception of what a theory is.

In an early essay Dewey explains the functional relation between theory and practice by using the example of an engineer building a tunnel. No matter how many times the engineer has constructed similar tunnels, what she is building is not a tunnel in general. "It is a tunnel having its own special end and called for by its own set of circumstances" (EW 3:156). However, because similar tunnels have been built under functionally similar circumstances one may develop theories or techniques that, because of their generality, can function as tools of analysis for particular cases. Hence, the general character of theories is not a limitation but the key to their possible functional importance for practice. To be sure, not all of the theoretical resources available to the engineer have the same kind of instrumental value. The most immediate ready at hand tools are principles or rules of thumb that provide a suggestion as to what to do when one is building this kind of tunnel. An engineer might also have a very general theory about the nature of the materials used to make the tunnel. Even if this theory makes no reference to the practice of building tunnels, it is not entirely divorced from or irrelevant to that practice.

In general, Dewey claims that theory cannot be divorced from the context of practice; for theory arises from, is informed by, and affects practice. It is true that theoretical moral inquiry has its own theoretical problems, very different in nature from the concrete moral conflicts that are the origin of personal moral deliberation. However, theoretical inquiry is not the quest for a "foundation for moral activity in something beyond that activity itself" (EW 3:94). To think otherwise is to commit the philosophical fallacy. For Dewey, moral philosophy is invariably and inevitably enmeshed in a particular context, that is, it is a function *of* and *within* moral life. The refined conclusions (i.e., secondary products) of moral theory are, like the theoretical resources of the engineer, instrumentalities by which we might be able to *indirectly* assist or illuminate the decisions and problems encountered in primary moral experience. When theory is conceived as something within practice it becomes a part of the available means for the intelligent amelioration of practice. "Theory located within progressive practice instead of reigning statically supreme over it, means practice itself made responsible to intelligence" (MW 4:48).

The conception of moral theory as somehow existing outside or above the context of moral practice is the source of recent skepticism about theory. Bernard Williams, for example, criticizes the history of moral philosophy for its futile attempt to find an "Archimedean point."[23] This is the place from which (1) one can objectively evaluate competing answers to how to live; or (2) one can discover universal criteria of right or wrong action; or (3) where one can argue that anyone (even the moral skeptic or anarchist) has reasons to live an ethical life. Indeed, traditional ethical theory usually assumes that to have a normative ethics is to have a philosophical answer to these issues. For Williams, as Susan Wolf explains, we must come to terms with the fact that our "point of view, even in philosophical reflection, is inevitably from *here*, and not from 'a mid-air position'."[24] This should deflate significantly our expectations in regard to what moral theory can do for moral practice. Williams asserts the Deweyan thesis that ethical theories "still have to start from somewhere, and the only starting point left is ethical experience itself";[25] but unlike Dewey, he doesn't derive constructive implications from the conception of theory within moral practice.[26]

THE EMPIRICAL-INSTRUMENTAL CONCEPTION OF MORAL THEORY

For Dewey the view that moral theory is both *in* and *for* moral life has important implications regarding how to evaluate ethical theories and their most productive functions. The most straightforward of these is that one cannot determine what an adequate ethical theory is without considering what kind of ethical theory is better for our moral lives. In other words, the worth of a theory is determined not only in terms of its intellectual consistency and coherence or its explanatory power, but also in terms of its instrumental and ameliorative powers in the context of practice. This allows us to propose hypotheses about when, and in what form, moral theory helps and when it hinders moral practice. Of course, any suggestion in this regard is ultimately an empirical claim, one that has to be tested in the moral lives of agents, remains open for future inquiry, and should be evaluated in light of the particular theories available at any given time. Dewey's own evaluation of some of the ethical theories of his time led him to some general hypotheses about this issue.

Dewey believed that our moral lives are better served if ethical theory becomes empirical. As we have seen this means primarily that ethics must take morally problematic situations in their qualitative uniqueness as the start and end point of inquiry, and avoid the adoption of any kind of axiomatic first principles. No ethical theory is final. It must have a dynamic, open, and learning relation with respect to the practice out of which it arises and within which it is embedded. However, one might accept the general claim that empirical theories are better than non-empirical ones and still remain skeptical about the point of ethical theory. For it is not clear what role there is left for ethics, once one gives up its traditional goals. Does this mean that philosophers should redirect their concern with theory to a more direct and exclusive concern with specific practical problems, as in what is today called applied ethics? This issue needs to be considered in order to avoid saddling a Deweyan approach to ethics with a narrow kind of instrumentalism about moral theory.

Ethical theory is not necessarily made more practical simply by having as its direct end a desire to be practical. In philosophy, just as in science, a constant fixation and concern with practical problems and ends could undermine practical effectiveness. One might argue that productive inquiry requires a division of labor where there are individuals who are directly involved in doing theory for theory's own sake. This is not to deny that there are excesses and dangers that result when intellectuals are so committed to their theories that they forget the place of theory within the context of moral practice. The failure to be empirical is perhaps the result of being seduced by one's interest as a theorist.

If the function of moral theory is to assist our moral practice, then the operations and selectivity of a theorist should be guided by purposes that enhance this function. However, the temptation of the ethical theorist is to guide her selectivity by theoretical or academic purposes that are irrelevant, secondary, or even counterproductive to the improvement of moral practice. For instance, selecting only those features of moral life that can be quantified, universalized, or made commensurable in terms of a theory is not in the best interest of morality as a lived practice. Moral theories are bad tools if they suggest that the complexity, uncertainty, and incommensurability that we experience in our moral lives are illusory. One is more likely to direct the changes in experience intelligently if one is faithful to its present traits.

Does ethics become more practical by limiting itself to applied ethics, that is, if it addresses particular problems instead of the usual general ones?

One cannot assume that the non-practical character of a philosophy is proportional to how comprehensive, general, and speculative it is. In conceiving of theories as tools, there is room for specialized tools as well as for tools that have a wide range of application and reference, and either one can be an obstacle or an aid to moral practice. Hence, philosophy cannot be disregarded as a speculative waste of time simply because it is concerned with formulating hypotheses of wide applicability. Of course, this is not to deny the futility of philosophical inquiries that are so abstract as to be completely detached from everyday moral experience. From a practical point of view, the problem with these inquiries is not that they are abstract or general per se, but rather that they usually reify their theoretical abstractions over aspects of ordinary experience. Dewey was aware of this common misunderstanding about pragmatism. He corrected C. I. Lewis once on this issue,

> Abstraction is the heart of thought; there is no way—other than accident —to control and enrich concrete experience except through an intermediate flight of thought with conceptions, relations, abstracta. What I regret is the tendency to erect the abstractions into complete and self-subsistent things, or into a kind of superior Being. (LW 7:216)

Here Dewey's view can be contrasted to that of Bernard Williams. Williams contrasts the thickness of ethical terms and the deliberations of concrete moral agents with the thinness of ethical theories. Williams believes that ethical theory can be discredited because it "looks characteristically for considerations that are very general and have as little distinctive content as possible."[27] For Dewey, the problem with the abstract and general categories of traditional ethical theories is not that they are thin or general, but that these reflective products are used to discredit, ignore, and replace the richness of concrete moral experience. The implication is that so long as ethical theorists recognize that our actual ethical lives are richer, more variegated, and thicker than our theoretical articulations, an ethical theory can be thin and speculative without undermining its legitimate instrumental function.

I do not want to suggest the equally implausible view that the degree of abstractness and generality or specificity of an ethical theory is totally irrelevant to its instrumental possibilities. It would be futile to try to lay out any universal and fixed rule about this issue; accordingly, Dewey proposes a general rule of thumb or vague hypothesis in this matter. He claims that the kind of ethical theory that is adequate and capable of functioning as a tool for our moral life has to avoid becoming either so general as to be abstract or so specific as to replace the particularity of our lived experience. In other words, ethical theories and rules can become bad tools when they are either too abstract or too specific. In one of his early ethical writings, Dewey wrote,

> The difficulty, then, is to find the place intermediate between a theory general to the point of abstractness, a theory which provides help to action, and a theory which attempts to further action, but does so at the expense of its spontaneity and breadth. I do not know of any theory, however, which is quite consistent to either point of view. (EW 3:155)

This is a claim that can be understood in terms of both the descriptive and the normative functions of ethical theories. A metaphysics of morals (as an empirical description of moral experience) is undesirable when it consists of excessively abstract generalities that "remain remote from contact with actual experience" (EW 3:159). Yet a metaphysics that can illuminate practice cannot be too specific. Dewey's reference to an empirical metaphysics as a "ground map of the province of criticism" provides a useful analogy to make this point (LW 1:309). A map can be general to the point of becoming a useless abstraction. On the other hand, a map that pretends to capture the uniqueness of the streets we travel or that tells us where to go becomes a bad tool. Furthermore, the fact that a map cannot have this kind of precision is hardly a good excuse for not using or making maps. Dewey uses this argument to support the construction and use of moral theory.

Ethical theories can become so abstract and general that they are of no use to moral practice; but the general character of theory is a precondition for it to inform and be informed by practice. It makes possible a dynamic relation between theory and practice where "the former enlarges, releases and gives significance to the latter; while practice supplies theory with its materials and with the test and check which keep it sincere and vital" (LW 2:58). Ethical theory can also be a tool for moral education. Like our best maps, it can orient us, but we must do our own traveling and learning. In both aesthetics and ethics a philosopher should be more concerned with a survey of the subject matter than with making judgments for others. "Then his surveys may be of assistance in the direct experience of others, as a survey of a country is of help to the one who travels through it, while dicta about worth operate to limit personal experience" (LW 10:313).

In sum, the alternative to either an ethical theory that stands totally aloof or one that pretends to lay down in advance fixed rules is an empirical theory concerned with the generic in moral experience, and that offers only indirect assistance to moral practice. These seem, so far, to be rather formal or methodological conditions of a theory. The type of theory that meets these conditions cannot solve moral problems. It cannot adopt the kind of standpoint where it convinces a moral skeptic that it is rational to be moral; and it cannot provide a rational proof that Hitler's conduct was wrong. Is there anything it can do? What sort of indirect assistance can be proposed? If one wishes to confront the skeptic about the possibilities of ethical theory once its traditional pretensions are abandoned, it is necessary to suggest some specific positive functions that a Deweyan ethics can perform. There are at least two. An ethical theory can function as a tool of criticism, and it can propose hypotheses about the conditions for living a better moral life.

Ethical Theory as Criticism

Philosophy is criticism for Dewey, and reflective criticism always takes place in the non-cognitive context of a situation that cannot be transcended. Nevertheless, effective criticism needs to begin with what we experience, and its point is to enhance, assist, and transform present experience. Let's consider how this entails a positive function or potential for ethical theory. Although too much reflective criticism might sometimes be harmful to moral practice, Dewey understood that without it, the quality (spirit and life) of our moral life suffers. Moral ideals degenerate into petrifications or mechanical rules when they are not subject to reflective criticism in light of present experience. It might be argued that, even if an examined life is better than an unexamined one, it does not follow that theoretical reflection is worthwhile or has a useful function in moral life. There is some truth to this, but theoretical reflection can provide a wider and broader perspective that is sometimes needed for effective criticism. This is why Dewey calls philosophy "criticism of criticism." To be sure, wider and broader does not mean or imply outside.

Dewey declared as illusory the notion of ethical theory as performing criticism from an outside privileged standpoint, but he never doubted the possibility of criticism from within. This is the possibility that seems to be ruled out or ignored by recent skeptics of theory, such as Richard Rorty and Bernard Williams. This has left them in an awkward position. For many have questioned whether the narrow role they have left for philosophical reflection is sufficient to engage (or make possible) the kind of social criticism and reflective moral life to which they seem to be committed. In effect, their repudiation of ethical theorizing is interpreted as a moral conservatism, insofar as it seems to imply that we should leave moral practice as it is. To be sure, Dewey did not hold the view that ethical theory is necessary for a reflective moral life; however, he hoped that, once reconstructed, it would be a potentially useful resource for such a life. This was a resource he used in his criticism of traditional moral philosophy and of the society and times in which he lived. The theoretical use of intelligence cannot make contextual decisions, but it might be able to undermine misleading assumptions and beliefs that are often operative in such contexts.

There are two different tasks for moral theory as a tool of criticism: the descriptive and the normative. The descriptive function is to provide a generic but faithful description of the generic traits of moral experience (the subject matter of part 2 of this book). The point is not to provide a picture of how things really are, but to provide a basis for reconstructing traditional notions of character, moral deliberation, and moral problems that usually presuppose dualisms. These dualisms are not mere intellectual problems; rather, they reflect or reinforce ways of conceiving moral life that are obstacles for the present amelioration of our moral experience. Furthermore, the descriptive-metaphysical task is an important precondition and basis for making any criticism of positive proposals about how to live. Dewey said, "The more sure one is that the world which encompasses human life is of such and such a character (no matter what his definition), the more one is committed to try to direct the conduct of life, that of others as well as himself, upon the basis of the character assigned to the world" (LW 1:309).

But descriptive criticism from the point of view of how things are can be complemented by normative criticism from the point of view of how things should be. "No just or pertinent criticism in its negative phase can possibly be made, however, except upon the basis of a heightened appreciation of the positive goods which human experience has achieved and offers" (LW 1:308). Hence, a moral theory can also articulate and make explicit a moral ideal (the subject matter of part 3) that can be used to criticize present beliefs and institutions. This also makes such an ideal both available and subject to criticism. This is the only way we can preserve the life and spirit of a worthwhile ideal, and this is what Dewey tried to do in regard to democracy. Still, there is bound to be some skepticism about the adoption of such a traditional notion as that of ideals by a pragmatist. How can this be compatible with the commitment to a situational contextualism?

Pragmatism recognizes the reality and necessary role of ideals in human life. They are "as natural to man as his aches and his clothes" (LW 1:312). They are real because potentialities and possibilities are part of experience. They are not made out of subjective matter, nor do they come from a Platonic heaven; they are active instrumentalities in experience.

William James said that ideals "ought to aim at the transformation of reality—no less."[28] For the pragmatist, ideals are ends but they are not ends in themselves, that is, ends that are not also means. They are not fixed or final ends, and they are subject to refinement or change. They are not states of ultimate repose, nor do they have antecedent existence. Dewey put this eloquently when he said, "Men do not shoot because targets exist, but they set up targets in order that throwing and shooting may be more effective and significant" (MW 14:156). Most of our ideals, like democracy, are inherited as possibilities from tradition. Our creative task is to use ideals to modify actual conditions, and to reconstruct ideals to fit the actual situation. In other words, both the actual and the ideal are open to modification and improvement by an experimental and continuous process.

Ideals can be distinguished from other ends by their inclusivity. In an ideal, constructive imagination puts together into a coherent whole values that have been previously experienced. Every ideal, Dewey says, "projects in a securer and wider and fuller form some good which has been previously experienced in a precarious, accidental, fleeting way" for the purposes of criticism. (MW 14:20) So, for example, by projecting the positive traits of actual forms of community life into an ideal, we can use the ideal to criticize undesirable features of our community and suggest improvement. Ideals serve as a "basis for criticism of institutions as they exist and of plans of betterment" (LW 7:349).

It is dangerous for ethical theory to take the formulation of ideals as its major task. Dewey warned us that "the trouble with ideals of remote perfection is that they tend to make us negligent of the significance of the special situations in which we have to act" (LW 7:273). However, a pragmatic understanding of the proper function of ideals makes the commitment to an ideal compatible with the commitment to the amelioration of present situations. For neither one of these commitments is a mere end for the other. Projected ideals and goals give a general direction; they provide an additional continuity from situation to situation in that our present efforts are served by an ideal. But ideals are also served and informed by their application. We can set up ideals in order to improve our actual conditions, but they do not demarcate the absolute limits of improvement, for they are themselves subject to constant improvement. Ideals give coherence and stability to our lives, but of a mobile sort, that is, the ideal itself unfolds and expands. Ideals can also become idle and impotent fantasies if we consider them independently of the means of their realization. It is through an explicit articulation and evaluation of ideals in terms of concrete existential requirements and the means of their realization that we can begin making ideals relevant and effective.

In today's intellectual environment the philosophical articulation of an ideal seems like a gratuitous theoretical and speculative indulgence. For Dewey, ideals are integral parts of any worthwhile philosophy. The contemporary resistance to associating philosophy with moral ideals is due to the neglect of the contextual nature of all philosophical reflection, and is based on the assumption that philosophy is just a "form of knowledge" (LW 6:43). Dewey pleads that we should return to the original meaning of philosophy as love of wisdom, that is, as involving moral concern or commitment. The present professional view of philosophy does not let us think of philosophers as intellectuals with a sense of a better kind of life to lead, or as those who use "the best knowledge and the best intellectual methods available in their day" for its articulation and support, and to persuade themselves and others of its reasonableness. (LW 6:44) One main premise of this work is that Dewey was just this kind of intellectual. By Dewey's standards most philosophers today lack the imagination and the boldness to propose ideals as tools for present amelioration and criticism. The last chapters of this book are my efforts to put together into a coherent whole Dewey's moral vision in terms of ideal character, relationships, communication, and community. I propose a hypothesis to be tested and modified by its means and application.

Ethical Theory as Inquiry into Conditions

Dewey hoped that ethical theory would shift its concern from trying to make decisions for individuals and reducing moral experience to abstractions, to the study of the conditions of these experiences and their betterment. The persistent attempt by ethicists to lay down rules or universal criteria is a misuse of intelligence and needs to be replaced by efforts to "devote themselves to studying the conditions and effects of the changing situations in which men actually live" (MW 3:57).

Inquiry into conditions in ethics assumes a conception of ethical theory within practice. It assumes that this kind of theory will be meaningful only to those who have had moral experiences. For those of us who are immersed within moral life, convincing an imaginary radical skeptic is at best secondary to inquiring into the conditions for improving experiences we already have.

The general inquiry about what would enhance or what would be obstacles to moral life can take many forms. Insofar as there are economic, biological, or cultural conditions to moral experience it may be appropriate to consult different disciplines. In moral philosophy, however, we can make an important functional distinction in a situation between the way of experiencing and what is experienced, that is, between method and subject matter. This needs to be done without abandoning the notion of a situation as the locus of moral experience.

The recognition that what is experienced is not independent of what we bring to a situation (e.g., our habits) was a great modern discovery. However, instead of using it to regulate the course of experience, philosophers have used it to defend the reduction of experience to experiencing, that is, to subjectivism. Experiencing has no existence apart from the subject matter experienced. We can distinguish the enjoyment from the objects enjoyed but "we do not enjoy enjoyments, but persons, scenes, deeds, works of art . . ." (LW 15:80). For Dewey, the purpose of this functional distinction is to provide some control over the direction or quality of our moral experience. The concern with conditions in morality is an attention to method, understood as the habits, character, or ways of life that determine how to interact with and participate in situations. Given the uniqueness of our characters, each one of us has unique ways of interacting in situations, but we can also distinguish generic ways. For example, approaching a situation with openness is a generic trait even though each one of us is open in a different way. Moreover, we can distinguish different levels of generality in how we interact in situations, for example, habits as particular ways of interacting, and character as a complex unity that defines how an organism interacts. We can even move to another level and speak of a way of life as a shared general way of interacting. These are abstract but very useful distinctions that I will rely on in presenting Dewey's views in the following chapters.

There are good reasons why ethics so understood should focus on character. In Dewey's ethics character and habits are central, but not because they have ontological or epistemological primacy. They should be the foremost concern of moral reflection and theory simply because habits are the most controllable factor we have among all the factors that come to determine the direction and moral quality of experience.

Principles (as empirical generalizations) and ideals (as comprehensive ends-in-view) are important resources at the foreground of moral inquiry. Habits determine to some extent our basic moral sensitivities in morally problematic situations and our way of thinking through them. Aristotle was right in emphasizing the importance of cultivating moral habits. I will argue that, for Dewey, the most important instrumentalities for morality, the cardinal virtues, are the traits of character that can improve moral habits and, more importantly, better assist us in determining what morality requires in particular situations. Dewey's contextualism thus advances a view about which habits are better in confronting moral situations, even if it does not prescribe beforehand what to do in these situations. Moral anarchy and chaos are not avoided by fixing moral rules, but by the proper cultivation of character. The kind of character we should develop is thus for Dewey a more important consideration than what decision procedure we should adopt. Character, however, is not under our direct control. You can no more transform (ameliorate) character by teaching the right rules of conduct than you can produce democracy by preaching its virtues. Ethical theory needs to come to terms with the indirect and uncertain aspects of its prescriptions. The transformation of character can be a slow and arduous process requiring the indirect change of environmental conditions.

THREE

The Normative Standpoint of Pragmatism

"How Should We Live?"

The functional distinction between experiencing—the *how*—and the subject matter experienced—the *what*—allows a pragmatist to recover the normative ethical issue of how one should live in a way that is consistent with her philosophical approach. The normative issue is about how one should interact in moral situations, rather than the one expressed by the question, "What is the good life?" Whereas the latter usually assumes an Archimedean point of view, the former merely assumes that our participation is one of the conditions of moral experience and that it can be evaluated. In order to have control in the direction and quality of our lives we can discriminate between how we should live (or between acceptable ways of life) and our circumstances, even if, concretely speaking, there is no ideal way of life independent of concrete living. This means that a philosophical investigation of this question starts from where we are. The question is not how we, as human beings or as beings with a human nature considered independently of present actual experience (i.e., of time, culture, and history), should lead our lives. In the context of experience the question that requires an answer is a matter of choice, rather than idle speculation; for it needs to be answered in terms of what our present living[1] options are, where we are, and what we can do. The issue is a momentous and forced one because we are not subjects who can stand outside the course of events; participation or engagement of some form or another is unavoidable. The only choice available to us is between modes of participation. As Dewey says, "one cannot escape the problem of how to engage in life, since in any case he must engage in it some way or another—or else quit and get out" (MW 14:58). This does not mean that we are trapped—unless we presuppose a non-relational, non-contextual notion of ourselves. However, it does mean that the question about how we should live cannot be answered once and for all; there is no final resting place, and no final answer, because our options and conditions can change. But this is not a good enough reason to neglect the question. Therefore the pragmatic approach has to be tentative.

It might be objected that once one gives up the Archimedean standpoint one also has to give up the normative task of being concerned with how one should live, since there is no justifiable and non-arbitrary standpoint from which to judge this issue. Richard Rorty claims that a pragmatist needs to admit that there is "no ahistorical standpoint from which to endorse the habits of modern democracies he wishes to praise," that there is no "demonstration of the 'objective' superiority of our way of life over all other alternatives."[2] For Rorty, the alternative to an ahistorical objective justification is not despair, but solidarity. We need to learn to be "ethnocentric" and to "privilege our own group, even though there can be no noncircular justification for doing so."[3] Since it is idle to want to stand outside our particular community and look down at it from a more universal standpoint, we should cultivate the desire to stand by our traditional liberal habits and hopes simply because they are ours. In the end, Rorty recommends a blind solidarity that merely justifies the status quo; in so doing, he places us in a false dilemma.

Dewey rejects the choice between ahistorical objectivity and solidarity, and thus rejects Rorty's dilemma. We do not have to stand outside experience or assume a God's-eye point of view in order to assess the options available to us. Neither is there a field of experience that provides all the considerations relevant to the evaluation of a mode of participation in experience. We can use past experience and our knowledge of actual conditions in order to evaluate our options. We need to start from where we are, but we can also learn from where we have been. The options we have today are not strictly the same as the ones our ancestors had, but neither are they so different that learning from past experience is impossible. Moreover, philosophers can generate hypotheses about which general ways of interacting in situations are better in light of the generic traits of present experience. Even if experience is fairly hospitable and tolerant to all types of character and ways of life, it might not lend itself equally to all ideals. For example, if change, novelty, and risk are traits of moral experience, can we not use this understanding to develop a hypothesis about what dispositions it would be better for one to have? Is it outlandish to claim that in a world of change, novelty and risk, one disposed to meet new demands, to embrace novel situations, and to be capable of constant readjustment will fare better than one with a fixed and static character? If moral experience is irreducibly plural in the sense that neither the right nor the good are reducible to each other, then we ought to pay attention to that fact instead of trying to live as if this plurality is illusory or as if an ultimate moral category exists.

I will demonstrate the thickness of Dewey's ethics in terms of the general and tentative proposals about how one should interact in situations; indeed, this is the only sense in which his ethics can be called normative. A proposal about how best to approach moral problems and engage in moral situations should be distinguished from the traditional ethical tasks of providing the answer to moral problems or of proposing a mechanical decision procedure by which we can solve all problems. Such methodological proposals are not universal or fixed prescriptions but rather are instruments at the disposal of persons already caught up in moral life. This weaker or more humble task can be as normative as the commandments of some ethical theories. There is a difference between a theory that states what one should do and one that recommends in a very general and tentative way how one can live a better life. Whereas the content of the first kind consists of rules, formulas or imperatives, the latter claims only general proposals that must ultimately be tested in the lives of individuals. In short, ethical inquiry can propose hypotheses about dispositions and instrumentalities that can assist individual reflection and are likely to improve or enhance moral life. These proposals are hypotheses of the form, "if you cultivate x you are likely to be better prepared to meet the demands of morality than if you do not."

If a Deweyan ethics can be normative in this humble sense, how can we evaluate the adequacy of such a view? We cannot test its adequacy via the usual use of counterexamples, for example, by considering whether it is able to judge as immoral the actions of someone like Hitler. Instead, it has to be the sort of philosophical inquiry that if successful provides good philosophical reasons why something is worth trying, and is presented with enough specificity to know when it is being tried. For Dewey, the most controlled environment for testing his hypotheses was the class-room; this is why he thought that moral theory and moral education were interdependent.

Dewey was fully committed to democracy as a moral ideal, that is, as a tool that provides some guidance without being the normative basis of all values, or without telling us what to do in a particular situation. Neverthe-less, I will argue in the last part of this book that a reconsideration of Dewey's view on democracy in light of his ethics discloses an even thicker description of democracy, one that goes beyond the vague commitments of Deweyans to notions like social intelligence, communal inquiry, and growth. Democracy is part of a general moral outlook toward the world and others. It is not merely a type of social procedure or mode of public deliberation; moreover, Dewey's defense of democracy as a way of life is not made from an Archimedean standpoint. He merely wants to win the consent of people who are already committed to certain values and who are challenged by certain concrete problems. Why must the only rea-sonable justification of democracy be the one that convinces an imagi-nary rational agent or a radical moral skeptic under ideal conditions? This again assumes a very questionable starting point for a philosophy of democracy.

The task of eliciting and articulating the thickness of Dewey's ethics in terms of the two general theoretical tasks just described will occupy us for the remainder of this study. But to some extent I have already begun. For I have unveiled Dewey's methodological commitments and hinted at some moral commitments behind his skepticism of traditional ethical theories. I have already indicated that his anti-theoretical views and his notion of principles cannot be understood independently of other assumptions that are part of his moral vision, for example, the function of intelligence and the artistic use of moral ideas. I will further explore the meaning and implications of these assumptions and the commitments they presuppose. But before moving into broad hypotheses about our moral lives I think it is important to reiterate why any adequate unfolding or examination of Dewey's ethical vision needs to begin and take as central the notion of a situation.

For Dewey, in our moral life we are always *in* a situation. His norma-tive proposals, no matter how general or abstract they might seem, are about how to participate in situations. Furthermore, if we wanted to summarize most of what Dewey's moral vision proposes, we could say that his moral philosophy encourages us to live *by* and *for* a situation. In other words, a concrete situation should be the means and end of morality. Let's begin to explore what this means.

Faith in Experience: The Situation as the Means and End of Morality

I have claimed that in the issue of moral decision making Dewey espoused a situation ethics. This position is based on a contextualist view about how acts acquire a moral cast or quality, and it is supported by Dewey's views about the relation between theory and practice. But there is a more important positive commitment that underlies and supports this view. The suggestion that we try a fresh and wholehearted use of intelligence for each situation that requires amelioration, instead of appealing to external authority or to ready-made rules, assumes a positive trust in the possibilities and instrumentalities available in a situation. Dewey claims, in other words, that the situation is not only the end but also the means of moral endeavor. Hence, a morally problematic situation can achieve its end through its own means.

This is an instance of Dewey's faith in experience or nature,[4] a commitment central to his philosophical vision. This is the idea that we do not have to look for guidance outside of experience because experience contains the resources for its own transformation. In *Logic: The Theory of Inquiry* (LW 12), Dewey presents the bold hypothesis that logical forms arise in the course of inquiry, a hypothesis very similar to that in his ethics about moral norms, standards, principles, and ideals. They "arise out of ordinary transactions; they are not imposed upon them from on high or from any external and a priori source . . . they regulate the proper conduct of the activities out of which they develop" (LW 12:106). Moral norms grow out of, and exert their normative force from, the moral inquiries that occur in the stream of situations that constitute our moral life. Their function is to transform indeterminate situations, that is, to help us with moral problems. Other resources available to an agent in a morally problematic situation are principles, ideals, and habits; more importantly, the qualitative context itself (in which we experience problems) can guide us, provided we are ready to listen.

Dewey's faith in experience is implicit in his advocacy for the kind of philosophical empiricism explained earlier, and he gave reasons for preferring his method to a non-empirical method in philosophy. For instance, the non-empirical method provides no test or verification for its conclusions, and it generates problems that are abstract, artificial, and act as "blocks to inquiry, blind alleys" (LW 1:17). But, more importantly, non-empirical philosophies "cast a cloud over the things of ordinary experience" (LW 1:40) and "obscure the potentialities of daily experience for joy and self-regulation" (LW 1:41). Hence, in proposing a method in philosophy he was suggesting more than the adoption of a formal procedure or a way of solving or dissolving problems in philosophy. He makes this clear when he prefaces the text of *Experience and Nature* with "If what is written in these pages has no other result than creating and promoting a respect for concrete human experience and its potentialities, I shall be content" (LW 1:41). The pragmatist's concern with experience is not parasitic on a prior concern with knowledge, as it is with the traditional empiricist; on the contrary, the pragmatist is concerned with knowledge only insofar as it is a means to enhance our lived present experience.

Dewey's work on metaphysics, logic, epistemology, aesthetics, ethics, and philosophy of religion affirms the potential of ordinary experience (concrete life) to be the source of amelioration, admiration, and inspiration. His metaphysics reminds philosophers that the tangled, complex, gross, macroscopic, and crude things we find in everyday life are real, for example, vagueness, ugliness, fantasies, headaches, illusions, spark plugs, a conversation with a friend, parties, diseases, stones, food, tragedy, a conflict with a roommate, a joke, playing backgammon with friends, measles, and marbles. His aesthetics is a philosophical reintegration of the aesthetic with everyday life that is, in effect, a celebration of lived experience. I will argue that his ethics is an affirmation of *morality as experience*. Dewey affirmed a "confidence in the directive powers that inhere in experience, if men have but the wit and courage to follow them" (LW 1:5), and thought that otherworldly and subjectivist views of morality are contrary to this affirmation. This is the basis of his faith in inquiry, intelligence, education, and democracy.

If there is today a lack of confidence in experience or in moral theory it is because we have had exaggerated and naïve expectations about our own capacities within nature. Because we cannot get what we want from lived experience with little effort and with the desired level of certainty, we have decided to rebel against it, either by trying to stand outside or above the context of our particular lived moral experience (as in many forms of objectivism), or by assuming that our moral ideals are protected from the course of natural events because they reside in the realm of our own human creations. The alternative to the traditional quest for certainty and an Archimedean objective standpoint is not that we are just humans talking to each other, trapped in our own language, culture, history, and inherited standards. Dewey's faith lay between these extremes.

> Men move between extremes. They conceive of themselves as gods, or feign a powerful and cunning god as an ally who bends the world to do their bidding and meet their wishes. Disillusioned, they disown the

world that disappoints them; and hugging ideals to themselves as their own possession, stand in haughty aloofness apart from the hard course of events that pays so little heed to our hopes and aspirations. (LW 1:314)

Dewey was not naïve. He believed that the course of events in nature and the quality of our moral life is not altogether under our control, but he didn't see this as a good reason to abandon an inquiry into what difference we can make. Dewey found it childish to abandon that which is in our power on the ground that we lack total control.

> We know that though the universe slay us still we may trust, for our lot is one with whatever is good in existence. We know that such thought and effort is one condition of the coming into existence of the better. As far as we are concerned it is the only condition, for it alone is in our power. To ask more than this is childish; but to ask less is a recreance no less egotistic, involving no less a cutting of ourselves from the universe than does the expectation that it meet and satisfy our every wish. (LW 1:314)

These passages assume a very delicate balance that is key to Dewey's vision. Dewey presents us with a "doctrine of humility" but also of "direction" (LW 1:373). He recognizes that we can only operate in a piecemeal fashion and from where we are. The way to rely on (lie back upon) lived experience is to rely on what is directly experienced. This requires that we open and trust our eyes, ears, and thoughts; but it must not be naïve, it is not a blind trust. We are no longer naïve, for example, about how undesirable racial or class-based prejudices can condition our immediate moral experience. We cannot question everything at once but we must nonetheless try to question. Dewey says, "An empirical philosophy is in any case a kind of intellectual disrobing. . . . We cannot achieve recovery of primitive naïveté. But there is a cultivated naïveté of eye, ear, and thought" (LW 1:40). Cultivated naïveté requires both trust and criticism. As I discuss in later chapters, the ideal is the balance between receptivity (appreciation) and criticism. We must be ready to doubt, but we must do so for the sake of cultivating our immediate experience. What we need to do in moral education is to foster the set of habits by which students can acquire cultivated naïveté instead of becoming absolutist or skeptics.

To summarize, I have suggested that Dewey's situation ethics is unintelligible apart from certain positive assumptions and commitments that I have been slowly revealing. The most important is his faith in experience and his commitment to taking the situation as the end and means of morality. We need to unfold Dewey's moral vision, for not just any moral life is consistent with these commitments. To anticipate what lies ahead:

Dewey's hypothesis is that the moral task of ameliorating the concrete, specific, and present situations that we are presented with might best be accomplished by efforts to participate in our moral lives in an intelligent, aesthetic, and democratic way. These three adverbial characterizations are general and related ways of describing Dewey's proposal of a better moral life, rather than three different and isolated aspects. A Deweyan moral life can maintain its own integrity without the support and guidance of fixed and external foundations, and it can sustain itself without falling into the dangerous extremes presupposed by what I have called the either/or dilemma.

To fully understand why this is Dewey's hypothesis, and in order to examine its plausibility, I need to more robustly and precisely characterize the kind of moral life Dewey proposed. I will do this in part 3, in terms of habits, traits of character, relationships, and general ways of interacting in communication and community. But his normative proposals were based on his view of moral experience. Therefore, I will turn first to how Dewey reconstructed traditional moral notions and provided a radical but more empirically adequate description of the generic traits and elements of moral life.

PART TWO

Dewey's View of Moral Experience

Morality as Experience

Among Dewey's most important contributions to moral thought are his criticisms of the assumptions of traditional ethical theory by means of a descriptive account of the generic traits and components of moral experience. Dewey's ethics is a promising and refreshing alternative to some of the narrow and reductionistic views about moral experience that dominate the history of moral philosophy. It points to dimensions of the moral life that tend to be overlooked and undervalued in much of modern ethical thought. His view of moral life is a result of his philosophical empiricism and is motivated by an effort to recover the notion of morality as experience.

The Alienation of Morality from Experience

Dewey argued that there is no area of our experience that has suffered more from distortion and misleading conceptions than moral experience. And among the most troublesome misconceptions has been the reification of morality into something that is separate from ordinary experience or nature. It has been cut off from lived experience and placed in an extra-experiential or subjective-human realm of its own. As Jerome Schneewind argues, modern moral philosophy arose as a reaction to the "traditional assumption that morality must come from some authoritative source outside of human nature."[1] The result of this reaction to tradition has been that it often turns morality into something merely human (in a subject or community) and not part of nature. Morality is thus either something externally imposed on human beings, or something internal that originates in them.

This understanding of morality, which has dominated Western culture, has been fostered in large part by the dualisms (such as that between fact and value) that have been assumed and nurtured by traditional philosophy. As a part of his goal of reconstructing traditional philosophy, Dewey attempted to heal these conceptual fissures. Just as he objected to the "museum conception of art" (LW 10:12) that isolates the arts from lived experience, Dewey warned against separating morality from relationships in the workplace, from the technical-scientific use of intelligence, from the material orientation of the business world, and from our natural biological drives and desires. If Dewey sometimes seems almost to conflate morals with science, industry or politics, it is because he wanted to "bring morals to earth, and if they still aspire to heaven it is to the heaven of this earth" (MW 14:16).

This persistent separation of morals from experience is one of the ways in which men and women seek to escape responsibility for their actions. If morality is perceived as something external or added to the material-natural realm of industrial and economic relations, then the instrumentalities of technology, science, and business are not properly perceived as tools that can be taken up and used to improve unsatisfactory moral conditions. This is a costly mistake because it diverts intelligence from the concrete situations where moral demands are encountered. If the continuity between morals and the rest of experience were acknowledged, however, then a fuller range of resources would become available for moral action.

In order to recover morality from objective but otherworldly views, on the one hand, and arbitrary subjectivist views on the other, Dewey engaged in a critical re-description of moral experience. He worked through the one-sidedness and vicious abstractions of past moral philosophy in an attempt to construct a view that was more adequate to actual moral experience. In these moral re-descriptions, Dewey had two concerns that may seem to be incompatible. Can he pursue the task of describing what is distinctively moral without undermining his concern not to separate morality from everything else in experience? There is no inconsistency. Although there are continuities, rather than dualisms, in experience, this does not mean that differences do not exist, nor does it mean that philosophers should abandon efforts to differentiate morality from the other areas of life. However intertwined morality may be in our everyday affairs, morality is experienced as different from, for example, the aesthetic or the religious. Because Dewey was so concerned to overcome the dualisms that separate morality from experience he took every opportunity to emphasize the continuities rather than the differences. Nevertheless, Dewey had no patience for reductionist theories that insist on "trying to explain away the distinctive traits of any type of experience" (MW 3:35).

How can a philosophical empiricism avoid conceiving of morality as a general and invariant phenomenon while remaining faithful to its particularity and context sensitivity? Dewey did not address this question explicitly but what he writes about other types of experiences is helpful here. If we are to discriminate between different modes of experience, we can do it in terms of the features that are predominant, controlling, or focal in a situation. For example, Dewey claims that "in a distinctively aesthetic experience, characteristics that are subdued in other experiences are dominant; those that are subordinate are controlling" (LW 10:62). Science, art, and morality are concerned with different materials and initiated by different problems even if there are continuities and they share general methods and traits. There are no clear and fixed boundaries between what is and is not moral experience, but it does not follow that the distinction between moral experience and other kinds of experience is meaningless or that it is an arbitrary and futile endeavor to discern these distinctions. We all encounter situations in which moral qualities are dominant and which we experience as moral. This was Dewey's starting point, and a description of these situations was the basis of his criticism and reconstruction of traditional notions of character, self, moral deliberation, principles, and moral problems.

A description of the generic traits of situations in everyday experience as it is lived became the basis of Dewey's metaphysics, thought of as a map of criticism. This map fits our moral, intellectual, and artistic activities because it is generic, that is, it omits the diverse and specific manifestations experience can take. Dewey's ethics is a generalized description or map of our moral experience. This map is generic in relation to individual and unique moral experiences, but it is specific relative to the more general ground map of *Experience and Nature*. My presentation of Dewey's map begins with two generic traits of lived experience that are often missing in traditional accounts of moral life, namely, the social and the qualitative. In the next several chapters, I provide some of the finer details of Dewey's map of moral life: chapter 5 is about moral deliberation and the specific problems, materials, operations, and phases that are dominant or central in those situations that we typically experience as moral; and chapters 6 and 7 are concerned with the role of habits, the self, character, and conduct in moral life.

Moral Experience as Social and Qualitative

Dewey thought that traditional ethics had become bankrupt because it begins with an isolated subject or self that has a purely cognitive apprehension of moral truths. This is problematic because it begins with an abstraction that ignores the social (transactive) and affective (qualitative) character of moral experience. In Dewey's ethics relationships are not conceived as secondary or derivative. "Morals are as much a matter of interaction of a person with his social environment as walking is an interaction of legs with a physical environment" (MW 14:219). There are occasions where we need to distinguish our self from our relationships, but it would be a vicious abstraction, an instance of the philosophical fallacy, to completely separate the self from these transactions and to claim that the self is metaphysically prior such relations. Indeed, the self lives through and by social relations. An individual has qualities and potentialities but these are not fixed or antecedent to its interactions. In fact, "the qualities of things associated are displayed only in association, since in interactions alone are potentialities released and actualized" (LW 3:41).

Morality is social, but this does not mean that it is not also personal or that, in Dewey's ethics, the individual is secondary. On the contrary, he claims that "morals are personal because they spring from personal insight, judgment, and choice" (LW 7:317), and his normative moral vision is based on a faith in individuals. But the character of an individual cannot be separated from the quality of his or her associations, and individuals become acquainted with and competent in moral activity through their participation in a community. As Todd Lekan has recently argued, "[t]he pragmatist approach maintains that morality is more analogous to nonmoral practical skills and arts like medicine, cookery, and baseball than has been acknowledge by most of the tradition of moral philosophy."[2] We acquire shared ways to be sensitive to moral considerations and how to respond to them, ways that are neither fixed nor necessarily controlling of our individual response to situations. They are revisable under new circumstances, and even when individuals embody shared ways of acting, they are expressed differently according to our individuality.

The subject matter of moral experience is also qualitative. This stands in sharp contrast to the predominant intellectualist readings of morality. The intellectualist holds that only if moral traits are objects of knowledge are they candidates to be part of reality. In other words, moral quality is part of the world only if it is justified or accounted for in the same way we account for our knowledge of physics. The problem of validating morals and the debate about moral realism become epistemological problems centered on questions about how we come to know moral values. But for Dewey, moral qualities, traits, or values are experienced; and insofar as they are experienced, they exist. Moral qualities require a perceiver, but they are not in consciousness; they are rather found in situations and reveal aspects of nature. Dewey's commitment to a version of moral realism is clear. He wrote,

> Instead of presenting that kind of mechanic naturalism that is bound to deny the "reality" of the qualities which are the raw material of the values with which morals is concerned, I have repeatedly insisted that our theory of Nature be framed on the basis of giving full credence to these qualities just as they present themselves (LW 14:63). If experience actually presents aesthetic and moral traits, then these traits may also be supposed to reach down into nature, and to testify to something that belongs to nature as truly as does the mechanical structure attributed to it in physical science (LW 1:13–14). Aesthetic and moral experiences reveal traits of real things as truly as does intellectual experience. (LW 1:27)

To be sure, this is a different sort of realism than the typical variety where moral properties exist independently of an agent's participation in a moral situation. Rather, moral qualities, such as those that we call good or right, are experienced and judged as objective features of a situation, even if further inquiry might change this or if there is disagreement about their presence.

This sort of realism is consistent with Dewey's contextualism. Moral qualities and moral decisions are context-dependent and have their home and meaning in a particular situation. This is true of all qualities. Color and sound are not qualities appreciated or discriminated in isolation, or self-sufficient elements that can be used to explain complex cases of sense perception. The situational context as a scene of action is what is experienced, where what we are directly concerned with becomes focal and meaningful because of that implicit field. "When objects or qualities are cognitively apprehended, they are viewed in reference to the exigencies of the perceived field in which they occur" (LW 12:153). Hence, the rightness, goodness, or moral necessity of an act is "not one property it possesses in and of itself, in the isolation of non-relatedness" (LW 14:77). It is true that moral qualities are not the subject matter of scientific inquiry. But the fact that moral qualities are not quantifiable or subject to predictive control does not imply that they are not real and important in the context of a morally problematic situation. This is the fallacy committed by recent naturalists who reject the notion that moral qualities are natural.[3]

In philosophy, the word 'quality' is usually associated with either some abstract metaphysical property or some subjective phenomena, as in emotivism. With Dewey, however, it simply points to our pre-theoretical and pre-cognitive experience in the world. A qualitative world of persons and things is the most basic and inclusive context where one finds language, knowledge, and all of our more discursive activities, philosophy included. "A universe of experience is the precondition of a universe of discourse" (LW 12:74).

The world of everyday experience also has tertiary qualities, that is, qualities that pervade all the parts of a whole. The quality that pervades a situation is what demarcates it as a situation. A situation is a "complex existence that is held together in spite of its internal complexity by the fact that it is dominated and characterized throughout by a single quality" (LW 5:246). To say that a quality pervades a situation is to say that the quality runs through every aspect and detail of a situation, gives meaning to each aspect, and binds them all together. "If the situation experienced is that of being lost in a forest, the quality of being lost permeates and affects every detail that is observed and thought of" (LW 12:203). This is relevant to the issue of designating what is moral in experience. Moral qualities should not be limited to single acts or agents. A situation may be experienced as predominantly moral, that is, as having the pervasive quality of demanding that one find out what one morally ought to do. When a felt moral perplexity controls and pervades the development of a situation, we can designate the situation and its corresponding inquiry as moral.

Although morality and art have traditionally been associated with the qualitative, serious thought and inquiry have not. This is because modern notions of thought neglect or downplay the importance of the qualitative. As a consequence, morality and art are disregarded as thought-less and arbitrary. In contrast, for Dewey, all thought is qualitative thought. Situations that demand reconstruction through inquiry are situations that are qualitatively experienced as unsettled, confused, and indeterminate. The transformation of the pervasive quality of this sort of situation is, in effect, the general function of any inquiry. This is not a subjective transformation. Situations in their qualitative immediacy and uniqueness are primary and prior to any distinction between subject and object. Dewey explains: "according to my theory, while the initial problematic situation

and the final transformed resolved situation are equally immediately qualitative, no situation is subjective nor involves a subject and object relation"
(LW 5:70). More importantly, "the immediate existence of quality, and of
dominant and pervasive quality, is the background, the point of departure, and the *regulative* principle of all thinking" (LW 5:261, my emphasis).

In my general characterization of moral life as a qualitative and social
process, I have not mentioned the elements, phases, and operations that
are experienced as an integral part of this process. In the next chapter, I
turn my attention to some of the finer and functional distinctions that can
be articulated about moral experience.

The "What" of Moral Experience

One of the broadest functional distinctions that can be made about lived experience is that between the subject matter experienced—*what* is experienced—and the experiencing of it—*how* it is experienced.[1] How we participate in morally problematic situations is one of the key features of such situations. In the next chapter, I will consider the function of habits and character in moral experience, that is, the how. In other words, I will distinguish our moral attitudes and dispositions from the moral situations in which they are operative. But I will first consider what occurs during the course of morally problematic situations. What are the generic traits and phases of these kinds of processes?

For Dewey, life is neither a homogeneous flux nor a succession of disconnected (atomistic) moments. It is "a thing of histories, each with its own plot, its own inception and movement towards its close" (LW 10:43). Each of these histories is a situation that begins with a disruption from the fluidity provided by our habits. From this initial phase we usually move to an intermediate phase in which we try to transform the unsettledness. In this second phase, we might engage in inquiry as a series of doings and undergoings with our environment. If successful, we arrive at a final phase of consummation where we establish a new equilibrium and a situation that is experienced as settled and determinate.

This general rhythm and pattern of experience adequately fits moral life. The life of a moral agent is one of being recurrently faced with decisions between conflicting moral forces or demands. These breaks in the flow of everyday life are situations that have the pervasive quality of being morally unsettled, confused, and indeterminate. The agent finds herself in a morally problematic situation that provokes the agent to engage in a process of moral deliberation, until she arrives at a judgment that results in a choice. It is in light of this process that Dewey provided novel and provocative reconstructions of the traditional notions of moral deliberation, value judgments, principles, and moral problems. I now turn to each of these matters.

The Nature of Moral Problems

According to the methodological commitments outlined in part 1, a radical empiricist approach to the nature of moral problems seeks a hypothetical-general but faithful pre-theoretical description of what moral problems are experienced *as* rather than an essence or a definition (i.e., necessary and sufficient conditions) of moral problems.[2] We do not, after all, experience moral problems in general. The problem of abortion, for example, can only be an abstract way of making reference to all the situations where a moral agent has to make a certain kind of moral decision. If, despite their uniqueness, moral problems are experienced as having traits in common (generic traits), then one can proceed to specify what they are.

Dewey thought that standard moral theories, regardless of their differences, usually shared a view of moral problems which was far removed from how they are immediately experienced. The root of the problem is that traditional accounts of moral problems rest on mistaken theoretical assumptions about experience in general, assumptions that are the result of a failure to be empirical, that is, the result of committing the philosophical fallacy. I will now consider some of the most common traditional assumptions about moral problems and how Dewey's empiricism led him to propose a more adequate and rich conception of the actual experiences that initiate moral deliberation.

ARE MORAL PROBLEMS PROBLEMS OF KNOWLEDGE?

When I am experiencing a moral problem it is more accurate to say that I am suffering a moral problem than to say that I know I am having a moral problem. This is not merely a verbal distinction; it points to different kinds of experiences.[3] Confusion results when, in the grips of a philosophical prejudice like intellectualism, one tries to reduce all experiences to knowledge claims.

A moral problem is something "had or experienced before it can be stated or set forth; but it is had as an immediate quality of the whole situation" (LW 5:249). Even if there is a point during a moral experience at which one wants to *know* what is right, that question occurs in a context that is initially experienced as immediately indeterminate regarding what should be done. The fluidity of everyday life is blocked and experienced as a unique ambiguity, confusion, disharmony, conflict, or pain that pervades one's situation. This indeterminate situation is a precondition for the more reflective phases that follow, during which one discursively inquires about the problem and figures out "what sort of action the situation demands in order that it may receive a satisfactory objective reconstruction" (LW 12:163).

Consider how different this account is from standard ones in moral theory. The most common account of the nature of moral problems begins with the assumption that they arise out of a conflict between objects of knowledge, that is, moral problems are about beliefs, propositions, rules, principles, values, or units of utility. Even if in hindsight a reflective analysis of a moral problem is carried out in these terms, can one honestly claim that what is directly experienced during the inception of a moral problem is a conflict between these refined abstractions? Just as when I experience a chair I do not experience a collection of sense data, so too when I experience a moral problem I do not experience a conflict of units of utility or a conflict of propositions.

When moral problems are reduced to knowledge problems, moral deliberation is conceived in terms of the standard philosophical models of knowledge or reasoning. If, for example, I am trying to decide if I should keep my promise, is this simply a matter of examining logical relations between factual beliefs and moral principles within my belief system? If moral problems arise out of indeterminate situations as non-cognitive experiences, then this has methodological implications about how to solve such problems. To be an empiricist in solving them requires that one be guided by the irreducible, concrete quale of the indeterminate situation that is suffered and that initiated inquiry. One fails to adopt an empirical attitude if one restricts one's data for moral deliberation to knowledge-facts or rules and disregards everything else as subjective and therefore irrelevant to a moral problem. How a moral problem is experienced and how it is felt are essential parts of the empirical data we have for its own transformation or rectification. For example, the extent to which I feel torn between keeping my promise to a friend and helping a stranger in need helps me determine what is relevant in reaching my decision. Moreover, the best qualitative indications that a problem has been resolved is when it is no longer suffered—not when we have acquired a certain knowledge or have met some antecedent formal criteria.

ARE MORAL PROBLEMS SUBJECTIVE?

The modern fallacy in philosophy which reduces experience to experiencing (set against an antecedent reality) is responsible for the view that moral problems are nothing more than the mind state of a confused subject who is ignorant about the right thing to do. Meanwhile, moral reality remains stable and unproblematic, waiting to be discovered. Successful moral inquiry moves from a confused subjective state to one that corresponds to the way things really are. According to this view,

> there is no situation which is problematic. There is only a person who is in a state of subjective moral uncertainty or ignorance. His business, in that case, is not to judge the objective situation in order to determine what course of action is required in order that it may be transformed into one that is morally satisfactory and right, but simply to come into intellectual possession of a predetermined end-in-itself. (LW 12:169–170)

Imagine a situation in which I am first frightened by a noise at the window and then after further investigation I find out that the noise is the shade tapping against the window.[4] A traditional view of experience would describe this situation as one where we move from the original fright as an imperfect-illusory-subjective cognitive state to one where we are face-to-face with reality. Dewey claimed that this is a distorted description of what we actually experience. When experienced, the frightening noise is as real as the eventual knowledge-experience of the cause of the noise. "Empirically that noise *is* fearsome, it *really* is, not merely phenomenally or subjectively so. That is what it is experienced as being" (MW 3:160). Insofar as the eventual experience is not misleading it is more true, but this does not make it more real. Similarly, moral problems are not experienced as internal or subjective. Insofar as a situation is experienced as morally problematic then it really *is* problematic. This situation might be transformed into one in which there is no longer a problem, but the second, transformed situation is no more real than the first one. For example, my initial experience of obligation to help a stranger is no less real than my realization afterwards that she does not need my help.

One's stance on this issue makes a difference. If moral problems are subjective, epistemic problems, then resolving them requires that we find out what is wrong with the experiencing subject, that is, what is the source of his or her confusion and ignorance, for according to this view, moral problems are only indications of our limitations as knowers. There is some comfort in the idea that moral problems are only our problems and are not constitutive of moral reality. Many want to believe that there is a right answer to moral dilemmas, in other words, that moral reality is uniform, stable, or in perpetual harmony, and that mistakes in moral decisions are "due merely to a personal failure to reduce the present case to the proper combination of old ones" (MW 13:12). For Dewey, this is a false sense of comfort.

If we find moral problems that are experienced as irresolvable and therefore tragic, then they *are* tragic and do not merely seem so. Their resolution requires scrutiny and transformation of all the objective factors (including ourselves) that are present in the transaction that constitute a situation. We cannot always transform a morally suffered problematic situation into one that is completely determinate and unproblematic. But this is not just a subjective problem caused by our human finitude; it is the way things really are. For Dewey, it is better to accept that there are tragedies than to flee from them by postulating an antecedent and conflict-free moral reality. In moral life we are in the midst of real moral conflicts and not in a phenomenal or subjective world. The moments when we are torn between irreconcilable obligations are as revealing of moral reality as the times when the right thing to do is obvious and unquestionable.

The Pluralistic Character of Moral Experience

In "Three Independent Factors in Morals" (LW 5:279–288), Dewey criticizes the tendency in moral theory to conceive moral problems as a conflict between a few commensurable factors or variables. This oversimplification derives from a self-serving characterization of moral experience by moral theorists and counts as an instance of the fallacy of selective emphasis. The casuistic power of a theory, that is, its ability to provide rules for decision making, depends upon its ability to reduce moral problems to a few commensurable elements, thereby facilitating decision making. But moral philosophy will remain abstract and detached from moral life if it is not critical of its own theoretical orientation.

Dewey argued that the history of moral philosophy is characterized by a one-sidedness caused by philosophers who have abstracted one feature of situations that are experienced as morally problematic, then have made that factor supreme or exclusive. "Whatever may be the differences which separate moral theories," he wrote, "all [philosophers] postulate one single principle as an explanation of moral life" (LW 5:280). Hence, moral theories have been classified according to whether they take the good (teleological-consequentialist theories), virtue (virtue ethics), or duty (deontological theories) as their central category or source of moral justification. But according to Dewey "each of these variables has a sound basis, but because each has a different origin and mode of operation, they can be at cross purposes and exercise divergent forces in the formation of judgment" (LW 5:280). The category of 'good' points to that part of our moral life that has to with our desires, wants, fulfillment and satisfactions; 'duty' with the demands that are part of associated living; and 'virtue' with the approval of conduct and character by others.

Good, virtue, and duty are all irreducible factors found intertwined and in conflict in moral situations. Hence, moral problems are very acute problems that border on the tragic. Dewey explains that "the essence of the situation is an internal and intrinsic conflict; the necessity for judgment and for choice come from the fact that one has to manage forces with no common denominator" (LW 5:280). One often associates moral struggle with situations where there is a conflict "between a good which is clear to him and something else which attracts him but he knows to be wrong" (LW 7:165), for instance, "the employee of a bank who is tempted to embezzle funds" (LW 7:164). But this is a very different kind of struggle than the ones that Dewey takes as paradigmatic of moral problems.

In moral problems the struggle is often "between values each of which is an undoubted good in its place but which now get in each other's way" (LW 7:165). For instance, should I support my country in a war that could benefit many but that nonetheless seems unjust? The elements of uncertainty and conflict between these two kinds of moral struggles are different. In the first kind of situation, the problem is how I can get myself to do what is morally right, or what means I should employ to minimize this evil and make that good prevail. But it is assumed that the morally right thing to do in that situation has been settled and is unproblematic. The question foregrounded here is about the best means to an antecedent, nonproblematic end. But in the second kind of case there is genuine uncertainty and conflict about what is the morally correct thing to do because incompatible courses of action are experienced initially as morally justified or as making a forceful claim upon the agent. Furthermore, each of these claims may belong to a totally different aspect of morality. My duty, my desire for good consequences, and my regard for virtue are each distinct and irreducible to the other even though one of them may end up becoming more pressing in the particular situation. Once moral inquiry is initiated, the experienced moral tension may or may not be eased.

Dewey's "Three Independent Factors in Morals" is a centerpiece of his moral thought. In a letter to Professor Horace S. Fries, Dewey acknowledged that in his early works "I followed the tradition in making ends, the good, the basic ideal," but that by 1930 it became clear to him that he had changed his view. His tripartite division of moral experience in this essay prefigures, among other things, his 1932 *Ethics,* where he placed good, duty, and virtue in separate chapters. It is clear in this essay how radical the situational and pluralistic thrust of his moral philosophy is.[5] His situation ethics is based on the view that each moral problem is unique and is usually constituted by an irreconcilable complexity. All three of the factors— good, duty, and virtue—have something to contribute, but their respective adherents in ethical theory have all latched on to one aspect of our moral experience. Dewey was concerned that this singularity does not encourage a generous survey of our moral problems. A narrow view of moral problems is responsible for the tendency in normative ethics to propose a single right way to reason in ethics. For Dewey, an appreciation of the nature of the conflicts that are the basis for moral theory and deliberation protects us from false pretensions about the power of single factors to resolve them. Dewey's faith in the instrumentalities of experience was tempered by the honest realization that the most intense moments of our moral life are tragic.

Moral Deliberation

Moral deliberation is not something that happens within one's mind. It is experienced as an intermediate phase in the process of transforming a morally problematic situation into one that is determinate. This does not mean that it is a discrete and independent phase. In moral inquiry the disruption that is felt as the engrossing whole that provoked it persists and evolves in the background; in other words, we are still suffering the problem even if the foreground or focus of attention is concerned with such questions as: what is the problem? What resources do I have at my disposal to settle this? How can I gather more evidence? To set up a problem that is not guided by some genuinely felt doubt or perplexity "is to start on a course of dead work" (LW 12:112). The overarching and final aim is to determine what I ought to do among alternative courses of action. In other words, the aim is *choice* as "the emergence of a unified preference out of competing preferences" (MW 14:134).

Moral deliberation is in this respect no different than any other inquiry that begins with "a forked-road situation, a situation which is ambiguous, which presents a dilemma, which proposes alternatives" (MW 6:189). Dewey's example is that of a man traveling in an unfamiliar region who is trying to decide which road to take.

> Having no sure knowledge to fall back upon, he is brought to a standstill of hesitation and suspense. Which road is right? And how shall perplexity be resolved? There are but two alternatives: he must either blindly and arbitrarily take his course, trusting to luck for the outcome, or he must discover grounds for the conclusion that a given road is right. (MW 6:189)

The moral problems that initiate moral deliberation are, of course, qualitatively different and more complex than the situation of the perplexed traveler. In a morally problematic situation we find ourselves with two or more actions that exert a different moral force or demand upon us. The gradual specification of the moral perplexity that has been felt is the key to finding out what is the best possible solution. Figuring out what the problem is requires that we get clear about what is in conflict or tension. We can easily get this wrong. We start with some immediate value judgment (valuing) about each of our conflicting options, but we may have to change our judgment after reflection (valuation) and a more careful survey of the situation. (I will consider later, in more detail, the important relation between valuing and valuation.) For example, what may first be experienced as a conflict between two duties may later be found upon reflection to be a conflict between a duty and what is good.

We do not, however, wait until we have a clear and definite formulation of the problem to entertain and examine possible solutions. In the midst of the ambiguity and uncertainty about what to do, we usually start with vague suggestions about the right action even though we are suspending a final judgment and are willing to revise this overall judgment (hypothesis) as inquiry proceeds. The intellectual task is to discover grounds for choosing one action over another in light of the present situation. How do we do this? We rely on whatever stable elements we can find.

> In the suspense of uncertainty, we metaphorically climb a tree; we try to find some standpoint from which we may survey additional facts and, getting a more commanding view of the situation, may decide how the facts stand related to one another. (MW 6:189)

95

The perplexed traveler relies on accumulated knowledge about similar situations, but must carefully scrutinize what is before him to find evidence to help him test a hypothesis that will ultimately help him decide between roads. He reasons to figure out the implications of some of his hypotheses, but his survey is also imaginative and emotionally laden. In any case, his final judgment is not merely a deductive derivation from some rule about what makes a road the best road.

If Dewey is right about the level of uncertainty and incommensurability that characterizes morally problematic situations, then the moral agent seems to face a more difficult task than that of the perplexed traveler. If, for example, an agent is torn between a good brought by her breaking her promise and a duty to keep her promise, then how can she weigh these incommensurable and forceful claims and reach a reasonable context-sensitive judgment? Where does she begin? What possible stable resources are available to an agent in a morally problematic situation?

We must first avoid the abstraction of the moral agent who comes to a situation morally neutral or impartial with respect to all her options. When one is in a problematic situation, it is not the case that all logically possible solutions are considered or stand on an equal level. Dewey explains that in most situations initial suggestions spontaneously occur to us, but there is nothing mysterious or arbitrary about this. It is what happens to an organism with habits funded by previous experience. "We do not approach any problem with a wholly naïve or virgin mind; we approach it with certain acquired habitual modes of understanding, with a certain store of previously evolved meanings or at least of experiences from which meanings may be educed" (LW 8:214–215). The initial suggestions that spontaneously occur to a mature moral agent or to those who have encountered similar situations are probably a better starting point than those of the immature and inexperienced. But the origins of the suggestions that arise in deliberation are not as important as the ability to test their pertinence to the problem at hand. Initial suggestions must also be developed into hypotheses that lead to further judgments. Let's consider what particular operations a moral agent can rely on in order to examine, criticize, improve, and modify her moral judgments.

In any process of inquiry we can make a functional distinction between phases of doing and undergoing as well as phases of analysis and synthesis. How these phases affect each other is the key to understanding how inquiry is a cumulative undertaking that guides itself to some final judgment. Analysis is what we do when inquiry is centered on making some finer discrimination of the parts that make up our problematic situation. Synthesis takes place when we are concerned with weighing how the parts contribute to making an overall judgment. These are mutually dependent phases throughout the different stages of moral inquiry. Reaching a hypothesis about the nature of the conflict is itself an act of synthesis from the more particular analysis of what the competing moral demands are in a situation and what particular features of the situation contribute to their rightness. Any tentative proposal about the nature of the problem provokes in turn an examination (analysis) of possible solutions that issues in a tentative overall judgment (synthesis) about the best solution; this may then guide further analyses and surveys of new aspects of the situation. The final judgment about what we ought to do is a synthesis that results from the analysis of the situation as a whole, but it is only the final step in a series of tentative overall judgments that have occurred throughout the entire process of deliberation.

This same process can be also described in terms of the phases of doing and undergoing in an experimental learning process. The consequences of different operations in the situation are perceived (appreciated) in order to guide subsequent ones. What we take to be the right course of action at any point in inquiry guides our survey of what we take to be the settled features, the facts, of the case (through observation or recollection of similar cases); this, in turn, may generate new suggestions and revisions of our judgment, which may in turn lead us to survey different aspects of the situation. In this process principles and habits have the function of bringing previous experience to bear. Reasoning provides us with the inferences needed to go beyond what we have, or it helps us elaborate our suppositions in light of other beliefs. Imagination in the form of a dramatic rehearsal helps us survey and test our options. Let's consider in some more detail some of these complex and interdependent operations and resources.

I explained the function of principles in Dewey's ethics in chapter 2. In the arts, cooking, or morals we often rely on principles and habits that are informed by previous experience in order to reach judgments. Principles may even help us with the task of deciding which facts are relevant in coming to a decision; but even in these cases, we have to ultimately rely on the guidance provided by the particular context of inquiry. For Dewey, even in the case of judgments reached in a court of law, where there is an explicit reliance on rules, "*the quality of the problematic situation* determines which rules of the total system are selected" (LW 12:124, my emphasis).

Judgment is required in deciding what principles apply. "There is no label, on any given idea or principle, that says automatically, 'Use me in this situation'" (LW 8:215). Judgment is required to find out what features of an action are morally relevant and which ones are a distraction. Principles can help but they are no substitute for the tact and discernment of a good judge. No rules can replace the power to seize the significant factors in a situation and the sensitivity to the quality of the problematic situation that is being transformed.

Moral deliberation can also rely on "reasoning" (LW 12:115), such as the examination of the implications of a proposed solution in light of its logical relations with other beliefs or meanings. This can be useful in developing and revising suggestions and considerations in such a way that they can be more easily tested. Moral deliberation is not, however, a deductive process. It is experimental insofar as the results of its operations are tentative and subject to confirmation or frustration as inquiry proceeds. Experimental thinking is not the exclusive domain of the sciences. The notion that empirical testing is the confrontation of ideas and hypotheses with the direct observation by the senses is a narrow form of empiricism. In moral life, many times it is only after one acts upon a choice (and judgment) that one can obtain the necessary confirmation or disconfirmation for one's choice. In fact, a judgment reached in a morally problematic situation is not final for it is a doing that might provoke further undergoings. Reaching a judgment about what to do is usually followed by experiences that either offer no resistance (a type of confirmation) or that generate a new problematic situation.

There is, however, no reason why testing needs to take the form of an overt experiment. For Dewey, the imagination plays a crucial role in the exploration and testing of our options in a situation. This provides an opportunity to have a preliminary test (trial) of our options in a morally problematic situation without suffering the consequences of acting upon them. In deliberation, the competing possible lines of action that are present in a morally problematic situation are tried out in an imaginative drama that includes the agents involved, possible consequences, and implications. Thus, Dewey often referred to moral deliberation as "a dramatic rehearsal" (MW 14:132). This is why he claims that what goes on in moral deliberation is closer to "an actor engaged in drama" than to a "clerk recording debit and credit items" (MW 14:139). Just as an actor engaged in a drama, moral deliberation may require imaginary role-playing, as well as taking seriously the standpoint or possible reaction of others. For example, my imagination may be provoked by the following questions: What are possible scenarios (or stories) if I support the war? How do they compare with the one of not supporting it and with regard to my duties? What would an impartial moral judge think? What good would be preserved or enhanced? How does the best-case scenario (in terms of consequences to us) look from the standpoint of someone who cares about virtue? Notice how in this imaginative exploration each of the independent factors in morals—good, duty, and virtue—plays a role.

The fact that deliberation includes the actual or the imaginary judgments of others and the principles we have inherited means that it is a social, not a solipsistic, process. That there are individuals who can deliberate without engaging in an actual dialogue with particular others hardly counts as evidence against this claim. For both Dewey and George H. Mead, thinking is an internalization of communal dialogue.

> In language and imagination *we rehearse the responses of others* just as we dramatically enact other consequences. We foreknow how others will act, and the foreknowledge is the beginning of judgment passed on action. We know with them; there is conscience. An assembly is formed within our breast which discusses and appraises proposed and performed acts. The community without becomes a forum and tribunal within, a judgment-seat of charges, assessments and exculpations. Our thoughts of our own actions are saturated with the ideas that others entertain about them, ideas which have been expressed not only in explicit instruction but still more effectively in reaction to our acts. (MW14:217, my emphasis)

If, in moral deliberation, imagination provides the dramas, then what provides the standard by which the possible courses of action are evaluated and tested? There is no perfect drama, or absolute standard, by which all imaginative dramas are judged, nor is there a set of intellectual criteria or rules (as in utilitarianism) by which one can choose one drama over another. For Dewey, the view that evaluation is reached by applying some set criteria of right or wrong (as the major premise in a practical syllogism) is a theoretical or abstract explanation that we may devise after we make actual judgments and decisions. But this is not how the most competent moral agents experience these situations. This is the case not only in morals but also in other areas of our practical lives where judgment is required. Good trumpet players and cooks may formulate in a set of rules or criteria the basis of their activities and decisions, but this is done for the purposes of the novice and does not come into their experience.

It is worth comparing the above account of moral deliberation to traditional ones in ethical theory. Dewey often contrasts his view of moral deliberation with two other views. The rationalist-intuitionist view identifies moral deliberation with a "separate non-natural faculty of moral knowledge" (MW 14:131). The undesirable implication of this view is a conception of morality as a separate and independent domain from our everyday life. Moral deliberation is conceived as a means by which we can have access to a moral reality behind experience. According to this view, the function of reflection is not creative or prospective; instead, its task is merely to copy, reproduce, and apply antecedent-fixed moral values or knowledge.

On the other hand, there are empirical views that claim moral deliberation is a mode of enlightened self-interested calculation, that is, "calculating what is expedient" (MW 14:132). Dewey had many criticisms of these views, views exemplified by utilitarianism. The notion that the function of deliberation is the calculation of future pleasures and pains is not based on what agents usually do, or on what can reasonably be expected of them. Dewey suspected that utilitarians confused the agreeable and disagreeable reactions to foreseen events that are presented in imagination with the calculation of future pleasures and pains. The former reactions are part of the agent's present situations, but future pleasure and pains are not. Therefore, utilitarians ask us to predict what is dependent on a complex set of contingent variables that are usually not subject to our control.

For Dewey, the function of deliberation is present rectification; it is not about a distant future or about figuring out "where the most advantage is to be procured. It is to resolve entanglements in existing activity . . ." (MW 14:139). Foresight of consequences is important in moral deliberation but it is used "to appraise *present* proposed actions" (MW 14:143, my emphasis). Even though we occasionally dwell on the effects of an action on our future feelings, to make this the paradigm of all moral deliberation is to make "an abnormal case the standard one" (MW 14:141). This is one of many reasons why the classification of Dewey as a consequentialist is a grave mistake. Dewey did emphasize consequences as a way to draw our attention away from notions of deliberation that appeal to a priori standards, but this has been misinterpreted as presenting a view that centers on maximizing good consequences as the goal or the standard. Later in life Dewey became aware of this misunderstanding. Consequences, he says,

> are important not as such or by themselves but in their function as tests of ideas, principles, theories. It is possible that at times, in opposition to ipse dixit intuitions and dogmatic assertion of absolute standards, I have emphasized the importance of consequences so as to seem to make them supreme in and of themselves. If so, I have departed from my proper view, that of their use as tests of proposed ends and ideals. (LW 14:74)

Utilitarianism was the prime example of an intellectual movement affected by the current money and business culture. "Its general spirit of subordinating productive activity to the bare product was indirectly favorable to the cause of an unadorned commercialism" (MW 12:184). It modeled moral deliberation on the calculation of future profit and loss in economic activity. This calculative model represents a narrow and limited use of our deliberative capacities. Furthermore, the utilitarian's instrumental view of reasoning does not allow for the evaluation of ends, which is an important part of morality. Utilitarians should be praised for insisting "upon getting away from vague generalities, and down to the specific and concrete" (MW 12:183), but they never questioned the idea that moral judgments must be based on some fixed criteria or final end. There is no genuine moral doubt ("no real and significant conflict," MW 14:149) about what to do when we know the end but are only puzzled about the best means. Moral deliberation is experienced as a genuine search and discovery, and it "is not an attempt to do away with this opposition of quality by reducing it to one of amount" (MW 14:150).

Because of the intellectualist fallacy and the linguistic turn in philosophy, moral judgments in ethical theory are often treated as, or simply equated with, propositions that are the result of other propositions. This process is conceived as one very similar to the linear process that occurs when we read a text or when we read statements in an argument written in a logic textbook. But for Dewey, a judgment is not a proposition,[6] a judgment is a practical act, affirmation, or assertion that "in distinction from propositions which are singular, plural, generic and universal, is individual, since it is concerned with unique *qualitative* situations" (LW 12: 283, my emphasis). As already noted, judgment and thought is qualitative for Dewey. In his contextualism, the control and guidance provided by context in inquiry is given by the underlying and pervasive quality of a situation that is being transformed. It is not surprising, then, that for Dewey art, far from being problematic, is in fact the paradigm of all thinking. "Artistic thought is not however unique in this respect but only shows an intensification of a characteristic of all thought" (LW 5:251–252). What is presented in imagination in art and morality is judged by the same means that we judge overt experiments: by our direct qualitative experience. "In imagination as in fact we know a road only by what we see as we travel on it. . . . in thought as well as in overt action, the objects experienced in following a course of action attract, repel, satisfy, annoy, promote and retard" (MW 14:134).

Dewey used science and art as metaphors to understand moral deliberation. This served the purpose of highlighting the continuity between morality and other modes of experience, and it provided a description of moral deliberation as an experimental, emotional, and imaginative process. Dewey's early concerns to reconcile ethics with experimental science led him to investigate the ways in which scientific inquiry and moral inquiry can share a way, or general method, of forming and justifying judgments. In his later works he came to rely more on an aesthetic model. This is most evident in his description of moral deliberation as a transformation into a unified consummatory experience and in his emphasis on the importance of the imagination and the emotions in this process. This is the aspect of Dewey's view on moral deliberation that seems most radical, considering the predominance of sterile rationalistic accounts of moral deliberation in the history of moral philosophy. It is also the most promising, considering the recent developments in cognitive science on the role of metaphor, imagination, and emotion.[7]

For Dewey, moral deliberation is not an intermediate phase where one moves from a conflict of qualitative material to a process of cold reasoning where qualities are transformed into quantities and propositions. Deliberation is not an intermediate phase where we close or suspend our access to the qualitative world. On the contrary, it is an opportunity to widen and enrich our qualitative experience. The access to the qualitative-richness of a situation is not limited to sense perception or observation. The function of imagination is to amplify perception, to open up the situation in ways that could assist us in coming to a judgment. Imagination "elicits the possibilities that are interwoven within the texture of the actual" (LW 10:348). It "puts before us objects which are not directly or sensibly present, so that we then may react directly to these objects" (MW 14:139). The capacity to deliberate signifies the ability to take an experienced conflict of possible actions and place them in an imaginative field so that they can be judged in light of what is qualitatively revealed in that field. Deliberation "is an attempt to uncover the conflict in its full scope and bearing . . . to reveal qualitative incompatibilities by detecting the different courses to which they commit us" (MW 14:150). And deliberation is not a phase of cool, detached inactivity or indifference. If there is no unified extrovert response while we deliberate it is only because different aspects of the situation are pushing us in different directions. Since these tendencies toward action are present, though inhibited, during deliberation, the resulting choice "is not the emergence of preference out of indifference" (MW 14:134). Hence, in Dewey there is no need to postulate the will as a separate faculty which pushes the agent in the direction dictated by deliberation.

It is also worth noticing how Dewey's account of how judgments are reached reverses the order assumed in many ethical theories. In these theories the final verdict about our "actual duty" (to use W. D. Ross's term) in a situation is something that is derived after we have first analyzed and evaluated what are the competing prima facie principles in the situation. There is a final verdict for Dewey, but like the conclusion of any inquiry, it is something that gradually emerges and is prior to its premises. Dewey explains how formal conceptions of logic often give the wrong impression about how we actually think.

> We say of an experience of thinking that we reach or draw a conclusion. Theoretical formulation of the process is often made in such terms as to conceal effectually the similarity of "conclusion" to the consummating phase of every developing integral experience. These formulations apparently take their cue from the separate propositions that are premises and the proposition that is the conclusion as they appear on the printed page. The impression is derived that there are first two independent and ready-made entities that are then manipulated so as to give rise to a third. In fact, in an experience of thinking, premises emerge only as a conclusion becomes manifest. (LW 10:45)

When we are in a morally problematic situation we start with some immediate unreflective judgment about what is right. There is a direct qualitative judgment that precedes the more definite recognition of what particular features of the action contribute to its rightness. We engage in analysis, survey, and reasoning in order to examine (test) or revise this preliminary reaction. The initial impression comes first, it changes as inquiry proceeds, and it serves to guide the subsequent phases of analysis and discrimination. Dewey explains how all inquiry starts with a hunch or impression but this is not something psychical or psychological. It is the presence of a dominant quality in a situation as a whole.

> To say I have a feeling or impression that so and so is the case is to note that the quality in question is not yet resolved into determinate terms and relations; it marks a conclusion without statement of the reasons for it, the grounds upon which it rests. It is the first stage in the development of explicit distinctions. All thought in every subject begins with just such an unanalyzed whole. (LW 5:248–249)

In moral deliberation the search for the reasons that ground our overall impression about what is right must involve a sincere survey of how the relevant features that make up a situation are related, and it may lead to assertions about what makes a particular action right or wrong. Articulating in propositional form what traits or features of a situation sustain one's moral judgment is key to justifying ourselves to others and in inviting them to consider for themselves the situation. In other words, it facilitates a more communal inquiry. More importantly, the phase of reflective analysis in moral deliberation may lead to a change in the overall qualitative judgment of what is right as inquiry proceeds.

In sum, deliberation is a process constituted by the same mutually dependent phases of doing and undergoing of any experimental and artistic process. The doing might involve acting to gather more evidence or the active operations of recollection and exploration. There is undergoing in the form of a constant receptivity to what is revealed by our doings or the reactions of others engaged in the process. Receptivity to the underlying and pervasive quality of the situation as it is being transformed is what guides the direction of inquiry. This is, however, a very generic description of the process. Moral deliberation is said to be specifically about moral values. Let's describe in more detail what goes on in moral deliberation in terms of judgments of value.

Valuing and Valuation

Moral deliberation results in a moral judgment—a decision to act in one way or another. But judgments are not static. They continue throughout the entire deliberative process, and they are transformed as deliberation proceeds. Within this process, Dewey distinguishes between the direct judgments of value, valuing, and the reflective judgments, valuations. The distinctions between valuing and valuation, between appreciation and criticism, and between play and work have as their basis two of the basic traits that appear in *Experience and Nature*: nature in its *finalities* (or consummations) and in its *relations*. Natural existences in their immediacy or qualitative existence have terminal qualities that are unique, unrelated, and final. Immediate and terminal quality is something *had* and that can be pointed to, rather than known or captured in a description. An object, event, or person either has the immediate and terminal quality it has or it doesn't; there is not much else that can be said about it qua having immediate quality. However, relations are also part of experience, so that any quality "may be referred to other things, it may be treated as an effect or as a sign" (LW 1:82). The significance of these distinct traits for inquiry is that there are two ways in which one can judge or apprehend anything in experience: in its immediacy (valuing) or in its relations to other things in experience (valuation). *Valuing* is the direct, spontaneous, and pre-cognitive operation where we appreciate something by its immediate quality before it is subject to reflection. But once the value of something is reflectively considered it is being considered in light of its relations, that is, in its connections as a means or as a sign. To think "is to look at a thing in its relations with other things" (LW 7:265). Reflection is comparative and attentive to conditions, relations of means and ends, consequences, implications, and inferences. The reflective process of arriving at this kind of judgment of value is called *valuation*.

About valuing, Dewey could have said that things have intrinsic qualities and that some of these qualities are moral. But he was aware that in philosophy intrinsic is usually associated with what is necessary, permanent, or universally belonging to a thing in virtue of its essence. But when Dewey says a quality is intrinsic he means that the quality is experienced as belonging to a thing as a "brute matter of space-time existence" (LW 15:43). In this sense, he said, "all qualities whatever are 'intrinsic' to the things they qualify at the time and place of the occurrence of the latter—provided only the things in question do genuinely 'have' them" (LW 15:43). Hence, to claim that a particular act of promise keeping is intrinsically good or obligatory is just to say that it is experienced as having that quality at that specific time and place. In this sense, any experienced non-problematic good is, as it were, an end in itself until the occasion arises where a choice has to be made. Value comparisons and the notion of better or worse acquire their meaning in the context of a particular situation where a choice needs to be made. "In the abstract or at large, apart from the needs of a particular situation in which choice has to be made, there is no such thing as degrees or order of value" (MW 9:248).

Since anything in experience exists in relation with some other thing, it can always in principle be compared, used, and valued as a means to something else. This is why there are no mere or essential ends-in-themselves. This is the basis for Dewey's criticism of the dualism of fixed separation of means and ends in philosophy. Anything can be valuable both as a means and as an end and there is a significant loss when we can only appreciate something as a mere means. This is an important antidote to misconceptions of Dewey as a narrow instrumentalist. Dewey held that a thing's instrumental capacity will be enhanced if it is (or has been) previously appreciated on its own account. He explained that

> If it is not, then when the time and place comes for it to be used as a means or instrumentality, it will be just that much handicapped. Never having been realized or appreciated for itself, one will miss something of its capacity as resource for other ends. (MW 9:249)

Valuation emerges from valuing but they do not always converge. For example, I might not immediately value recycling, although I come to reflectively judge that it is a good practice. However, most of the situations that Dewey has in mind when he makes the distinction between valuing and valuation are those in which one of these judgments of value emerges, transforms, and is organically related to the other. When the terminal or immediate quality of a thing is enhanced because a process of judging it in its relations precedes it, then it acquires consummatory value. For example, my effort to understand and explore the benefits of recycling may actually transform my immediate experience of it.

Let's consider an example about a controversial moral value. There are people who claim to experience in an immediate way (valuing) homosexual acts and persons as immoral, or at least with some negative moral value. Among these people there may be disagreement about the particular moral value. For instance, are homosexual acts experienced as a vice, as the violation of a duty, or as just bad? I am, however, someone who has yet to experience any kind of negative moral value about homosexuality.

I will admit that, perhaps because I am heterosexual, I sometimes find homosexual acts immediately repugnant but definitely *not* in a moral sense.[8] I have yet to experience homosexuality with the same kind of immediate negative moral value that I usually experience when witnessing acts of injustice or when people harm others for fun. This makes me wonder if, perhaps, those who are against homosexuality on moral grounds are just confusing two different kinds of experiences. This gives me hope that I can make them become aware that their negative valuing, though real and genuine, is not of the moral kind. This may not be easy. It is not as if I can defend, or present them with, some definite criteria about what is and what is not a moral valuing. The best one can do when faced with this sort of disagreement is to invite and assist the person in making a sincere survey of their lived experiences and hope they will realize on their own that there is a qualitative difference between their valuing experiences about homosexuality and those other valuing experiences they have had in their lives that are distinctively moral. This is no different from the challenge of trying to make someone see that there is a qualitative difference between their negative aesthetic valuing of a movie and their negative moral valuing. We are all vulnerable to a failure to make or become aware of more subtle but important discriminations about what we immediately experience, but as Dewey says "Moral decline is on a par with the loss of that ability to make delicate distinctions, with the blunting and hardening of the capacity of discrimination" (LW 5:280).

Since I am a contextualist, I am open to the possibility that I will experience the homosexuality of a person or of an act as either contributing to what is morally wrong or as being of negative moral value in a situation. But contrary to some, I have yet to experience any recurrent or meaningful connection between homosexuality and negative moral value. Therefore, my disagreement with people who object to homosexuality on moral grounds is not just at the valuing level. As much as I have reflectively considered the issue (i.e., engaged in valuation), I have yet to be convinced that there is anything morally wrong with homosexuality. None of the arguments offered by others or considered on my own have any validity. It is possible that in some future reflective consideration of the issue I will change my mind. If so, then it is also probable that I will also change my valuing about homosexuality. A change in the contrary direction is also a possibility. I may come to have new valuing experiences that may affect significantly my valuation.

For Dewey, our valuing should be subject to constant and even intense criticism, but critical reflection (inquiry) is not a contextless and rationalistic process that can guide itself by logic and facts alone. My critical reflections about homosexuality may end up changing my valuing, but it starts, takes place, and is guided by whatever valuing experiences I happen to have. In other words, valuation is not an impartial and rational process that requires that the immediate valuings be bracketed or left behind, perhaps because they are considered mere appearance or subjective. These valuings are not objects of knowledge (e.g., propositions) but they function as initial data and are regulative as moral deliberation proceeds. (I discuss this further below.) And one does well to remember that what is revealed from the valuing standpoint (from the practical engaged point of view) is moral reality, rather than our inner moral feelings toward actions. As Dewey says, "It is not experience which is experienced, but nature—stones, plants, animals, diseases, health, temperature, electricity, and so on" (LW 1:12). My valuing experience of an act of injustice as wrong is about a value that I find in the same world where I also find plants and stones. To dismiss the importance of valuing in inquiry because it is merely subjective or a mere psychological reaction is to assume a dualism or to presuppose the supremacy of the theoretical standpoint in revealing what is real.

Dewey's view on judgments of value has important implications about the nature of moral disagreements and what resources are available to deal with them. Suppose I am having a discussion with some who oppose homosexuality on moral grounds. Let us assume (and this is not a small assumption) that we are all fairly committed but open-minded individuals infused with the Deweyan democratic spirit to genuinely learn from each other (more about this in part 3). Each of us thinks that she is right, but we are willing to be convinced otherwise about the moral value of homosexuality. My role in this communal inquiry is to try to convince others but, if Dewey is right, the challenge takes a lot more than argumentation. I must, of course, engage others as much as I can in serious reflective examination of the issue. We should try to examine together possible arguments in favor of or against homosexuality in light of their logical validity. We have seen, however, that for Dewey, there is a lot more to deliberation than reasoning. We could imaginatively consider a variety of actual and possible cases, that is, construct a dramatic rehearsal. There may also be a legitimate role for the use of stories, metaphors, and emotional appeals.

Dewey is not so naïve as to think that even in the best of circumstances we will reach total agreement in our judgments. I am not even sure that one can change someone else's moral stand on issues so easily. But unless the situation is one where an immediate consensus must be reached there is no good reason to put so much emphasis on consensus as the outcome. It would be significant enough if at the end of the communal inquiry both parties recognized some of the weakness in their arguments. It would be even better if both sides learned about some significant considerations that they had overlooked in reaching their judgments. The parties in the dialogue are learning even if no one convinces the other. Outcomes matter and we want to convince others, but people often do not change their minds about moral matters from one day to the next. It requires a longer process of gestation where the objections and the new considerations gradually make one less convinced about some moral issue. But if Dewey is right, valuation is not enough. To significantly affect or change the stand of someone on some moral issue requires more than changing their minds (i.e., valuation). What good is it to have convinced someone intellectually that there is no good argument against homosexuality if in their everyday moral engagement they continue to immediately experience and value it as always wrong (i.e., valuing)?

For Dewey, learning and deepening our appreciation of values requires that there be a mutually affecting and beneficial relation between valuing and valuation. This presupposes that one has the sort of character that allows this to happen. There may be people whose valuings are usually at odds with, or unaffected by, their more reflective valuations, in other words, they are unable to learn and improve their value experiences. In chapter 11 I will be concerned with what it takes to have the ideal sort of character. But was Dewey naïve about the actual power of valuation to affect valuing? Emotional or unconscious prejudices sometimes run so deep that no amount or quality of reflection may make any difference. Dewey can accept this possibility, but it is also important to mention that he did not think the only way to change valuing is through valuation. As much faith as he had in reflection, he recognized the power of changes in one's environment, that is, in the tools we use or our communal rituals, to change valuing. These changes must still be subject to criticism and reflection to be justified, but this opens the doors to more effective ways of effecting moral change in our society than just dialogue or reflection. Women have come to be experienced as the moral equals of men (valuing), not just as a result of philosophical arguments that prove their moral equality (valuation), but as an indirect result of a change in social and economic conditions. The development of new technologies, such as birth control, has facilitated the movement of women into certain social roles that has, in turn, affected the valuings of men, that is, how men experience women. Sometimes changes in environmental conditions are more effective than the best-argued objections to provoke the sort of criticism that is needed to change people's valuings. It could be argued, for example, that it was not until Louis Braille worked out his basic 6-dot system for the blind to communicate, read, and participate more fully in society that many people reconsidered the immediate valuing of the blind as idiots or as not deserving of the respect and dignity as other humans.[9]

In estimating the power of valuation over valuing in changing moral judgments it makes a difference how one conceives the role of reasons and arguments in moral deliberation. In the process of reflectively considering the moral value of homosexuality we can exchange arguments, but is the goal and hope of such an exchange that others will reach our conclusion by making a logical inference from certain premises? We do not change people's judgments by this sort of process because this is not how reflective judgments are reached. The way we can contribute and affect someone's reflective judgments of value is not by reasoning alone but by bringing up considerations or reasons to which they have hitherto not fully attended. Reasons are considerations to look for in the survey of one's situation, rather than premises in an argument. Arguments are important but they are just one of the resources available to make others reexamine on their own the subject matter to be judged. It is part of the method proposed by Dewey to extend an invitation to others and provide the conditions by which they can have the experiences that confirm or reject our assertions. You may also contribute to someone's dramatic rehearsal by provoking him or her to consider similar cases or to adopt an imaginary impartial standpoint. None of these resources may in the end be effective in a particular communal inquiry, but Dewey's view of what it takes to be reflective about value is more heterogeneous and resourceful than the anemic rationalistic conceptions of moral deliberation and intelligence that predominate in ethical theory.

Dewey held that an organic relation between valuing and valuation can lead to the kind of integration of means and ends present in artistic activity. This is an ideal of human conduct that I will explore later, but it is important to appreciate that it is the possibility of a dynamic and integrative relation between valuing and valuation which explains why Dewey believed that moral life is a process of *creating* or *transforming* value, and not merely of accepting and living by given or former values. The process by which valuings are subject to reflection (valuation) has as its end an enhanced valuing or appreciation. In valuation "former goods are subjected to judgment" but "the end of judgment is to reinstate some immediate value" (MW 13:6). Here is how Dewey explains this transformative process:

> The new value, dependent upon judgment, is, when it comes, as immediate a good or bad as anything can be. But it is also an immediate value of a plus sort. The prior judgment has affected the new good not merely as its causal condition but by entering into its quality. The new good has an added dimension of value. (MW 13:6)

Dewey emphasized the importance of valuation because in a precarious world the relations of events in experience are important from the point of view of control. Moreover, to acknowledge valuation is to recognize that moral values can be subject to reflective criticism and are not subjective or arbitrary. However, one must not underestimate the importance for Dewey of value that is immediately had and non-reflective. Valuing is important because "the realm of immediate qualities contains everything of worth and significance" (LW 1:94).

Criticism and reflection depend for their material resources upon the problematic context that is immediately had, and upon prior direct appreciations; but their ultimate function is to bring about qualitative transformation. "Appreciation, or taste, must supply the material for criticism, while the worth of criticism is tested by its power to function in a *new appreciation* which has enhancement, new depth, and range of meaning because of the criticism" (MW 13:7, my emphasis). Criticism and reflection, the examined life, are important constituents of moral life because they are capable of enriching its immediate quality and not because they lead us to the Truth or to actualize some essence. This insight is crucial to understanding his normative moral vision.

Before I consider in more detail the function of valuing and valuation in the context of moral inquiry I must make some very general but important qualifications.[10] Empiricism commits one to begin with "situations having value-quality" (LW 2:73) and not with value as something independent. Moreover, what we find in experience are not values as such; rather, as Dewey observed,

Speaking literally, there are no such things as values. . . . There are things, all sorts of things, having the unique, the experienced, but indefinable, quality of value. Values in the plural, or a value in the singular, is merely a convenient abbreviation for an object, event, situation, res, possessing the quality. (MW 15:20)

Value is an abstract and vague term that can be used to refer to qualities beyond those that are moral, for example, aesthetic and prudential value, and even within the moral ones one can make some finer discriminations. Dewey often adopted this manner of speaking because it provided him the level of generality that he needed to assume in such works as *Experience and Nature* and the *Logic.* It also served his purpose of criticizing the theories of values that were current.[11] However, to take Dewey's theory of value, as it appears in such places as *Theory of Valuation* (LW 13:189–254) and the chapter "The Construction of the Good" in *The Quest for Certainty* (LW 4), as central or as good summaries of Dewey's mature moral thought is a mistake. These general and abstract discussions about value leave out or do not do justice to what is explicitly recognized in his 1930 essay "Three Independent Factors in Morals": that there are at least three distinct and incommensurable qualities designated by moral value. This pluralistic view of moral values will be taken for granted as we proceed to consider the function of valuing and valuation in moral deliberation and the nature of the resolution of this process.

The Function of Valuing and Valuation in Moral Deliberation

The distinction between valuing and valuation has to be understood in terms of their function in the process of moral inquiry. Valuing and valuation correspond to undergoing and doing phases that hold a mutually supporting and effective relation in the process of transforming a morally problematic situation.

Valuation arises because valuing turns problematic, that is, "experience raises the question whether the object in question is what our esteem or disesteem took it to be" (LW 7:264). Therefore, it is not always the case that "qualitative immediacy is subject to judgment" (LW 15:80). But once doubt arises, valuing judgments provide the initial material for deliberation. Although they are immediate and precede the more reflective operations of inquiry, we cannot assume "that they are always superficial and immature" (LW 5:250). For when they proceed from a well-developed character they are judgments funded by previous experience. Dewey explains that "they may also sum up and integrate prolonged previous experience and training, and bring to a unified head the results of severe and consecutive reflection" (LW 5:250). It is important to understand that in making the distinction between valuing and valuation we are discriminating between phases of a continuous process.

> If there is in direct valuing an element of recognition of the properties of the thing or person valued as *ground* for prizing, esteeming, desiring, liking, etc., then the difference between it and explicit evaluation is one of emphasis and degree, not of fixed kinds. *Ap-praising* then represents a more or less systematized development of what is already present in prizing. (LW 15:105)

The move toward a more reflective judgment and phase of inquiry is not a jump to a separate objective domain or to receiving the guidance of a reality independent of experience. Instead, "when it is said that a thing cognized is different from an earlier non-cognitionally experienced thing, the saying no more implies lack of continuity between the things, than the obvious remark that a seed is different than a flower" (MW 3:166). Valuation (the flower) emerges from within the same initial valuing situation that provoked it (the seed). An initial conflicting or disturbed valuing experience evokes reflection (valuation) and guides the possible solutions to be tried out. Any eventual correction or improvement of a present experience comes from the same experience in need of reconstruction. Dewey's empiricism is committed to the view that "whatever gain in clearness, in fullness, in trueness of context is experienced must grow out of some element in the experience of this experienced as what it is" (MW 3:164). This became the basis of Dewey's faith in experience. We need to trust the potential of any present experience to carry the seed of its own transformation. We detect and correct illusoriness "because the thing experienced is real, having within its experienced reality elements whose own mutual tension effects its reconstruction" (MW 3:164). If a moral problem has a solution, it must emerge from guiding our inquiry by its initial direct and unique problematic character. It is untrue that without some external criteria of right and wrong we are lost and cannot transform the situation.

This early insight was later refined and elaborated as Dewey became more interested in the logic of artistic construction and appreciation. The initial immediate experience of a work of art as good, for example, is "relatively dumb and inarticulate yet penetrating" (LW 5:249). It is neither knowledge nor a mere state of a personal feeling, but it is an initial valuing that serves as the reliable basis (the seed) to any subsequent reflective analysis that may or may not result in confirming, rejecting, or enhancing the original valuing experience. In this process, we examine and sometimes make subtle discriminations about what makes that particular thing aesthetically good; but to take these reflective discriminations as criteria or determinants of its quality is to commit the philosophical fallacy. Granted, analysis of why things are good may help me enhance my immediate experience of their goodness, but what is primary and the ultimate test of value is their immediate qualitative value. Dewey makes this clear in his comments about art:

> Upon subsequent analysis, we term the properties of a work of art by such names as symmetry, harmony, rhythm, measure, and proportion. These may, in some cases at least, be formulated mathematically. But the apprehension of these formal relationships is not primary for either the artist or the appreciative spectator. The subject-matter formulated by these terms is primarily qualitative, and is apprehended qualitatively. Without an independent qualitative apprehension, the characteristics of a work of art can be translated into explicit harmonies, symmetries, etc., only in a way which substitutes mechanical formulae for esthetic quality. (LW 5:251)

We have examined the nature of the transition between valuing and valuation in moral inquiry, but what brings about the resolution? How do we know we have arrived at a final judgment? It is no different than in the process of artistic production. In both moral and artistic activities the agent is engaged in a process of continually shaping and reshaping (doing and undergoing) until she qualitatively appreciates that the present product (a course of action or a work of art) meets the demands presented by the developing situation that has been explored. When this happens, the experienced relation between one's product and the context can be described as one of fittingness or appropriateness to the situation. In other words, the final judgment that "I ought to do X" is the qualitative appreciation and assertion that, in light of the terrain imaginatively explored, this is the act that is morally called for by the situation; it is not, however, a deduction from propositions or an application of a universal criterion. To acquire the habits capable of making these kinds of context-sensitive judgments is to have practical wisdom (moral intelligence).

Notice what this entails. The qualitative instructions telling whether one has come close to fulfillment in aesthetic and moral activity are not to be found outside of the particular unique qualitative situation that is experienced as needing transformation. "The making comes to an end when its result is experienced as good—and that experience comes not by mere intellectual and outside judgment but in direct perception" (LW 10:56). In a morally problematic situation, there is no pre-established formula, indicator, or criteria that we can rely on to discriminate which act is called for by a particular situation or whether our inquiry is headed in the wrong direction. The traditional quest in ethics and aesthetics for some ultimate criteria of right and good neglects the fact that the situation itself gives the agent a pervading qualitative sense of relevance and a satisfactory closure during the process of reconstruction.

Let's consider next a philosophical debate about value that is usually based on neglecting the situational context that guides our judgments.

Value and the Objectivist-Subjectivist Debate

Are moral values objective? This issue is important because it seems that a negative answer would commit us to the view that morality is not something to be taken as seriously as other areas of experience. Dewey was committed to defend the metaphysical and logical objectivity of moral-ity on empirical grounds, but he was opposed to the sort of metaphysi-cal realism "that locates 'objectivity' of value in 'objects' that are so-called because of lack of any connection whatever with human behavior" (LW 15:63). On the other hand, he affirmed his "opposition to those views which admit a human factor in values, but which interpret it in such a way that the result is skeptical denial of the possibility of any genuine judg-ments about them" (LW 15:63).

In the metaphysical or ontological understanding of the issue of objec-tivity, objective is equated with what is real. But this presupposes the same dualism that underlies the realism versus non-realism debates. Moral val-ues are either out there in the objective world, understood as an antecedent independent reality that we do not affect, or they are in our heads, under-stood either as in a person or in their culture or society. We will not get caught up in this issue if, as with Dewey, we start with the primacy of lived situational experience rather than with this inner/outer picture.

Objectivity about moral values seems impossible if it requires that there be a self outside the course of events that does not affect anything. The self as an organism is one among other things transacting in a situa-tion, and it therefore makes a difference to the qualities that emerge in experience; this, however, does not mean that qualities "inhere exclusively in the subject; or as posing the problem of a distortion of the real object by a knower set over against the world" (MW 10:26). One can discern one's contribution to having certain experiences in an effort to study the condi-tions of having them. "The 'subjective' factor (using the word to designate the operations of an acculturated organism) is, like 'objective' physical subject-matter a condition of experience" (LW 14:199). That, for example, one's character is usually one of the conditions of what is qualitatively had in valuing experiences does not warrant the conclusion that values are subjective. To make this mistake is to commit the philosophical fallacy, that is, the "conversion of a condition of an event into an inherent property of the event itself" (LW 15:75).

Of course, Dewey cannot hold the view that there can be universal agreement about a fixed set of values regardless of who we are or what characters we bring to situations. But this does not make him a subjectivist, though perhaps it makes him a kind of relativist: one who subscribes to a relativism to situations and to the factors that come to constitute them. However, this is an objective relativism in the sense that things actually have the value-qualities we experience them as having.[12] According to the postulate of immediate empiricism, things are what they are experienced as. Valuing judgments are experienced as qualities found in a particular situation (as manifestations of nature[13]) and not subjective projections, the content of one's consciousness, or the manifestation of the culture to which one belongs. If I experience "x" as morally repugnant in a particular context, then it *is* morally repugnant even if I later hypothesize that I would have experienced it differently had other attitudes been operative or had I been some other person. Perhaps humans would not experience acts of cruelty as wrong if they were not brought up in a certain way, but this does not make these acts less wrong when they are experienced as such. It is puzzling why anyone would find this sort of relativism objectionable in morals but not in regard to other non-moral qualities. For example, colors are also relative in the sense that we would not experience them if we did not bring into a perceptual situation certain optical organs, and certain linguistic conventions regarding colors. But this is not usually considered problematic, and we all admit that there can be genuine disagreement about the color of things.

The reality of moral values has been considered problematic on other grounds. John Mackie, for example, held that moral values couldn't be objective or "part of the fabric of the world" because if they were then they would have to be very strange things, "queer" as he famously put it.[14] If one starts with the assumption of a valueless world, then moral values as qualities would indeed seem queer sorts of entities. From this metaphysical outlook all judgments of values are suspect and in need of an explanation. Mackie explains it in terms of how humans project values onto the world and learn to live with the deception that they are objective. Other philosophers have accounted for value judgments in terms of how a subject applies some criterion upon the more natural traits of things. In other words, value qualities and judgments must supervene on or be derived from the more objective traits of the world, otherwise the alternative seems to be the sort of emotivism that makes value judgments mere expressions of our subjective preferences.

For Dewey, of course, there is no need for an explanation. The only thing queer about values is how anyone could question their existence, for, insofar as 'value' is a term that points to what is directly and immediately qualitative, everything is value-laden. In particular, moral judgments are as natural and as descriptive of the objective world as any other judgment. Moral qualities are not experienced as things added to a world that is morally neutral.[15] This is, at best, a theory. To be sure, the fact that we find ourselves in a qualitative world of moral value does not mean that, as implied by some forms of objectivism, we can only copy what we find. As I noted above, inquiry has the power to change what we directly perceive or judge as valuable, but what has been transformed is the same objective world of tables and chairs.

In general it is a favoritism toward objects of knowledge that has discredited the objectivity and reality of moral experience. Contributing to this is a particularly narrow conception of knowledge where science and math are the models of objective discourse. This reflects deep-seated dualisms where science and art are polar opposites. On this view, art is clearly subjective since it is concerned with expression and creation of values, whereas science is the discovery of what is the case independently of human values. Dewey explains how this picture makes moral values especially problematic and how it generates the subjectivism versus objectivism debate.

> Between these two realms, one of intellectual objects without value and the other of value-objects without intellect, there is an equivocal mid-country in which moral objects are placed, with rival claimants striving to annex them either to the region of purely immediate goods . . . or to that of purely rational objects. (LW 1:304)

This general picture is based on misconceptions about science and art, as well as of the general activities of discovery and creativity. It assumes that we either *discover* the world as a passive spectator of an antecedent reality or we *construct* it in the sense of inventing or making it out of nothing. But discovery and creation are two mutually dependent phases of any inquiry and are themselves multifaceted endeavors. Artistic activity requires receptivity, paying close attention to the grain of things, and discovering the qualities of the raw materials to be transformed. On the other hand, discovery requires selective searching and creative ingenuity. Dewey's view of scientific inquiry is one in which not even facts are given in the sense of being antecedent to human interest or contextual purposes. Similarly, in morality there is both discovery and creation of value; this was implicit in my explanation of the dynamic relation between valuing and valuation in moral inquiry.

Objectivity also has epistemological and logical aspects. The objectivity of moral values has been questioned on the basis of their validity or genuineness as judgments. How can moral values be objective if there is so much disagreement about them and there is no Archimedean standpoint from which to settle them?

Is there really more disagreement about moral values than there is about other qualities in experience? This is an empirical issue. It is true that the conditions for aesthetic and moral qualities, in comparison with other qualities, are less stable and uniform, and that their apprehension depends heavily on how the agent participates in a situation (i.e., as one of its conditions). Dewey knew this. "In the case of aesthetic and moral goods, the causal conditions which reflection reveals as determinants of the good object are found to lie within organic constitution in greater degree than is the case with objects of belief" (LW 1:321). It is also true that moral and aesthetic qualities cannot be measured, quantified, or subject to predictive control. But this cannot be taken as evidence of the subjectivism and arbitrary character of these dimensions of our experience. From Dewey's point of view, it is to be expected that disagreement and change is more common in moral and aesthetic matters. But this was not for him a fall from grace, because he did not believe that morality should only be taken seriously if moral values are universal and absolute. On the contrary, the complexity of our moral and aesthetic experiences is a reason why we must be more sensitive, careful, and thoughtful in our judgments and why we must study their conditions.

More than the purported fact of disagreement, what seems to raise doubts about the objectivity of morality is presumably the lack of any objective means to resolve moral problems. As Sydney Hook observed, "The most common objection to naturalistic humanism is not that it has no place for moral experience but that it has no place for an authoritative moral experience."[16] If there is no authoritative Archimedean standpoint and no criteria-based procedure to settle disagreements about morals, then moral values are subjective. For Dewey this is a false dilemma. Disagreements in morality can only be handled in the same way as other disagreements in everyday experience. We can engage in a common inquiry that appeals to experience and that guides itself by the same problematic situation in which the disagreement is embedded. This, of course, assumes that the people involved have some of the virtues (habits) needed for this task. (I will have more to say about these virtues later.) In experimental inquiry in science, art, and morals the general method is the same: we *try* to change each other's judgments (and are open to modify our own) by consulting objective features of our situation. The key to guidance is a closer attention to the situation and the use of our shared resources, rather than any attempts to step outside of the situation. Reaching agreement about general rules (e.g., about what usually makes actions right) may help carry inquiry along in some cases, but this does not replace judgment, which is unique and qualitative. Although there are more quantifiable means to test hypotheses and resolve disagreements in science than in morals, that does not make scientific thought less qualitative and morality subjective. In science, art, and morals we can guide others toward having experiences in a situation that can confirm or reject our hypotheses.

The opposition between objectivism and subjectivism in value theory is one more instance of the "common occurrence in the histories of theories that an error at one extreme calls out a complementary error at the other extreme" (LW 13:240). The subjectivist starts with the assumption of isolated desires as sources of valuation; there is thus no way to test values, no possibility of intellectual control, and values become arbitrary. In response to the subjectivist, a diametrically opposed theory is constructed, one in which values are ends-in-themselves or outside of experience. "This theory, in its endeavor to escape from the frying pan of disordered valuations, jumps into the fire of absolutism" (LW 3:241). From Dewey's standpoint, in spite of the opposition, the error is the same: both assume the "same fundamental postulate of the isolation of valuation from concrete empirical situations" (LW 13:241). Without the qualitative context of a situation there is no basis in experience for control, guidance, and experimentation in regard to values; we must either go outside of experience for a standard or make values subjective. Subjectivism troubled Dewey because it made criticism, appreciation, and cultivation in matters of value arbitrary or absurd. But for Dewey "educated interest or taste is, ultimately, supreme, the *unum necessarium*, in morals" (LW 2:76). And "The saying 'De gustibus, non disputandum' . . . is either just a maxim of politeness or a stupid saying" (LW 2:95).

For the subjectivist, to be valued is to be enjoyed or desired. But valuings are about things in the world and not mere reports of our internal affective or appetitive states. Valuing judgments can become problematic, and then become subject to objective criticism (i.e., valuation) without having to appeal to anything outside of experience. Inquiry into relations and conditions is as applicable to valuings as it is to scientific matters. To be sure, value judgments differ from other judgments in their subject matter and in the usual importance they have in directing conduct, but there is nothing inherent in the nature of values that precludes them from the general method of inquiry. Hence, intelligent and objective criticism of existing values is possible even if it is always relative to what is available in the particular situation, rather than from a God's-eye point of view.

Today, one could argue that any proposal for objective means to resolve moral disagreements is seriously challenged by the growing awareness of how radical the disagreement is across the world. The "ineliminable diversity of moral convictions among the peoples of the earth"[17] seems to support a cultural moral relativism. The cultural relativist is in a better position than the subjectivist to propose a way to settle disagreements. According to this view, moral judgments are not mere expressions of our subjective preferences, but neither are they representations of an antecedent reality. Instead, moral judgments are ultimately grounded in the standards of a community. The existence of these standards provides a sufficiently stable basis to settle intra-cultural disagreements, thus rescuing morality from the charge of arbitrariness. It is another matter whether moral relativism has much to offer when it comes to moral disagreement across cultures or societies, especially when the moral relativist assumes that moral incompatibilities between groups of humans are radical and incommensurable. Some moral relativists, aware of this challenge, have proposed ways to settle conflict that are coherent with their views. One tactic is to suggest an objective way to deal with cross-cultural conflict that is based on prudential reasons that the conflicting parties can accept. According to Joseph Margolis, the best we can hope for is "to find whatever viable forms of practical tolerance may help us avoid the worst imagined disasters."[18] The quest for neutral, non-moral grounds to resolve irresolvable moral conflict among a plurality of moral traditions is common in the history of political liberalism. One could question the moral neutrality of such proposals and the underlying assumption that humans agree more on prudential than on moral grounds.

Is Dewey in a better position than the moral relativist to propose something positive or promising that could settle radical moral disagreements without presupposing cognitive privilege, as in traditional forms of objectivism? One could argue that because of the way Dewey conceives of moral disagreement, he has more resources to offer. Many philosophers, including objectivists and relativists, assume that moral disagreement is an opposition or conflict between moral convictions or judgments as norms or propositions that are either true or false. This starting point determines the range of options available to ameliorate moral disagreement because the inquiry centers on the plausibility of possible ways to adjudicate between conflicting propositions or belief systems. Is there something that makes moral propositions true or false outside of one's culturally inherited moral norms?

Since Dewey has an entirely different starting point, moral disagreement happens in a situation, so that even if people in moral disagreement do not share beliefs, they share the situation of unique and particular disagreement as something that is outside of discourse and without propositional content. If we start with moral conflict as a situation that is experienced by participants as having the quality of radical disagreement, a quality that is unique to each conflict, then that starting point opens the possibility of more shared resources for amelioration. We thus start with more to rely on than our moral beliefs and languages. Even if one cannot convince others by arguments or test their convictions by reasoning, one can guide others outside of the discourse to have certain experiences. This is not a sure thing. Our experiences may still be very different, but there is also the possibility of guiding dialogue by the unique unsettling quality of the situation of disagreement. For Dewey, if there is any hope to ameliorate a situation, it must come from within the same indeterminate situation.

It is not my purpose here to demonstrate the superiority of Dewey's view to relativism or objectivism. Instead, my goal has been to show why any full consideration of Dewey in ongoing debates in ethics must confront the most basic assumptions about the nature of moral disagreements, judgments, and the starting point of philosophical inquiry. As much as Dewey shares with moral relativists, moral judgments for him are not derivations from general norms of warrant, generated in the context of intersubjective discourse. This would leave out situations, the concrete non-cognitive and non-linguistic context in which these norms and discourse are found and can be tested. "Any one who refuses to go outside the universe of discourse . . . has of course shut himself off from understanding what a 'situation,' as directly experienced subject-matter is" (LW 14:30–31). This is why Dewey would be suspicious of the preoccupation of some neopragmatists with the norms of warrant within conceptual schemes.[19] As David Hildebrand has recently argued, they share a "theoretical approach that makes 'language games' or 'conceptual schemes' more basic to inquiry than life or 'situations.' "[20] For Dewey, if there are norms of warrant, then experienced situations are their ultimate measure. Our present formulas are constrained, facilitated, and guided in unpredictable ways by a qualitative world that never appears that way within discourse or inquiry. Inquiry and judgment of better or worse are controlled by reference to a situation.

SIX

The "How" of Moral Experience

What occurs in moral experience is a choice of conduct that arises out of deliberation in the context of an evolving morally problematic situation. I have given separate description of the phases within this process. First, I considered the nature of the kinds of problems that disrupt the fluidity of moral life, and then of the process of moral deliberation that issues in a choice. However, a description of Dewey's ground map of moral experience is incomplete without considering the role of the agent in the process I have described. "No complete account of what is experienced, then, can be given until we know *how* it is experienced, or the mode of experience that enters into its formation" (LW 5:228). The agent is part of the context and does not stand outside the process of reconstructing a situation. Postulating a moral self that is outside the process and locating the process as somehow within the mind of a self (subjectivism) are the causes of many of the problems of moral philosophy. For Dewey, these problems are dissolved if we begin with the self as a constitutive part of moral situations.

Dewey shared with George Herbert Mead the view that the self emerges from a natural process of social interaction, but he focused more on describing the self as an organization of habits. All of our habits at any given time in the process of living constitute our characters. Character is the "working interaction of habits" (MW 14:30), the "enduring unity of attitudes and habits" (LW 7:258), that is expressed in the continuity of a series of acts. This might seem like a narrow view of character, yet the pragmatist notion of habit is a very rich one.

Habits

Through the process of socialization, an organism channels its impulses, that is, it learns habits. Habits include not only one's routine way of doing things, but a broad spectrum of tendencies and dispositions, dominant ways of acting, ways or modes of response, abilities, attitudes, sensitivities, accessibilities, predilections, and aversions. "Habits are the fibre of character, but there are habits of desire and imagination as well as of outer action" (LW 9:187). Habit is a word that expresses "the kind of human activity which is influenced by prior activity and in that sense acquired" (MW 14:31). However, when one develops a habit, what one has acquired is not a possession within the confines of a self but a *way of interacting* within a social and natural environment. Since some pre-existing association is prior to any particular human being, many of our habits are common ways of feeling and believing, or what Dewey called "custom."[1]

Habits have to be understood in terms of their function in the life-process and in situations. They are the most basic instrumentalities of any organism in its environment. Organisms depend on habits for sustenance, control, and continuity. One trait common to human beings is that most of our habits are not instinctive; they are instead acquired through our constant interaction with an environment that is social and processive. Our ability to acquire habits is due to the original plasticity of our nature.

Habits permit the everyday unreflective flow of action. The disruption of a habit in meeting present conditions marks a state of crisis for an organism. A morally problematic situation is in effect a disruption of the fluid function of our habits, that is, a blockage of effective overt action. In these situations, there is shock and confusion. Disruption of habits is an occasion for deliberation, in other words, thinking or inquiry comes about when habits no longer work. The outcome of this process is the recovery of the same kind of stability, equilibrium, and fluidity of conduct provided by previous habits in a stable environment. However, some habits remain operative and stable through this process.

In a morally problematic situation, different habits are operative at different levels depending on whether they are in the background or at the foreground of our reflective awareness. The contextual background is temporal and spatial. It is temporal because what is present proceeds or is a culmination of previous inquiries; there is, in other words, a narrative or history. In the background we are usually carrying forward ways of interpretation and observation that are part of a tradition or a culture. The contextual background is also the contemporary spatial setting in which thinking occurs. There are no exact boundaries that delineate the contextual scene or arena of a situation, but its vagueness does not imply that it is unimportant. Dewey explained its importance with an analogy,

> This contextual setting is vague, but it is no mere fringe. It has a solidity and stability not found in the focal material of thinking. The latter denotes the part of the road upon which the spot light is thrown. The spatial context is the ground through which the road runs and for the sake of which the road exists. It is this setting which gives import to the road and to its consecutive illuminations. The path must be lighted if one is not to lose his way; the remoter territory may be safely left in the dark. (LW 6:13–14)

In a morally problematic situation, the inclusive situation does not become the object of focal awareness, which is usually concerned with what is unsettled. What is in the background in a situation might become an object of thought, but the whole contextual background does not all come into question at once. Hence, we need to abandon the Cartesian illusion that we can doubt everything. We can only start where we are, with all the moral beliefs and habits that we have inherited from our social environment. This is not, however, a reason to despair. What may appear to be a limitation is for Dewey a resource. Without the stable or settled aspect of the background, we would not have the experiential resources to think and reconstruct what is unsettled. "If everything were literally unsettled at once, there would be nothing to which to tie those factors that, being unsettled, are in the process of discovery and determination" (LW 6:12). The background habits in a situation are the ones we count on because they provide the necessary stability to operate at the foreground reconstruction of the habits that have been ruptured (at the more precarious and shifting level of our experience). There are also the habits of exploration and imagination that are needed to engage in a process of moral deliberation that can issue in a resolution. In short, habits are necessary and active instrumentalities by which we experience the world. As Dewey said, "concrete habits do all the perceiving, recognition, imagining, recalling, judging, conceiving, and reasoning that is done" (MW 14:124).

In *Human Nature and Conduct*, Dewey argues against the misconception that habits are essentially conservative. Habits can have the tendency to become self-perpetuating and mechanical, but not all habit is the "enslavement to old ruts" (MW 14:48). There are habits that, though persistent, can adapt themselves to new conditions. Dewey referred to these flexible habits as "intelligent" or "artistic" (MW 14:52). Moreover, the thinking capacities that are needed to reconstruct and reform habits that are old ruts are themselves habits. An intelligent organism is capable of modifying and improving her habits so that they can become relevant to this and similar situations. With time, an intelligent organism not only learns to adapt her habits to present situations, but also learns to learn; she can, in other words, modify her present tools, but she can also create tools to modify tools.

Situations and habits do not constitute separated isolated compartments of experience. Habits are not formed in a vacuum and we cannot think of them as an exclusive property of a self. Just as "breathing is an affair of the air as truly as of the lungs" (MW 9:15), habits require the cooperation (interaction) of the organism and the environment. On the other hand, situations are what they are and have their uniqueness because they are a result of the interaction (transaction) between the habits and attitudes of the organism and its environment. There are two sides to the relation (interaction) between our habits and the situations in which they operate. With the attitudes and habits we bring from previous experience to a particular situation we affect the quality of the resulting situation, but these same attitudes and habits are also affected by the situation. This ongoing, bi-directional process provides the basis for *continuity* in the development of experience. But it also forms a continuity that, in a certain sense, is educative or cumulative. In Dewey's words,

> The basic characteristic of habit is that every experience enacted and undergone modifies the one who acts and undergoes, while this modification affects, whether we wish it or not, the quality of subsequent experiences (LW 13:18). Every experience affects for better or worse the attitudes which help decide the quality of further experiences. (LW 13:20)

The fact that habits are the tools funded by previous experience makes them one of the more dependable and stable aspects of our moral life.

Character as an Organic Whole

Habits interact not only with things in the environment, but also with other habits. A habit is a trait of character, not to be thought of as an isolated compartment, but rather as "one phase of an interpenetrated

whole" (LW 7:258). The habits that constitute character are always operative, though some might be more overt than others depending on the
situation. That is, most of our conduct is an expression of the coordina-
tion of several habits, though occasionally one habit predominates.

There is continuity in conduct because of character. "Were it not for
the continued operation of all habits in every act, no such thing as character could exist. There would be simply a bundle, an untied bundle at that,
of isolated acts" (MW 14:29). Character is not a fixed thing, but is in a
continuous process of transformation. "There is always in character the
possibility of change, of development."[2] The habits that are constitutive of
a character are not all plastic or persistent to the same degree. Those that
persist and resist change form the most stable aspects of our characters.

It is because of his organic model of character that Dewey resisted the
approach to ethics and to moral education that consists in listing and
cultivating a set of moral positive traits of character or virtues. He said,

> The mere idea of a catalogue of different virtues commits us to the
> notion that virtues may be kept apart, pigeon-holed in water-tight com-
> partments. In fact virtuous traits interpenetrate one another; this unity
> is involved in the very idea of integrity of character. (LW 7:283)

Because of the relation of mutual dependence between the habits of a
concrete character, it is possible that a habit or virtue that is cultivated in
isolation can turn into a vice. For example, when temperance is cultivated
independently and in isolation, it can become a negative kind of inhibition. And when courage is taken as independent of achieving or maintaining positive ends in conduct, "it shrinks to mere stoical and negative
resistance" (LW 7:116).

Dewey recognized the practical function of the language of virtues.
Habits are as a matter of fact evaluated as either positive (virtue) or
negative (vice) in the everyday approval and disapproval that takes place
in human relationships.[3] This is important as grounds for praise and
blame in moral development. Using traits of character to describe how
someone dispositionally responds, behaves, and interacts under certain
circumstances can serve other purposes, but a concrete character is not the
sum of its parts. Because of its unique history, circumstances, and interactions among its habits, the total integration of the habits that make up a
character is unique. Hence, there can only be a very rough functional
sameness among characters. Although we classify and discriminate between people and virtues for instrumental purposes, one commits the
philosophical fallacy if one assumes that these classifications exhaust the
nature of individual persons.

Another implication of Dewey's notion of character is that we can no longer establish the traditional fixed demarcation between the moral and the non-moral virtues. If character is an interactive whole, then moral conduct can never be the sole expression and operation of one, or one kind of, habit. For example, how my stomach and eyes react to a morally problematic situation might be as integral a part of moral inquiry as the habit of remembering moral principles. Moral conduct is not guaranteed simply by acquiring a specific set of moral habits and allowing those habits to guide our lives. For instance, doing honest acts when they are morally called for in a situation requires more than a general disposition to be honest. It also requires all the thinking habits that help me determine whether honesty is really called for in the situation, as well as all the other habits in my character that are supportive of my individual actions. It is precisely because many of our moral failures result from automatically following moral habits that Dewey insisted on emphasizing the habits of inquiry required to find out what a present morally problematic situation calls for. He said:

> Wide sympathy, keen sensitiveness, persistence in the face of the dis-agreeable, balance of interest enabling us to undertake the work of anal-ysis and decision intelligently are the distinctively moral traits—the vir-tues of moral excellencies. (MW 12:173–174)

The virtues that are often considered to be distinctively moral in concrete experience (e.g., sympathy, truthfulness) are virtues because they are intimately connected with other habits. Hence, Dewey concluded that

> To call them virtues in their isolation is like taking the skeleton for the living body. The bones are certainly important, but their importance lies in the fact that they support other organs of the body in such a way as to make them capable of integrated effective activity. And the same is true of the qualities of character which we specifically designate virtues. Morals concern nothing less than the whole character. (MW 9:367)

For Dewey, if one considers the nature of intellectual activity, then this opens the door to challenging the separation of the intellectual virtues from the moral virtues within character. Such activity is not something purely mental or the exercise of reason, but a social transaction, a certain kind of communication. Therefore, intellectual activity cannot be separated from the virtues that are usually labeled moral. While the canons of deductive and inductive logic are integral to intellectual communication in philosophy and in the sciences, traits of personal and social morality that make possible a democratic and cooperative process are also important. Dewey was aware of the inseparability of moral values from our more intellectual activities.[4] Philosophers such as Jürgen Habermas and Alan Gewirth have also acknowledged this inseparability. Gewirth, for example, says that without some "moral traits of character and social interaction, the very operation of intellectual inquiry becomes impossible."[5]

The distinction between and separation of moral and intellectual virtues is counterproductive in moral education. With respect to the aims of education, Dewey maintains that "no separation can be made between impersonal, abstract principles of logic and moral qualities of character. What is needed is to weave them into unity" (LW 8:139). More important than education by "direct moral precept" (MW 6:388), that is, learning moral rules or principles, is the indirect learning that comes from engaging students in open, communal, and sensitive inquiry. The openness and tolerance that I might encourage in my students by examining together different moral systems is of more moral importance than the information they learn.

If character is an organic whole, then this opens the possibility of being able to evaluate habits in terms of their interactive effect upon other tendencies that one cherishes or in terms of how they contribute to the whole character. Different habits of a character might reinforce each other or they might function at cross-purposes. There are persons who lack integration, where different habits or compartments of their character are relatively isolated from each other. A specialized habit might endure and become more efficient in its area of application in virtue of its relative seclusion from others. But this confinement does not really work in a world where one does not have control over one's environment or in situations that may call for other conflicting habits. The character that allows for the mutual modification (interaction) among its habits opens itself to the possibility of making readjustments that might resolve conflicts among habits and at the same time enrich the whole character.

To be sure, the hypothesis that it is better to have an integrated character than one that is compartmentalized is not based on the assumption that integrity or unity are worth achieving for their own sake. Character is one of our most reliable tools in a situation. The integrative ideal signifies the fullest and most productive use we can make of our characters in a situation. I will return to Dewey's conception of an ideal character in part 3.

So far, I have described character in terms of its constitutive habits, but it must also be understood in its relation to conduct and social environment. The specific reactions, habits, and dispositions that make up a character are evoked, confirmed, nurtured under the influences of associated life. The quality of our characters is affected by our associations, and the quality of our associations is affected by the characters partaking in them.

Character is also said to be "whatever lies behind an act in the way of deliberation and desire" (MW 5:188). A moral act involves choice and therefore it is the expression of a formed and stable character. Character and conduct designate two organic and inseparable elements in moral experience. However, the distinction between character and conduct has been the source of a fundamental dispute between moral theorists. Dewey thought his view could overcome this divisive issue. I turn to this issue in the next chapter.

SEVEN

Character and Conduct

Dewey and the Great Divide in Ethics

One important consequence of the resurgence of virtue ethics is a more comprehensive way to classify ethical theories than the usual choice between deontological and consequentialist views. It has been assumed that the great divide in ethics is between act-centered views, ethics of doing, and character-centered views, ethics of being;[1] in other words, morality should be conceived as a matter of doing good or being good. (I hereafter use the expression "the divide issue" to describe this issue.) Though this seems like an issue that has been recognized only in contemporary ethics, John Dewey anticipated it and evaluated its legitimacy. Dewey undermines the grounds for the divide issue, and he proposes a way to move beyond the debates between character-centered and act-centered ethics, by having a different starting point and metaphysics for his ethics. An examination of this contemporary issue will reveal how inclusive but radical Dewey's view of moral life were, and spotlight his contemporary relevance.

William Frankena explains the divide issue as "To be or to do, that is the question. Should we construe morality as primarily a following of certain principles or as primarily a cultivation of certain dispositions or traits?"[2] To answer this question philosophers have turned to two other questions: (A) what is central to moral discourse, evaluation and justification? and, (B) what is the primary concern or end of moral activity?

If the answers to (A) and (B) are that the moral self is primarily concerned with what sort of person she ought to be, and that character considerations are the primary source of moral justification in moral discourse, then moral life is character-centered. This stands in contrast to act-centered views where the primary concern and source of moral justification is the moral rightness or goodness of our conduct. Let's examine the basis of this debate.

Moral Discourse as the Basis for the Divide Issue

Character-relevant discourse is about judgments of virtues and features of the agent such as one's ideals, dispositions, and motives. On the other hand, conduct-relevant discourse is identified with moral judgments of conduct based on features of the act, such as furthering certain ends or complying with certain rules. On the basis of these two sorts of discourse the divide issue admits of two different formulations. The first assumes the independence of each sort of discourse to the other or, in other words, the *autonomy* of each. It then raises the question: which sort of discourse represents the distinctively moral concern? The second formulation of the issue assumes that both sorts of discourse are genuinely moral but that, therefore, one must be more *basic* in some manner to the other. As I explain below, Dewey rejects both of these approaches.

THE AUTONOMY CLAIM

Dewey believed that both Kant and Mill based their ethical views on the differences and divergences between judgments of character and judgments of conduct in situations. Mill claims that one can get the same objective good act from different motives, even from bad ones. On the other hand, Kant believes that the goodness of a good will does not depend on the rightness of its actions. In general, the act theorist would argue that, for example, an act can be judged dishonest or wrongful even if it is performed by a person of honest character. Therefore, character has nothing to do with morality. Meanwhile, the virtue theorist claims that virtues, such as honesty, are independent of and cannot be reduced to judgments or rules of good conduct.

Dewey of course acknowledged that there are times when we invert our judgments of the doer and the deed, for example, an honest person can do a dishonest act. But the only way a philosopher can establish that the moral goodness of a trait of character is somehow independent of the assessment of the activities of that person is if she stipulates a narrow definition of human action. For example, only if it is assumed that honesty is a property of the inner confines of the self and not a tendency to interact in a situation in a certain way, can one claim that the goodness of honesty is independent of conduct. But, for Dewey, there is no basis in experience for such a dualism and there is a good explanation for the disparities and differences between judgments of character and those of conduct.

Character is a working interaction of habits. We cannot always accurately assess the character of a person by assessing his or her conduct, even after a long period of time. However, this is not because character is something inner that may or may not cause external action, but simply because there is no certainty about when our actions are expressions of stable dispositions (habits) and when they are accidental reactions to an undetermined number of contextual factors. Judging traits of character can be difficult, uncertain, and complex but that does not mean that they are other than tendencies to interact in a certain way in a situation—habits. We cannot judge character without considering actual or possible conduct.

But what about moral judgments of action? Are they not autonomous from character-relevant discourse? This seems on its face more promising. It is clear, for example, that sometimes one can judge an act to be honest without considering the honesty of someone's character. Moreover, many ethical theories and moral traditions have made reference in their list of moral precepts to acts, such as stealing and lying, regardless of who the actor might be. Does it then follow, however, that moral judgments of conduct as they are made in everyday moral experience can disregard the agent and her character?

To what extent character-considerations of the agent are relevant to the final moral judgment of an act is something that will depend on the context, but they are a necessary part of that context. As Dewey noted, "intent is a normal part of a moral situation" (LW 7:167). In judging moral conduct, one needs to consider if it is an expression of the self, that is, if it embodies "the interest and motive of the self."[3] To be sure, Dewey makes these claims not because he has or wishes to have a theory that centers on character, but because he is a contextualist. To evaluate an act by taking into account the actor is part of what is required in order to judge an act in light of its concrete context. Of course, philosophers can always perform the intellectual exercise of assessing acts in abstraction from their agents, but there is no obvious reason why we should do this. Moreover, it is unclear why we should think that this is the way in which acts acquire their moral cast in the concrete context of moral life.

In sum, Dewey holds that we can distinguish judgments of character from judgments of conduct without assuming that they are about separated domains of moral discourse or moral experience. On the contrary, the way we make moral judgments suggests that character and conduct are mutually dependent and inseparable facets of our moral experience. Dewey claims that "There is no character excepting as manifested in conduct, there is no conduct excepting that which expresses character."[4]

But even if the autonomy claim were true, this does not by itself provide support for making the divide issue a meaningful one. Why must one decide which discourse represents the distinctively moral one? It seems that only an unstated dualism would make one assume that character and conduct cannot be brought together in an integrated view of moral life, or that a moral agent cannot attend to both virtue and the moral goodness of her actions without suffering from a type of moral schizophrenia.

Perhaps aware that claims about autonomy are difficult to support, recent philosophers have instead couched their centeredness claims in terms of the primacy in morality, rather than in terms of exclusion. Let's briefly consider this recent way of arguing for the divide issue.

THE BASICNESS CLAIM

Even if one cannot judge character without conduct (and vice versa) one might still make the claim that one of these judgments must be basic. There are two ways to understand this issue, neither of which is sound from the point of view of Dewey's ethics.

The issue of basicness has sometimes been understood as being about which kind of judgment is susceptible to theoretical explanation and reduction by the other. For example, if virtues are reducible to moral rules of conduct but not vice versa, then the latter are basic.[5] But in this way of understanding the issue, it seems that what is basic is decided by how good one is at performing conceptual reductions. This kind of reductionism is indicative that perhaps the interest in ethical theory on the divide issue arises out of a theoretical demand for conceptual economy and elegance, and not because it has anything to do with anyone's actual moral experience.

Is there any way to make sense of the issue of basicness from the point of view of moral agents making moral decisions? Which kind of judgment is *derivative* to the other in terms of its justificatory role in moral deliberation? This is a loaded question. In order to engage in debates that center on this issue one has to assume a certain model of moral reasoning and justification. It reduces, without an argument, all morally relevant considerations and judgments to two, that is, to act- and character-centered ones. But the content of people's actual moral deliberation is a lot richer and more varied than proponents of both sides of the divide issue seem to allow. More importantly, it assumes that *either* the inherent goodness of certain types of character *or* the moral quality of certain kinds of actions determined by some rule is the source of all moral justification and value. The theoretical appeal of this assumption should be obvious. But Dewey would argue that this is an oversimplification of moral experience. Moral philosophy "should frankly recognize the impossibility of reducing all the elements in moral situations to a single commensurable principle" (LW 5:288).

In Dewey's contextualist view of moral justification, neither character-judgments nor act-judgments have an inherent primacy or foundational role in moral reasoning independent of the particular context of a situation. The relative weight of each judgment in coming to a final decision of what one ought to do will depend on considerations of the unique and specific features of the situation under consideration.

Being Good and Doing Good: Which Is the End of Morality?

If the defenders of the divide issue are not able to defend the meaningfulness of this issue by appeals to moral discourse and justification, they might still reformulate the issue as a response to the following general question: what is the primary end of moral activity? This question is ambiguous. It might be asking about the primary *concern* of moral agents when they are engaged in moral activity. But it could also be about the theoretical issue of the ultimate *end* of morality. Let's consider both of these interpretations of the divide issue from a critical Deweyan perspective.

Why must moral theorists decide if becoming a good character or doing right actions is the end of our moral life? The demand to find out which end is primary follows from what Dewey called the "doctrine of fixed means and ends."[6] This is the view that in moral life there are fixed means and ends, and that the task of the philosopher is to find out which one is which. Hence, is moral conduct the means by which we express and cultivate a good character (or the good life), or is it the end for which virtues are the means? For Dewey this is not a meaningful issue because the distinction between means and ends is a functional one. Doing good and having a good character are two phases of moral life, and either one can be a means or an end relative to where we are in the process. Furthermore, and more importantly, this issue ignores the organic and mutually dependent relation in moral life between the quality of our characters and the quality of our actions. Let's consider more closely this view.

For Dewey, the problem with moral theories that begin with (and focus on) discrete acts or the qualities of agents is that they begin with an abstraction from the concrete processional context where both character and conduct acquire their quality and significance. Being good and having a certain character, although by no means a guarantee that we will always do good or do what ought to be done, does nonetheless increase our chances. The good habits we bring to a situation are part of the means by which we find out and do what is right. But it is also the case that it is only by doing what we ought to do that we can improve our habits. This is based on the important dynamic relation between habits and situations already explained.

Moral life would not be educative and capable of improvement through its own means if it were nothing more than the succession of isolated, independent, and hermetically sealed situations or events. But there is continuity and "every experience affects for better or for worse the attitudes which help decide the quality of further experience" (LW 13:20). An important implication of this for moral education is that the most important learning a person can acquire in a situation is not information (or rules), but the indirect cultivation of the habits that are going to affect the quality of future situations. A growing, educative moral life requires both improvements of the habits that will determine the quality of present experience as well as improvement of the present experiences that will determine the quality of our habits.

If there is an important relation between doing good and being good in moral life, then why have philosophers insisted on separating and taking sides between the goodness of our character and good conduct? Dewey speculates that it is because of a quest for certainty which is not content with any view that affirms a contingent relation. That a good will tends to do good is insufficient for Kant; he therefore saves morality from the vicissitudes of time and change by restricting it to the confines of the will. On the other hand, utilitarians want morality to depend on an objective and certain calculation of pleasures and pains.

The relationship between character and conduct is not as tight as many philosophers would want it. But for Dewey this is not a reason for disappointment or to deny their relation. The disparities between being and doing good count as evidence of the role of luck, accident, and contingency in our moral lives. Having the virtues (or having the right sort of character) at any particular time is no guarantee that we are going to do the right thing, but this is hardly a good reason not to cultivate virtue.

If Dewey is right about the relation between the quality of our character and our conduct, then we cannot settle (or make meaningful) the issue of whether morality is centered on character or conduct, and whether one is the basis of the other. But perhaps we have misunderstood the divide issue. Perhaps the issue is: what defines the concern of a moral agent qua moral? Is it a concern to be the right sort of person (being) or to act consistently with certain rules (doing)?

Which Is the Primary Concern of Moral Agents?

In considering this final formulation of the divide issue we could once again raise the questions: why are they the only possibilities? And why are they mutually exclusive? It seems that the easiest way to dismiss this issue is simply to assert that there are plenty of moral agents in the world for which becoming the right sort of person and acting consistently with certain rules defines or is part of their moral concern in situations. Once again, defenders of the divide issue are better off if they base their claim for primacy or centeredness on comparing concerns rather than on excluding them. This is in effect the tactic of many in contemporary virtue ethics.

The recent resurgence and interest in virtue ethics is a consequence of the recognition that concerns about being are in some sense bigger or more inclusive moral concerns than the narrow concerns about doing of modern act-centered views. Furthermore, they have claimed that one's moral life must center on being because otherwise one suffers the constricted and alienating moral lives that are entailed by the act-centered outlooks. We need to consider these arguments because they are the ones used by virtue ethicists to support the importance and meaningfulness of the divide issue.

Virtue ethicists have argued that concerns about being are more inclusive by comparing the question of act ethics, What is the right thing to do? with questions such as, What sort of person should I be? or What is the good life? They have claimed that the latter two questions must be primary for an account of morality because they recur more frequently and are of much broader scope. The issue of recurrence is an empirical one, namely, that these questions become the object of conscious concern in the lives of moral agents more often than do questions about actions. Virtue ethicists argue that it is an error to center morality on moral quandaries about what to do because moral problems so conceived only occasionally occur in moral life. Louden, for example, says that

Moral problems do not permeate every moment of our existence: occasionally, we are unsure about what to do . . . but thankfully, such quandaries are the exception rather than the norm in day-to-day life. However, if the primary moral question is not what is the right thing to do in
a problematic situation? but what is a good life for a human being?
morality suddenly seems to invade all corners of life.[7]

This recurrence claim can be challenged on empirical grounds. Virtue
ethicists tend to underestimate how often moral agents experience moral
problems. In fact, it seems plausible to believe that the incidence of moral
problems increases with moral maturity since we become more morally
sensitive. In any case, this appeal to recurrence is hardly a good reason to
establish the primary question of morality. Should we decide the divide
issue on the basis of popularity? Our moral life could then just as well
center on a question that is asked every 50 years.

On the other hand, the issue of the primary question of morality
might be decided on the basis of scope. Here the virtue ethicist seems to
have a better argument. But this is only because the act theorist's primary
question usually presupposes a narrow view of our moral life. According
to Dewey their narrowness is a consequence of assuming an atomistic view
of our moral experience. Act theorists conceive of our moral life as discrete and isolated quandaries where the question What is the right thing to
do? is understood as an evaluation of a selfless act from the impartial or
impersonal point of view of a set of rules. If this is what is meant by this
question, then questions like, What should I be? or How should I live? are
better because they are more inclusive of important aspects of our moral
experience. But a better question in this sense does not make it the central
question of morality, nor does it entail that moral theory must give pri-
ority to being over doing.

Dewey was, in fact, suspicious about the alleged inclusivity or broad
conception of morality entertained by character-centered theorists. He
consistently argued against views of our moral life for which "moral goodness is identified in an exclusive way with virtue" (LW 7:285). This is not to
deny that virtue is important in moral deliberation. If what we do has
consequences for our character, in confirming and weakening habits, then
moral agents should be attuned to this. I will call this the virtue concern
since it is a central feature of virtue ethics. But moral concern is not
reducible to a concern with our characters, or with questions about the
nature of the good life. This is because the present or future state of our
character (or virtues) is not always relevant in moral situations. Some
decisions are more trivial than others with respect to the formation of our

characters, but this does not mean that they cease to be moral decisions. There are also situations where the virtue concern is overridden by other moral considerations, situations in which one is aware that what one morally ought to do might adversely affect one's character. For Dewey claimed that the virtue concern is only one among many other independent and irreducible moral demands, such as duty and good, that characterize morally problematic situations. None of these demands can claim an inherent primacy over the others.

Virtue ethics may claim to have a broader scope in moral matters because it is concerned with seemingly larger issues, such as the nature of human flourishing and the good life, or how one should live, but it is not thereby a richer or more inclusive view of morality. But perhaps the claim of a broader scope is based on the context or standpoint from which these questions are asked. Bernard Mayo, for example, explains the context of "What I ought to be" as ". . . where a man's perplexity extends not merely to a particular situation but to his whole way of living."[8] The assumption seems to be that certain questions entail the abandonment of the situationalist and particularistic thrust that has characterized act theory. But there is nothing about the content or meaning of these questions that make them transcend the particular contexts within which questions about what action to undertake are asked. Even such far-reaching decisions as "to be brave" or "to be a good human being" are as situation-specific for Dewey as any other decision. They arise out of a particular problematic situation and not from some wider standpoint or context.

Virtue ethics is a reaction to the act-theorist view of moral life as a succession of isolated situations. For the virtue ethicist, the solution to this atomistic conception of our moral life is to posit a moral self who is primarily concerned with her life as a whole. This concern is meaningful to Dewey, but it always takes place in a particular situation and for a self that is in a process of continuous formation. Virtue ethics wants to recover the sense of continuity in our moral lives but for this we do not have to postulate one concern that pervades all moral situations or a standpoint from which a growing self can survey her moral life as a whole. A standpoint that is wide but nowhere in particular might be bigger but if it has nothing to do with our concrete experience as moral agents it has nothing to contribute to a rich conception of morality. What these two views share, in spite of their opposition, is the theoretical starting point (discussed in chapter 1) of gazing at atomistic actions or moral life as a unified whole. From within moral life things are experienced differently.

Virtue ethics has taken advantage of the general disillusionment with act theories in order to support their centrality claims. The appeal or strength of the divide issue might not be based on a careful examination of the issue on its own terms, but rather on the historical fact that character theories have been conceived as the only alternative to act theories. Sometimes the issues that divide philosophers owe their legitimacy and liveliness to the fact that no one has suggested an alternative view. If this is true, then the divide issue will continue to be assumed in philosophical debates as long as no alternative to the character- or act-centered views is proposed. Dewey's view is thus important because he proposes just such an alternative, one that is richly detailed and true to our moral lives. This makes Dewey's ethics an alternative worth considering and developing.

What is peculiar about Dewey's conception of moral life is that it recovers the importance of character (and related concerns) without falling into the excesses and reductionism of contemporary virtue ethics. On the other hand, it stresses the situational aspect of living morally without falling into the atomistic view of our moral life detailed by act theorists. In other words, it offers the possibility of an ethics that is neither a virtue ethics nor an act-centered ethics, and it recovers the strengths of both views.

On Dewey's account, moral life is a series of continuous situations. Morally problematic situations are the events where we gain focal awareness of the moral dimension of experience. "The moral life has its centre in the periods of suspended and postponed action, when the energy of the individual is spent in recollection and foresight, in severe inquiry and serious consideration of alternative aims" (MW 5:375). It is in this context that we come to consider among other things the favorite considerations of act-centered and character-centered ethics. When they are present in a particular situation they are both instrumental to the more inclusive moral concern: to find out what we morally ought to do. Therefore, if morality is centered anywhere, it is on morally problematic situations. Does taking situations as the starting point of ethical theory or as the end of morality not entail a narrow or scaled-down view of moral experience? On the contrary, Dewey thought that much of the reductionism and oversimplification in contemporary moral theory was caused by a failure to consider the complexity and richness of moral experiences as they are had in unique situations. The history of moral philosophy is characterized by one-sidedness because philosophers have abstracted one feature of situations which are experienced as morally problematic, then made it supreme or exclusive. But, for Dewey, good, virtue, and duty are all irreducible features found intertwined *in* moral situations.

Moreover, the particularistic thrust of Dewey's moral philosophy is not incompatible with some of the broad and general concerns characteristic of virtue ethics. For, as I noted, our moral life is not merely a succession of isolated situations; there is continuity and the possibility of learning in our moral development. Moral ideals and character, for example, have a place in Dewey's ethics. However, he is able to incorporate these concerns in his ethics without postulating abstract notions that are antecedent to concrete situations. Ideals are part of the means of a situation. Virtues are to be examined as habits operating in the context of situations and not as means to abstract notions of human flourishing. Dewey would even agree with virtue ethicists that moral theorists should concern themselves more with providing hypotheses about the traits of character that might be worth cultivating than trying to construct rules of action. But this does not mean that character is central to morality or that we should make character and its flourishing the primary conscious aim of our moral life. From time to time we need to reflect about our moral character. However, to make the state of our character the moral end and everything else the means to improving character is to elevate character as antecedent to the context from which it emerges and has its importance. For Dewey this is not only a philosophical mistake, but if put into practice, can lead to one of the worst forms of moral life. Agent-centered views encourage what he called "spiritual egotism," that is, it produces people who "are preoccupied with the state of their character, concerned for the purity of their motives and goodness of their souls. The exultation of conceit which sometimes accompanies this absorption can produce a corrosive inhumanity which exceeds the possibilities of any other form of selfishness" (MW 14:7).

Making the goodness of our character the conscious object of our moral concern can in fact be counterproductive. Too much concern for our character can become a distraction or block to fruitful character-building activity. The best way to improve our moral characters is to attend to what we ought to do in a particular situation. Dewey thought that just as there is a hedonistic paradox, there is a moralistic paradox: "the way to get goodness is to cease to think of it—as something separate—and to devote ourselves to the realization of the full value of the practical situations in which we find ourselves" (MW 5:318).

We need to shift the emphasis in moral philosophy away from rules of action. However, in Dewey this is done by shifting the emphasis toward the concrete and unique situations of our moral experience and not toward virtues and notions of the good or human flourishing. Does the claim that the locus of our moral life is in situations where one has to decide what one ought *to do* commit Dewey to an act-centered view? The answer is "no" for several important reasons.

First, the reason why the question What ought I *to do*? is primary is because in a morally problematic situation it is always a choice about a particular course of conduct which is being considered. This does not imply anything about giving inherent primacy to rules, standards, or any act-centered type of evaluative commitment in making such decisions. Furthermore, Dewey holds that among the legitimate and irreducible moral demands considered in trying to answer or resolve a morally problematic situation is the state of one's character (i.e., the virtue concern). Third, and most important, Dewey's particularism is a contextualism that does not share with act-centered positions the atomistic view of acts and of moral experience. His ethics begins with situations as individualized contexts that, though unique, are continuous with each other in an open-ended process. Acts are not contextless events or mere external effects of a self. In fact, for Dewey moral conduct is an expression of the moral self. This relation is so intimate and direct that, in a sense I will soon explain, questions about what one ought *to do* are in effect also questions about what one ought *to be*. But before turning to this view of moral conduct, I must consider one more argument used by character theorists to defend the view that one's moral life must be centered on a concern with being. Some recent ethicists have claimed that one's moral theory and moral life must be centered on character because otherwise one suffers the constricted and alienating moral life that is entailed by the act-centered concern. Let's examine the problem of alienation and consider if this warrants the conclusion that moral philosophy should center on character and whether Dewey's ethics is susceptible to this problem.

The Problem of Alienation and the Moral Self

Character-centered views criticize modern act-centered views because their abstract view of acts and rules tend to alienate concrete moral selves from their acts. Bernard Williams, for example, has argued that utilitarianism's regard for moral actions as merely "happenings outside one's moral self" and their evaluation from an impartial and abstract point of view "alienates one from one's actions."[9] Utilitarianism fails to capture the sense in which moral persons identify with their actions. The notion that character is only, at best, a means to right conduct presupposes a distance or separation between the moral self and its acts that is counterintuitive to those who live meaningful moral lives.

Dewey agrees with this last criticism, but he does not think this entails that morality should be agent-centered as Williams and other virtue theorists seem to think. On the contrary, his diagnosis of the problem reveals that insofar as character views presuppose the same view of the moral self as act views, they are susceptible to the same criticism. As Dewey sees it, the problem is a consequence of starting ethical theory with a certain theoretical conception of what it is to be a self in moral experience, namely, the spectator view of the moral self.

For a moral self as a subject-spectator, conduct is an external consequence of its deliberation, itself an inner cognitive process. Therefore, the relation between the self and its conduct is, at best, one of cause and effect. This is troublesome because the relation between a moral self and what she does seems in moral experience to be more intimate, that is, moral conduct is an expression of a moral self. In effect the spectator view of the self alienates the moral self from its own activities. The implications about alienation of this view are perhaps more evident in act-centered moral theories, for they usually assume that acts are atomistic contextless events subject to external demands, rules, duties, or principles, which hold no special relation to the one who effects them.

What agent-centered views, such as that of Williams, overlook is that their attempt to anchor morality in the agent (or character) might not resolve the problem of alienation between the moral self and its acts. Can the self genuinely identify with her actions if they are merely an outward expression of some personal moral project or a mere means to achieving virtue? Possessive attitudes toward an activity can be as alienating as impersonal ones. Consider, for example, how alienating is the experience of students who think of learning merely as a way of getting good grades or becoming a good future professional. Virtue theorists assume an account of moral reasoning that rests on a hypothetical imperative where the antecedent is a desire to be a certain sort of person. In other words, the condition for engaging in moral activity (finding and doing the right thing) is an antecedent concern for one's character. How is this better than rules in regard to alienation? On both views my identification with what I ought to do in a particular situation is mediated and conditional upon a concern that is somewhat removed from the concrete and specific issue at hand. Moral conduct is not a direct expression but only a consequence of caring for something else.

If the only alternative to the abstract concern to abide by rules is the exclusive concern to become the right sort of person, then alienation seems like an unavoidable trait or danger of living morally. The problem seems unavoidable as long as we assume a separation between the self and its acts, and make one a means to the other. If there is in moral experience a more intimate relation between the moral self and its acts, then the problem of alienation is a further reason to reject the divide and its options. As Dewey noted, "The key to a correct theory of morality is recognition of the essential unity of the self and its acts" (LW 7:288). The noble intention of virtue ethics is to recover the personal character of morality from modern rule theorists, but this does not have to be done by reducing morality to a concern with one's character. It can be done by recognizing, as Dewey did, that moral conduct is a direct expression of a moral self.

The Unity of the Moral Self and Its Acts

In Dewey's ethics there are at least three reasons why moral conduct is an expression of the moral self: (1) because moral conduct is an expression of intention; (2) because moral conduct reveals acquired character; and, (3) because in some fundamental ontological sense what I do is what I am. I will consider each of these in turn.

Moral conduct is an expression of the self since it is the manifestation of an intended and voluntary choice. This is why the "self is more than a cause of an act in the sense in which the match is a cause of a fire" (LW 7:287). The fire is not an expression of the match, not because the match has no soul, but because it does not choose and has no intentions. Moreover, insofar as this response or choice is influenced or shaped by our previous experiences, it is also expressive of the habits that have been acquired by the self. Not all of our actions stem from acquired dispositions to the same degree. But usually where there is a "formed and stable character," a moral act is also an expression of that character, it "*reveals* the existing self and it forms the future self" (LW 7:287, my emphasis).

But there is a more fundamental sense in which moral conduct or activity is the expression of the moral self: there is no ready-made self prior to activity, therefore conduct is not something that can be separated from what we are. This is not a form of behaviorism, as this would assume the sort of mind and body dualism that is rejected by Dewey. From the practical starting point the self is experienced *as* a participant in activity. We sometimes reflectively establish a distance between our self and our acts, and even make distinctions between our capacities as agents (i.e., characters) and the environment, but this is only because of a temporary obstruction in our fluid and immediate identification with our acts. When a person is engaged and absorbed in what she is doing, she is not conscious of her self as something apart from the activity; instead, "the self is in what he is doing."[10]

If the self is a spectator causing some outer action, then moral action is *for* the self. That is, moral activity is instrumental to some end, purpose, or interest of the self, for example, the attainment or expression of virtue, the maximization of happiness, or compliance with a universal duty. On this assumption, self-realization and moral activity are usually conceived in terms of *getting* something *for* the self. Hence, it is not surprising that one of the predominant tendencies in the history of moral philosophy (e.g., that of utilitarianism and virtue ethics) most criticized by Dewey was a possessive and acquisitive view of morality. He said whether it be pleasure or

> getting happiness, or culture, or experience, enriched life, or more morality, or perfection for the being which is already in existence; it throws the emphasis on the side of acquisition and of possession. I do not see that it makes much difference what a man gets as long as you define moral life from the standpoint of getting.[11]

For Dewey, "morality consists in not degrading any required act into a mere means towards an end lying outside itself, but in doing it for its own sake, or, again, in doing it as self" (EW 4:52). The alternative to the notion of living morally *for* the self is living morally *as* the self. This means that the self is directly identified with what she ought to do, that morality is "finding the self in the activity called for by the situation" (EW 4:51).

Morality, as Dewey understands it, is thus a matter of a being that is doing. Therefore, although concerns about what one ought to do convey that in a morally problematic situation it is always the choice of a particular course of conduct that is being considered, this is not something independent from what an agent ought *to be* in that situation. Only an agent view of the self implies the kind of identity between the self and its acts that avoids the problem of alienation endemic to both character-centered and act-centered views.

The notion of the self as a passive spectator that is moved to moral activity by something outside itself[12] has also led to narrow views of moral motivation. When the unity of the self and its acts is not recognized, it is assumed that concern for moral activity is either *for* the self or it is the impartial and impersonal motivation of act-centered views. It is as if, apart from wanting virtue or wanting to comply with rules, the moral self would be indifferent to each particular moral task. This mistake is avoided by starting with the experience of concrete moral selves as they are genuinely engrossed in present moral activity instead of starting with abstractions. What is ruled out is that a self can be *directly* interested in or concerned with present moral activity. But this is precisely the type of moral self and engagement that Dewey describes as the model of having a moral experience. Once again it will be useful to draw from the similarities with art as experience.

The moral self, like the genuine artist, while engaged in the process, defines and identifies herself with what she does; there is no distinction between herself and the activity (process). In the absence of this kind of engagement and direct absorption in a situation, any other special commitment to a value, ideal, or purposes can be a narrow and distracting indulgence. It is like the artist who lets personal projects and agendas, such as fame or the desire to become a better artist, get in the way of the artistic process.

For Dewey, this model of the self needs to be studied and fostered in moral education. He was concerned to undermine the divide issue because of its implications for moral education. The view that moral training in schools is a matter of discipline to act according to certain pre-established rules of conduct, and the view that what is important is that students have a good character or a good will were dangerous and one-sided. The former produces characters that are so rigid and mechanical that they lack the spirit of morality; the latter encourage characters who limit their moral tasks to meaning well and perfecting their characters. For Dewey, these alternatives reflect not only dualisms, but also a society unable to encourage the optimal sort of engagement from individuals to deal with moral problems.

What virtue ethics tries to recover is what might be called the personal character of morality. But it has assumed that the way to recover from legalistic and impartial models of morality is to shift the focus of ethics away from problematic situations and toward character. But Dewey provides an alternative view that recovers the personal character of morality and gives character its due without giving up the situational thrust of our moral experience. The moral agent who is aesthetically engaged in present moral activity has a direct personal identification with the specific conduct that is morally required of her in a situation. For this kind of self, moral activity is a matter of self-expression and not an external imposition (of obeying rules) or a matter of "getting" virtue (or any moral good). In my account of the ideal self in part 3, I will discuss the characteristics of a self capable of this sort of engagement.

In conclusion, in spite of similarities, it would be a mistake to regard Dewey's ethics as a form of virtue ethics. This mistake is costly since it precludes the appreciation of the distinctive character of Dewey's ethics. His ethics is an alternative that avoids the atomistic view of acts, the legalistic form of morality, and the neglect of the self and communal context that characterizes many modern act-centered views. Dewey would not deny that moral agents are or can be concerned with character considerations (virtues, ideals, projects) and also with act considerations (rules, principles, consequences), but there is no reason to take either one as defining the paradigm of moral engagement. In fact, both are instances of a more general concern of a moral agent: to search and to choose what each particular and unique morally problematic situation requires. For a moral self, each situation presents a unique moral task, the execution of which is its immanent end, even if its resolution happens to produce wonderful instrumentalities for future experiences. Our moral life is composed of situations with their own unique and meaningful development. Hence, morality is more than following rules, but it is also more than a quest for virtue.

One more feature of Dewey's view of moral experience that is sometimes implicit in his criticisms of traditional views but that must be emphasized is how he places the locus of moral endeavor in *present* experience. Considering this final aspect of Dewey's conception of moral life, as well as the issue of meaning, will serve as a bridge to the more normative aspects of his ethics considered in part 3.

EIGHT

Present Activity and the Meaning of Moral Life

In the history of moral philosophy, present moral activity has been taken as a means to a future remote goal, virtue, happiness, a universal duty, or the good life. Moral life has been conceived as a cumulative process where present situations are important only to the extent that we can acquire something from them, such as the goodness in our characters, happiness, or compliance with a general rule. Several things can account for this commonly shared assumption.

The view of moral life as acquisitive and product-oriented has been supported by socio-economic practices. Dewey was alert to the close relation between, for example, utilitarianism and capitalist institutions which subordinated "productive activity to the bare product" (MW 12:184). Socio-economic conditions have contributed to the belief that satisfaction and fulfillment are future possessions—products—that can be separated from present productive activity. But Dewey also diagnosed how in philosophy a mistaken notion of the self and of the temporal in experience contributed to making these assumptions about moral life seem like common sense. Let's first consider the issue of time.

The importance a philosopher might give to the present or to the future in morality depends, in part, on her assumptions about time. The notion of time as it is lived and experienced, and the notion of time as it is surveyed from a spectator standpoint represent two different starting points of philosophical inquiry. The theoretical starting point for many philosophers is the God's-eye or bird's-eye point of view, a view that assumes that there is a non-temporal point of view from which we can gaze at past, present, and future as relative points in a spatial continuum. From this perspective the present is only an ephemeral point where we are in relation to the past and the future. The present is, so to speak, that place in the continuum that will be part of our past. While what counts as present is constantly fading and shifting, the past has been written. According to this picture of time, the present cannot be the significant center of reference for moral life; Dewey and proponents of process-oriented views disagree.[1]

According to the radical empiricist, this last view of time, although useful for many purposes, is a picture or an account of *things* but not of *time* as it is experienced. In a certain sense the only time that is experienced is the present; the future is experienced as present possibilities and anticipation, the past as present memories and instrumentalities. Hence, the present is of the utmost importance. What one retains and what one expects are used as guides in the present. Making an effort not to be troubled about one's past or worried about one's future is for the sake of one's present. This is not to deny that in everyday life we are intellectually concerned with the future. But this does not prove that we are all directly aiming at controlling a distant future or that we should. As a matter of fact, Dewey states,

> thought about future happenings is the only way we can judge the present; it is the only way to appraise its significance. Without such projection, there can be no projects, no plan for administering present energies, overcoming present obstacles. (MW 14:183)

Moral views that emphasize the present as a mere means to a remote future lack a certain wisdom. After all, the present is what is most under our control, while the future is not. Therefore, to subordinate the present to the future "is to subject the comparatively secure to the precarious, [to] exchange resources for liabilities" (MW 14:183). For Dewey this was "the element of truth in Epicureanism" (MW 14:201). The problem with Epicureanism lay in its "conception of what constitutes present good, not in its emphasis upon satisfaction as the present" (MW 12:201).

But should we not make an effort to control the future? Is it not prudent and even morally required to sacrifice present enjoyments for future and more worthwhile ones? Dewey would agree that control of the future is a precious goal, since we live in a precarious and changing world. But it is incorrect to believe that the best way to achieve something is to always directly aim at it. Even if we want future improvement and control as a result of present action, this does not mean that we should thereby directly aim our actions at securing future improvement. On the contrary, there are reasons to believe that reflective overconcern with future improvement is the surest way not to attain it, because such overconcern results in a halfhearted "attention to the full use of present resources in the present situation" (MW 14:183), which is detrimental to any future state. Dewey claimed that the surest means to attain anything in the future is "to attend to the full possibilities of the present" (MW 14:183) and that "such enrichment of the present for its own sake is the just heritage of childhood and the best insurer of future growth" (LW 8:348). Dewey says,

> control of future living, such as it may turn out to be, is wholly depen-
> dent upon taking his present activity, seriously and devotedly, as *an end,
> not as means.* (MW 14:184, my emphasis)

The necessity of subordinating the present to the future in morality has also been supported by the modern separation between reason (and its foresight) and present-focused impulses and desires that are presumably the sources of moral temptation. Hence, to live for the present has been associated with an immoral and self-indulgent life. However, Dewey points out that

> moralists have spent time and energy in showing what happens when appetite, impulse, is indulged without reference to consequences and reason. But they have mostly ignored the counterpart evils of an intelligence that conceive ideals and goods which do not enter into *present* impulse and habits. (MW 14:188, my emphasis)

Perhaps the most common modern assumption that conspires against making present activity the locus of moral effort and meaning is the spectator view of the self. For a self, as a fixed and isolated subject separated from its acts, present activity is a mere external means *for* the self. This self should be committed to present activity only to the extent required to obtain what she needs for future use or to initiate powers that come from within the self. From this point of view, halfhearted participation of the self in present activity is not necessarily bad because the self is antecedent; whereas too much involvement is dangerous because the self can lose itself in activity and forget that the present is only a means. However, as already noted, Dewey's view of the moral agent implies that the self cannot be ontologically separated from present activity; moreover, it achieves self-expression by being directly concerned and immersed in it.

Any consequentialist or teleological interpretation of Dewey's ethics ignores his attempt to shift the center of gravity of morality to concrete present situations. Consequences and ends are, of course, important, but they are only part of our present resources for present reconstruction. As Dewey writes,

> growth of *present* action in shades and scope of meaning is the only good within our control, and the only one, accordingly, for which respon-sibility exists. The rest is luck, fortune. And the tragedy of the moral notions most insisted upon by the morally self-conscious is the relega-tion of the only good which can fully engage thought, namely present meaning of action, to the rank of an incident of a remote good, whether that future good be defined as pleasure, or perfection, or salvation, or attainment of virtuous character. (MW 14:194, my emphasis)

Views that have "made the present subservient to a rigid yet abstract future" (MW 14:284) understand moral progress and growth in terms of an approximation to a fixed and remote ideal or standard. One version of this is when moral progress is conceived as a cumulative and linear pro-gression toward a final "stable condition free from conflict and distur-bance" (MW 14:285). These views interpret change and our present moral struggles as signs of our human limitations, and as incentives to work toward a world where these aspects of existence are diminished until we reach moral stability, perfection, fulfillment, and completeness.

As Dewey sees it, the dogma of approximation runs counter to the general pattern and rhythm of moral experience. Moral life does not have this linear pattern. There is, of course, continuity and many instrumen-talities are carried forward and improved, but moral life is "no uniform uninterrupted march or flow. It is a thing of histories, each with its own plot" (LW 10:42). Even when we talk as if our lives were a cohesive, on-going story for us to make, we do so as a way of understanding and making meaningful the present episode. We experience life as a continuous pro-cess but not as a single, all-inclusive, and evolving situation. Furthermore, it is wishful thinking to assume that moral life will become easier and more secure with every solved moral problem and with every improve-ment of character; this view assumes a uniform environment without the possibility of unforeseen new problems. But every accomplishment—each resolution of a morally problematic situation—introduces new conditions that generate new and sometimes even more complex problems. Dewey asks us to admit that "no matter what the present success in straightening out difficulties and harmonizing conflict, it is certain that problems will recur in the future in a new form or in a different plane" (MW 14:285). New struggles and failures seem inevitable. The way toward a conflict-less, trouble-free, stable, and final state of affairs could only be achieved if it were possible to go back to a state of primitive simplicity or to follow the Buddhist's renunciation of desire, action, and attainment.

It is not surprising that pessimism is one of the consequences of conceiving of moral life as an approximation to moral stability and perfection. With such high expectations, one's moral struggles to ameliorate present situations seem to be in vain. For many, the only way to avoid pessimism and to keep the dogma of approximation intact is to subscribe to a form of transcendentalism where the desired trouble-free, stable condition is found outside of space and time. That is, moral life is finite, illusory, but perhaps a necessary evil and bridge to a transcendent moral reality.

Dewey's disagreement with this view is more than an empirical issue about what moral life is or can offer. Even if such an approximation to a perfect and stable end were possible he would consider it almost inherently unappealing, for he shared with William James the idea that an existence without struggle lacks meaning. First, the concepts of success, growth, and fulfillment would be unintelligible in a world completely devoid of struggle and failure. More important, an existence without struggle lacks meaning; it is a pointless and unbearable kind of existence. For as James said, "need and struggle are what excite and inspire us; our hour of triumph is what brings the void."[2] Dewey and James did not understand how a trouble-free existence can be a source of moral aspiration or motivation.

Even if we agree with Dewey's criticisms of any final and future telos, this does not mean that he has provided an alternative view that has answered adequately all the important questions. How does his view avoid pessimism? If all there is to moral life is the rhythmic pattern of unending problems, then how is this any different than the meaningless life of Sisyphus repeatedly rolling the rock up the hill? What could be the point of moral life if it is not cumulative, or if it ends up in nothing? Moreover, if there is no final end or outcome to the present process, then how can we judge the quality of the present process? How do we know if in the present we are headed in the right direction? Let's consider these issues since they point to commitments that ground the normative vision I discuss in part 3.

Consider first how one is able to judge present experience without a fixed and final standard. This objection is important because it suggests that Dewey might not be able to avoid the implication that in moral experience there is no non-arbitrary way to determine better from worse. This implication follows if one assumes that the quality of any present process can be judged only by the quality of its future end-product. The future is the only standard for the present. But Dewey was critical of this commonly held assumption in the American school system and workplace. Outcomes, especially quantifiable ones, are important but they do not determine the quality of the present process. Present learning can be directly experienced and judged as a meaningful and worthwhile experience regardless of what may come from it.

The apparent need for a future and fixed end to judge the present may well be the result of having an abstract and narrow view of the resources that are found in the present situation. But as Dewey notes, the present is not a "sharp narrow knife-blade in time" (MW 14:194) and it includes not only what is present to observation but also a complex of working habits, memory, and foresight. To rely on present experience to judge its own ongoing quality means that one needs to rely on character, inherited moral principles, and present possibilities (including goals or ends-in-view). Moreover, the present is a qualitative context that we can synchronically rely on to determine better from worse. In other words, we experience whether we are making progress during a moral problem as a pervasive quality of the present situation without deliberately applying some antecedent standard or criteria. Dewey claimed that if moving into the better "cannot be told by qualities belonging to the moment of transition it can never be judged" (MW 14:195). He insisted that

> there are plenty of negative elements, due to conflict, entanglement and obscurity, in most situations of life, and we do not require a revelation of some supreme perfection to inform us whether or no we are making headway in present rectification. (MW 14:195)
>
> Every situation has its own measure and quality of progress. (MW 14:195)

Once again, we cannot overestimate the importance of the qualitative in Dewey's ethics. The qualitative context is "the background, the point of departure, and the regulative principle of all thinking" (LW 5:261). This is why, as I later discuss, sensitivity to the pervasive quality of the situations that demand moral reconstruction is a virtue. No matter how good our knowledge-based resources (i.e., rules or criteria) are in a given situation, without this sensitivity we are lost and without any sense of what is or is not relevant to the problem at hand.

Dewey's attempt to shift the emphasis in ethics to the present and to the quality of the process was motivated by a concern that if we do not give the present its due attention, the quality and meaningfulness of life suffers. Criticism of moral theories that legitimize the separation of means and ends and products and process is needed because these dualisms keep individuals from living more meaningful moral lives. Product-oriented views of morality overemphasize our acquisitive capacities at the expense of the creative ones. If the best we can do with our present moral struggles is endure them for the sake of some remote end, then present experience is a mere means, and moral life is experienced as unaesthetic drudgery. This is, in fact, how many in today's complex conditions already experience their daily lives. For Dewey there is another possibility: moral life can have aesthetic quality. This is the possibility that I will explore in part 3. But before turning explicitly to Dewey's normative proposals, I will end this chapter with a reminder about the kind of proposals we can expect and the broadest commitments on which they are based.

There is in Dewey a general but clear prescription to give up thinking of "some parts of this life as merely preparatory to other later stages of it" (EW 4:50) and to instead aim at the "fullest utilization of *present* resources, liberating and guiding capacities that are now urgent" (MW 14:185, my emphasis). This does not mean that we ought to rest on previous accomplishments. He says that "morality is a continuing process not a fixed achievement. Morals mean growth of conduct in meaning . . ." (MW 14:194). To live fully in the present means that the past should be used as a "storehouse of resources by which to move confidently forward" (LW 10:23). On the other hand, the future "consists of possibilities that are felt as a possession of what is now and here" (LW 10:24). In short, foresight, hindsight, and present observation are all done *in* the present *for* the present. He said,

> memory of the past, observation of the present, foresight of the future are indispensable. But they are indispensable to a present liberation, an enriching growth of action. (MW 14:182)

The quest for fixed and final ends ought to be replaced by an effort to attend to the needs and possibilities within a unique and present situation to the best of our abilities. At one point Dewey summarized his moral outlook by saying,

> if we wished to transmute this generalization into a categorical imperative we should say: "so act as to increase the meaning of *present* experience." But even then in order to get instruction about the concrete quality of such increased meaning we should have to run away from the law

and study the needs and alternative possibilities lying within a unique and localized situation. (MW 14:196, my emphasis)

This shift of focus toward present situations, and the rejection of overarching ends, rules, absolute standards, and promises, cannot be separated from Dewey's faith in experience, that is, the hope that the same present and unique situations that require amelioration can be the sufficient source of both guidance and inspiration. He did not think that in moral matters the potentialities of daily experience for self-regulation had been sufficiently tried. This makes his view susceptible to a number of skeptical challenges. Even if one does not question the capacity of experience for self-amelioration, there is still the issue of finding this a sufficient source of inspiration. Is it a good enough reason to find moral life and its hardships worth the trouble? Compared to the customary noble or cosmic purposes attributed to morality, Dewey's view does not offer hope for a final convergence or consummation. In fact, the sort of episodic character of moral life seems like the meaningless life of Sisyphus. How is Dewey's view not one that leads to pessimism?

The Sisyphus analogy does not really fit Dewey's view of moral life simply because of the element of uniqueness in moral problems. In moral life we never push the same rock up the same hill. In any case, the objection that relies on this analogy seems to beg the important question: why would the absence of a final consummation make our present efforts pointless?

Dewey did not think his view was pessimistic. In fact, pessimism and optimism struck him as "paralyzing doctrines" insofar as they are based on a certainty that one will succeed or fail in the future. Instead, his view was based on meliorism, that is, "the belief that the specific conditions which exist at any moment, be they comparatively bad or comparatively good, in any event may better" (MW 12:181). Dewey hoped that we would find, like he did, something very positive, encouraging, and inspirational in the idea that although we do not have complete knowledge of, or control over, the course of events, we are nonetheless active participants in the making of an unfinished world. Moreover, we may find intelligent ways of participating that might make things better in some respects in a particular situation. We do not affect or transform the world in general but rather only in the particular and unique situations in which we find ourselves. Hence, "while there is not a single end, there are also not as many as there are specific situations that require amelioration" (MW 12:174–175).

Is this piecemeal, melioristic faith sufficient to support and inspire the efforts required to confront the unavoidable moral struggles and problems of life? For Dewey it was, but he would have to recognize that there may be individuals who need more than the present meaningfulness of the journey or struggle. Dewey would of course question whether the need for more is grounded on prejudice or on a failure to give the present a chance. But all he can do as a philosopher is argue that the faith that underlies his moral vision is possible and reasonable. The activity of creating and re-shaping present moral experience can be meaningful and of value without the guarantee or hope of an independent and long-term final end. We do not have to aspire to acquire something outside of experience in order to make our melioristic efforts meaningful or to engage in the creative pro-cess of transforming existing situations. The present trouble, strife, mo-notony, limitations, and suffering in a situation *can be* sufficient reasons and motivation to pursue the task of reconstruction. Dewey said that "men have constructed a strange dream world when they have supposed that without a fixed ideal of a remote good to inspire them, they have no inducement to get relief from present troubles, no desires for liberation from what oppresses" (MW 14:195). He would even argue that it is pre-cisely the search for fixed, absolute, and final goods that is an obstacle to effective amelioration. The pursuit of general fixed goods such as truth, knowledge, health, and justice can make one overlook the specific, con-crete, and unique situations where such goods are at stake. For "in declar-ing that good is already realized in ultimate reality tends to make us gloss over the evils that concretely exist" (MW 12:182). Dewey hoped that the abandonment of the quest for universal and fixed rules and ends in morals would enable us to employ all our resources and focus our "attention to present troubles and possibilities" (MW 14:198). He would agree that our efforts to improve present conditions are and should be sometimes in-spired and guided by ideals (e.g., the ideal of democracy). But he would not understand why such ideals need to be fixed, final, or absolute. They can be nothing more than present means of present amelioration.

Does this commit Dewey to meliorism as the end of moral life? I would rather characterize it as a faith. If meliorism is an end, it would have to be something so broad and general that it would elude a fixed determi-nation of its content. Just as seeking health can only mean that one tries to live healthily, so too does seeking meliorism mean living melioristically, that is, doing our best to make things better. But what does this really come to? If it presupposes any particular rule about what counts as making things better, then there is not much difference between meliorism and any other ethical view that presupposes a fixed standard. Consistency requires that Dewey holds that 'better' is context dependent, that is, its meaning depends on what particular problems and potentialities are present in a particular situation. Furthermore, the judgment that things are better is a qualitative determination in and of the particular present situation.

Does the piecemeal and situational thrust of Dewey's ethics entail unrestrained licentiousness or irresponsibility? On the contrary, he thought of it as a call for more work and responsibility than other ethical views. In trying to redirect our efforts toward what is specific and presently lived, Dewey claimed that his view "does not destroy responsibility; it only *locates* it" (MW 12:167, my emphasis). Neither did he believe that this shift of focus entailed the end of ethical theory. Instead, there has to be a change in its scope and intent.

Instead of looking for criteria and final solutions, ethics should be concerned with method, that is, with how we can become better prepared to obtain qualitative guidance in making good decisions in the difficult and complex situations that we confront. Since certain habits and dispositions are our main tools, as well as the most controllable factors we have, we can hope for *amelioration* by encouraging certain virtues. Philosophical inquiry into the possible conditions for improvement is not the search for the set of habits that will solve all our problems, or that will help anyone in any situation. Nor is the task to find those dispositions and attitudes that will lead us to the good life; rather, the task is to find those which offer some reliability for achieving a better life. There is no predetermined formula for a better life and it is not altogether under our control. But these were not sufficient reasons for Dewey to abandon his melioristic faith.

NINE

Conclusion

The Need for a Recovery of Moral Philosophy

I have been presenting Dewey's view by contrasting it with some of the ways in which other moral theories that assume a theoretical starting point have portrayed moral life. Dewey's reconstructive approach generously builds on even the most blatant mistakes in philosophy. Indeed, he considers non-empirical views as a source of instruction because even "the most fantastic views ever entertained by superstitious people had some basis in experienced fact" (LW 1:357).

Rule-centered and act-centered ethics are based on the fact that we can formulate and, to some extent, rely on moral generalizations in spite of the uniqueness of our circumstances. However, such views take principles as rules and thereby ignore the importance of flexibility and of non-cognitive resources in a situation. Rule-centered ethics end up portraying moral life as a mechanical or legalistic process, where morality is a system of restrictions, constraints, impositions, or limitations in someone's life. In "negative morals," as Dewey put it, the "practical emphasis falls upon avoidance, escape of evil, upon not doing things, observing prohibitions" (MW 14:6).

Subjectivist and character-centered views, on the other hand, appreciate the personal and human aspect of morality, especially the fact that we qua moral agents are ourselves a condition of moral experience. But by committing the philosophical fallacy they have portrayed morality as a self-centered endeavor or, worse, they have reduced moral experience to the act of experiencing or to the content of consciousness.

Contemporary moral theories appreciate the linguistic, cultural, historical, biological, and communal character of morality. From the standpoint of Dewey's ethics, this is a welcome trend, but it is not a significant improvement on subjectivist views if it leads one to commit the philosophical fallacy. Moral experience cannot be reduced to its conditions. The view that moral life begins and ends inside a language, a conceptual scheme, or a culture is a theoretical presupposition that is not supported by life as it is lived considered from a practical, engaged standpoint. Furthermore, such a narrow view tends to portray moral agents as trapped in their own creations, without the possibility to test or judge specific moral claims without begging the question. From this perspective, it seems as if the only way to save morality from arbitrariness is to jump "into the fire of absolutism" (LW 13:241).

Dewey thought that the history of ethics was dominated by family quarrels and by the recurrent oscillation between extreme views, each trying to compensate for what the other had failed to emphasize. Dewey thought that there is a need for a recovery of moral philosophy. This recovery requires the abandonment of certain common assumptions about moral experience that are made by non-empirical philosophies. It is helpful to contrast some of the assumptions in non-empirical philosophies with Dewey's view of moral experience.

1) Many of the debates among ethical theories center on whether it is certain acts, traits of character, rules, goals, motives, feelings, or obligations that provide the basis for distinguishing morality from other aspects of life. For Dewey, all of these elements are integral to moral experience, since they are found in the context of a situation. The basis for distinguishing morality from other dimensions or modes of experience is the subject matter, problems, and pervasive quality of certain situations. There is no criterion that is antecedent to the sheer having of these experiences. Hence, in principle, anything in experience can be experienced as having moral significance and can also be continuous with other ways of immediately experiencing the world (aesthetically, politically, religiously). The locus of moral experience is a present situation, thought of as a qualitative whole that is susceptible to dramatic

structure, that is, one with patterns, rhythms, and phases. Situations are the ultimate context of our problems, inquiries, ideals, and resources.

2) Moral experience is not subjective. To describe moral experience is not to describe the content of an agent's consciousness. Furthermore, there is more to moral experience than what, at any given time, is cognitively discerned and at the foreground of attention. In the context of a morally problematic situation there is the foreground where moral problems and inquiries are taking place, but there is also the temporal and spatial background upon which we rely and that we take for granted. Moral experience per se is not knowledge, although knowing experiences are part of it.

3) Many of the traditional polemics in moral theory start with a dualism, for example, between subject and object, or character and conduct. For Dewey, we can recognize the functional basis of these distinctions while being faithful to the integrity of moral experience. In fact, the distinction between what is experienced and how it is experienced in a moral situation, or between conduct and character, is important for an effective ethics.

4) Many traditional views of moral experience start with the abstraction of an antecedent subject whose conduct is merely an external effect. For Dewey, the moral self is an embodied and acculturated agent with habits, and engaged in processes; moreover, the self is inseparable but distinguishable from its relationships and acts. When the moral agent is engrossed in moral reconstruction, conduct is an expression of the self, that is, there is a unity of the moral self and its conduct.

5) Moral deliberation is often conceived of as an inner cognitive search for moral truths, or as reasoning with propositional content that centers on the application of antecedent rules to current situations. For Dewey, however, moral deliberation is a qualitative, experimental, social, and imaginative process that requires operations to transform situations which carry their own seeds of reconstruction.

6) For Dewey, judgments are not propositions. In ethics, it is commonly assumed that the normativity or reasonableness of our specific moral judgments is derived from a general standard of appropriate conduct. Debates center on whether these general standards are grounded in some ahistorical, objective standpoint, or are rather the result of communal, intersubjective agreement. For Dewey, this gets it backward and puts the emphasis in the

wrong place. Judgments are individual acts and concerned with a unique qualitative context. Rules, criteria, standards, and reasons are instrumentalities that derive their validity from particular moral judgments. The morally wise among us rely on these instrumentalities only when her habitual response to situations is not sufficient, or after a judgment in order to justify herself or to invite others to consider for themselves the situation. Dewey's bottom-up view of moral experience has support from recent research in social and cognitive psychology. According to Jennifer Wright,

In social psychology, a growing body of research has begun to offer an alternative picture of moral judgments, one in which moral agents engage in moral judgments from the "bottom up" instead of the "top down." Such research suggests that moral judgments are primarily intuitive, "gut-level," emotionally-guided evaluations. These evaluations appear to be able to both identify morally relevant issues and provide insight into appropriate action without requiring explicit deliberation or reference to moral principles. In fact, appeal to such principles, if it occurs at all, happens (as in Kohlberg's studies) only after the fact, when moral agents are called upon to explain and/or justify judgments already made. Thus, such research suggests that moral judgments and actions are not typically guided by principles, but are in fact prior to them.[1]

7) There is no general problem of value, in the sense of accounting for the existence of values. We live and begin inquiry in a qualitative world, and the only problem for ethical theory is what discriminations are worth making and what difference we can make. Things are immediately experienced in their individuality as well as in their relations. Moral values are more irreducibly plural and complex than hoped for by ethical theorists. Duty, good, and virtue have no common denominator, nor is there a set hierarchy among them. There is nothing subjective or otherworldly about moral qualities; they are as natural as any other quality found in the same objective world of persons and things.

8) The traditional view of moral experience has been affected by the atomistic and monistic modern views of experience in general. Because there are habits and continuities in moral experience, the situationalist and particularistic thrust of Dewey's view commits him neither to an episodic atomistic pluralism—where our moral life is a mere succession of isolated situations—nor to a monistic view of moral life that assumes that there is standpoint from which moral life can be gazed at as a unified whole.[2] There

is no unifying telos to moral life, but there is significant continuity and interaction to make the quality of habits, character,
and associations interdependent.

9) Morality is a mode of experience that is practical and concerned
with choice and self-expression; it is not, as it has been traditionally portrayed, a matter of passively getting, possessing, or
collecting antecedent knowledge or goodness. Instead, morality
is a creative, experimental, and prospective process which is personal without being subjective; and it is objective without presupposing a God's-eye view or fixed and universal standards.

10) In the traditional view of moral experience, the present is just a
place in between the past and the future. For Dewey, moral life is
experienced as an open-ended and continuous process in which
the past and the future are integral to the present. Thus, ethics
must shift its attention to the quality of the present process instead of to goals, consequences, or any criteria. Meaning and
guidance can be found in the present journey.

11) Because of the philosophical fallacy that infers reality from superior value, philosophers deny the reality of one or more of the
following traits of moral experience: immediate quality, appreciation, change, contingency, uniqueness, novelty, risk, and uncertainty. They think that such traits are subjective, or a sign of
human limitations. On the other hand, they identify moral reality and objectivity with the aspects of our moral life that are most
cognitive, stable, orderly, distinct, and explicit, namely, rules,
universals, quantifiable subject matter, and propositions (or any
object of knowledge). Dewey, in contrast, affirms the reality of
the former traits and shows that the only basis for the distinction between these traits and the traditionally favored traits is
functional. Moral experience is an intermixture of stable and
precarious elements and its direction is not altogether within
our control. Moral tragedy is likely, even with the best of resources and intentions. Novelty and uniqueness are aspects of
every moral situation. Nevertheless, there are always stable elements upon which we can rely. The most stable elements are
habits, rather than rules or any of the discursive resources preferred by traditional theorists. Habits reside in the background of
a situation, but even they are not fixed and can change in their
application to concrete circumstances. What is stable, recurrent,
and relational in a situation can be said to be primarily from the
standpoint of control over the direction and quality of moral life.

"Standardizations, formulae, generalizations, principles, universals, have their place, but the place is that of being instrumental
to better approximation to what is unique and unrepeatable"
(LW 1:90). Habits and principles are the means (though not the
sole means) by which we can enhance our experience of what is
unique, unrepeatable, local, qualitative, transitory, and ineffable.
In emphasizing these other traits of moral experience, Dewey
seems to be reversing the order of importance assumed by traditional moral philosophy. The reconstruction of each moral situation is more important than the knowledge of moral truths. "The
local is the ultimate standard and as near an absolute as exists"
(LW 2:369).

Dewey's departure from the traditional ways of conceiving moral life,
as well as his methodological commitments, entail a change in the tenor
and nature of the questions considered central to moral theory. The change
of scope toward present activity and concrete situations signifies that,
instead of asking about the human telos or the good life, the moral philosopher should be concerned with an investigation into those conditions that
may improve and make meaningful present moral activity. What are these
conditions? Is there, in Dewey, any hypothesis about the ways of participating that might make things better in moral life? These are some of the issues
addressed in part 3.

PART THREE

The Ideal Moral Life

TEN

The Intelligent, Aesthetic, and Democratic Way of Life

Dewey did not have a theory about the good life, a notion antithetical to the pluralistic and contextualist thrust of his moral philosophy. Nevertheless, his ethics is unintelligible apart from some normative commitments and hypotheses about the conditions and instrumentalities for a better moral life. Dewey wanted us to give each moral situation the attention and care that it deserves and to assume a positive trust in the possibilities and instrumentalities available in a situation. The moral life that he envisioned is one that relies on experience for direction, illumination, and motivation. He was not, however, always explicit about his ideal. I will be occupied, in the remainder of this book, with articulating in a coherent way this normative vision. This chapter begins with the most general description of the kind of moral life that Dewey thought was worthwhile in light of his preoccupation with the quality of present experience. Then, in the last two chapters, I consider the kind of self and community that, according to Dewey, are constitutive of such a life.

The broadest possible characterization of Dewey's ideal is that he advocates living a moral life that is intelligent, aesthetic, and democratic. These three adjectives characterize mutually dependent aspects of a single moral vision, and they collectively describe a moral life that promises to be the most meaningful and fruitful general form of engagement in experience.

To say that a moral life has a dimension of intelligence is to say that one who lives the moral life can educate herself (i.e., learn) and transform morally problematic situations through her own moral resources. What Dewey called "experimental intelligence" involves those habits of inquiry by means of which hypotheses are tested and by means of which working connections are found between old habits, customs, institutions, beliefs, and new conditions. With respect to moral life, intelligence refers to a way of reaching moral judgments and appropriating a moral tradition. Dewey contrasts intelligence with the practice of guiding our lives by authority, custom, coercive force, imitation, caprice, or drift. To live a reflective moral life is not to live in accordance with reason but to have "the power of using past experience to shape and transform future experience. It is constructive and creative" (MW 11:346).

The aesthetic dimension of moral life refers to its qualitative aspect and to the inherently meaningful forms of engagement exercised within it. Moral reconstruction is undertaken in an aesthetic manner. Dewey contrasts the aesthetic with the mechanical, the fragmentary, the non-integrated, and all other non-meaningful forms of engagement. To engage a situation intelligently is to engage it aesthetically. It is in this way that "moral life is protected from falling into formalism and rigid repetition. It is rendered flexible, vital, growing" (MW 12:180).

The democratic aspect of moral life means that living the moral life involves a certain way of interacting with others, a certain kind of communication and community. Dewey understands democracy as a form of moral association in which a certain way of life is instituted in the relations and interactions of its citizens. "It is primarily a mode of associated living, of conjoint communicated experience" (MW 9:93). His notion of democracy is an outgrowth of his ideas about moral experience, and the democratic way of life involves the intelligent and the aesthetic community.

Although an important part of my task is to show how the ideal moral life is supported by and consistent with Dewey's philosophical commitments (e.g., his faith in experience) it would be wrong to suppose that this ideal logically follows from them. To do this would be to neglect context (i.e., commit the philosophical fallacy) and assume a view of ideals that is foreign to Dewey's philosophical outlook. Inquiry about how to live takes place in the context of a felt discontent with present ways of living. Let's briefly consider the problematic context that generated and gives meaning to Dewey's ideal.

The Impoverished Character of Contemporary
Moral Experience

We live in a world where we are recurrently confronted with situations in need of qualitative improvement. The problems, challenges, and demands we find are always unique and particular, but we can nonetheless have a general concern about how we are confronting and living in such situations. If Dewey had a general concern as an ethical thinker, it was about how a complex array of contemporary problems and conditions have contributed to the impoverished quality of moral experience. He was concerned about the disoriented, uncontrolled, compartmentalized, rigidly segregated, alienated, isolated, mechanical, superficial, drudgery-filled, capricious, arbitrary, and disintegrated character of contemporary life.

His opposition to dualisms or any of the traditional rigid separations favored by philosophers was based on a practical concern that they reinforce the compartmentalized lives we are living. About the rigid separations between what is intellectual, emotive, imaginative, and volitional, Dewey says,

> The result of these divisions has been the creation of a large number of problems which in their technical aspect are the special concern of philosophy, but which come home to every one in his actual life in the segregation of the activities he carries on, the departmentalizing of life, the pigeon-holing of interests. Between science's sake, art for art's sake, business as usual or business for money-making, the relegation of religion to Sundays and holy-days, the turning over of politics to professional politicians, the professionalizing of sports, and so on, little room is left for living, for the sake of living, a full, rich and free life. (LW 2:104)

Dewey was also troubled by the lack of meaningful and intelligent engagement in human relations, and the way many attended to the unique moral and social problems they faced. What passes for public deliberation about shared problems is hardly effective in ameliorating these situations. Although we must try to undermine the sources of moral evil in the world and confront moral disagreement in a growing and pluralistic world, there are better and worse ways to accomplish these tasks. Dewey was concerned that the quest for certainty, in the midst of a precarious world, had led many to adopt habits of thought that, though comforting, oversimplify the problems they encountered. For instance, the habits of thinking in terms of exclusive and dualistic categories such as good/evil and us/them, as well as the quest for one easily definable source of all moral evils and problems, work against democracy. The way that people attended to moral situations was troublesome to Dewey because it meant that moral possibilities remained dormant and unexplored, and that we have failed to try to make the best out of experience. Dewey had a melioristic faith that a more intelligent and qualitatively enriched moral and social life was possible under present conditions, and his posited ideal was an attempt to point us in the right direction.

Dewey was not naïve about the complexity and plurality of contemporary conditions—educational, economic, and political—that would have to be examined in order to adequately diagnose and ameliorate individuals, relationships, and communities. He noticed, for example, how formal education, with its emphasis on information, passivity, compartmentalization, and specialization, produced characters whose intellectual and imaginative capacities are at odds with each other. Dewey was worried about the dogmatism encouraged by many religious institutions. He was also critical of the ways in which our economic system has affected the quality of our interactions as well as encouraged habits and attitudes that run contrary to the spirit of our moral life. Our society has also accepted the sharp divisions (dualisms) that we live by—between ends and means, morality and business, values and facts—as a matter of course. This problem is aggravated by the fact that in a time of unprecedented complexity and rapid change we experience the demand to integrate and secure values that demand one's loyalty but that seem in conflict or mutually exclusive. For example, how can one secure and adjust both freedom and organization, or moral stability and openness, in today's complex conditions?

Dewey did not aim to provide a solution or a complete diagnosis of these and other general problems, for his methodological commitments demanded the avoidance of a fixed, final, or a single-minded approach. Furthermore, there are dimensions of the problem that are way beyond the scope of philosophy. But what can philosophy do? In part 1 I argued that although Dewey was not naïve about the powers of philosophy, he found significant uses in its general character and critical function. Philosophy might not be able to fully solve situated and concrete problems, but it could criticize methods, that is, detect or rectify mistakes in methodology or inquiry when dealing with problems. Mistakes in method are obstacles to effective amelioration. Therefore, the empirical philosopher can warn theorists in different fields about the dangers of intellectualism, reductionism, dualisms, and other non-empirical vices. But, more importantly, philosophers have much to reconstruct and rectify within their own discipline. Let's consider why.

Even if philosophy has not created any of the problems above, it has helped to perpetuate them through erroneous intellectual validations. Dewey thought that traditional moral philosophies provide support for dualisms that can paralyze genuine efforts at reconstruction. Moreover, philosophers have obstructed the possibility of a better moral life because, in one way or another, they have provided moral views that denigrated the capacity of qualitative and situational everyday experience to guide and rectify its own moral problems and challenges. In conceiving of morality as either otherworldly or subjective, non-empirical philosophers "have denied that common experience is capable of developing from within itself methods which will secure direction for itself and will create inherent standards of judgment and value" (LW 1:41).

Historically, morality is an area of our experience directed by the force of custom or tradition. However, contemporary conditions—science, pluralism, technological innovations, and new interactions among societies—have undermined its stability. Conflicts between moral traditions have created problematic situations where individuals and institutions can no longer count on the absolute stability of custom. But the failure of custom to guide us has been interpreted by philosophers either as evidence that morality is subjective, or as a failure to recognize the true source of absolute moral authority.

Philosophers concerned to protect the seriousness of morality have appealed to reason or rationality for the finality and immutability of custom. "Confusion ensues when appeal to rational principles is treated as if it were merely a substitute for custom, transferring the authority of moral commands from one source to another" (LW 7:166). Meanwhile many have ignored that the source of the problem might not be custom per se but its absolutistic and rigid character. If it is true that we are suffering from laxity of habit or unregulated impulsiveness, it is due to the fact that our moral habits and principles have failed to grow and adapt to new experiences. In other words, Dewey would say that morality has failed to grow guided by the same kind of experimental intelligence operative in other areas of our life. This is a mistake in general method or in how we should live and cope with contingency, change, pluralism, indeterminacy, and uncertainty. The implicit recommendations of traditional moral philosophy in regard to these integral features of morality have been either to downplay them or deny their reality (as in objectivism), or to affirm their reality by excluding any stable basis, other than the present consensus of a community, to guide us (as in relativism). Dewey criticizes these philosophical positions by uncovering their assumptions and presenting an alternative ideal.

How we should approach or respond in general to the kinds of situations present in moral life is an important issue, one that can determine the quality of present moral experience. This quality has suffered in part because of extremism in dealing with moral and social problems. To be torn between the rigidity of absolutism and the laxity of relativism is to be torn between qualitatively poor ways to live and conceive of moral life. By Dewey's lights, both alternatives reflect a general distrust in our everyday moral experience and a failure to use the resources and potentialities of experience.

Dewey sought to undermine the dualistic and otherwise mistaken philosophical views that sanctioned the idea that we are stuck between extreme options. He said, "The modern world has suffered because in so many matters philosophy has offered only an arbitrary choice between hard and fast opposites" (MW 12:137). Philosophy as criticism is needed to unearth these prejudices and to suggest better ways to live.

Philosophy and Extremism

In his *Lectures on Ethics, 1900–1901* Dewey notes that most problems in philosophy center on two categories that he believed "come up everywhere."[1] These categories are a family of oppositions. If we add to the family of oppositions presented in this early text the many other ones that appeared in Dewey's later works, we get the following list:

A	B
universal	particular
necessity	contingency
order	spontaneity
permanence	change
stable	precarious
recurrent, dependable, common	unique, novel
work	play
means	ends
relations, instrumental	finalities
cognitive	emotional
actual	ideal
fact	value
product	process
social	individual
interdependence	independence
unity	diversity

Notice how the items in each column are related in a loose but nevertheless meaningful way, as if they shared an underlying generic mode of experience.[2] For Dewey, not all of the items in columns A and B are conceptual abstractions, for many of them designate contrary tendencies or generic traits that have to be dealt with in nearly every dimension of experience. In fact, many of these traits became part of the ground map of experience that he provided in *Experience and Nature*.[3] I will argue that the relation between them is important to the philosophical issue of how to live.

Typically, the philosopher takes the opposition of A and B as problematic. Hence, the task of inquiry for such a philosopher becomes one of finding, once and for all, a way to theoretically overcome, reconcile, downplay, or solve the oppositions by determining which side of the opposition is ontologically primary. For example, the monism-versus-pluralism debate assumes that all things are either interdependent or independent. Universalists and nominalists assume either that particulars can be explained by or reduced to universals, or the contrary. The absolutist-versus-relativist debate usually assumes either that moral principles are fixed or that anything goes. Dewey was concerned to diagnose why philosophers tend toward these polemical extremes.

The fundamental mistake of the traditional philosopher is that she misconstrues the nature of the concrete problems where A and B are in tension, thus confusing a practical tension in actual situations with a theoretical issue about what is real. This is the philosophical fallacy.[4] We live in world that is a mixture of A and B, where we can distinguish them without setting them dualistically apart. However, this does not mean they coexist in some sort of pre-established harmony. The practical problem is that A and B are sometimes in an undesirable tension in the context of a problematic situation. The challenge is not to get rid of the tension but "to find the limits or balance between these two things."[5] For example, in our moral life there is a recurrent experienced tension between the stability and order of our acquired habits (and principles), and new conditions, on the other hand. But the practical problem, if taken for what it is, is not how we should get rid of the opposition and tension. From the point of view of the everyday person, the concrete problem is a matter of *proportion,* that is, of determining how much flexibility should be allowed in specific areas of our moral practice, or deciding what has to be changed and what does not.

Philosophers have ended with extreme views because they have confused matters of *proportion* with an abstract ontological problem. If there were no opposition, the sides of the tension would lack meaning and, more importantly, would lead to undesirable consequences. For instance,

Identity without difference is a stagnation, permanence which does not mean anything. Difference without identity gives absolute disintegration and conflict; it does not mean anything either, because unrelated particulars cannot have any meaning.[6]

For the "ordinary man," as Dewey put it, it is of practical importance that the balance between A and B should obtain. Dewey explained that

the ordinary man would say that you must not let one factor unduly predominate over the other, that you get disintegration if you allow the individualistic factor to go too far; you lose public spirit, the sense of solidarity. . . . On the other hand, if you carry out authority too far you get despotism, arrest of freedom of thought and action, and fossilization of society.[7]

It is clear that Dewey uses the ordinary man to propose a normative thesis that remained central to his philosophy: that we ought to seek an integrative balance between A and B, and that wisdom usually lies in avoiding the tempting simplicity of extreme philosophical views. Although even a short acquaintance with his works would confirm this general thesis, he never explicitly and systematically defends it. Instead, it is implicit in his treatment of particular oppositions present in different areas of philosophy. Not enough attention has been given to balance as a normative notion in Dewey. Balance is a feature of ideal activity, the ideal moral self, and the ideal community.

Dewey's Notion of Balance

Dewey's qualitative, interactive, and processional interpretation of balance must be distinguished from the customary, quantitative one. Quantitative balance is the maintenance of a certain measurable proportion between things. Usually the proportion is one of equality, that is, the same magnitude, quantity, degree, or worth. To seek this kind of balance requires that we seek equal amounts of x and y. Here excesses and deficiencies are measured and corrected by adding or subtracting accordingly. Balance in this sense does not entail that the elements to be balanced must interact or affect each other in any significant way; in fact, it does not require that the elements in question coexist. One can achieve balance by a compensation that takes place across time. An excess of x at time t can be balanced by a deficiency of x (and perhaps an excess of y) at some other time. For example, one might say "I am going to spend three days engaging in excessive play, to compensate for the last two days of drudgery." Dewey entertained a rather different conception of balance, informed by the influence of biological and aesthetic models. Let's consider how these models contributed to a distinct notion of balance.[8]

Although for Dewey the balance achieved in aesthetic experience is the paradigm and highest expression of this notion in experience, it is a development continuous with the basic balance we seek as biological organisms.[9] An organism's life can be regarded as a continual rhythm of disequilibrations and equilibrations. From Dewey's generic descriptions of this process we can abstract two features that are central to his general notion of balance:

a) Balance is a relation between forces in opposition or tension.
b) Balance is an interactive process where these forces are transformed in a tension-filled but reinforcing relation.

Balance in the life of an organism is something temporal and dynamic that is not achieved for all time; it is, rather, like riding a bicycle: individuals continuously correct tendencies to tilt excessively in one direction or the other. The restoration of balance is not a return to a prior state of balance. In fact, no particular balance is ever strictly speaking the same balance. In the shift from imbalance to balance, there is a transformation of the factors in opposition. Moreover, this transformation is not one in which the factors are dissolved into a new, undifferentiated unity, one where there is no longer tension. There is instead an organic unity: "Organic unity must be interpreted in terms of the interaction, of actual reinforcement between the parts, and not in terms of any one thing which somehow includes all others."[10] This notion of balance as a unity where tension is preserved is present in art. In art "equilibrium comes about not mechanically and inertly but out of, and because of, tension" (LW 10:20). But there is more to learn from art about balance:

c) Balance is excellence in proportion that is inseparable from rhythm.
d) Balance is a relation between elements of an organic whole that avoids excess and deficiency.

In *Art as Experience* Dewey argues that since balance is "the equilibrium of counteracting energies, [it] involves rhythm" (LW 10:183). The inseparability of balance and rhythm is something that an artist understands very well. The rhythm between the factors in tension affects the quality of their balance. For example, if the factors recur without any variation there might be balance but not the kind that is characteristic of great works of art. Some balances are therefore better than others depending on their constitutive rhythms.

In the balance of an organic whole the parts are interdependent in that what happens to one affects the other. This is true even when there is an imbalance. When there is an excess of one of the parts there is also a deficiency of some other part. Dewey explains this in works of art. "There is no such thing as a force strong or weak, great or pretty, in itself. . . . To say that one part of a painting, drama, or novel is too weak, means that some related part is too strong—and vice versa" (LW 10:185). This is important for someone who seeks cues from experience about when balance might be threatened or how to maintain it. The artist becomes aware that he has introduced too much variation only when he experiences not enough order. Not enough stability or order might be a sign that we are being too flexible. What is sometimes referred to as the excessive individualism of our American society is in fact experienced as a deficiency in our communal bonds.

There are many possible relations between the elements that make up an organic whole. One reason for preferring a one-sided, unbalanced relation is that it is often assumed to be a sign of strength. There are works of art that succeed in getting notice because of an "effort to get strength by exaggeration of some one element," but Dewey believes that "such works do not wear . . . no real strength is displayed, the counteracting energies being only pasteboard and plaster figures. The seeming strength of one element is at the expense of weakness in other elements" (LW 10:185). The problem with excesses is that they are usually accompanied by, or lead to, deficiencies. Painters and writers have the problem of keeping one part "down" so that other parts can be kept "up." This does not mean, though, that all parts must remain equal, as required by the quantitative notion of balance. In Dewey's organic conception, a relative predominance of one element over another is compatible with balance. But the strength or excellence of this element must significantly take into account, be affected and reinforced by, the other parts that make up the whole, even if they are downplayed and in tension with it.

An excess or a deficiency is a problem that results from the relative seclusion, confinement, oppression, and suppression of one element over another in an organic whole. Therefore, balance is not the mean between extremes as a fixed equidistant midpoint that we either attain else we are out of balance. There is an indefinite number of ways in which one can stay within the balance without falling into an extreme. The balance of a bicycle rider is such that, at different times, he can tilt to one side more than to the other without falling down. In art, this is done on purpose. The artist might add a touch of disorder to add emphasis, without falling out of balance. She takes advantage of the room she has between extremes.

She does not know beforehand how much room she has, therefore she has to rely on experimentation. Those who take more risk in artistic production are those willing to test the limits, that is, to try to find out how much of one element they can get away with without falling off balance. Dewey thought that being able to achieve this dynamic variation within balance is a mark of great works of art. "The greater the variation, the more interesting the effect, provided order is maintained" (LW 10:169). This is balance that is maintained in spite of changes in rhythm. In great works of art there might be periods of relative predominance of disorder and novelty, but they do not lead to chaos or confusion, that is, "it does not prevent a cumulative carrying forward from one part to another" (LW 10:171).

Balance as the Ideal

A and B are generic traits, tendencies, or phases that we distinguish in dealing with a tension-filled situation. We become fully aware of their relation when experience turns problematic. In fact, the most generic description of our most important problems in life is that they are about the relation or proportion between A and B. Dewey explains that "the significant problems of life and philosophy concern *the rate and mode of conjunction* of the precarious and the assured. . . . On the cognitive side the issue is largely that of *measure,* of the *ratio* one bears to others in the situations of life. On the practical side, it is a question of the use made of each, of turning each to best account" (LW 1:50).

Although eradicating the presence of A and B in experience is not really an option, how to respond to them and relate them can be a matter of choice. This issue would not be so important if it did not determine the quality of our present experience. But Dewey claims that the overall quality of our lives depends on how we deal with, accommodate, and mutually adapt these features.

> Structure and process, substance and accident, matter and energy, permanence and flux, one and many, continuity and discreteness, order and progress, law and liberty, uniformity and growth, tradition and innovation, rational will and impelling desires, proof and discovery, the actual and the possible, are names given to various phases of their conjunction, and *the issue of living depends upon the art with which these things are adjusted to each other.* (LW 1:67, my emphasis)

Hence, the traditional philosophical question of how to live is reconstructed by Dewey as how to live in a world where A and B are present and intermixed. This is not as simple as how to survive. In fact, our problem is that as organisms we are not content with mere survival; we procure things, for example, A and B, that do not automatically reinforce each other but that seem necessary for meaning and quality of living. Dewey explains, for example, that "the live creature demands order in his living but he also demands novelty" (LW 10:171). "The organism craves variety as well as order" (LW 10:173). But what can philosophy contribute to this important issue and why did Dewey favor balance over relations of excess or deficiency between A and B?

For Dewey, philosophy requires metaphysics, that is, disclosing the general character of the world in which we live; but philosophy is also about wisdom. "Love of wisdom is concerned with finding its implications for the conduct of life" (LW 1:50). It is in its capacity as wisdom that philosophy must take a stand on how to respond to these traits of existence. In this respect Dewey thinks there is a basic split between those philosophies that are life-affirming and those that are not. He said, "ultimately there are but two philosophies. One of them accepts life and experience in all its uncertainty, mystery, doubt, and half-knowledge and turns that experience upon itself to deepen and intensify its own qualities" (LW 10:41). We live in a world that constantly challenges us with tendencies and traits that seem to point in irreconcilable directions. We can either acknowledge and accept this while trying to make the best of it, or we can turn our backs upon the world, disillusioned by the lack of a pre-established balance. Dewey opts for the former. He stands on the possibility that with our efforts an integrative *balance* between elements in tension might be achieved. To take up the unavoidable tensions present in experience as the resources by which a productive balanced relation could be worked out requires a faith in experience. This does not mean that Dewey believes that we will always find balance or that balance will always be better than the alternatives. But neither is Dewey's hope unfounded or arbitrary wishful thinking. It is based on lived experience. He relies on the following general hypothesis: the balance between A and B is the relation that can make experience educative, enriching, and esthetic. Excess and deficiency, on the other hand, characterize our most unfulfilling, meaningless, and non-educative moments. These are lives that are, for example, too mechanical or too random and chaotic, too easy, or too hard. "Only persons who have been spoiled in early life like things always soft; persons of vigor who prefer to live and who are not contented with subsisting find the too easy repulsive. The difficulty becomes objectionable only when instead of challenging energy it overwhelms and blocks it" (LW 10:172). People who live under extreme, wretched conditions so crave stability and serenity that they might hold as ideal a life without struggle, difficulties, and pain. But Dewey would argue that this is not what they really want. A life of too much struggle and challenges is undesirable, but so is a life without enough challenges and struggle.

Dewey's affirmation of the hypothesis that balance makes for a better lived experience can be demonstrated by showing how balance is essential to his descriptions of ideal activity in all of the different dimensions of human life. For example, in *How We Think* Dewey claims that "the best thinking occurs when the easy and the difficult are duly proportioned to each other" (LW 8:350). He also characterizes the extremes. "Too much that is easy gives no ground for inquiry; too much that is hard renders inquiry hopeless" (LW 8:350). However, nowhere is it clearer that the notion of balance is ideal for Dewey than in his aesthetics and ethics. In fact, art is his paradigm of balance. Art is the highest achievement of experience. It represents the complete integrative balance of those tendencies and generic traits of experience that philosophers have erected into dualisms because they are in a tension-filled relation. "In art as experience, actuality and possibility or ideality, the new and the old, objective material and personal response . . . are integrated in an experience in which they are all transfigured from the significance that belongs to them when isolated in reflection" (LW 10:301). Moreover, Dewey holds that balance is key to any human activity with aesthetic quality. The ideal moral life, in other words, has aesthetic quality.

The Ideal of a Balanced Moral Life

Dewey lamented the unaesthetic character of most paradigms of morality. Discontent with the mechanical and rigid conception of morality, with its hopeless task of finding fixed rules and ideals in a changing and complex world, can lead one to a different unaesthetic extreme. One might decide to live aimlessly, drifting according to external pressures, accepting as right or wrong whatever might seem convenient at the moment.

Disillusionment with life and with morality would seem justified if we could choose only between these two unaesthetic extremes. Both extremes seem to assume that universality, stability, order (A traits) are irreconcilable with particularity, novelty, and change (B traits). For Dewey, there is much we can learn in morality from art. Dewey said, "the assumption that there are no alternatives between following ready-made rules and trusting to native gifts, the inspiration of the moment and undirected 'hard work,' is contradicted by the procedures of every art" (MW 9:178). In ideal moral engagement one has to have the same kind of balanced flexibility of the artist who uses acquired knowledge (stabilities) as a tool for present individual creation. The extreme forms that our moral life can take are not straw man philosophical positions to be dealt with only within philosophy proper. They represent liabilities of living. For even if we might not be able to point to any one who can be said to wholeheartedly embody these extremes, they are two opposite tendencies our characters and community can take if we do not attend to the difficult task of reflective moral life. There is always the risk that acquired habits and any inherited or past moral knowledge can become mechanized and rigid when they are taken as direct guides to action. But there is also the risk that flexibility in moral matters might descend into a lack of respect for any moral standard.

Perhaps these risks are more evident when we think about the moral education of our children. No matter how true the moral principles are which we wish to inculcate in our children, we should also be concerned about *how* they are going to adopt and apply them to their unique circumstances. There is no guaranteed or simple method to prevent our children from becoming either too flexible or too rigid and dogmatic in moral matters. We can only hope to create the conditions which may enable them to steer between undesirable extremes. Some of these conditions are the habits of intelligence.

In his writings on philosophy of education Dewey describes the ideal in terms of the balance between "the work attitude and the play attitude" (LW 8:347). He claims that, "To be playful and serious at the same time is possible, and it defines the ideal mental condition" (LW 8:347). In morals, just as in art and science, there should be a merging of playfulness with seriousness. There is no intention on Dewey's part to establish a dichotomy; as he says, "there is no distinction of exclusive periods of play activity and work activity, but only one of emphasis" (MW 14:211). In play, one is engaged in the present activity for its own sake, for "interest centers in activity, without much reference to its outcome" (LW 8:346). Play is "free, plastic," imaginative, and requires a "serious absorption" in present activity. The presence of play signifies tendencies of curiosity, flexibility, and openness. In work, on the other hand, the direction of one's interest is in the product in which the activity terminates, therefore "the end holds attention and controls the notice given to means" (LW 8:346).

When there is excess or deficiency of either play or work, or an isolation of one from the other, the outcome is undesirable, that is, it is an unaesthetic vice. On the side of play the vice is "fooling," namely, "a series of disconnected temporary overflows of energy dependent upon whim and accident" (LW 8:346). Excessive playfulness becomes the kind of indulgence that becomes an arbitrary and aimless fancy. The excessive flexibility and openness in play can lead to dissipation or disintegration. On the side of work the vice is drudgery. When work becomes drudgery, activity that was "directed by accomplishment of a definite result" becomes activity "undergone as *mere* means by which to secure a result" (LW 10:283). In drudgery, the agent is not emotionally or imaginatively involved in present activity, and it becomes routine and mechanical. An exclusive interest in outcomes results in "activities in which the interest in the outcome does not suffuse the process of getting the result" (LW 8:346). In drudgery, the present activity is taken as if it were a necessary evil. When ends are *external* to the means, the process of doing loses all value for the doer.

The occurrence of any of the above vices is often followed by the other. For when there is excess or isolation on the side either of play or work, the other develops in isolation. When most of our daily activities fail to engage our emotions and imagination, the few opportunities for play usually degenerate into aimless amusement, that is, there is a "recourse to abnormal artificial excitations and stimulations" (MW 14:113). Hence, for Dewey, a society where passive entertainment and drudgery are the predominant modes of daily engagement is a sign of a problem. He also diagnosed that in our product-oriented and class-structured society, social and economic conditions tend to make "play into the idle excitement for the well-to-do, and work into uncongenial labor for the poor" (MW 9:214).

But are there not things one has to do without the direct interest characteristic of play? Of course, but ideally even in this kind of situation work activity can be more than mere means. The alternative is that interest in and appreciation of the value of the end suffuses and informs the present means; in other words, a sense of its value is transferred to the means. The process is appreciated as constitutive of the product. In ideal work "activity is enriched by the sense that it leads somewhere"; there is "interest in an activity as tending to a culmination" (LW 8:287). This is different from situations of drudgery where it is only the thought of completion—to earn a reward or avoid punishment—that keeps you going. Artistic activity, again, is Dewey's model: "Work which remains permeated with the play attitude is art—in quality if not in conventional designation" (MW 9:214).

Dewey thought that moral philosophers had either conceived moral activity as a playful, arbitrary, and subjective creation or tried to recover the seriousness of morality at the expense of associating it with drudgery; in other words, morality conceived of as a rigid and emotionally sterile activity that subordinates the present, or that is based on externally imposed rules. He envisioned the possibility of a moral life with aesthetic quality as one that achieves a balance between the tendencies and traits associated with play (i.e., B) and with work (i.e., A). This balance is also the key to an intelligent moral life. Intelligence requires that the self or community be capable of carrying forward the habits funded by previous experience while keeping them open to modification; such is a society capable of integrating means with ends. It must be creative but receptive, unified but expansive, working but playful. This is our best hope for a meaningful moral life that can maintain its own integrity without the support or guidance of fixed and external (transcendental) foundations. A moral life that is lived merely by finding the best means to fixed ends is neither aesthetic nor intelligent.

Criticisms of Balance as Ideal

Let's consider some arguments that can be used to discredit the notion that wisdom lies in the balance between extremes. One easy but fallacious way to argue in support of an extreme is to attack the opposing extreme on the assumption that this is the only alternative. This kind of argument usually relies on selecting from the historical evidence the most grotesque or undesirable instances of A or B that one is trying to undermine; it is to stereotype one side of the opposition with an unbalanced and extreme instance of it. For example, those who oppose play in education narrowly conceive of play as mere amusement. Those who argue against the role of emotions in morality support their view by appealing to extreme cases in which we are swayed and misled by strong emotions; emotions are here thought of as impeding, rather than aiding, reasoning. Those opposed to the role of communities in social and political thought are quick to point out that communities have historically oppressed individuals.

If these arguments are persuasive in everyday life, it can only be because a paucity of imagination or circumstances has prevented us from conceiving alternatives beyond the available extremes. At best, they show why one extreme is better than another, but not why a more balanced situation might be a better option. To effectively argue against Dewey, the extremist must give reasons why one-sidedness in regard to A and B is better than balance. Let's consider some possible arguments.

One might concede that in principle there could be instances where A and B are reconcilable, that is, where one achieves a reinforcing relation that constitutes balance. However, these situations are rare and in any case ephemeral. They are so ephemeral, and achieved at such a high cost, that for all practical purposes the effort to maintain a balanced integration and avoid one-sidedness is, in the long run, impossible and counterproductive. For one who sees the desirability of one extreme, the attempt to introduce balance tends to lead further and further into the opposite and undesired direction. For example, those who endorse freedom and spontaneity might claim that any attempt to add order or objective control to our lives leads eventually to fixity, a clear threat to freedom. Therefore, if we really care about freedom we need to be ready to pay the price of laxity or anarchy, if that were to occur. In other words, there is no lasting integration by which we can secure at the same time the values gained by freedom and order. We live in world where we must make a tragic choice between extremes. The quest for balance amounts to delaying or disguising the difficult choice that must be made; meanwhile, we are not able to reap the full benefits of taking a one-sided, wholesale stance. Wisdom requires that we make a *practical* choice regarding which of the elements of the A-B opposition should be primordial.

We could extend this argument to the more general disputes about our moral life. Those philosophers who describe our moral life primarily by using A categories are perhaps concerned that allowing (or trying to integrate) change, flexibility, and precariousness as features either of reality or of our basic principles, character, morality, and society will eventually lead to decay, disorder, chaos, and anarchy. In other words, a departure from immutable standards leads to a lack of fixity in habit and principles. On the other hand, those who endorse B-traits are concerned that the stability, commitment, and security characteristic of the opposite extreme lead to conformity, stagnation, lack of creativity and spontaneity, and all the possible evils that derive from self-righteousness. Notice that in all of these arguments the notion of balance is undermined by a slippery slope argument; in other words, attempts to balance opposing tendencies eventually lead to a vice or failure. Therefore, since one cannot have the best of both tendencies we should embrace one. In this debate, both sides claim that any compromise or balance is deceptive or open to suspicion. Dewey was in fact criticized from both sides. People at contrary extremes perceived Dewey's position as a disguised threat to their endorsed extreme.

One has to admit that each of the extremist philosophers in this imaginary debate points to authentic concerns about the dangers of living under their opponent's assumptions. However, such slippery slope arguments only show the risk and difficulty involved in trying to keep a workable balance; they do not, however, prove that the possibility envisioned by Dewey is unworkable. Of course, to add more flexibility to the moral stabilities that we count on might lead to a chaotic and unprincipled moral life, but this is not a good reason to adopt one-sidedness. On the contrary, for Dewey this is a reason to try to study the conditions by which the kind of balanced relationship that he envisions might be achieved and maintained.

As I have explained, balance is not something achieved for all time or something antecedent to human effort and experimentation. Dewey cannot claim to know that there will always be a workable and lasting balance by which we can secure at any time the values gained by A and B respectively. Moreover, there are many situations in which, even with our best efforts, we will fail to achieve balance and will have to embrace an extreme. Dewey was not naïve. He was aware that his proposals were difficult to implement. But he was not ready to assert that it was impossible or that we must resign ourselves to a life of extremes.

One could argue that it is too much to ask that we make balance the aim of all of our conduct. But making balance an ideal does not entail this. The only kind of activity where balance is usually a conscious aim is art. Art serves as a paradigm because in it we are concerned with balance and rhythm for their own sake and enjoyment. The artist takes as her subject matter and concern something that is implicitly present in all ideal activity. But the fact that the achievement of balance outside the realm of art is relegated to the background does not make it less important in those activities. Most of moral life is directly concerned with unique, morally problematic situations and there may well be situations where extreme solutions are called for. To hold balance as an ideal is not to set it up as a criterion, standard, or end of morally correct action. That is determined by the particular context. Dewey only claims that a balance between our doings and undergoings, means and ends, etc., is the optimal condition for confronting morally problematic situations. Balance is key to a more meaningful and enriching moral life, but it is not morality's explicit end. In fact, a moral agent who makes balance the direct conscious aim of all her situations will likely preclude the sort of balance that Dewey thinks is needed in attending wholeheartedly and intelligently to moral problems. Indeed, even in art the artist usually achieves balance by attending directly to materials and their relation, rather than by making balance the conscious end. A moral agent might make balance her conscious concern but this is only when a serious imbalance is experienced and one is concerned with improving one's method or character (i.e., the "how" of experience), such as when one has become too rigid in dealing with moral problems and one wants to re-balance oneself. Similarly, in social and political inquiry one is typically concerned with very specific social and political problems. Balance becomes a direct and conscious issue only when, for example, one experiences problems that indicate that one's society is becoming overly individualistic in its approach to problems. In these situations, one craves an opposing element, even though, properly understood, what we really crave is more balance. Hence, we move between extremes because we mistake the nature of the problem.

On the other hand, one might argue that what is objectionable about Dewey's view is that it is not demanding enough or sufficiently ideal. If a life of balance is one in which we try to avoid excellence or strength in any one thing or aspect, then this seems to be a life that aims at mediocrity. How can this be ideal? But we have seen that Dewey did not identify balance with moderation. Not all instances of seeking strength or excellence of one part undermine the balance of an organic whole. What is crucial to Dewey's notion of balance is that the counteracting parts have a mutually supportive relation, not that they have equal weight. The person who tries to be moderate by avoiding excellence in any aspect avoids the risk of falling into an imbalance, but her life does not have the intense tensions, remittances, and variations that Dewey considers ideal. The positive basis for this ideal is the promise of a more enriched and meaningful life, not merely the fear of extremes or the avoidance of certain risk.

One could still try to find an inconsistency in Dewey's view. Is a life that is always in balance not something monotonous? Isn't this, by Dewey's own standards, undesirable? Should we not then consider a life where we fall in and out of balance ideal? This would be the case if we could easily attain and maintain balance, but Dewey's prescriptions for balance are conditional upon a certain view of the world. Imbalances do not need to be sought; they are unavoidable in a world of constant change. Balance is not a state of rest but a matter of correcting tendencies that push us in different directions. The risk of falling into imbalance is constant. Situations require that we tilt to one direction rather than another. Our desire to emphasize and excel also demands that we tilt. But, again, we have no safeguard or antecedent prescriptions that can help us secure balance or know when we have gone too far toward an extreme. For example, how much emphasis on individuality can our society take before it falls into systematic anarchy and disintegration? How much order should we impose in our classroom before it turns into a petrifying environment? On these and many other questions we have to rely, like the good artist, on good judgment (practical wisdom) acquired through sensitivity and experimentation.

Given Dewey's notion of balance, his view of ideal activity is demanding and challenging. Balance is not achieved by obtaining equal amounts or by correcting excesses and deficiencies with mere addition or subtraction. His ideal is not achieved by compensating periods of excess with periods of deficiency (or vice versa). We tend to fall into this pattern because while experiencing one excess its contrary seems desirable. The desired excess might represent the direction toward which we should aim, but we must not confuse direction with final aim. It is true that a life lived as the alternation between extremes has rhythm and therefore might be better than the monotony of living under one extreme. But Dewey hoped we could do better. We can try to maintain a balance where there is significant variation and rhythm, aware of the risk we are taking. Extremism is appealing because extremes are easily noticed and they seem to represent a position of strength. But Dewey argued otherwise. It is when we live within an extreme that we are the most vulnerable because we are more likely to compensate by shifting to the opposite extreme.

In sum, Dewey's view about balance is important to his philosophical outlook. It sheds new light on the importance of undermining philosophical dualisms. Dualisms, more than just roadblocks to inquiry, are obstacles to rehearsing in practice a more beneficial relation between opposing elements in experience. The consequences of dualisms are usually seclusion, isolation, suppression, one-sidedness, excesses, and deficiencies. His task as a philosopher was to keep our options alive and open. As long as we continue to believe that extremes exhaust our options we will fail to try what he thought deserved to be tried.

Dewey's ability to stand somewhere between apparent oppositions on almost every issue has led to the view that he was the great American unifier and reconciliator. Alan Ryan, for example, has recently claimed that Dewey's "views gratify a familiar American longing to unify opposites."[11] Although there is some truth to this, we must be clear about the nature of Dewey's solution or proposal regarding the oppositions that are present in philosophy and experience. It is a simplification and misunderstanding to suggest that he only sought to remove dualisms or that he unified by dissolving tensions. Rather, he sought a more balanced relation that relies on and affirms the tensions found in everyday experience.

Thus far, my characterization of Dewey's ideal is too general for our purposes. What in particular needs to be in balance in a moral life that is aesthetic, intelligent, and democratic? What kind of self and community is required? What specific habits are required in order to achieve the balanced integration between doing and undergoing, play and work, needed in morality? In the remainder of this book, I will provide a sketch of the kind of moral self, virtues, relationships, and community that were constitutive of Dewey's moral ideal.

The Ideal Moral Self

The particularist thrust of Dewey's moral philosophy is not incompatible with the broad concerns of virtue ethicists. Philosophical hypotheses about an ideal self and its virtues are no more than sophisticated ways of preparing the agent for what each situation requires. Dewey resisted making explicit claims about specific virtues even though it is obvious that he prescribed a certain kind of moral character. This resistance is understandable given that his understanding of character discourages this kind of compartmentalization. Nevertheless, Dewey found a number of different ways to describe the qualities that he thought were characteristic of agents genuinely and creatively engrossed in present moral reconstruction. These different descriptions complement each other. I will begin with a specification of some of the general dispositions and sensitivities needed in our moral life. Then, I will gradually move to a consideration of how these elements are integrated in a certain kind of character, taking part in certain kinds of relationships and communities.

The Concept of a Virtue

A pragmatist approach to the virtues has to be contextual, instrumental, pluralistic, and experimental. Recall that Dewey's view of a positive trait of character is tied to habits and their function in experience. Character is our primary tool in situations. If virtues are positive traits of character, then according to a pragmatic analysis the distinction between a virtue and a vice is the distinction between a good tool and a bad tool. A virtue is a functional disposition or habit in a character that, upon evaluation, is positively appraised and therefore worth cultivating. But we cannot over-stress the fact that the focus of the instrumentality of a virtue is the concrete ongoing situations of life, that is, the more inclusive context of experience. For a pragmatist view has to be distinguished from other instrumental but contextless and fixed views about virtues, which usually proceed by first postulating an a priori or overriding goal, end, or ideal for all our dispositions (e.g., truth, the actualization of human nature, human flourishing, or the good life), then comparing all dispositions in terms of their capacity to reach these ends.

Furthermore, a pragmatic approach has to be distinguished from a contextual but teleological view, such as that of Alasdair MacIntyre. The predominant teleological views take the following general form: X is a virtue if and only if it enables us to acquire, appropriate, or possess a good of type Y. It seems to be a common fallacy to suppose that a tool is not a good tool if it does not lead to the acquisition of some already established good. But, as a matter of fact, we often cherish and preserve certain tools without having any idea of the specific goods they will provide. We might think of a disposition as a positive instrumentality simply because it helps us remake other instrumentalities, or because it leads us to experiences of a certain kind (e.g., aesthetic or moral). We might have learned that given the contextual setting in which they might be used, they are likely to be very productive. A pragmatist would argue that, given certain assumptions about the general traits of the concrete context in which dispositions operate, one can construct a hypothesis about which general dispositions are better than others. For even if experience is fairly hospitable to all dispositions, it might not lend itself equally well to all of them.

A pragmatist approach also has to be pluralistic, in the sense that there is no good reason why an evaluation of a disposition (as a virtue) should be restricted to how it functions in some particular dimension of our lives, or how it exclusively serves some end.

Finally, a pragmatic approach to the virtues has to be experimental in the important sense that ultimately the only possible test of whether or not a disposition is a virtue is in acquiring it and incorporating it in a general way of life. This last condition points, once again, to the fact that dispositions are not in separate compartments but are concretely intertwined with other dispositions to form character in someone's life.

For a pragmatist there is no automatic criterion by which we can distinguish, once and for all, a virtue from a vice. But the abandonment of the notion of a single criterion does not entail that any disposition is as good as any other or that there is no point in inquiring into reasons why certain dispositions might be worth approving, cultivating, and trying out. After all, the issue is a matter of forced choice. One can wait to arrive at the single criterion if one likes, but meanwhile our characters are being formed in one way or another.

For Dewey, openness, courage, sensitivity, conscientiousness, and sympathy are virtues. This is not an exhaustive or fixed set but I believe an explanation of their nature and relation is sufficient to demonstrate the thickness and organic coherence of Dewey's moral vision. They are some of the habits constitutive of an aesthetic, intelligent, and democratic way of life. The reasonableness of this hypothesis is contingent upon the character of our moral experience. In other words, these habits would not be virtues if experience was other than what it presently is.

Openness and Courage

Dewey had reasons indigenous to his moral philosophy to consider open-mindedness and courage as complementary virtues. Moreover, the importance of these virtues becomes revitalized under his view of experience. Let's begin by illustrating how Dewey's account of openness differs from the usual philosophical accounts and defenses of this virtue that appeal to the intrinsic value of traditional epistemological goals.

OPENNESS

Open-mindedness is a neglected virtue in moral philosophy. A probable reason for this neglect is that too many epistemologists have kidnapped the notion of open-mindedness and claimed it as a merely epistemic virtue.[1] This is a misconception that can prevent one from appreciating the moral and social importance of this virtue for pragmatism. How specific can we get in determining what open-mindedness is? It is uncontroversial to say that it is the tendency or disposition to act open-mindedly. But how do we determine if an act is of the open-minded kind? We cannot say without circularity that such an act is just one which is performed by an open-minded person. As a contextualist Dewey must claim that what does and does not count as acting open-mindedly is ultimately determined by the contextual features of a situation that cannot be specified by a set of definite rules. Nevertheless, a contextualist approach does not preclude a philosopher from delineating some general marks of paradigm cases. In such an analysis, however, vagueness should be expected to rear its head. For example, basic to open-mindedness is a willingness to revise or reconsider one's views and commitments if necessary. But there is no exact answer to the question of when we should expect an open-minded person to revise her views or to retain them. Another reason why precision tends to elude us is that openness seems to be a matter of degree. There is a difference of openness between one who looks at objections only if they arise and another who actively looks for weaknesses in his view; this is the difference between one who welcomes new ideas when they arise, and another who actively seeks new experiences.

Given the variety of forms open-mindedness takes, and since it is not merely an intellectual trait, it is more appropriate to describe this virtue in terms of a general attitude, one Dewey describes as an attitude of *hospitality toward the new*. To be open is to be free from rigidity and fixity, but "it is something more active and positive than these words suggest. It is very different than empty-mindedness" (LW 8:136). It is a receptivity and plasticity that comes from an *active accessibility*, from "alert curiosity and spontaneous outreaching for the new" (LW 8:136).

Open-mindedness means a capacity to interact. It is to welcome new experiences, but in the strong sense of a *willingness to be affected* by participation with the new. As Dewey says, it is a "willingness to let experiences accumulate and sink in and ripen" (MW 9:183). Openness is not just letting the other person have her say but actively listening to her. Openness is almost the contrary of a defensive attitude. In being open we become exposed, susceptible, sensitive, and therefore *vulnerable*. Because open-mindedness constitutes the lived rejection of absolutism, there is a peculiar humility to the open-minded character, an implicit recognition of one's limitations and vulnerability. For a pragmatist, it points to a recognition of the precarious and open-ended character of experience.

Dewey had reasons to consider openness and courage habits worth cultivating. They are virtues because (1) they are part of intelligence, understood as the concrete set of habits which make possible the amelioration of experience through its own means, and (2) a balance between these dispositions is required for an aesthetic moral life, one that avoids the extremes of moral absolutism and moral anarchy.

Recall that Dewey's faith is that betterment might result if we do what is in our power. The power to improve the habits which interact with the demands, possibilities, and enjoyments of present experience is under our control. An intelligent organism has the capability to modify and improve a disrupted habit so that it can become relevant to this and all similar situations. With time, an intelligent organism not only learns to adapt her habits to present situations but learns to learn; in other words, not only can she modify her present tools, but she can create tools to modify tools. However, the habits involved in the effort to readjust disturbed habits are general and second-order habits of habits. Whereas first-order habits operate and are applicable only at the level of the particular situation (they are specialized tools), second-order habits are general in the sense that they operate with respect to many kinds of situations.

A general name for the operation of second-order tools is intelligence. When a pragmatist like Dewey refers to intelligence or experimental reflection, he is pointing to the workings of a very complex but concrete set of habits and attitudes which make possible the ability to learn from and reconstruct experience. Some of these habits are wholeheartedness, persistence, sensitivity, single-mindedness, sympathetic curiosity, unbiased responsiveness, sincerity, breadth of outlook, and balance of interest.[2] But I want to claim that openness and courage are two of the most important second-order dispositions of this ideal character.

The most important learning a person accomplishes in a situation is not amassing information, but the cultivation of habits which are going to affect the quality of future situations. A present experience can, for example, promote the formation of secondary habits and attitudes that prevent the enrichment of future experiences; for example, it might engender callousness or a lack of sensitivity and responsiveness. Hence, as far as moral education is concerned, the cultivation of secondary dispositions to improve old habits is more important than teaching information or a set of rules. But which dispositions are worth cultivating?

If the very existence of habit signifies a tendency toward recurrence and self-preservation, then the ability to modify and improve old habits requires, first of all, an openness, plasticity, or flexibility in the face of new experiences. Without plasticity there would be a non-pedagogical fixity, a self-imposed stability, which is not faithful to the precarious and changing character of experience. But without an active, stable determination nothing can be carried over to guide us and to be tested in subsequent experience; continuity and learning would be impossible. In terms of an ideal character, it means that both open-mindedness and courage are complementary virtues. Openness makes a character flexible and adaptable when a change of direction or modification in our beliefs and habits is called for.

Courage, on the other hand, is needed to stand by one's convictions in spite of our openness and the unavoidable presence of risk in experience. But what is needed is not only their presence, but their balance. Dewey holds that "convictions must be firm enough to evoke and justify action, while also they are to be held in a way which permits the individual to learn from his further experience" (LW 8:98). Too much or too little of either habit is detrimental to learning and conducive to unaesthetic extremes. The person who is willing to modify her moral principles in the face of any prima facie counterevidence is as ill-equipped for moral life as one who remains committed to them no matter what.

For Dewey, a society, community, or character that is not averse to change and that remains stable is a live option. He proposed the development of the kind of character and community that is faithful to both the stable and precarious traits of experience. With regard to character, we can develop dispositions that not only accord with these traits but that turn them into conditions for a self-regulative and self-educative moral life. Two of the required dispositions for this are openness and courage. Of course, we do not form these habits in a vacuum; certain social conditions and environmental and communal activities make certain dispositions possible. For example, open-mindedness requires engaging in activities characterized by open communication. The experimental ideal character can only flourish in a democratic environment and community. This is why open-mindedness and courage are operative instrumentalities in Dewey's democratic ideal community, an ideal that I will consider further in the last chapter.

To what extent do openness and courage acquire greater moral significance under pragmatic assumptions? Would they not be considered virtues even if experience had a different constitution than that assumed by Dewey? Perhaps, but notions of courage and openness in many traditional moral philosophies are lifeless because of the views of experience implicit in these philosophies. When moral life is conceived as "primarily a knowledge affair" (MW 10:6), and as a passive representation of a finished world, these virtues cease to be important. But if moral experience is "reaching forward into the unknown" (MW 10:6), then there is a central role for courage. Courage is needed for more than the few heroic moral acts we will do in our life. Courage is needed at every step of the way for the instability, indeterminacy, and uncertain possibilities inherent in every moral situation. For Dewey, moral situations issue demands and offer possibilities that usually have no common denominator; and these situations involve a certain degree of uncertainty about the consequences of our actions. But we must have the courage to choose and stand by our choices, even if it means going against the moral authority of custom. More importantly, courage is required to confront the vulnerability that comes with being open.

What about openness? To what extent can openness be considered a virtue under a traditional view of experience? In a fixed world where experience is the subjective content of our consciousness, the flexibility of our tools—habits and beliefs—provided by openness is useful only until we have arrived at *the* fitting set of tools, the set that corresponds to or copies an antecedent moral reality. Openness is needed to get to know antecedent moral truths, that is, the way the world really is. On such a view, an unstable and changing child is living in what unbeknownst to him is a stable and fixed world. The child's openness is a sign of insufficiency; he is open because he needs to grow; he lacks something. The improvement of our habits and beliefs is measured in terms of an approximation to a state of affairs where we are in harmony with the fixed truth or the world. But, in principle, once this harmony is established we can once and for all rest on this achievement, and flexibility and openness are no longer virtues. On the contrary, they only become a threat to desired stability. According to this view, openness is no longer required or valuable once children have become acquainted with moral truths. All that is then required is the will to apply them to concrete circumstances.

However, if, as Dewey holds, what we morally ought to do can change depending on what new aspects arise in each unique situation, then openness is always required. We live in a world where what has been good cannot be taken for granted—otherwise it can become bad. If experience is open-ended and still in the making, openness is also an asset because we are more at home in experience by virtue of it. For we have embodied in our characters a feature that is a generic trait of moral experience. If we habituate ourselves to a "hospitality toward the new," then we welcome change and openness as features of the world, rather than just of our minds.

In a world where there is novelty and risk, openness is one of the dispositions that can give character the only kind of control possible in such a world, namely, a flexible control. Openness is necessary for the kind of productive character that welcomes untried situations and is capable of constant readjustment. The best and only preparation for coping with future experience is learning from present experience. To cultivate the general disposition of openness is the only guarantee we have that we are going to learn what there is to learn from each experience.

We are more familiar with the arguments against fixity because we have probably had the opportunity to experience the results of such a tendency. We know that times characterized by fixity result in periods where there is lack of freshness, creativity, and originality. The observation that somebody has settled down or is set in his ways has a negative connotation. But the worst criticism of fixity is that it produces characters who are self-righteous and hold immutably to their views. The only argument for fixity of character is one that suggests that any lack of fixity can lead to extremes that are more dangerous, for example, an irresponsible moral relativism or skepticism. But such arguments usually assume that openness is incompatible with a serious, stable commitment, and this is to confuse open-mindedness with neutrality or with a laxity of character.

One might object that the pragmatist's view about open-mindedness and courage commits him to a narrow, instrumental view of virtues. But, again, I have not claimed to have exhausted all the reasons why openness is worth encouraging and cultivating. And there is no reason why the instrumental, pragmatist view of open-mindedness is limited to saying that it is merely a good tool for dealing with moral problems, just as there is no limit to the reasons we might value a tool. For example, we might even enjoy its use and simple presence; we might want to claim that there is something beautiful about somebody who is open-minded, or that it is more pleasant or easier to live with someone who has this disposition. What seems most plausible is the claim that openness enriches our lives in a way that stiffness and rigidity do not, for with increased openness usually comes not only adaptability but increased susceptibility, sensitiveness, responsiveness, and enjoyment. Openness is a condition of the ability to learn to enjoy more things. It is a constitutive part of the aesthetic, intelligent, and democratic way of life that was central to Dewey's thought.

Sensitivity and Conscientiousness

Dewey's paradigm of deliberation is one where its operations—such as selection, observation, rejection, determining relevance, and experimentation—are guided by the qualitative features of the situation as it is transformed. In an earlier chapter, I noted how in this process pre-reflective initial judgments (valuings) are reflectively judged (valuation) in light of the present situation. This presupposes the operation of certain habits or virtues. When in moral life valuings develop and become an expression of a positive disposition or habit, it becomes or is part of a character that has *sensitivity*. In the case of valuation it becomes thoughtfulness or *conscientiousness*. For Dewey, a balanced relation between sensitivity and conscientiousness in a character is the best preparation one can have to meet the moral demands of situations and to give direction to our moral life. Let's consider each of these virtues separately.

SENSITIVITY AND CULTIVATED APPRECIATION

In our initial confrontation with a morally problematic situation the *emotional* direct and spontaneous response to situations is indispensable for moral inquiry. The development of sensitivity to the felt problem that evokes inquiry, as well as to the pervasive quality of the context of inquiry as it is transformed, is our best preparation for obtaining qualitative guidance from experience. Dewey wrote,

> nothing can make up for the absence of immediate sensitiveness; the insensitive person is callous, indifferent. A person must feel the qualities of acts as one feels with the hands the qualities of roughness and smoothness. (LW 7:269)

Our more reflective valuations depend on sensitivity for their qualitative material, but our sensitivity changes as it is affected by particular valuations. Growth of character and education depend on the extent to which there is this kind of nurturing relation between our present inquiries and our cultivated appreciation or sensitivity. This is how we develop taste: "The formation of habits is a purely mechanical thing unless habits are also tastes—habitual modes of preference and esteem, an effective sense of excellence" (MW 9:244). Our more important habits are not skills, they are tastes. For in developing taste we are forming the implicit standards that will be operative in later experiences.

> If the word [taste] be used in the sense of an appreciation at once cultivated and active, one may say that the formation of taste is the chief matter wherever values enter in, whether intellectual, aesthetic or moral. (LW 4:209) The formation of a cultivated and effectively operative good judgment or taste with respect to what is aesthetically admirable, intellectually acceptable and morally approvable is the supreme task set to human beings by the incidents of experience. (LW 4:209)

The ideal condition is one in which a character is immediately appreciative of values approved by reflection. There is no better safeguard against the temptations of immediate desire and urgent passion. Hence, "the need of fostering at every opportunity direct enjoyment of the kind of goods reflection approves. To deny direct satisfaction any place in morals is simply to weaken the moving force of the goods approved by thought" (LW 7:210).

In moral education Dewey stressed that learned standards and rules are no substitute for firsthand vital appreciation of the moral quality of an act. He distinguished between representative experience, which is an indirect experience that is dependent on signs, and direct experiences "in which we take part vitally and at first hand" (MW 9:240). When the representative and informative are overemphasized there is a danger for "the tendency of technique and other purely representative forms to encroach upon the sphere of direct appreciations" (MW 9:241). The capacity to directly appreciate certain features that is built into character because of previous direct experience is a more effective moral tool than moral knowledge thought of as handed-down information. To know the abstract proposition that "kindliness is usually a good thing" is different from being able to appreciate its truth firsthand in concrete situations. Dewey said, "A youth who has had repeated experience of the full meaning of the value of kindness toward others built into disposition has a measure of the worth of generous treatment of others" (MW 9:243).

Dewey admired how the Greeks stressed the "exercise of the affections and how aesthetic qualities were the 'chief instruments'" to "create a direct feeling of the beauty of the good" (MW 6:386). He lamented that we had lost the aesthetic as a "moral force" and had failed to see the importance of "an acute and sensitive direct response" (MW 6:386). Moral appreciation or sensitivity is, however, a habit that cannot be taught. The best we can do in moral education is to provide the conditions for its emergence by, for example, surrounding the child with the proper activities and environments. Even artistic activities in schools might be more consequential for encouraging the development of a morally sensitive character than the study of moral maxims.

In sum, moral sensitivity is for Dewey a better guide to what is morally required in a situation than any set of moral rules. Through a cultivated sensitivity we retain in a more organic and effective way the lessons of past moral experiences. Our characters also determine our qualitative access to the moral richness and depth of situations. Those without moral sensitivity do not experience moral problems. This does not make them fortunate; instead, they are handicapped by lacking a dimension of experience that is as real as any other. There are, however, limitations to relying exclusively or excessively on moral sensitivity in our moral life.

Direct appreciations are partly dependent upon our upbringing, that is, upon how our previous experiences have affected and funded our receptive habits. The positive implications of this, for both Dewey and Aristotle, are that "the immediate judgments of good and evil of a good man are more to be trusted than many of the elaborately reasoned out estimates of the inexperienced" (LW 7:266). But this also means that there are some characters for whom "the warped and distorted might seem natural" (LW 7:267). Moreover, even the best among us (i.e., the morally good person) is fallible and subject to the unavoidable elements of novelty and complexity in moral situations. Intuitive moral appraisals are "dependable in the degree in which conditions and objects are fairly uniform and recurrent. They do not work with equal sureness in the cases in which the new and unfamiliar enters in" (LW 7:267). We cannot then rely exclusively on our acquired sensitivity to meet the demands of morality.

Moreover, too much reliance upon our moral sensibilities can lead to an unaesthetic moral life in which our habits do not change. Exclusive trust in our immediate appreciation does not let us grow and learn from new situations. As Dewey puts it, "extreme intuitionalism and extreme conservatism often go together" (LW 7:267). In a world of change and novelty, in which each situation is unique, our direct appreciations are fallible even if they have a "presumption of correctness" (LW 7:267).

The limitations of the good and sensitive character can only be ameliorated by supplementing its immediate appreciations with a disposition to engage in reflective valuations. "The direct valuing which accompanies immediate sensitive responsiveness to acts has its complement and expansion in valuations which are deliberate, reflective" (LW 7:271). In terms of moral character this means that sensitivity should operate in a balanced relation with "conscientiousness" (LW 7:271).

VALUATION AND CONSCIENTIOUSNESS

When moral valuation develops into a positive moral disposition it becomes conscientiousness.[3] Conscientiousness involves a thoughtful concern, a disposition to reflectively seek relations and connections in the sense of conditions, consequences, possibilities, and moral implications of an act. It is "the habit of bringing intelligence to bear upon the analysis of moral relations—the habit of considering what ought to be done" (EW 3:364). It is this willingness and readiness to evaluate our immediate moral apprehensions that keeps the good character from falling into ruts. The good character could rest on her oars if novelty, uniqueness, precariousness, complexity, and change were not generic traits of our moral life. But since they are, and there are no ready-made rules that can tell us when our immediate moral assessments should be subject to valuation, it is important that we are rightly disposed. The conscientious character is willing to reconstruct, revise, improve, and deliberate when readjustment is required. This is a different disposition than the excess, "overconscientiousness," which is a "constant anxiety as to whether one is really good or not, a moral 'self-consciousness' which spells embarrassment, constraint in action, morbid fear" (LW 7:272). We need to be reflective in moral life because our actions occur in a context with relations and implications that we sometimes do not apprehend until after the deed is done. We often blame ourselves for not being more thoughtful when making a particular decision; and we also blame our children because, even if they are not at fault for something they did not intend to do, we want to teach them that there are relations in their experience that they need to consider before they act, that is, they should be responsible.[4] Of course, one is not always to blame for not foreseeing the consequences of one's actions. What will actually happen is not altogether under our control, but this does not excuse us from doing the best we can and being conscientious.

The habit of reflectiveness is important because the moral rightness of a particular sort of conduct can change depending on the actual and changing relations that an act sustains with other things within its present but changing context. The same sort of act of charity that I performed ten years ago might have different moral implications and moral qualities today. One cannot take for granted the moral worth of a line of conduct that one has decided to pursue. Sometimes the relations that are relevant to the moral evaluation of a particular line of conduct do not reveal themselves until we act. One must then be ready and willing to make adjustments as these relations are disclosed in further experience.

To be sure, what Dewey meant by conscientiousness is not a detached, impartial thoughtfulness but the kind that is characteristic of those who are genuinely concerned with the moral dimension of their conduct. Conscientiousness is "intelligent attention and *care* to the quality of an act" (LW 7:273, my emphasis). It is manifested as an "interest in the discovery of the true good of the situation" (MW 5:363). This concern is not incompatible with a concern for the state of one's character. On the contrary, we have already seen how for Dewey being good and doing good are mutually dependent phases and concerns of a growing moral life. The way to actually improve one's habits is through an attentive care to present situations.

In sum, sensitivity and conscientiousness are complementary and mutually dependent functions in moral intelligence. Moral life is experienced as a recurrent tension between the old, familiar, and stable conditions, and the new. A balance between conscientiousness and sensitivity allows a good character to use the habits funded by previous experience while being attentive to new relations and conditions. Many of our moral failures can be traced back to a failure to be thoughtful or sensitive. These are distinct failures that can only be avoided if we cultivate a corresponding disposition. Each of these dispositions can lead to distinct excesses and deficiencies when not in a balanced relation with the other. Our sensitivity becomes warped, stagnant, and predictable if it is not properly affected by a disposition to inquire, criticize, and search for new relations. On the other hand, conscientiousness becomes morally callous and impervious to experiential input if it is not checked and informed by sensitivity.

Aesthetic engagement in moral experience requires a balance between a capacity to be receptive—sensitivity as an instance of undergoing—and a willingness to seek reflectively what ought to be done, that is, conscientiousness. Conscientiousness keeps a character from falling into ruts and from a drudgery-filled moral life. And sensitivity keeps it from being unaware of moral relevancies and qualities in experience; without its guiding function, in fact, our moral life would be aimless and arbitrary.

Sympathy and the Virtues of a Richer and Wider Experience

Moral philosophy often assumes that one must aim at objective thinking in the sense of a neutral standpoint that one can get to by putting aside or dispensing with affective and imaginative capacities. But for Dewey,

> there is care, concern, implicated in every act of thought. There is someone who has affection for some things over others; when he becomes a thinker he does not leave his characteristic affection behind. As a thinker, he is still differentially sensitive to some qualities, problems, themes. (LW 6:14)

This should not be a cause of despair but a reason to learn to discriminate between better and worse habits of affection and imagination. As Dewey said,

> one can only see from a certain standpoint, but this fact does not make all standpoints of equal value. A standpoint which is nowhere in particular is an absurdity. But one may have an affection for a standpoint which gives a *rich and ordered landscape* rather than for one from which things are seen confusedly and meagerly. (LW 6:14–15, my emphasis)

Which "habits of desire and imagination" (LW 7:187) one brings to a situation will determine one's selectivity, and hence the scope and depth of the present situation that is being immediately appreciated and reflectively examined. Hence, there is a way to assess particular habits of imagination and affections in our moral life. There are habits that provide the agent with a rich, broad, and wide landscape upon which to deliberate and act, and there are others that in comparison are constraining, one-sided, and narrow. Dewey prescribes "the fostering of those habits and impulses which lead to a broad, just, sympathetic survey of situations" (MW 14:144).

Thinking is the capacity to consider an act in its bearings and relations. But there is more to moral deliberation than reasoning or exploring logical relations between abstract propositions. Recall that for Dewey one does not fully examine the relations of an act unless one engages in inquiry as an imaginative process of constructing and testing hypotheses. In this process, relations with past experience, present events, and possible consequences are explored. One can do this better or worse according to whether one has a vivid imagination, but a more important determinant of one's success in inquiry is the breadth, width, and flexibility of one's imaginative field. At one extreme is the agent who only considers the consequences of a single proposed act with respect to one person (usually him or herself), without considering other possible acts and their consequences. Equally narrow from Dewey's perspective is the experience of someone—a utilitarian, for example—who in deliberation can only consider the relation between alternative actions and one predetermined fixed end. Moral agents can do better. They can develop the kind of habits that allow them to have a wider experience in that they open themselves in deliberation to several sometimes incommensurable ends and their relations, and thereby entertain a rich field of considerations. Sympathetic imagination and openness are thus two valuable undergoing habits.

I have already considered how openness expands or welcomes our reach toward new experiences. But whether our experience is wide or narrow depends also on the extent and depth of our sympathies. "Every widening of contacts with others, every deepening of the level of sympathetic acquaintance, magnifies in so much vision of the good" (MW 5:379). What Dewey meant by sympathy is closer to what feminist writers today have identified as empathy.[5] To understand sympathy we must distinguish it from other more casual and ordinary considerations. It is one thing to consider how a possible course of conduct will affect others, quite another to consider how those affected others would look at it from their standpoint independently of our own. Of course, this capacity is a matter of degree and will likely vary as a function of the level of acquaintance, the nature of the relationship, and one's powers of imagination. But this ability does not presuppose the existence of some mysterious or independent faculty. For Dewey and George Herbert Mead alike, the natural basis of sympathy is the way we acquire a sense of a self as an individual. The self is not given; it emerges out of "taking on the attitude of the other."[6] With proper conditions an individual can also develop the capacity to perceive the needs, interest, hopes, and dreams of others from their own standpoint. It becomes a virtue when it is used with other dispositions in moral inquiry.

Sympathy functions best in moral life when employed as a means in moral deliberation. "The emotion of sympathy is morally invaluable. But it functions properly when used as a principle of reflection and insight rather than of direct action" (LW 7:251). Sympathy is a special kind of sensitivity. Through sympathy we obtain material for moral deliberation that cannot be obtained through other means. To emotionally and imaginatively put oneself in the place of another is the only way to widen our intellectual horizon in moral situations and to determine effectively what ought to be done. It is the most "generous thought . . ." (MW 5:302), as it "widens and deepens concern for consequences" (LW 7:251). On the other hand, "a person of narrow sympathy is of necessity a person of confined outlook upon the scene of human good" (LW 7:270). This widening of experience is not quantitative. Someone who has sympathy, even to a few, may have wider experience than the utilitarian who considers many people as abstract loci of utility.

The rationalist tradition in moral theory has assumed that the avoidance of a distorting partiality in moral deliberation to guarantee considerate and just treatment of others requires the adoption of a universal and objective standpoint provided by moral reason. Both Dewey and recent feminists cannot make sense of an impartial and universal standpoint.[7] However, Dewey holds that the closest we can get to a similar broad intellectual standpoint that might be useful for moral deliberation is with the aid of sympathy. "Sympathy, in short, is the general principle of moral knowledge . . . because it furnishes the most reliable and efficacious *intellectual* standpoint. It supplies the tool, *par excellence,* for analyzing and resolving complex cases . . . sympathy supplies the *pou sto* for an effective, broad, and objective survey of desires, projects, resolves, and deeds" (MW 5:303). The concern implied by a genuine sense of justice cannot be accounted for by the intellectual capacities associated with the impartiality of reason; it also requires sympathy. "A person entirely lacking in sympathetic response might have a keen calculating intellect, but he would have no *spontaneous sense* of the claims of others" (LW 7:270, my emphasis). Failure to treat others beyond one's social group as equals is not a deficiency in the ability to perform a reasoning process from a formal principle of justice, nor is it a result of failing to intellectually and abstractly grasp the respect in which all people are equal. James Tufts argues that it is not a matter of logic:

what we shall set up as our units—whether we shall treat the gentile or the barbarian or negro as a person, as end not merely as means, or not, depends on something quite other than reason. And this other factor is not covered by the term "practical reason."[8]

Although Kant in his ethics expressed a democratic ideal, his intellectualism did not allow him to see that it requires sympathy, not reason alone, to treat others as ends. Tufts continues,

> The defect of his statement is that the rational process as such has never treated and so far as can be foreseen never will treat human beings as ends. To treat a human being as end it is necessary to put oneself into his place in his whole nature and not simply in his universalizing, and legislative aspects.[9]

There is no prima facie reason why humans can be the only objects of sympathy. Although Tufts and Dewey do not address this issue, it is a lack of sympathy, rather than a failure to cognitively acknowledge rights, that may be the reason why many humans fail to treat other animals as ends. A Deweyan ethics, with a more global or ecological scope than Dewey himself acknowledged, would encourage humans today to deliberatively consider other creatures in a sympathetic way and not merely from the point of view of human needs.

Dewey warned us that "when a legal type of morality is current" (LW 7:373), justice is "the working of some fixed and abstract law" (LW 7:373) and is separated from sympathy or care. But justice ceases to be a virtue if it is not fused with sympathy. It is through sympathy that one can appreciate what justice demands because it makes us understand what each person needs in a vivid and more reliable fashion. Hence Dewey claims that "to put ourselves in the place of another, to see things from the standpoint of his aims and values . . . is the surest way to appreciate what justice demands in concrete cases" (LW 7:251).

For Dewey, moral thought that is sympathetic is integral to the considerate and just character. Sympathy "is the surest guarantee for the exercise of consideration, for examination of a proposed line of conduct in all of its bearings. And such complete interest is the only way in which justice can be assured" (LW 7:259).

I should anticipate the important role of sympathy in Dewey's ideal democratic community. He claims that "the political action of citizens of an organized community will not be morally satisfactory unless they have, individually, sympathetic dispositions" (LW 7:300). Sympathy makes possible the kind of moral life and community where the interests, demands, and needs of others are vital and moving realities in one's moral deliberation, rather than abstract variables in a cold utilitarian calculation or in the application of a formal law. When sympathy becomes fused with other virtues, such as openness, it becomes part of the democratic readiness to listen to others and look at things from their point of view whether we agree or not. The morally reasonable person in Dewey's moral vision is not someone who listens to reason, but one who sympathetically listens to others. The ideal moral community is one where agents treat each other as ends in the sense that each has the willingness and imagination to take account of others from the point of view of their needs, desires, and circumstances.

Moral education should aim at developing in students the habits that make them capable of examining for themselves the nature of the practical situations they will face. Foremost is "the formation of a sympathetic imagination for human relations in action; this is the ideal which is substituted for training in moral rules" (EW 4:57). The cultivation of character is not an easy task, for sympathy can only grow out of having certain communal experiences. This is why Dewey thought that the most important kind of moral education in the school is the creation of the conditions for a certain kind of community. He objected to the emphasis in schools on absorption of information and competition because it goes against the required social spirit needed to cultivate the "habits of social imagination" (MW 4:284). The presence of these habits is a prerequisite for any significant moral lessons to be conveyed in the classroom. These lessons "amount to something only in the degree in which pupils happen to be already animated by a sympathetic and dignified regard for the sentiments of others. Without such a regard, it has no more influence on character than the information about the mountains of Asia" (MW 9:364).

I have distinguished sensitivity, conscientiousness, courage, open-mindedness, and sympathy as some of the virtues required in an intelligent, aesthetic, and democratic moral life. But they are not virtues unless they are integrated into a certain unity of character.

The Constituents of Moral Character and Their Function

In his lectures on moral education, Dewey addresses moral development by distinguishing three constituents of character: the intellectual, the affectional-imaginative, and the volitional. Each one plays a different but indispensable active function in an ideal moral character. These functional distinctions help one appreciate how the elements of character that Dewey stressed at different times, including the few virtues I have considered, form part of an integral whole.

THE INTELLECTUAL

Commenting on the intellectual aspects of character, Dewey wrote that "it has been the fortune of this element to suffer from both over-appreciation and extreme depreciation" (MW 6:383). In modern moral philosophy, the intellectual has been overappreciated at the expense of the active and emotional phases simply because experience has been conceived of as a primarily cognitive affair. For Dewey, intellectual habits are tools of reflection needed for general learning and to estimate in particular situations what one ought to do, that is, to reach judgment. In education Dewey stressed that the mere passing down of information or knowledge does not affect character in a way needed to affect good judgment.[10] Judgment is the "power to perceive the bearings of what is known" (MW 6:382), it "is equivalent to valuation, appraisal, estimation" (MW 6:383). To reach judgment one must engage in a process of inquiry. To adequately engage in this process requires all the habits that can make a character critical, experimental, and able to follow the leads of experience wherever they may go. When one develops the disposition to apply these thinking tools to moral experience, it becomes conscientiousness.

The importance of cultivating the more intellectual constituents of our character is that they make possible a relative control of changes based on the relations or grain found in experience. The habits of critical reflection make it possible for us to deliberate over the means to achieve our ends, as well as the ability to assess our ends in light of our means. The disposition to think and judge signifies the ability to reconsider and reshape present habits—that is, to engage in criticism—thereby preventing us from resting on our oars and living an unaesthetic moral life. Dewey explains that "through judging, we get above the mere routine of habit; through judging, we get above being mere imitators, copiers, and followers of others; through judging we get above caprice, above random activity" (LW 17:338).

THE EXECUTIVE

For Dewey, the executive is not like the will, that is, a faculty that moves the self into action after deliberation. If the self is an agent in process (and not a spectator), then the will developed in our character cannot simply be the capacity to initiate activity out of a state of inactivity. For Dewey, we are always doing something and the only meaningful question is how we are doing it: are we aggressive? Assertive? Willing to go as far as we can? Willing to experiment or disposed to become inhibited in the face of risk?

In general, what is designated as the executive in experience has to do with how to sustain and control both support and resistances from the environment. In moral life we find that things happen that are congenial with our wishes and others happen that are not. The disagreeable—pain, hardship, obstacles, resistance—tends to inhibit conduct, thus highlighting the importance of courage. The agreeable, on the other hand, might sway us and make us overindulge at the expense of other impulses and possibilities. Hence the importance of self-control or temperance.

Dewey is opposed to the conception of temperance that supports a negative view of morality, namely, a morality that is focused on restraining all impulse and passion because they are the source of wrongdoing. Neither is he in favor of training the moral will in the Kantian sense of a self-disciplined inhibition of tendencies and inclinations so that we can follow abstract duty. Dewey thinks that the only effective self-control is based on more, not fewer, passions and on positive goals. The alternative to asceticism and random indulgence is a particular relation between habits and desires in a character. This will become clear when I later consider the notion of a balanced-holistic character.

Moral life requires the development of the executive habits needed to work out things for ourselves and to face responsibility in the face of obstacles. These include initiative, self-control, courage, and efficiency. These are habits that enable us to direct changes and confront their consequences in experience. As Dewey understands it, the commonsense idea that if one means well, then one is morally excused is only true if one has gone as far as one can in execution. But a good will is often faced with resistance, unfavorable conditions, and the possibility of failure. Hence the importance of persistence and courage. As Dewey says, "the chief ally of moral thoughtfulness is the resolute courage of willingness to face evil for the sake of the good" (MW 5:379).

With respect to moral education teachers have the difficult task of cultivating "habits of efficient action so that the person won't be a mere day-dreamer or theorist, or a wasteful or incompetent person, but to get that unity with certain affections, and desires and sympathies and with power to carry on intellectual plans" (LW 17:82). An educational system that appeals merely to the absorption of information encourages worthless passivity. The ideal is a "character which is not satisfied with being simply a spectator, or passive absorber, but that strives earnestly to put right intention and good desire into actual and concrete effect" (MW 6:388).

THE AFFECTIVE AND IMAGINATIVE

The affective and imaginative are the areas of moral experience that have been most devalued and neglected in traditional Western ethics. Dewey would have agreed with many of today's feminist writers in ethics who are reclaiming for the affective and imaginative their proper place in our moral life.[11] The affective is central to an adequate account of moral inquiry and of a good moral character. This is evident in the previous account of sensitivity, openness, and sympathetic imagination as modes of direct and emotional undergoing in experience. These dispositions underlie the function of the affective in providing the necessary qualitative material in inquiry.

The dualism between reason and the emotional or the imaginative, as well as a narrow view of the latter, have led to views in moral education and ethics that take emotion and impulse as sources of vices because they do not allow us to "look far enough ahead" (MW 14:137). But for Dewey, blindness and narrowness result from a lack of the affective and imaginative. To have an affective relation with someone or some situation signifies access and sensitivity to a landscape that would not be available otherwise. Dewey explains,

> We cannot know the varied elements of value in the lives of others and in the possibilities of our own save as our affections are strong. Every narrowing of love, every encroachment of egoism, means just so much blindness to the good. (MW 5:379)

The emotional aspects of experience are always the result of a transaction between the organism and the environment. Emotional appreciation is about something that in a situation is experienced as having certain qualities. Our sensory reactions are not the only means or access to knowledge of the world, and they are not even essential to our acquaintance with and knowledge of persons. Instead, our "emotional reactions form the chief materials of our knowledge of ourselves and of others. Just as ideas of physical objects are constituted out of sensory material, so those of persons are framed out of emotional and affectional materials. The latter are as direct, as immediate as the former, and more interesting" (LW 7:269–270).

But the role of the affective in Dewey's ethics is not limited to providing the initial data for moral deliberation. The affective pervades and guides the entire process of deliberation. Recall that this process relies on making qualitative judgments, rather than on making deductive inferences from moral axioms or on calculating future pleasures and pains.

> Any actual experience of reflection upon conduct will show that every foreseen result at once stirs our present affections. . . . There is developed a running commentary which stamps objects at once as good or evil. It is this direct sense of value, not the consciousness of general rules or ultimate goals, which finally determines the worth of the act to the agent. (LW 7:275)

Good moral deliberation is one that comes from a good character, and a good character is one that even in imagination responds with the "right emotional stamp" (MW 5:255).

What Dewey admired in Greek philosophers is how they stressed "direct emotional susceptibility to values presented in experience," and how aesthetic qualities, like rhythm, grace, and balance, were considered the "chief instruments" to "create a direct feeling of the beauty of the good" (MW 6:386). All this is lost in most modern educational practices and theories.

> The modern mind has been much less sensitive to aesthetic values in general and to these values in conduct in particular. Much has been lost in direct responsiveness to right. The bleakness and harshness often associated with morals is a sign of this loss. (LW 7:271)

The neglect of the aesthetic and affective factors ("direct sensitiveness") in American education is "the greatest deficiency in our educational systems with respect to character building" (MW 6:386).

Dewey also believed that imagination had been underappreciated in moral education. It is usually identified with the fanciful and imaginary, but when properly understood, it can be the capacity to experience the reality of possibilities present in a situation. Hence, "imagination supplements and deepens observation" (MW 6:356). It makes possible the "warm and intimate taking in of the full scope of a situation" (MW 9:244).

> The imaginative is not necessarily the imaginary; that is, the unreal. The proper function of imagination is vision of realities and possibilities that cannot be exhibited under existing conditions of sense-perception. Clear insight into the remote, the absent, the obscure is its aim. (MW 6:355)

A good imagination is required for moral deliberation. This is how we can try out the implications and consequences of an act in order to determine its moral worth. Moreover, to be able to reach beyond one's narrow view of things and understand others through sympathetic communication requires imagination, rather than the mere manipulation of information. Without the development of our imaginative capacities deliberation is reduced to calculation and a drudgery-filled task. "The imagination is the medium of appreciation in every field. The engagement of the imagination is the only thing that makes any activity more than mechanical" (MW 9:244).

The functional classification into constituents of character allows us to formulate the following thesis found in Dewey: the ideal state is for these constituents to be in a certain organic relation to one another and as parts of character in an integral whole. It is only then that the virtues we have distinguished can in fact function as virtues.

The Balanced Holistic Character

Dewey's organic view of character lets him evaluate character in terms of how its constitutive parts relate to each other. The key relation is one of balance and it is instructive to contrast this ideal with views that have assumed otherwise. For example, a notion of rationality that recommends putting aside affective aspects of our experiences to achieve objectivity suggests discrimination, isolation, and exclusiveness. For Dewey, these attitudes can only suggest irrationality, or a very unconstructive kind of repression of indispensable parts of our experience as moral agents. Rationality has more to do with the attitudes of generosity and inclusiveness; it is the result of an interactive process among the plural demands and aspects of experience where a relation of mutual reinforcement is achieved.[12]

Views of rationality that emphasize objectivity and impartiality assume that the rational agent is a detached spectator, wary of any type of emotional involvement. Pragmatists, on the other hand, recognize the importance and need of both detachment and involvement, of both reflection and emotional sensitivity and commitment. To those who emphasize "bloodless reason" Dewey responds that too much reflection can also be a vice. It is true that a strong passion can sometimes make us unreasonable. We are so absorbed that we allow no room for alternatives and we are not sensitive to the complexity of the situation. However,

> the conclusion is not that the emotional, passionate phase of action can be or should be eliminated in behalf of a bloodless reason. *More "passions,"* not fewer, is the answer. To check the influence of hate there must

be sympathy, while to rationalize sympathy there are needed emotions of curiosity, caution. (MW 14:136, my emphasis)

It is easy to react to narrow views of the rational moral agent by overemphasizing the role of the affective and imaginative. But this is equally mistaken and dangerous. Views that express a tyranny of the intellectual over the emotional (or vice versa) usually assume a dualism or atomism between elements of our character. We can only avoid falling into extreme views if we entertain an organic-interactive conception of character. Under this conception the fundamental concrete unit is the whole character, and the traits that we can discriminate in such a whole are not self-sufficient, isolated compartments.

On this model any trait or power of character—no matter how important or central to moral life—can become a vice if it is not checked, informed, or fused with other dimensions of our character. When conscientiousness is cultivated in isolation it becomes a "morbid anxiety about the state of one's virtue" (LW 7:116). When justice is not pursued in concert with other virtues it turns into something mechanical, quantitative, impersonal, and harsh. Sympathy is only protected from sentimentality and other evils if it is fused with other dispositions—for example, openness and thoughtfulness—that give it the proper perception of conditions and possibilities. However, it is equally important to note the transforming and protective effect that affective-sympathetic powers have on other dispositions. In this regard Dewey says that they influence other attitudes and interests in such a way as to transform them "into a single and moral interest," for it gives them "social quality and direction" (MW 5:272–273).

Dewey would welcome the emphasis that many feminists put on sympathy and care. Care that is rightly fused with other traits of character does not fall into the kind of harmful care that stultifies the growth of those being cared for. What we must make room for in morality is not just altruistic emotions but the organic interaction between them and other virtues of character, that is, a balanced character that achieves an active "union of benevolent impulse and intelligent reflection" (LW 7:298).

The cultivation of a balanced character is consistent with, expands, and adds content to the very general claims I have made so far regarding the ideal moral life. The balanced character signifies the "full participation of *all* our powers in the endeavor to wrest from each situation of experience its own full and unique meaning" (LW 10:273, my emphasis). Balance among the virtues and constituents I have distinguished is needed to live an aesthetic, educative, and meaningful moral life. It is not enough to have good habits such as conscientiousness, openness, and sympathy, or to try to cultivate them in isolation. Only when there is a balanced relation among them do we have a good chance to save our moral life from both drudgery and aimlessness. Excesses and deficiencies of any of them usually restrict the capacity of a character to learn from experience. It is not easy to avoid excesses or one-sidedness in our character especially when our contemporary ways of living encourage compartmentalization, specialization, and fragmentation.

If what Dewey means by intelligence in morals involves such a complex and total integration of all the dimensions of our character, then it is tempting to conclude that he, along with the Greeks, believes that ignorance is vice. Moral ignorance is more a condition of our character than it is a lack of information or true beliefs. Morally ignorant would be the individual who has a lot of information about right and wrong but who lacks moral sensitivity. Dewey was very explicit about this,

> The modern counterpart to the Socratic doctrine that ignorance is the root of vice is that being morally "cold" or "dead," being indifferent to moral distinctions, is the most hopeless of all conditions. One who cares, even if he cares in the wrong way, has at least a spring that may be touched; the one who is just irresponsive offers no leverage for correction or improvement. (MW 5:377)

The ideal character has an emotional responsiveness and capacity to make judgments that is missing in the character who is merely a knower of epistemologically justified moral truths. Dewey explains this difference.

> It is difficult to put the quality into words, but we all know the difference between the character which is somewhat hard and formal, and that which is sympathetic, flexible, and open. In the abstract the former may be as sincerely devoted to moral ideas as the latter, but as a practical matter we prefer to live with the latter, and we count upon it to accomplish more in the end by tact, by instinctive recognition of the claims of others, by skill in adjusting, than the former can accomplish by mere attachment to rules and principles which are intellectually justified. (EW 5:80)

One final observation about the ideal character is in order. There is hardly any reference in Dewey's ethics to many of the dispositions that are usually considered moral virtues in ethics textbooks, for example, honesty, truthfulness, compassion, etc. Instead, one finds a strong and almost exclusive emphasis on the complex array of habits that allow one to sense, explore, and find the right course of action in a situation. To be sure, Dewey does not wish to exclude the usual moral virtues from his account of a good character. They are not emphasized in his texts because he wanted to discourage a certain view about moral character. It is often assumed in moral theory that there is a defined number of virtues that are exclusively moral, such as honesty and truthfulness, and that the habits that allow us to explore situations are only intellectual means and therefore non-moral and external to morality. But this dualism between moral and intellectual virtue is for Dewey unacceptable. The reason why we tend to associate moral virtues with such virtues as honesty and truthfulness is because they play a crucial role in our everyday moral relationships. But, as Dewey said, to treat these virtues as the moral virtues is "taking the skeleton for the living body . . . morals concern nothing less than the whole character" (MW 9:367). Furthermore, to take the virtue of intelligence as a mere external means to a core of moral virtues assumes a primacy and self-sufficiency of the latter not warranted by our moral experience. If one has acquired the habit of honesty, it is because of honest acts. But what counts as an honest act and when or where it is called for requires the context-sensitive reflection provided by the habits that Dewey identifies with intelligence. Without the habits required to sense and figure out what I ought to do in particular moral situations there cannot be the development of morally well-formed characters. This is why they are the most important instrumentalities in moral life. The cardinal virtues are the traits of character that make it possible to determine what morality requires here and now.

Let me summarize my progression up to this point. My presentation of Dewey's ideal began in the previous chapter with a very broad characterization in terms of a way of life. In this chapter I have specified what sort of character is involved and some of the virtues that it requires. But Dewey occasionally expresses his normative vision in terms of a certain kind of self. I now consider that characterization of the self.

The Moral Self as the Morally Interested Agent

Dewey was concerned with the spirit of morality, that is, with how one should be engaged in moral experience. He often spoke about how the virtues I discussed above are integral to a self that has a genuine interest in moral activity. This is not the self that is interested in the sense of expecting an external stimulation, such as pleasure, virtue, or salvation from moral activity. The dependence on external gratification in effect reflects a serious lack of integrity and commitment to morality. As I noted, Dewey thought there is in moral life the possibility of a more intimate relation between the moral self and its acts. He had a different paradigm of a moral agent committed to morality. The moral agent who is aesthetically engaged in present moral reconstruction has a direct personal identification with the conduct that is required of her in a situation. To attend to and try to ameliorate the moral difficulties and demands as they present themselves in a specific situation is the interest of a moral agent qua moral agent. This includes having a concern for good, duty, or virtue. What is not as clear is what makes someone's interest in morality more or less genuine. There is a normative component here that needs to be elucidated.

One mark of genuine interest for Dewey is wholeheartedness, which is one of the "traits which must belong to an attitude if it is to be genuinely an interest" (LW 7:256). The ideal engagement in any activity is a "serious absorption" (MW 9:212) that is expressed in conduct that is wholehearted, integrated, and that "moves by its own urge to fulfillment" (LW 10:46). There is a lack of character in someone who is partial, divided, and lukewarm. Wholeheartedness means that the whole character comes into play, that is, the self can put all of her powers and constituents in a relation of mutual reinforcement in the process of resolving a morally problematic situation. Halfhearted engagement is less than the full transaction required to have an "active and alert commerce with the world" (LW 10:25). Dewey's paradigm of integral involvement in some person or cause is love. In love there is a "totality of interest" (MW 5:363).[13] Wholeheartedness can turn into a vice if it is not checked and balanced by other traits of character. There is such a thing as becoming overly absorbed. Hence the importance of having some of the virtues already mentioned, for example, a willingness to reflect generously and with openness. Balance is the key to keeping the genuine interest in moral reconstruction a virtue.

Dewey distinguishes between two different sorts of cases of genuine interest in any activity. The most direct kind are cases of immediate engrossment where "there is no gap in space nor time between means and end" (EW 5:125). On the other hand, there is indirect or mediated genuine interest. These are cases where an activity that functions as the means is suffused and saturated by the interest we have in the end.[14] These are different from cases of non-genuine interest where the means are experienced as remote, external, and separated from the end, and therefore the moral agent is only mechanically or externally interested in moral action.

That there are cases of genuine mediated interest allows Dewey to affirm that interest in far-reaching ideals can be part of a moral life that has as its locus present experience. A moral self can be wholeheartedly engaged in resolving a morally problematic situation and at the same time care for ideals that transcend the present problem. Where there is a balance between work and play, enthusiasm with wider aims and ideals is integral to the interest in present reconstruction. Again, Dewey takes the artist as the paradigm of genuine interest in an ideal. "When the thought of the end becomes so adequate that it compels translation into the means that embody it, or when attention to the means is inspired by recognition of the end they serve, we have the attitude typical of the artist, an attitude that may be displayed in all activities, even though they are not conventionally designated 'arts'" (LW 8:348).

The above account is vague and does not capture an aspect of the ideal genuine moral interest that is very important to Dewey. It is not enough that the self be wholeheartedly or *aesthetically* engaged in moral reconstruction. The interest of the self must also be authentic in the sense of not being the result of blindly adopting or following a moral tradition. This is why the ideal moral self is also *intelligent* in the sense of having the habits of critical reflection necessary to effect a working connection between what is inherited and what is new. For Dewey, criticism is needed for authentic appreciation and commitment to tradition, otherwise we become mere imitators, followers, or agents who drift. It is through inquiry that one is capable of maintaining the proper spirit of a moral life that has aesthetic quality and is democratic. Individuals who come to appreciate the moral truths of their moral traditions as a result of their own critical inquiries appreciate and identify themselves with these truths in a very different way than those who just collect and repeat them. Moral conduct that is not the outcome of one's moral deliberation lacks the kind of appropriation and interest that comes from engaging in a creative problematic process. But all of this requires a community and an education system that allows and fosters individuals to work out for themselves the solution to morally problematic situations. This is the positive freedom integral to a democratic way of life. I will have more to say about this in the next chapter.

Moral Interest and the Egoism vs. Altruism Debate

Dewey noticed that most discussion about the place of interest in morality usually centers on preoccupation with the issues of egoism and altruism. The shared assumption in this debate is that self-interest and altruism are the only motivations relevant to the issue of moral motivation. This assumption has been questioned by Kantian philosophies that postulate a moral motive beyond our natural interests, that is, morality is about finding and doing the right thing in a *dis*interested manner. The assumptions of modern ethics seem to place us in the following dilemma. It seems as if we cannot preserve the idea that our moral life is emotionally interested and self-affirmative without assuming or being accused of support-ing a morality of self-interest. This is one reason why moral philosophers have shied away from taking a mother's care toward her children as a source of insight about morality.[15] Is the only way to avoid a self-interested model to endorse moral conduct as unemotional, disinterested, and self-denying? Dewey questions the underlying assumptions that lead to such odds results.

First, why should one assume that there is a single motive that deter-mines the boundaries of morality? There are, for instance, situations in which "intense emotional regard for the welfare of others, unbalanced by careful thought, may actually result in harm to others" (LW 7:295). The unwarranted identification of altruism with moral conduct is another unsuccessful attempt to set a fixed criterion for moral conduct. Whether, and to what extent, there should be regard for others or for ourselves is determined by the particular context.

An even more questionable assumption according to Dewey is the idea that we are naturally moved to moral action by any of the motives appealed to in this debate. This assumes a narrow and simplistic view of our experience as interested agents. Both self-love and altruism are ac-quired dispositions. If there is a natural motivation it is that most of the time we are unreflectively and directly interested in activities and things without any reference to our selves or to others. Our native impulses and acts "are not actuated by conscious regard for either one's own good or that of others. They are rather direct responses to situations" (LW 7:293).

Furthermore this more direct or natural interest makes for a better moral life than one in which individuals have to consider in their daily activities whether or not it is for the good of others that they are acting. Dewey says, "the scholar, artist, physician . . . is interested in the work itself; such objective interest is a condition of mental and moral health" (LW 7:297). When there is too much of a deliberate concern to make the good of others or of ourselves the end of our activities these ends be-come extraneous and possible obstacles to the wholehearted engagement needed to find out what a situation morally requires. In any case, Dewey suggests that just as there is a hedonistic paradox there may be an altruistic paradox, that is, "before he can really do good to others, he must stop thinking about the welfare of others; he must see what the situation really calls for and go ahead with that, and the reason is the same in both cases. Whenever one makes his own good or the good of others the end, it becomes an extraneous end."[16]

Dewey diagnoses the contemporary preoccupation with egoism and altruism on different levels. Historically, it reflects a concern of many with the rugged individualism of a capitalist society. Since the everyday trans-actions "taught that each man was actuated by an exclusive regard for its own profit, moralists were led to insist upon the need of some check upon this ruthless individualism, and to accentuate the supremacy of morals (as distinct from business) of sympathy and benevolent regard for others" (LW 7:299). But for Dewey the antidote to the narrow pursuit of profit is not to claim that altruism is the distinct end of all moral conduct. The problem that many business institutions have of subordinating all of their present operations to the one and only goal of maximizing profit is not resolved by setting aside a separate moral goal like benevolence, corporate responsibility, or the good of society. The setting of altruistic fixed quotas that have to be met at the end of the day usually results in an external relation between means and end. When this happens, Dewey writes, it usually

> means that there is no adequate moral criterion within the business itself. It means that it does not carry its own moral standard and justifi-cation with it. At every point you must get away from your business and think about the welfare of other people; and in that outside consider-ation, which is more or less remote and external to the thing you are doing, you must seek for justification and for guidance.[17]

For Dewey, an effective moral transformation of our business institutions requires that community well-being, or any other moral concern, be or-ganically integrated to the everyday operations and deliberations of that industry.

From a philosophical perspective the preoccupation with the egoism vs. altruism issue is a consequence of the same starting point in ethics that created the being vs. doing debate. If the self is a fixed subject, then any object of one's interest is always external to and a mere means for the self, that is, "action is selfish just because it manifests an interest" (LW 7:295). If to this you add a hedonistic conception of the affective that accentu-ates the acquisitive and possessive (as in utilitarianism), then all interest and emotional concern is directly or indirectly *for* the self and therefore amoral or selfish. The same Cartesian starting point that in epistemology leads to the problem about the epistemic states of other knowers, leads in ethics to the problem of accounting for emotional, direct, and genuine in-terest for other things—including other persons—that are outside the self.

If, as Dewey thinks, the self is an agent (relational, interactive, and processional), then all interests are self-centered but only in the sense that they are organically related to a self. For Dewey, interest means "the active or moving identity of the self with a certain object" (MW 9:362). A person can be *directly* interested in whatever may be the object of her interest as an affirmation of what she is. Hence, moral life can be conceived of as emotionally interested and self-affirmative without assuming a morality of self-interest. Those who are moral exemplars of a moral life dedicated to others are as wholeheartedly interested in what they do as those whom we consider selfish. The difference between them lies in what they are interested in, and in the different selves this expresses. "It is absurd to suppose that the difference between the good person and the bad person is that the former has no interest or deep and intimate concern (leading to personal satisfaction) in what he does" (LW 7:296). This posture allows Dewey to avoid the terms of the egoism and altruism debate and instead propose an alternative way to evaluate a self according to whether the self is wide or narrow.

The Wider Self

If "the kind and amount of interest actively taken in a thing reveals and measures the quality of selfhood which exists" (MW 9:361–362), then there are no fixed boundaries to the engaged self; put differently, the self can be extended beyond the traditional boundaries of the body and its mental states. For Dewey, to have our interest and identity limited to these boundaries is to have a narrow self. The only sort of self-centeredness that can be a threat to morality is the unreflective and undue absorption of a narrow and closed self. This is the self that has "a narrow vision of the situation."[18] Dewey explains that "the judgment that a man is selfish means that he ought to be defining himself on the basis of a wider situation, that he ought to be taking into account factors which as a matter of fact he is neglecting."[19] This may lead to wrongdoing. On the other hand, the generous or wider self is the self whose interests, care, and concern are expansive, open, and inclusive. In the present experience of a self there are horizontal edges in moving from one situation to another, just as there are vertical edges that define the extension of the present arena of action. This distinction allows us to discriminate between two different aspects of the wider self. In the horizontal dimension, the wide self is someone interested in continuous readjustment and open to unforeseen and new experiences. This is an accomplishment because the natural tendency is to have an aversion toward the new, unexpected, distant, and unfamiliar. "There is a tendency to identify the self—or take interest—in what one has got used to" (MW 9:362). To fall back on the achieved self is the easy course but results in a failure to face and be nurtured by the recurrent demands and opportunities for growth, learning; in short, it leads to a stagnant and unaesthetic life.

In the vertical dimension, the wide self is one who has a willingness to be faithful, receptive, and concerned with one's relationships "instead of drawing a sharp line between itself and considerations which are excluded as alien or indifferent" (MW 9:362). To be sure, the idea of having interests in others or the good of others is very ambiguous. It can mean an interest in others mediated by an interest in being altruistic (having virtue), achieving the best possible happiness for all, or obeying an altruistic rule. These are very different interests and therefore express different selves. But for Dewey none of these abstract altruisms is as genuine and as effective for moral life as the moral care or interest expressed when there is a self that has a "direct interest in the welfare of others for their own sake" (MW 5:267). Dewey anticipated contemporary feminists in taking direct care as the paradigmatic example of the kind of direct interest characteristic of a healthy and growing moral life. This is not another ethical theory that emphasizes benevolence. For Dewey, benevolence becomes a deliberate conscious aim only in situations where it is not at work in the everyday direct relationships among people, for example, in caring relationships within the family and among friends. An adequate moral life is not lived by making some kind of happy compromise between concern for ourselves and an abstract concern for others. These are really secondary to a direct personal interest in particular others and the relationships one shares with them.

How far are we capable of extending our selves beyond our immediate and intimate relationships? Does the ideal of the wider self entail that the wider our concern the better, regardless of how weak are the connections one establishes? Dewey recognizes that our interest in others varies depending on the intimacy of the relationship. Hence "it would be mere pretense to suppose that one can be as much interested in those at a distance with whom one has little contact as in those in whom one is in constant communication" (LW 7:257). Moreover, Dewey claims that the strength and intimacy of our relationships is as important as how inclusive our concern is or how many relationships we have. The extent (scope) of our relations and their depth (strength) are two distinguishable but equally important factors that determine the quality of one's present experience. "An activity has meaning in the degree in which it establishes and acknowledges *variety* and *intimacy* of connections" (MW 14:202, my emphasis). This is why Dewey stresses in moral education the importance of fostering the conditions for widening and *deepening* the experience of children. The deepening and expansion of one's relationships can be conflicting goals. The self that overreaches takes the risk of sacrificing depth in her relationships. For Dewey, the ideal moral self can strike a balance. Strong ties in our close relationships, as well as extending our interest beyond them by means of habits of social imagination (including sympathy and openness), are necessary in order to have a wide, rich, and meaningful landscape upon which to inquire and act.

The self lives through and by social relations. This has significant implications for how an ethics should formulate its normative prescriptions and hypotheses. An account of Dewey's ideal character would be incomplete if it left out the kind of relationship and community it assumes. Dewey's ideal character has to be envisioned in the context of an ideal net of interactions that Dewey qualified as democratic. Hence, the appeal to communication, community, and even way of life is necessary for a fuller picture of Dewey's view.

TWELVE

Democracy as the Ideal Moral Community

> The deepest source of happiness in life comes to one, I suppose, from one's own family relations; and there too, though I have experienced great sorrows, I can truly say that in my life companion, in my children, and in my grandchildren, I have been blessed by the circumstances and fortunes of life.[1]

No formulation of Dewey's ideal moral life is complete without addressing his views about democracy. Moreover, his views about democracy are incomplete and subject to misunderstanding, oversimplification, and underappreciation without an adequate understanding of his ethical thought. I plan here to bring Dewey's ethical thought to bear on his views about democracy.

One could characterize the ideal moral community as one in which people have the type of character that I presented in the last chapter. This would be true but insufficient, and perhaps misleading. It could suggest that the notion of a community is the sum of individuals prior to their associations. For Dewey, the quality of our character, and the quality of our associations, may be distinguished but they cannot be separated.

Dewey's concern with character is thus a means and end to the task of enriching the quality of associations, and both are integral to the more inclusive goal of ameliorating the quality of present experience. Whereas in the previous chapter I articulated some of the traits of character needed for an ideal moral community, in this chapter I am concerned with the kind of community and communication that is required for an ideal character to flourish.

Democracy as Experience

It is well known that Dewey objected to the customary but narrow view of democracy as a political mechanism, and preferred that we shift our attention to democracy as a way of life or as a form of moral association. But what does this shift really mean? Most commentators are content to add a moral dimension to Dewey's ideal, but ignore the importance of experience, and in particular, his views of moral experience. My claim is that if one takes Dewey's views on democracy as integral to his ethical thought, then one has to attribute to him a more radical and richer view of democracy than is usually done.

The impoverished quality of present moral experience was the underlying concern behind Dewey's democratic vision. This is the context that gives Dewey's ideal its plausibility and function. In fact, the relevance of Dewey's ideal today can be attributed to the fact that our society still suffers from the same generic ailments that prevent us from having a better quality of shared experience. When Dewey is read today he sounds prophetic, for he mentions fragmentation, a lack of unity and variety, a heterogeneity that leads to isolation, a homogeneity that stifles, polarization, absolutism, drudgery, relativism, drifting, suppression, consumerism, triviality, superficiality, blind impulse, and impersonality as present threats to the spirit of democracy. Dewey was a philosopher concerned more with the problems of a society that is democratic in form, but not in spirit, rather than with the theoretical problems of democratic theory.

A complete diagnosis of why the current ways of living, even in a society that calls itself democratic, are unfulfilling must be pursued on many fronts. Dewey addressed multiple fronts, including the economic, sociological, and political dimensions of the problems of his era. He warned us that the hope of a democratic culture could be corrupted by a growing money culture that subordinates the quality of the present process of living to some future quantifiable product or end. This is a culture in which the emphasized value is market value, the only freedom it procures is an economic one, and the only virtues it encourages are those associated with financial entrepreneurship and competition. Dewey was also concerned about how rapid changes in technology and the means of communication threatened traditional beliefs and strained the quality of our everyday interactions with each other. "Changes in domestic, economic, and political relations have brought about a serious loosening of the social ties which hold people together in definite and readily recognizable relations" (LW 7:233).

Dewey's discontent with present conditions did not lead him to a simplistic diagnosis of a truly complex array of interrelated problems. His role as a philosopher was instead to criticize the dualisms that continue to affect the ways we approach these problems and the narrow notions of democracy that do not allow us to envision better possibilities.

In this problematic social environment, the notion of democracy as a mere political mechanism that safeguards individual rights, or as a system of open and inclusive elections, seems inadequate because it fails to address how the impoverished character of our experience is tied to our everyday interactions. Improvement of the political machinery and protection of constitutional rights are good things, but how do they reconstruct the ties that have been strained by contemporary conditions? Why does aimless obedience to custom, force, or propaganda predominate in some political democracies? In other words, democracy, conceived strictly as a political system, is compatible with an unaesthetic and unintelligent way of life in which there are no strong communal bonds and the people are not really free to lead their own lives. The generic ailments of a society that considers itself democratic in form, but which still lacks a democratic spirit, are more telling of a deeper meaning of democracy.

The presence in democratic societies of detached and lonely individuals, and whole groups that conform to the mob spirit, are not for Dewey evidence against democracy. Instead, they are the reason why we must reconstruct the ideal of democracy. Legal and formal guarantees of freedom and equality for isolated individuals do not guarantee a more democratic experience. A philosophy of democracy must also turn its attention to habit, character, interaction, communication, and the qualitative dimension of situations. It must take as its starting and end points the present lived process and the struggle for democracy. Democracy as experience means that the primary and ultimate test of democracy as an ideal is the amelioration of presently experienced problems. It also means that democracy strives to have certain enriching and meaningful experiences. Democracy must be conceived as a complex array of transactions where each individual has a high quality of shared experiences; where, for instance, others are spontaneously and directly experienced in a certain way.

The tendency toward extremes of a society that wants to be democratic is not, from Dewey's standpoint, surprising. It is rooted in tensions present in the very nature of experience. Democracy is, for Dewey, partially a proposal about how to deal with these tensions. It is about how to preserve order, unity, and stability while recognizing uncertainty, change, individuality, and pluralism. This is not just the challenge of democracy, but also the challenge of how to live in a world with those generic traits; in other words, when democracy is understood in the context of Dewey's ethics, it becomes an answer to the perennial issue of how one should live. Recall how Dewey redefined this issue. Although the quality of present experience is not totally within our control, how we engage life usually is. The uniqueness of situations precludes universalism and situation-specific prescriptions by philosophers, although one can inquire into better and worse general methods. Hence, democracy as an ideal is not a blueprint of the good life, or a set of norms (e.g., for an ideal communication), but it is a set of instrumental proposals about how to engage in life in light of its generic traits. To be sure, democracy is an ideal about how best to elect a government. However, to appreciate the deeper possibilities of democracy, we must extend its meaning to include how to make collective decisions, how to treat and experience others, how to communicate, how to confront problems and disagreement, how groups must interact, how to engage in rituals, and how to attend to experience in general.

Dewey's ideal of democracy thickens the general description of the ideal way of participating in experience that I have been discussing, one that is intelligent and aesthetic. It is a task or process that requires the creative integration in a community of opposing tendencies, traits, and general values that are hard to maintain in a balance. To demonstrate this, I will consider the specific interactions that are essential to democracy and, whenever possible, highlight the particular tensions that must be balanced and the particular extremes to which it is susceptible. Dewey's conception of balance is critical to understanding his democratic vision.

Democracy as the Balance between Individuality and Interdependence

Democracy is based upon the possibility that the values associated with individuality can coexist in a tensile balance with those associated with community. This tension is part of the very nature of things. In all of experience, tendencies toward solidarity coexist with tendencies toward differentiation. "Human nature, like other forms of life, tends to differentiation, and this moves in the direction of the distinctively individual, . . . it also tends toward combination, association" (LW 13:77–78). Let's consider the specific values on each side of this tension beginning with those associated with individuality.

POSITIVE FREEDOM

In the ideal democratic community there is an environment of free thought, information, and discussion. It is free insofar as everyone is not prevented from participating and expressing themselves. This freedom from interference, or "negative freedom"[2] as it is called, rules out censorship, suppression, or any type of restraint by an external authority or privileged minority. Although this freedom is necessary, it is not sufficient for a democracy. Dewey criticizes traditional liberalism for assuming only this narrow view of freedom, and he provides a historical and a metaphysical diagnosis of this mistake.

Historically, it is understandable how liberty became synonymous with the absence of restriction at a time when the elimination of the repressive external force of government on individuals and societies was paramount. Metaphysically, the narrow view of freedom rested on an erroneous conception of the individual. Philosophical defenders of liberalism assume that individuals come to the world atomistically and already endowed with positive capacities "which then proceeds to unroll as a ball of yarn may be unwound" (LW 14:103). On this view, all that is required to actualize individual freedom is the removal of external obstacles for the unwinding to occur and the protection of the individual from the demands of association. In Dewey's metaphysics, nothing has inherent potentialities independent of its context and relation with other things. The development of potentialities is not an unfolding of what previously existed; they are rather called out through interaction and cannot be known beforehand. Therefore, association, far from being a threat to individual freedom, is its very condition. Some forms of association are educative and empowering to individuals, others are not. Positive freedom is the capacity of an individual to carry out a course of action; it is accomplished by creating certain habits in a particular social environment, but it is not something with which we are born.

Negative liberty is a precondition for positive freedom. External constraints that do not let individuals work out for themselves the solutions to problematic situations are not conducive to adequate habit formation and empowerment. But merely leaving one alone is not sufficient to produce individuals in a community who are capable of self-government, or at least not the sort implied by the notion that truly democratic individuals exercise individual responsibility, initiative, and independence of judgment. Democracy requires the creation of the conditions that nurture individuals who are equipped with the executive and intellectual habits I discussed in the previous chapter. It requires, for example, citizens with the habits of critical intelligence as the means to self-government. What good is my negative freedom to do and consume when I am unable to intelligently reflect and choose? Democracy requires more than the capacity to go to the mall and choose between varieties of goods.

The distinction between negative and positive freedom has more potency, and is closer to Dewey's intent, when it is understood in terms of the quality of public discourse in a democracy. As he said, "the conceptions and shibboleths which are traditionally associated with the idea of democracy take on veridical and directive meaning only when they are construed as marks and traits of an association which realizes the defining characteristics of a community" (LW 2:329).

When one compares democratic and authoritarian methods, one might characterize the difference as one between discussion and violent imposition of views. Dewey insisted that we need to think of democracy as more than free, untrammeled discussion. "I would not minimize the advance scored in substitution of methods of discussion and conference for the method of arbitrary rule. But the better is too often the enemy of the still better" (LW 11:50). Communication where there is positive freedom and learning is better than one that functions merely as a "safety valve" (LW 7:361) where everyone can talk but no one is listening. For Dewey, mere communication is insufficient, and nothing less than intelligent discussion by individuals with positive freedom should be our ideal.

Dewey was concerned about the consequences of limiting the conception of democratic communication to mere negative freedom of speech largely because of the growth of unprecedented forces of technology, propaganda, and commercialism. A community without censorship may still be controlled by a few who can rely on propaganda and entertainment to pacify the public.

> We seem to be approaching a state of government by hired promoters of opinion called publicity agents. But the more serious enemy is deeply concealed in hidden entrenchments. Emotional habituations and intellectual habitudes on the part of the mass of men create the conditions of which the exploiters of sentiment and opinion only take advantage. (LW 2:341)

This problem is not resolved simply by getting rid of the few that control opinion. A useful way to understand this condition today is by contrasting Orwell's prophecy with that of Huxley. Those who champion negative freedom for a democracy may be content with the fact that there is no Big Brother in the form of a government, corporation, or group that controls the minds of the people through the primary means of communication. In contrast, Huxley envisions a society without Big Brother yet which is nevertheless impotent to direct its own destiny because an insatiable appetite for amusement and consumerism enslaves it. There are many who believe that Huxley's dystopia is much like our situation in America today. Neil Postman in *Amusing Ourselves to Death,* and Ronald Collins and David Skover in *The Death of Discourse* have argued that the quality of public discourse has deteriorated because of our highly consumerist, television-centered culture. In a Deweyan fashion they attribute the problem partly to a constricted understanding of the freedoms protected by the First Amendment. Collins and Skover conclude that

> triumphantly, America has survived 1984 and is less fearful of Orwell's dark determinism. But our Orwellian perspective hinders us from focusing on an equally menacing and more realistic threat to the First Amendment—the evil identified in Aldous Huxley's *Brave New World.*[3]

Dewey anticipated the Huxleyan evil, and diagnosed the problem in terms of positive freedom and inquiry in public discourse. For him, communication does not become public, democratic, or even discursive merely by releasing the powers that may control it, or by allowing maximum freedom of expression. What good is a society where everyone is allowed to speak but no one is listening and genuinely learning from each other? As Cornel West has recently claimed, "The major problem [today] is not the vociferous shouting from one camp to the other; rather it is that many have given up even being heard."[4] What good is a society where no one is prevented from participating, but where no one bothers to, where one can be a citizen, but no one cares to be? Can the public govern itself, or even have a sense of its own identity, if everyone only cares about the freedom to consume? From a Deweyan perspective it is disturbing that we continue to associate democracy with negative freedom provided by our means of communication. This problem is clear in discussions about cyberspace as the new hope for democracy. This hope seems justified when it is compared to television as a public medium. However, this may be one of those cases where "the better is . . . the enemy of the still better" (LW 11:50). I am afraid that most of the hope, enthusiasm, and defenses of this medium are based on a narrow view of democracy. Jon Katz, for example, says, the online world is the *freest* community in American life. Its members can do things considered unacceptable elsewhere in our culture. They can curse freely, challenge the existence of god, explore their sexuality nearly at will, talk to radical thinkers from all over the world. They can even commit verbal treason.[5]

There is no doubt that the Internet, as a technology, has facilitated negative freedom. The fact that we now have a medium by which it is possible to have instant, unfiltered information and communication while avoiding Big Brother would be celebrated by Dewey as a step in the democratic direction. But if cyberspace is to become a democratic space, or a tool for democratic citizenship, it must become a lot more than a place where free information is exchanged. Without this Deweyan criticism of our new means of communication we may fall into the sort of complacency that Dewey thought was endemic to democratic progress.

Rights-based views of democracy assume that freedom is an end-in-itself, something that is valuable and to which one is inherently entitled. For Dewey, freedom is a means as well as an end. It is one of the necessary conditions for the sort of meaningful engagement that we should strive for in a democracy. It is only when you have a certain amount of freedom that there can be genuine learning, enrichment, and responsibility. Legal and formal guarantees of freedom by institutions amount to nothing if in the everyday classroom and workplace, rules are imposed on individuals that constrain their creativity and interest in participating.

EQUALITY

There are quantitative and legalistic notions of equality that Dewey criticizes as formal or narrow. They are a consequence of the same assumptions made by visions of democracy centered only on negative freedom. If a community was composed of atomistic individuals, each with inherent potentialities requiring the same obstruction-free conditions for development, then equality of opportunity would only require the removal of these same external conditions. On this view, equality also means that at the very core of every self, in spite of our differences, we are all made up of the same substance. For utilitarians and for those who hold views that center on human rights as an original possession, equality means sameness. Historically, these views are reactions to aristocratic ones that claimed that some individuals are inherently superior to others. In Dewey's alternative view, equality negates fixed hierarchical inequalities while maintaining the reality of irreducible differences among actual individuals.

Dewey's understanding of equality is based on the uniqueness of each person and means that every one in a community can appreciate every other one beyond a comparative and quantitative scale–type judgment. So understood, equality does not mean that beyond our classifications and plurality of identities everyone is alike. Instead, it means that beyond them there is something irreducible and incommensurable about everyone. Equality means "effective regard for whatever is distinctive and unique in each, irrespective of physical and psychological inequalities" (MW 12:329–30). And further: "Moral equality means incommensurability, the inapplicability of common and quantitative standards" (MW 13:299).

A community with Dewey's ideal of equality does not homogenize, since it takes differences as unavoidable and irreducible. Diversity is celebrated not just at the level of social groups but at the level of individuals. Pluralism in Dewey goes all the way down. This appreciation of individuality is a social good. It tends to improve the quality of communications and relationships. Equality is more than an empty slogan when it operates as the assumption that no one has an inherent privilege in communication or can be reduced to the group, class, or culture he or she represents. Each participant has something unique to contribute and to gain from participation. William James and John Dewey hoped that the denial of a privileged universal standpoint by anyone would lead to an appreciation of the particular and unique location each of us inhabits in experience. James said: "Hands off: neither the whole of truth nor the whole of good is revealed to any single observer, although each observer gains a partial superiority of insight from the peculiar position in which he stands. Even prisons and sick-rooms have their special revelations."[6] And equality as uniqueness must not only be recognized, it must be fostered. A community nurtures its own means of improvement when it makes it possible for everyone to develop their own unique voice. This is more than allowing everyone to speak.

The shift from democracy as a political system to democracy as experience means that there is more to equality than legal and institutional guarantees. It has to go beyond judging others according to some impartial standard. Equality is an abstract name for something that can be qualitatively and directly experienced in our relations with others. We must appreciate others as individuals who have grown out of unique conditions and transactions, and also as having unique possibilities for future growth and development. Democratic respect is not only about how we treat others (a doing) but also about how we experience them (an undergoing). It is, in effect, the most generous experience we can have of others. In our deliberations and judgments of others we must be as sensitive as possible to their unique circumstances. This is the key to democratic generosity.

Traditional liberalism assumes that individuals can be "split up into a number of isolated and independent powers, all of which can be compared, one by one, with like powers of others so as to determine their equality" (LW 7:335). But this abstraction neglects the context of concrete individuals. We cannot really determine what is due to someone, and whether her freedom is furthered or interfered with, unless we consider the wholeness and uniqueness of her character, environment, and relations with others. Dewey does not deny that, to some extent, we all share the same general and minimal conditions for individual development (e.g., a minimal education), but he stressed that these conditions may change and, more importantly, inquiry about this issue must be as sensitive as possible to the uniqueness and wholeness of each individual. This sensitivity is the more fundamental meaning of equality for Dewey, and it is part of the general sensitivity to context of his ethics.

Is this understanding of equality not a very difficult requirement for us to live up to, even if we wanted to? Some of the apparent unreasonableness of this demand may disappear if we think of this requirement in terms of degrees, instead of an all-or-nothing affair. An ideal is, after all, "the tendency and movement of some thing which exists carried to its final limit" (LW 2:328). In many situations, it may be practically impossible to consider everyone in the context of their unique circumstances, but this does not mean that we must not try, nor that we should instead rely on some quantitative notion of equality. To resort, for example, to a utilitarian calculation, where everyone is in some abstract sense the same, is to betray the spirit of democracy.

The foundations of democratic respect are, for Dewey, a certain way of experiencing *everything*, not an exclusive and abstract regard for human rights or justice that is independent of nature. For the truly democratic character, "every existence deserving the name of existence has something unique and irreplaceable about it" (MW 11:51). Since each "speaks for itself and demands consideration on its own behalf" it "must be reckoned with on its own account" (MW 11:52). This is the sort of natural piety that Dewey hoped for as a consequence of abolishing hierarchical ways of looking at the world. Instead, philosophy has replaced these hierarchical views with democratic visions that rest on an atomistic individualism that absolutizes every human individual as having rights, and that set humans apart from other animals in nature. Needless to say, Dewey's vision points to an ecological democracy with consequences for environmental ethics.[7]

This general sensitivity to individuality that Dewey thought ideal has to be contrasted with the customary way we experience the world. Our habitual ways of experiencing and judging individuals in our society is "not as individuals but as creatures of a class" (MW 13:295). Uniqueness is a trait of experience, a fact often overlooked by us in our eagerness and practical need to classify, label, and quantify the world. Many of us live in cities where the kind of superficial undergoing we have of others is recognition rather than perception. Dewey explains the difference:

> In recognition there is a beginning of an act of perception. But this beginning is not allowed to serve the development of a full perception of the thing recognized. It is arrested at the point where it will serve some other purpose, as we recognize a man on the street in order to greet or avoid him, not as to see him for the sake of seeing what is there. In recognition we fall back, as upon a stereotype, upon some previously formed scheme. Some detail or arrangement of details serves as cue for bare identification. (LW 10:58–59)

When most of our day is consumed in routine and mechanical relations, and when even the most intimate of our relations is taken for granted, there is the sort of stable comfort—a lack of tension—that does not arouse a vivid consciousness of the other. But when perception replaces recognition, we experience others in a pregnant sense. Dewey said, "even a dog that barks and wags his tail joyously on seeing his master return is more fully alive in his reception of his friend than is a human being who is content with mere recognition" (LW 10:59). Perception, just as openness, is an active receptivity that makes a significant difference in the quality of our relationships. The point of these distinctions is that there are degrees in the quality of our transactions that affect how we judge and listen to others. A deeper, fuller receptivity of the other may also require the sensitivity Dewey called sympathy, an ability to assume, and not merely infer, the standpoint of the other. As a political system, democracy does not address the issue of how we should experience each other. And legal guarantees of equality, however important and necessary, are no substitute for equality as something that is spontaneously felt in a particular social environment.

FRATERNITY

James Gouinlock is not exaggerating when he makes the following claim about Dewey: "It would be hard to find a philosopher (I think, in fact, that there is none) who identified a more profound value in the experience of intimately associated life."[8] This may lead some today to label Dewey a communitarian, but that word fails to capture the uniqueness of his vision. In particular, it misses the importance of what is local and direct in Dewey's political philosophy. One consequence of an empirical philosophy—one that begins and ends in primary experience—is that "the local is the ultimate universal, and as near an absolute as exists" (LW 2:369). It is the quality of the most direct and intimate interactions that is the key to democracy.

> I am inclined to believe that the heart and final guarantee of democracy is in free gatherings of neighbors on the street corner . . . , and in gatherings of friends in the living rooms of houses and apartments. (LW 14:227)

This is advice on method and a warning against taking community too broadly and abstractly. It is a warning against taking the usual abstractions about democratic society as antecedent to the unique, direct, and qualitative relations people hold with each other in situations. It would be more accurate to say that a democratic society is one that is composed of democratic associations than to say that a democratic association is one that exists because of a democratic society. "Democracy is a form of government only because it is a form of moral and spiritual association" (EW 1:240). Therefore, pragmatist ethics and politics, rather than being communitarian, are interactionary or based on an ethics of democratic relationships.

Local relationships are both the means and the end of democracy. They are the means by which the democratic character is formed. The ideal is to have characters competent to participate in the comprehension and intelligent control of indirect consequences of the larger society. But this competence can only be developed in the context of a local community. It is also through local and personal ties that our sense of duty and loyalty emerge. Dewey attributes contemporary moral laxity to the loosening of these ties rather than to a failure to adhere to absolutes. "In countless ways the customary loyalties that once held men together and made them aware of their reciprocal obligations have been sapped" (LW 7:234). The truth of this diagnosis demands that any solution involves a revitalization of our relationships. We live in an individualistic society where individuals are generally more ready to claim their rights than to acknowledge their obligations. Instead of pretending to ameliorate the problem by appealing to the direct inculcation of abstract moral rules and virtues, or a universal sense of duty, Dewey suggests that we find ways to "develop new stable relationships in society out of which duties and loyalties will naturally grow" (LW 7:234).

Dewey pleaded for the revitalization of local associations as a condition for the "Great Community" (LW 2:327). Does this mean that he conceived of local communities as a means to a great one? Furthermore, how can society on a mass scale ever be a community in any meaningful sense of the word? The United States, for instance, is simply too big and diverse to create the sort of community that Dewey hoped for. What is possible on a small scale may not be on a larger one. These are important challenges, but they misconstrue what Dewey meant.

Dewey was keenly aware of the limitations posed by size and distance in relationships. He said, "The Great Community, in the sense of free and full communication, is conceivable. But it can never possess all the qualities that mark a local community. . . . Vital and thorough attachments are bred only in the intimacy of an intercourse which is of necessity restricted in range" (LW 2:367). Nevertheless, he believed that we are capable of extending our selves beyond our immediate and intimate relationships, as in his notion of the wider self, but he never addressed the issue of how far. But is this a problem for his view? Why must he specify in advance how far the precious qualities found in the local can be extended beyond its boundaries? Why is it not sufficient to say that we must extend ourselves as far as we possibly can?

Even if Dewey's Great Community is only conceivable, this is hardly an excuse for failing to try to extend to whatever degree possible at least a generic sense of "we", that is, of social unity or communal experience. Indeed, this seems necessary to have even the weakest form of community needed for democracy. In order for a pluralistic, scattered, and mobile public to take charge by regulating the indirect consequences of local interactions, individuals must extend the reach of their sense of "we" beyond their local group; in other words, one must first experience their identity as that of the people. This does not mean, however, that we should expect the Great Community to have the same depth in its affective ties as the local ones; rather, the distinct "we-ness" of the local is irreplaceable.

A further problem with this last objection is that it assumes that the democratic task is an approximation to a certain ultimate or grandiose state of affairs—for example, the Great Community—and that a failure to obtain it means a failure of the overall task. In Dewey's ethics, the emphasis is, however, on the process. There are no promises about ultimate outcomes. Whether or not there will ever be such a society is not the ultimate concern. We must keep striving for it, understanding that a final realization of that goal is not the point. If it were, we'd surely give up. Our ideals are nothing more than ends-in-view that can help us improve present experience.

A rebuttal to the objection may be that we cannot even speak meaningfully of a wider sense of "we" in any degree beyond the local. But whether it can or cannot be done is an empirical issue, that is, of having or not having the "we" experience. It is clear that Dewey thought that a sense of "we" could be expanded well beyond our immediate community. In fact, he even makes reference to the possibility of experiencing oneself as a citizen of nature. Works of art and our communal bonds can elicit the religious feeling or quality of belonging to the "larger, all-inclusive, whole which is the universe in which we live. . . . This whole is then felt as an expansion of ourselves [that] we are citizens of this vast world beyond ourselves" (LW 10:199). To become aware of our continuities not only with others but also with nature had, for Dewey, religious quality. But experiencing this sort of natural piety does not require an equal intimacy or concern for everyone in a Great Community, or that this bigger association should be our sole end. It may well be that instead of seeking these experiences in what is remote and bigger they "can be found only in the vital, steady, and deep relationships which are present only in immediate community" (LW 2:368–69). In other words, it is through *and* by the local that I can acquire this sense of connection with what is beyond it.

Democracy, just as with the experimental method, must grow out of but continue to return to what is local. The consequences of effective social reform at the broadest level should be measured ultimately by the effects upon the quality of the experience of individual, concrete relationships. Social institutions should be judged according to the degree to which they do or do not foster exploitative relationships, and whether they contributed to the development and qualitative enhancement of associated living.

Democracy must grow from within, that is, from what is local, spontaneous, voluntary, and direct. This includes the neighborhood, family, classroom, workplace, and grass-roots movements. We may not know beforehand if the process of democratization can reach as far as the present and impersonal political, economic, and intellectual relations of the wider society, but we must avoid sacrificing the quality of what is had locally merely for the sake of reach. Our previous discussion about the ideal wider self made it clear that Dewey is not one to make this sort of compromise, at least as part of the ideal. The difficult balancing task is to improve our present experience with further depth and intimacy, while enhancing variety and reach without sacrificing one for the other. This is a different ideal than that of trying to achieve community on a broad national scale by any means.

Dewey's emphasis on the local is not without difficulties. He often referred to this as "face to face intercourse" (LW 2:367), but this seems outdated and nostalgic today, when people form friendships over the Internet. The notion of the local needs to be reconstructed in a way that preserves Dewey's insight. The functional distinction that Dewey stresses is between local versus non-local relationships. From a methodological and metaphysical perspective, the pivotal point of reference of what is local in Dewey's philosophy should be clear. The location in which and from which I live is always a situation. From this shifting place, I philosophize and eat cereal, but it is also where I have different relationships. Some of them are closer or more distant than others, but there is an ambiguity about how this is understood. Even if one could make the case that physical approximation and bodily interaction make relationships closer and in some ways better, there is no necessary correlation. The difficulties with using face-to-face interactions as the paradigm are avoided if we instead contrast our personal relations with our more impersonal and formal ones.

Dewey's point is that democracy as a political system stresses these latter relationships too often, and therefore narrows the time and the places where democracy is relevant. It puts the emphasis on political activity performed only every four years (by voting) instead of something that needs to be worked at every day through our everyday interaction with each other in contexts such as the classroom, the workplace, and the living room. Dewey believes that ultimately the most important relationships in our lives are the personal ones.

More has to be done to clear up these conceptual distinctions. Dewey can be criticized for failing to make some subtle distinctions in his democratic vision. It is not clear, for example, that the word community is helpful. Between family and friends, which are usually the most local and intimate, and our relations with remote groups and institutions, there are many voluntary groups that vary in size. Today we speak of community of interest, communities of professionals, and Internet communities. Are these all communities? Where are we supposed to locate them in the continuum between friends and the society at large?

Is Dewey guilty of underemphasizing the importance of the wider, more indirect impersonal associations that we form as membership of a larger society? Dewey knew that too much emphasis on personal associations is an excess to be avoided, for it could result in neglect of the wider social relations and political decisions which might then eventually affect our most personal and direct associations. He was not especially concerned about this possibility simply because he did not perceive this as the most present danger to American society. However, it is the responsibility of followers of Dewey to ponder whether things have changed enough to prompt concern about a different extreme than Dewey did. Nevertheless, democratic reconstruction starts for Dewey where we are in the midst of a web of local relations, and may extend as far as we can reach.

Dewey assumes that the sort of communal loyalty and civic-mind-edness needed in a democracy can emerge as a natural outgrowth of strengthening and nurturing local ties. Is this correct, or is it a problematic generalization that may only apply to certain places or cultures? In places like Latin America and Italy, personal relationships are emphasized, but if anything they tend to work against the civic-mindedness needed in a democracy. In a recent study, Seymour Lipset and Gabriel Lenz claim that many of the cultures found high on the scale of corruption are also places that value strong family bonds.[9] In these cultures, loyalty to family, friends, and groups seems to work against any loyalty to the wider community and a sense of civic responsibility. Even if these cultures could achieve a wider experience of the "we," they would still lack the dutiful sense of social consciousness that civic-mindedness seems to entail. What is missing is not openness, tolerance, or inclusivity but a general sense that there are certain things one must do as a citizen for the anonymous, generalized other. For some reason, some cultures have this problem more acutely than others. I am suggesting that, in his effort to emphasize what was missing in his own society, Dewey may have overestimated the impor-tance of certain things and taken for granted others as conditions for the sort of interaction needed in a democracy. Nevertheless, his contextualism is a good safeguard against prescriptions about democracy that do not take into account deep cultural and historical differences among people.

Democracy as Communication with Aesthetic Quality

A community is created through participation and interaction in com-mon rituals and practices. In a democratic community, these rituals and practices provide an order and stability that is not rigid or oppressive to individuality. The participation of individuals is aesthetic and not me-chanically imposed. Dewey hoped that a certain quality of discussion experienced in local associations could be encouraged and extended to other areas of life.

The optimal sort of communication can be described as intelligent in order to emphasize the role of inquiry in controlling the direction of the discussion, but communication must also have an aesthetic quality. There must be a balance between activity and receptivity that steers between extremes. The licentious classroom environment, where each student says what he or she feels but "without paying much attention to what another is saying," or without any sensitivity or receptivity to "the limits imposed either by the subject matter or the input of others,"[10] is one extreme. The communication may be free and between equals, but fails to be the full transaction that can make the process educative, enriching, and self-regulative. Communication is full whenever it is reciprocal, a genuine transaction where everyone involved is affected by the process. Letting every voice speak is good but it is much better when everyone is listening in a wholehearted manner where learning and sharing occurs. Genuine listening, especially to those who speak against our beliefs, does more on behalf of participatory democracy than voting. The strength of full transactions and receptivity in communication is a matter of degree. At one end of the ideal is a classroom where students in the process of discussion mutually modify not only their thinking but their whole selves.

Much has been made of cooperation to describe Dewey's conception of democratic deliberation,[11] but there are cooperative discussions that can fall short of the ideal envisioned by him. Compromise and bargaining are cooperative processes but they do not represent the highest possibilities in human association. In negotiation, the end of the discussion is to get concessions and consensus from each side. Each must be willing to give some ground to the other, but at the end of the discussion there may not be a significant change in the participants or their views. Taking a part in a discussion where we imaginatively enter into the experience of the other requires more than that we meet each other halfway. What we want is a deeper interaction. It is a truism that in a democracy, conflict is resolved by discussion, yet there is a difference between mere bargaining and the sort of discussion where members reexamine their values and interest in light of all others.[12] In a community of inquiry, there is more than the taking, adding, or subtracting of viewpoints to reach some decision; it is not a zero-sum game. Ideally there is a transformation of the views that came into the dialogue.

In procuring freedom of communication, democracy makes itself vulnerable to the dangers of becoming unruly and capricious. But for Dewey, the solution is not to gravitate to an equally undesirable extreme. It is easy to react to the possibility of a permissive or unrestrained classroom by creating a constricted one where interaction is totally controlled by pre-established goals (such as standardized content) or the orders of a teacher; on this model, students are merely passive recipients of information. The results are also unaesthetic: in a classroom environment where discussion is routine and mechanical, drudgery predominates. To be sure, creating this sort of extreme does not require an external force (like the teacher or Big Brother) that controls the discussion. A discussion with excess receptivity (undergoing) can be one where there is much following but little initiative, spontaneity, reformulation, criticism, and power of judgment (i.e., positive freedom). A classroom where the teacher is a tyrant is as bad as one where the students are nothing more than passive recipients of information with a singular external interest in grades, because in both there is no chance to have an aesthetic discussion. This is also the danger in a society where everyone is a consumer but no one a citizen. In improving the quality of discourse, it is tempting to shift between extremes because doing so is much easier than facing the challenges posed by the democratic ideal.

Dualisms often get in the way of imagining how the freedom, playfulness, and spontaneity of our best discussions can be reconciled with control, order, and direction. Indeed, what seems puzzling to many about democracy is that it is unclear what can control the direction of discussion where freedom of expression is allowed and encouraged, and claims to inherent authority are denied. Dewey argued against such skepticism by appealing to our ordinary experience. We would have more faith in democratic discussion if we paid attention to how many of our ordinary free discussions actually unfold. In them, just as in moral deliberation, the present qualitative process guides its direction, that is, the control comes *from within* the discussion. Consider our best moments in a classroom discussion. They are not the ones that are mechanical and controlled by objectives or particular individuals. Rather, they are the ones where no one in particular controls the discussion because control comes from everyone attending to the subject matter and to what others say as the process unfolds. The dialogue develops through the mutual modification of the original contributions of its participants. The same thing happens to a sensitive artist in her interaction with materials. However free her interaction is, there are limits imposed by the subject matter she is trying to transform, and this is what serves to control and direct the process of production.

What the conditions and obstacles are for having the optimal sort of communication is a complex issue that Dewey hoped we would never stop discussing. The freeness and fullness of communication needed in democracy is not possible when there is intolerance, marginalization, fragmentation, polarization, and segregation. Racism, sexism, ethnocentrism, and all "barriers that divide human beings into sets and cliques, into antagonistic sects and factions" (LW 14:227) remain culprits in today's environment. Dewey writes that every way of life "that fails in its democracy limits the contacts, the exchanges, the communications, the interactions by which experience is steadied while it is also enlarged and enriched" (LW 14:230).

Whatever social and political reforms we need for free and full communication, it is clear that we also require wider selves with the complementary virtues presented in previous chapters. To rely on some explicitly formulated rules may sometimes be necessary, but this is a sign of a failure to habitually experience each other in a more significant way. Communication is free when tolerance is a central virtue among individuals, but it is not full unless there are also the receptive dispositions of openness and sympathy. This last virtue plays an important function.

Sympathy is responsible for the sort of deliberation where participants take the roles of speaker and listener. It is only when individuals in communication are able to emotionally and imaginatively take the role of the other, and be willing to be affected by it, that significant learning and shared experience occurs. What is precious and distinctive about democratic communication, as George Herbert Mead and Dewey conceived it, is that the common experience is not based on sameness. As Mead put it: "A difference of functions does not preclude a common experience; it is possible for the individual to put himself in the place of the other although his function is different."[13] The idea that we cannot understand or communicate with each other at a deeper level unless we are the same, or that communication is better when difference is removed, is simply false. As an ideal, democracy is the possibility that individuality and difference can flourish and meet in common experience.

The role of openness in a democratic communication should be obvious. A community of people who are merely tolerant but not open-minded has built up internal barriers to the fullness of discussion. They may be able to compromise and bargain, but will not learn from each other. Democracy requires more than letting others have their say; it also requires a certain kind of vulnerable but committed participation in a constant dialogue. Genuine undergoing requires the kind of openness and receptivity that may affect who we are. This is not easy. "It involves reconstruction which may be painful" (LW 10:48). It takes courage to have a willingness to be affected in this way. This is very different from paying lip service to others doing their own thing when we are already convinced that there is nothing important to be learned from them. One must habitually listen with care to the concerns of even those who oppose one's views. This is a standard by which we may judge today's cyberspace communications. Insofar as the Internet as a medium gives the power to individuals to communicate with like-minded individuals, it is a tool that can be used against democracy. Communication between parties where each has as the primordial goal the validation of what they already believe is superficial (i.e., not full), unfruitful, and dull.

Character is something that is formed in the context of local communications, but the process of communication must not be conceived as a mere means to virtue or any predetermined goal. When people communicate solely in order to solve their problems, or to reach consensus, or for the sake of democracy as a remote end, they risk turning that discussion into drudgery. More important, they miss something that Dewey thinks is unique and precious: the present and the intrinsic enjoyment of sharing. In Dewey's view of participatory democracy, just as in his ethics, the emphasis is on the quality of the present process. Ideal communication is both fertile and immediately enjoyable; it is neither mere work nor mere play. Communication may or may not come to something, but when it is immediately meaningful, it is more likely to be productive in terms of future efficacy than when it is not. "When the instrumental and final functions of communication live together in experience, there exist an intelligence which is the method and reward of the common life, and a society worthy to command affection, admiration, and loyalty" (LW 1:160).

Dewey's strong emphasis on the quality of communication and on shared experience does not imply a sacrifice of individuality. Dewey's communitarian values are based on the hope of "enlarging and deepening the range of our individuality" (LW 17:322). In democracy, the values we routinely separate are in fact interdependent. The liberation and appreciation of individuality (equality and liberty) are done in and through associations (fraternity), but the improvement of these associations is dependent on the voluntary nature and power of judgment of all its individuals as well.

> Only when individuals have initiative, independence of judgment, flexibility, fullness of experience, can they act so as to enrich the lives of others and only in this way can a truly common welfare be built up. (LW 7:348)

This is not the view that there is a pre-established harmony between these values, but it does presuppose that there is no dualism that precludes possible degrees of harmonization. It is based on the possibility that the values that are associated with individuality can co-exist in a tensive balance with those associated with community.

Democracy as the Celebration of Continuities and Differences

Democracy is a task that can be metaphorically described as a process of balancing centripetal with centrifugal forces. Local communities must be sustained by loyalty and solidarity while also remaining receptive to the continuities within the larger context of a pluralistic society. Moreover, there must be a balancing act that allows differences, diversity, pluralism, and independence to flourish while also celebrating and building commonalities, unity, continuities, and interdependence. This is the act of balancing needed to widen and deepen everyday experience.

The difficulty of this proposal, even in the most favorable of conditions, should be obvious. Overemphasis on differences has a centripetal effect, one that leads to isolation, exclusivity, and divisiveness. This unbalanced response is supported by atomistic ways of conceiving the world which deny that relations and continuities are fully real. This can take the form of the atomistic individualism that Dewey criticized, or of today's cultural atomism. Let's consider the latter for the purposes of illustration.

Cultural atomism is the assumption that cultures are pure, discrete, and singular wholes. It is a view that is sometimes assumed in debates about multiculturalism. Insofar as multiculturalism is a move away from monistic and hierarchical ways of conceiving the status of cultural differences in our society, it is well intended. The problem, however, is that in its extreme forms, it assumes a pluralistic ideal that is also separatist. According to such views, protecting, sheltering, and separating all cultures preserve a multicultural society. Each culture is incommensurable and entitled (as if by right) to be protected and left alone. This is the best we can hope for on such views because any other alternative may produce a society where the larger group obliterates the culture of small groups, or where all cultural differences are homogenized. Is this true?

Contextualism dictates that one must be open to the possibility that, in a particular time and place, these are the only options. One must not ignore political and historical realities. A defensive provincialism, ethnocentrism, or protectionism on the part of certain groups may well be the only adequate response in a particular situation. But Dewey would not see this as ideal or the best we can hope for. The best we can hope for is a society composed of an indefinite variety of cultures whose free and full interactions enrich the lives of all. This equality of cultural interchange is an ideal that goes well beyond mere cultural tolerance.

When the only competing ideals are that we are either all the same or radically different, there is usually an assumed metaphysics that denies the reality of continuities. An empirical philosophy, on the other hand, recognizes that similarities and differences coexist in the continuum of experience. One cannot appreciate differences without also appreciating similarities. Moreover, identity and difference are functional rather than ontological designations. For some purposes, I must ignore the differences among groups or cultures; for others I must affirm them. This does not mean that they are arbitrary or artificial, but only that they are not radical or fixed. The pluralist-separatist has chosen to select—exaggerate, in fact—the differences between groups and ignore their continuities. This is an instance of the fallacy of selective emphasis. However, the obliteration or denial of such differences is not the only alternative to their overemphasis. Both overemphasis and denial are extreme stances toward difference, and both are mistaken. The mistaken denial of difference, for example, is evident in the sort of universalism that denies differences by postulating a human essence, or in the ideal of melting all of our differences together. When differences are exaggerated and not conceived as a matter of degree they contribute to isolation, exclusivity, and (possibly) racism.[14] The democratic ideal entails that we should transform differences from sources of friction to sources of enrichment. And for this we need to develop characters with suitable dispositions (e.g., open-mindedness and sympathy) that welcome and are nurtured by what is experienced as new and different.

Differences and continuities each have different functions in an ideal community. Individuals and groups should be encouraged to be different because this contributes to the whole. It adds the variety needed to work against both boredom and an atmosphere of suppression. General uniformity or homogeneity produces stability but one that leads to fixity and mechanical interaction. On the other hand, a celebration of diversity that forbids interaction, sympathy, the making of connections, and the exploration of commonalities seems to rule out any basis for a sense of "we." It is also a waste of resources since only in interaction are potentialities discovered and developed. We can avoid separatism and homogeneity by maintaining a balance between emphasizing our differences and our continuities. A pluralistic community that incorporates this in its daily communication nurtures itself with differences and change, and at the same time experiences a common life. The stability procured is rhythmic and developing. It has the dynamic variation within balance that for Dewey characterizes great works of art.

In general, one of the most difficult balancing acts in a democracy is to know when and in what proportion differences among individuals or groups obstruct democratic communication. Deficiency and excess in, for example, social differences such as economic class and knowledge tend to affect the quality of communication. Insufficient variety often results in stagnation, homogeneity, and a lack of creative tension in the relationships. But too much variety or too many differences can also undermine the possibility of having mutually enriching democratic communication. It may result in an undesirable power relation where it is impossible to imaginatively take the standpoint of the other, as occurs, for example, when large economic or class differences exist.

As a good contextualist, Dewey does not tell us precisely when and in what proportion differences are detrimental to democracy. But the lack of specificity should not prevent us from appreciating how distinctive his approach is to problems related to gaps in knowledge and economics in a democracy. These problems are evaluated in terms of how differences may affect the quality of the concrete relations among individuals in communication, rather than in terms of rights. A Deweyan approach can appropriate rights talk but only as a tool to effect societal and political changes that would ameliorate our concrete relationships.[15]

Dewey welcomes knowledge-related differences among people and he is aware of the need for experts. There is, of course, the provision that everyone in a democracy possess minimal knowledge and thinking skills to be a participatory citizen and to exercise positive freedom. Nevertheless, there is a difficulty that Dewey did not address. It is because of the knowledge gap between experts and clients that clients are vulnerable to exploitation and that communication can easily deteriorate. Even if everyone was equipped with the habits needed to be critical of experts, we must ultimately rely on trust in democratic communication. The expert must be worthy of trust and the client must be willing to trust. Trust is what democratizes communication and other practices. This is a democratic virtue absent in Dewey's moral and political writings that he should have stressed. That he assumes it as integral to the democratic way of living is clear in the following passage: "Merely legal guarantees of the civil liberties of free belief, free expression, free assembly are of little avail if in daily life freedom of communication, the give and take of ideas, facts, experiences, is choked by mutual suspicion" (LW 14:228). Dewey should have considered how difficult it is to extend this virtue beyond the local level. It is the sort of difficulty that can make people skeptical about the prospects for democracy.

Democracy as the Intelligent Community

Intelligence for Dewey is not a faculty, but a general way of interacting by which a social organism develops the means within experience to inform and guide ongoing experience. The intelligent self can be described in terms of having certain habits, but the corresponding intelligent community is best characterized in terms of the predominance of a certain type of communication: one that comes to decisions and judgments guided by inquiry.

Dewey's qualification of democracy as intelligent serves as a point of contrast with communities that, for example, relied merely on authority, tradition, impulse (caprice), or imitation as methods for addressing problems and regulating and directing its own affairs and decisions. But, more importantly, it allows him to distinguish his view from other conceptions of democracy. Democracy must be more than a collective consensus by majority rule or the mere counting of votes. This last procedure, if required in democracy, must be the culmination of a process of inquiry where participants may change their views at any time in light of new evidence and arguments. The quality of this process or method is more important than reaching any preconceived result. "The question of method to be used in judging existing customs and policies proposed is of greater moral significance than the particular conclusion reached in connection with any one controversy" (LW 7:338).

Dewey thought that intelligent inquiry, although exemplified in the sciences, had yet to penetrate into the ways we handle matters in religion, politics, and morals. This is why in many of his texts and essays about religion, politics, and morals, he promotes rather than articulates his conception of intelligence. This is regrettable since readers of his ethics not acquainted with his logic are left without the more systematic and formal bases of the method Dewey called intelligence. Meanwhile, those acquainted only with his writings in logic and epistemology may be left without a clear idea of how intelligence is actually operative or embodied in the process of making moral and political decisions. To bridge this gap, one must keep in mind that the context of the process of inquiry presented in the *Logic* is not the mind but a situation where there is a dialogue with the world and others. The pattern, forms, operations, and propositions of Dewey's logic are theoretical abstractions from intelligence as a concrete inquirential process where there is concomitant communication among individuals equipped with certain habits (virtues). Dewey explicates the common patterns of successful inquiry more systematically than he does the common traits of good communication (or of the ideal community), but there is no doubt that the former presupposes the latter.[16] Among the habits or general attitudes presupposed by inquiry are sensitivity to context (i.e., to the indeterminate situation), a genuine disposition to listen and learn from others (openness), and a general willingness to let experience decide. Communication where these attitudes are present has a different quality than communication that is merely the confrontation of ideologies or an attempt to compromise regardless of how much tolerance is exhibited. Dewey occasionally chooses scientific discourse as exemplifying some of the habits and general qualities he wished would become part of public discourse. But artistic communication is also a model. In music, for example, listening to each other and to the subject matter, experimenting, cooperating, and thereby learning are crucial traits of the interaction between musicians.

I have contrasted intelligence as method with reliance upon caprice, prejudice, or authority but there are more subtle ways in which much of public discourse today fails to be intelligent from Dewey's point of view. Take, for example, the requirement of sensitivity to context. This means that communication must be regulated and guided by the specific and unique problem that brought the parties into dialogue. To set up an antecedent end to the process, even one as vague and as desirable as reaching a consensus, is to risk failing to guide the analysis, construction of hypotheses, and possible solutions by attention to and care for the specific situation.

A community of inquiry that is not centered and guided by the unique problem at hand usually deteriorates into a mere conflict of ideologies without the fullness of interaction required for learning. Moreover, this leads to an oversimplification of concrete social problems and often to faulty solutions. For Dewey, one of the most important threats to intelligent, context-sensitive communication in a democracy is the opposition between individualism and collectivism in attending to problems.

The ideological opposition between individualism and collectivism in social matters has a long history. Political theorists who focus on individual natural rights and the notion of negative freedom are suspicious of all collective action for it tends toward regimentation, mechanical and mass uniformity, censorship, and suppression. Collectivists, for their part, consider collective organized action as the source of all that is good and civil in nature. Both views assume an untenable dualism between the individual and the social but, more importantly, they share the same dogmatic approach to problems. For the individualist, social organization (government) is at best a necessary evil and it tends to be oppressive. Therefore, social problems are analyzed in terms of how individual initiative, freedom, incentives, and independence have been suppressed by some collective action or organization. The collectivist, on the other hand, tends to analyze problems in terms of the disintegration and instability created by a rampant individualism that has undermined social order or communal bonds. Depending on who represents the status quo in this debate, one accuses the other of the present problems but neither one cares to examine situations on their own merits. Hence, Dewey refers to them as dangerous opposing doctrines that seem to exempt us from the responsibility and hard work of ameliorating social problems in light of their contextual uniqueness. "The person who holds the doctrine of 'individualism' or 'collectivism' has his program determined for him in advance" (LW 2:361).

These opposed camps or schools of thought would be of only historical interest if they did not continue to this day. But these oppositions persist and are exemplified in the way many liberals and communitarians analyze and seek solutions to concrete problems. This is not the place to assess this ongoing debate, but I trust that what has been said is sufficient to make anyone suspicious of efforts to interpret Dewey as belonging to either camp.[17] Instead, Dewey was simply a contextualist who, however much he cherished community, avoided prejudicing the communal over the individual good. For the same reasons, I would also resist characterizing Dewey as a socialist. Dewey was a contextualist democrat. Even if he may have sided during his time in favor of a more socialized economy, his approach to means and problem-solving is a radical, non-partisan contextualism. Every question regarding what should be socialized or otherwise left to be solved by market forces must be considered on its own merits. Dewey was clear about this:

> We have to consider the probable consequences of any proposed measure with reference to the situation, as it exists at some definite time and place in which it is to apply. There cannot be any universal rule laid down, for example, regarding the respective scope of private and public action. (LW 7:336)

Being a contextualist about the appropriate means to democratize our experience is not an easy position to hold in today's political climate. Consider the implications. It may require that we resolve one problem by market means and another through government intervention, or even that we treat the same problem differently at different times. Such an approach by a politician would probably be perceived as a sign of indecision or lack of character. Nowadays, political integrity is identified with standing by one's ideological and pre-conceived way of dealing with a problem. Granted, insofar as both seem flexible, a genuine contextualist politician may at times be difficult to distinguish from one who operates capriciously, but for Dewey there is a profound difference in method and result.

Sensitivity to context presupposes that democratic communication must take experience as its guide. Aristocratic and hierarchical ideals operate under the assumption that guidance, standards, and solutions must come down either from outside or from above the ordinary communications we hold about the problems we share. "Every other form of moral and social faith rests upon the idea that experience must be subjected at some point or other to some form of external control; to some authority alleged to exist outside the process of experience" (LW 14:229).

In democratic communication, no one has an a priori or absolute authority, but not all points of view are equally valid. If the expert or professional is granted more authority in some aspect of everyday life, it is only because of her accumulated experience and not because of some inherent authority. Her credibility is always open to question and revision. The ideal is for decisions and problems to be addressed by engaging in a process of inquiry where everyone has implicitly agreed to let experience decide, and they have therefore agreed to remain equally vulnerable to the lessons or authority of experience.

To accept experience as the authority is to believe in the self-sufficiency and potentialities of communal inquiry. In other words, in a democratic community the control and direction of a discussion comes from within itself as it unfolds. "The final issue of empirical method is whether the guide and standard of beliefs and conduct lies within or without the sharable situations of life" (LW 1:391). But this should not be confused with the sort of relativism that proclaims that there is no authority beyond our language, culture, conceptual scheme, or human consensus. Communal inquiry is devoted to making ourselves answerable to the world, to how things really are, to follow the evidence wherever it leads and not just to find out what the majority wants. This is an aspiration beyond consensus or the reinforcement of one's ethnocentric beliefs, but not one beyond experience. A view of reality as a world in the making with humans as participants does not entail that we can make reality what we wish. On the contrary, "it will indeed recognize that there is in things a grain against which we cannot successfully go" (MW 11:50).

Dewey's robust view of public discourse is what allows him to insulate himself from the traditional objection that democracy can be nothing more than the tyranny of the majority. For it is through inquiry that individuals in a democracy can be heard and can criticize the judgments made by a majority. Dewey thought it was imperative to "create the conditions which will enable the minority by use of communication and persuasion to become a majority" (LW 7:362). In any case, he thought that the fear of the tyranny of the majority in democracy had been exaggerated. "The world has suffered more from leaders and authorities than from the masses" (LW 2:365). For him the real culprit most of the time is a powerful minority that suppresses a majority who stands by passively (e.g., as mere consumers) and permits it to occur. Hence, he stresses the importance of educating the general public to be both active and critical.

But is the majority capable of such high-quality public discourse and activism? Are the people capable of good judgment? If it is impossible to raise the quality of public discourse of the masses then we might as well let an intelligent elite rule. Dewey worried about this sort of objection to democracy, which was raised by Plato, Alexis de Tocqueville, and Walter Lippman. Dewey was not naïve and he recognized that the ignorance, bias, and levity of the masses are liabilities for democracy. But for him the actual limitations of the people at any given time and place are not fixed by nature or fate. This may not be satisfactory to those skeptics who claim that democracy has built-in features that militate against achievement of the ideal. It lends itself to widespread manipulation of mass opinion by political and financial elites. This debate may and should continue, but it certainly reveals Dewey's deep faith in the intelligence of the people once proper conditions are provided. This generous belief in the possibilities of everyone as a human being irrespective of race, color, sex, or class is basic to the democratic faith. Dewey explains what is required: "Generosity in judgment of others as distinct from narrowness is largely a matter of estimating what they can grow into instead of judging them on the basis of what conditions have so far made of them" (LW 7:348).

Democracy and the Balance between the Stable and the Precarious

In Dewey's metaphysics, tendencies toward association and continuity are usually the source of stability, while tendencies to differentiation and individuality are the source of novelty and the precarious. There is thus an even broader way to characterize the democratic way of life. The democratic community is one that is able to maintain, in its everyday transactions, a productive balance between the stable and the more precarious aspects of experience. This is also a consequence of its intelligence or reliance on the experimental method. For it is the sort of community that, although it relies on the stabilities inherited from the past (tradition, habits, precedent, institutions, etc.), is also ready to engage in criticism and is receptive to new conditions.

Dewey's democratic community allows for moral rebels, but maintains "a presumption in favor of principles that have had a long career in the past and that have been endorsed by men of insight" (LW 7:330). It is because a principle may no longer be valid and may need to be revised that a democratic community must allow moral rebels. "Some persons persecuted as moral rebels in one period have been hailed as moral heroes at a later time" (LW 7:230). Of course, the sort of moral rebel that Dewey imagines is one who genuinely cares about morality and has the virtues integral to communal inquiry and learning. In other words, he must be open and willing to accept that the burden of proof is upon him. Dewey explains,

> In asserting the rightfulness of his own judgment of what is obligatory, he is implicitly putting forth a social claim, something therefore to be tested and confirmed by further trial by others. He therefore recognizes that when he protests he is liable to suffer the consequences that result from his protesting; he will strive with patience and cheerfulness to convince others. (LW 7:231)

On the other hand, Dewey is fully aware that one of the problems with developing a democracy is that "the majority is always hostile to permitting a minority to develop ideas which are opposed to its own" (LW 7:362); therefore, "If patience, cheerfulness, freedom from conceit, self-display and self-pity are demanded of the moral non-conformist, there is a correlative duty imposed upon conformists: namely the duty of toleration" (LW 7:231). For Dewey, the continued vitality of communal inquiry requires a "creative tension"[18] between its participants, rather than the harmony that comes from the consensus of homogeneity. This tension may require a diversification of the functions or roles among the participants. The function of the conservative is to stand on precedent or on what is generally accepted, whereas the radical is more critical and open to change; but what brings everyone together is the "positive willingness to permit reflection and inquiry, to go in the faith that the truly right will be rendered more secure through questioning and discussion" (LW 7:231). Moreover, one could generalize and claim that the important function of the individual in communal inquiry is usually to provide the novelty and experimentation, while communal bonds provide the needed stability. As James once said: "The community stagnates without the impulse of the individual. The impulse dies away without the sympathy of the community."[19]

The rigidity and solidity of a community that is not open to change usually results either in maintaining the stability by repression and confinement that ultimately does not work, or it leads eventually to such a violent enthusiasm for the new as to encourage complete rupture from previous experience. To maintain a community that is both faithful to tradition and experimentation is a never-ending challenge. For new experiences that result from open and wide communication are often perceived as a threat to the traditional beliefs and accepted code that form the basis of a community's stability. On the other hand, a community that cherishes change and experimentation often perceives tradition as a threat to creativity and freedom, or as the source of stagnation.

The sort of community Dewey endorsed must be enthusiastic and hopeful about inquiry. But this also makes it vulnerable to overconfidence and naïve optimism. An overly optimistic quest for control leads to disillusionment and a passive pessimism in a universe where "when all is said and done, the fundamentally hazardous character of the world is not seriously modified, much less eliminated" (LW 1:45). There is no certain way to avoid this vulnerability except by maintaining a deep sense of the tragic. The democratic community cherishes stability and control, but this must be balanced by an appreciation of the precarious character of life. Dewey's criticism of traditional ethics is based on the hope that more people would come to appreciate incommensurability, disagreement, risk, and uncertainty as features that are at the very heart of morality and not as mere appearances or products of human ignorance. The readiness to ameliorate life through the use of our best resources (tools and funded experience) needs to be balanced out by a keen sense of the ambiguities and novelties of the world that are beyond our control, even with all of our hard facts and predictive methodologies. "Because it recognizes that contingency cooperates with intelligence in the realization of every plan, even the one most carefully and wisely thought out, it will avoid conceit and intellectual arrogance" (MW 11:51). This is the basis of democratic humility that contrasts with the self-assurance and arrogance of aristocracy. For Dewey it was humility, not pride, that was needed for democracy. When the values of democracy are used arrogantly by a leader or a nation to express superiority and self-sufficiency, it betrays the very spirit of democracy.

Pride and conceit in its many manifestations (e.g., of the learned, the wealthy, of those with status, or of those who profess a special connection with a spiritual world or the good) usually leads to isolation, exclusivity, and divisiveness. Democratic humility presupposes equality in that no matter what our differences in merit and achievement are, we are all subject to the precarious. The sense that we are dependent and living in the same precarious context can reinforce the experience of shared life and interdependence that is key to democracy. "A sense of common participation in the inevitable uncertainties of existence would be coeval with a sense of common effort and shared destiny" (LW 4:246). For Dewey, the highest achievement of this experience of interdependence takes on a religious quality. "Whether or not we are, save in some metaphorical sense, all brothers, we are at least all in the same boat traversing the same turbulent ocean. The potential religious significance of this fact is infinite" (LW 9:56).

Democracy as a Task

If believing in democracy is just a matter of accepting some theory, then it seems as if the inherent tensions projected in the ideal of democracy present a serious challenge to its reasonableness. John Patrick Diggins observes that "democracy is too full of tensions and contradictions to be subsumed under logical formulas . . . if there is a logic to democracy, it is the logic of contradiction."[20] But Dewey stressed that part of what is meant by calling democracy a moral ideal is that it is an endeavor, part of a program of work, rather than a theory or something already given and ready-made.

Democracy as a way of life means that one takes on the task of working out and ameliorating actual tensions that are integral to democracy's ideal in concrete and particular situations; it is not a matter of proving its coherence or validity at the abstract level of ideas. In a democracy we want things that, although necessary for meaning and quality of life, do not automatically reinforce each other. History does not prove the futility of our democratic hopes, but it does teach us that the built-in values of democracy contain tensions that are not easily reconciled. Dewey explains, for example,

> that there is no automatic criterion of liberty and fraternity with each other. How can fraternal relations be secured without putting individual freedom under restraint? History proves also that liberty and equality do not automatically tend to generate and support one another. (LW 7:349)

Indeed, the situation of a community where tendencies toward solidarity coexist with tendencies toward differentiation is tense and continuously challenging. How can a community that celebrates agreement and shared experience also encourage disagreement, individuality, and diversity? How do we encourage openness while preserving loyalty to tradition; how do we encourage both work and a spirit of play, both action and receptivity? How much freedom should we give up for the sake of more order and security? These are some of the never-ending challenges posed by democracy. But with Dewey's account of balance in place, we know that the challenge is not met by trying to dissolve all tension; rather, to live in democracy is to learn to embrace conflict and tension.

The difficulty of the democratic endeavor lies in the fact that the risk of imbalances is constant as new conditions require adjustments. Balance is not guaranteed by the simple addition or subtraction of the elements in tension. Moreover, the values that are supposed to be balanced are not antecedently given. We have seen that freedom and equality, for instance, require appropriate conditions and concerted effort for their emergence.

Democracy as a task also means that, beyond merely theorizing about the coherence or philosophical foundations of the ideal, intellectual work is needed to spell out what contemporary problems it entails in light of present conditions. This is why Dewey insists that democracy as an ideal "poses, rather than solves" (LW 7:350) problems. For example, what conditions are needed at a particular time to sustain a stable community capable of readjusting or reexamining the habits and principles inherited from previous experience? Although this must be left to a specific inquiry of the particular case, one can speculate about some general conditions. It seems necessary to have in the community the proper means to pass along and reinforce the valuable habits, traditions, and lessons of experience. Hence, communal bonds and rituals must be strong. On the other hand, for a community to remain experimental and self-corrective, it must not take any policy as final nor exclude anyone's interest from continued consideration. It would be the kind of community that secures a flexible readjustment of its institutions and rituals, not for change's own sake, but because change is inevitable and the demand for remaking old habits and institutions is recurrent. This presupposes the operation of some of the virtues I have outlined.

Another problem posed by democracy as an ideal is how we achieve, in light of present conditions, a way of life where there is an organic and nurturing relation between all individuals and the social wholes (relationships, institutions) to which they belong. Dewey describes this as "a postulate in the sense of a demand to be realized: That each individual shall have the opportunity for release, expression, fulfillment, of his distinctive capacities, and that the outcome shall further the establishment of a fund of shared values" (LW 7:350). There are no easy formulas or guarantees that we can get close to the balance described. Neither is this something to be achieved once and for all, nor is this the point of the endeavor. Working for balance requires the constant meeting and solving of new and unforeseen problems in particular situations. Even if all goes well in a democracy, we cannot rely solely on our past accomplishments because "the conditions and the concrete significance of liberty, of equality, of mutual respect, and reciprocal service, change from generation to generation, in some degree from year to year" (LW 7:350).

Dewey diagnosed many problems that he believed were undermining the democratic ideal during his time; these included distrust of government, indifference, corruption, control of the public by propaganda and entertainment, a system of formal education that does not cultivate democratic habits, economic inequalities, and the present "walls of privilege and of monopolistic possession" (LW 7:348) that do not permit individuals to develop and contribute to society. These same general problems are still with us, but in different form or manifestation.

Democracy as a task means that one must never stop identifying the structural obstacles to democracy, but also that one must always confront and attempt to dismantle these obstacles. This requires interdisciplinary research and on-the-ground activity. This is one of the goals of Public Agenda, a nonpartisan public opinion and citizen engagement organization. It works with community-based organizations, school districts, corporations, government officials, and citizen-leaders to foster substantive public engagement that produces civil, productive dialogue on difficult issues of public importance. The public intellectuals in this organization, like Alison Kadlec and Will Friedman, are doing research and experiments with new design principles for deliberative forums that may help overcome the gridlock, divisiveness, and power relations that undermine meaningful democratic communication.[21]

Is making the ideal our task something that contradicts the contextualist approach that is so crucial to Dewey's method? Yes, but only if we take ideals as ends-in-themselves, and not as means for present reconstruction. The task is here and now. One has an end-in-view that points in the direction in which we need to go; the point of the direction is not to arrive at some final place, but to assist us in the journey. The ideal can do much for us in terms of general guidance and inspiration, but it says nothing about what must be done for a particular case. For example, there are times and places where more unity, solidarity, and tradition may be the intelligent response; at others times more pluralism, individualism, and openness might help. One can have this sensitivity to context (practical wisdom) while holding that highly uniform societies and highly individualistic societies are usually undesirable extremes. Recall also that balance for Dewey does not require that we aim at or even obtain a win-win situation among the elements in tension. A balanced society may well be more individualistic than community-oriented.

The recent wave of communitarianism and calls for civic responsibility in American society can be interpreted as a reaction to the rampant individualism that has affected us since Dewey's times. These calls for change would cease to be intelligent if they ignored context and set up a universal and fixed ideal. By making community values the only and final aim, we may fall into the opposite extreme. We tend to fall easily into this pattern of compensation (i.e. alternating between extremes) because, under the experience of an extreme, the contrary excess seems desirable. Dewey hoped we could do better. We can try instead to maintain rhythmic variation within a balanced relation to a particular context, where the danger of extremes (because of tensions) is always present. This requires that we become sensitive to imbalances and that we be willing to experiment in trying to reconcile tendencies that seem to lead us in different directions. More importantly, even if we succeed in our endeavor, we must be humble and accept the vulnerability of the balance to the contingencies of experience. The easiest task and temptation is to take an extreme. Extremes are appealing because they seem simple and final solutions to problems that require persistence and context-sensitive reflection. Since they are easily noticed, they seem to represent a position of strength. But Dewey argues otherwise. It is when we live under an extreme that we are the most vulnerable and when we are more likely to compensate by shifting to the opposite extreme.

For the democratic task, we are going to need a lot of imagination, especially since we are living in a time of cynicism with much "disillusionment about all comprehensive and positive ideas" (LW 5:277). In order to be able to envision the goals of freedom and equality in balance with fraternity, we need to give up not only dualisms but also the competitive market metaphors that underlie political rhetoric about freedom and equality. One of these is the notion that the ideal society takes place in a field where everyone has the same capacities and freedom to run a competitive race. Westbrook has suggested that we should instead think of a basketball team as the appropriate metaphor of the type of communal association needed for democracy. For "the game calls upon players to develop some common skills and virtues while at the same time specializing in some of each in accordance with individual talents and desires and to coordinate these talents with other members of the team to advance common goals."[22] I would suggest that an even better metaphor is jazz. This is usually the sort of music where an organic relation between interaction, common goals, and individuality is cherished. It is the type of music that often achieves a balance between stable elements (perhaps in melody, harmonies, or rhythm) and more precarious ones (in experimentation or improvisation). Here is how jazz pianist Brad Mehldau describes what should happen in a jazz trio setting: "Improvisation takes place not only in performance but in the way the band develops. There is a group decision perpetually taking place, a collective intelligence that wants everyone to express themselves."[23]

Dewey's Ethics and Contemporary Political Theory

I warned the reader above that I have presented Dewey's views about democracy based on his ethics and overall philosophy, rather than in contrast to current debates in democratic political theory. There is, however, a resurgence of interest in Dewey in democratic political theory, so I must address some of the consequences of my inquiry for the present use of Dewey's philosophy in political theory.

Engaging Dewey in present debates in democratic political theory without his ethics would count as a failure to confront the most fundamental and thought-provoking differences that confound present dialogue. Doing so would mean that we have not used Dewey's thought in its most productive way, for many of the current debates in political theory center on issues that have to do with morality. We must make the assumptions about moral life explicit in order to determine where Dewey would stand on these issues. To illustrate matters, I will consider two recent issues. My aim here is not to fully analyze these issues, nor to assess the proffered answers; at best, I want to use Dewey's ethics as a way to suggest some promising avenues for future inquiry as they bear on the problems that concern political theorists today.

DEWEY AND DELIBERATIVE DEMOCRACY

In recent years, political theory and socio-political philosophy has experienced what has been called a deliberative turn. Many of the members of this movement have proclaimed John Dewey as a predecessor, an influence, or as a founding father of deliberative democracy.[24] There is no doubt that deliberative democratic thinkers share with Dewey the concern that the quality of deliberation in political democracies continues to deteriorate. Moreover, they share the concern that traditional liberal theory has neglected the importance of public deliberation. Democracy is in need of rehabilitation through an emphasis on a more robust notion of democratic deliberation. Communal deliberation and judgment can be more than the aggregation of private preferences, or the competition among fixed preferences and standpoints. Deliberative political theorists have argued, as Dewey did, for the power of dialogue to transform the preferences and views of participants. However, in examining the recent deliberative turn in political theory, a Deweyan must be critical of the notion of deliberation that is often assumed.

Iris Marion Young has recently argued that many deliberationists still operate under a traditional rational and epistemic model of discourse: an exchange of propositions, reasons, and arguments governed by rules and reasoning.[25] This focus entails the exclusion of emotional-imaginative methods and reasons that are not traditionally associated with rational speech. This is problematic because it is a bias toward the mode of speech of certain groups and it leaves out much that is essential to good deliberation and communication.

This recent criticism of deliberative democracy, and the quest toward a less restrictive notion of proper public deliberation, dovetails with Dewey's robust notion of deliberation and democracy, and is an alternative worthy of consideration. As his ethics reveals, Dewey does not restrict deliberation to argument and rational speech; instead, it is a qualitative process and transaction that includes emotional and imaginative elements. The recent emphasis on deliberation is a good corrective against narrow views of democracy, but political theorists must avoid the intellectualist temptation that has plagued the history of philosophy: the reduction of experience to the cognitive realm. Furthermore, there is more to democratic experience than democratic deliberation. How we experience each other in our everyday local and direct interactions is something more inclusive than how we talk and inquire together. Democratic discourse takes place in the non-discursive context of our democratic relationships. Hence, as important as public deliberation was for Dewey, the turn that he hoped for in the philosophy of democracy was toward a view of *democracy as experience.*

Dewey's alternative conception of democratic deliberation is worth reexamining and developing especially in light of the present threats and obstacles that distort democratic deliberation. For instance, there are new forms of emotional persuasion that are the consequence of the medium in which dialogue in public life is had. We live in a world in which images and other non-cognitive and non-verbal means preclude or guide inquiry. The mass production and consumption of images that please and deceive have taken center stage in public discourse. This non-propositional content is easily dismissed by rationalist deliberationists as irrational, psychological, and beyond the realm of logic. This is the same sort of magical safeguard that Dewey criticized in philosophy: label something as unreal or irrational and it will go away. A Deweyan view of public deliberation is not as prone to this mistake because it holds that what is emotional, qualitative, imaginative, non-cognitive, or non-verbal is an important aspect of any genuine process of deliberation. A Deweyan approach would not pretend to repress what cannot be repressed. Dewey would be skeptical that the solution to our problematic situation lies in a return to a print-centered culture where propositions and their logical relation are the means to truth and knowledge and are the main vehicles of public deliberation.

Does Dewey, however, provide any practical advice about how to avoid the dangers of a society where public discourse is susceptible to the distortions of emotional appeals and manipulation? If one explicitly includes in democratic deliberation the non-propositional and emotional factors, then how can we avoid all of the obvious dangers and evils that come with that inclusion? The dangerous aspects of rhetoric and emotional persuasion are more significant today than during Dewey's time. The problem with public discourse in America is that emotional reasons and rhetoric are used to reduce the quality of collective intelligence. The people are often swayed by irrelevancy, amusement, and fear. They are seduced by images, propaganda, and demagoguery instead of by the force of the better argument.

This is not the place to fully pursue a Deweyan response to these serious contemporary challenges, for Dewey did not provide answers to the problems that affect us today. There are, however, important lessons from my reconstruction of Dewey's ethics worth considering in any future inquiry. For Dewey, good judgment and deliberation depend on the cultivation of habits. Encouraging certain virtues in a community is the best way to prepare for particular collective decision making. The best way to counteract the seductive lure of images, coercive rhetoric, wishful thinking, and appeals to fear is to work on the conditions required to encourage individuals who have the capacity to be critical. Instilling virtuous traits is the alternative to the imposition of proper rules or restrictions on public discourse, and this is the reason why Dewey put so much faith in education. This is the most democratic solution because defenses against the anti-deliberative forces emerge from within democratic culture instead of being something external to or imposed on particular situations and communities. But is Dewey not just saying that we need to work on making people more rational? Is making people more rational not just a new form of rationalism? Dewey's notion of the ideal character is, however, so inclusive and so distant from the traditional use of the word 'rational' that even 'intelligence'—the term he preferred—seems narrow and misleading, and its use distracts from appreciating the uniqueness of his view.

According to Dewey's view of the ideal character, we need more, not fewer, emotional and imaginative habits to counteract the seduction of images and emotional appeals that distort inquiry. Pragmatists under-stand the force of habits. The simple awareness of being emotionally manipulated is insufficient to protect us from such manipulations. What we need is the development of a character that is emotionally receptive to doubt and that has a habitual passion for criticism. To counteract the craving and comfort provided by absolutism and dualisms, we must learn to habitually find some emotional zest and thrill in facing uncertainty and contingency. One might even claim that, if we want to protect ourselves from the seduction of images, we need to develop characters that can negotiate and interact with more, not fewer, images. Visual literacy, com-munication, and criticism may well have their own logic and the proper place in the sort of education that is needed.

Proponents of deliberative democracy prefer to describe the ideal dia-logue in terms of an exchange of reasons bounded by certain norms and conditions. Some are concerned that this model yields an overly formal normative vision of democracy. As Frank Cunningham notes, "deliberative-democratic theory may be seen to overcome the formalism of liberal democracy: by introducing the idea of deliberation and its con-ditions, substantive content for abstract democratic rights can be justified. A question that poses itself is whether deliberative democracy might not itself be too formal."[26]

Dewey presents an alternative. To avoid the same sort of formalism that is common in ethics, democratic theory should formulate its norma-tive prescriptions in terms of certain types of relationships and habits, rather than in terms of rules. If people are genuinely engaged in demo-cratic deliberation, it is because they have certain habits and not because, as Jürgen Habermas claims, they are committed to certain implicit rules of discourse.[27] Virtues as embodied habits, or ways of interacting in a de-liberative situation, are better than the mere following of rules in describ-ing and capturing the spirit of democracy deliberation. Democratization takes more than improving rules. We must, for example, be asking about the proper imaginative and emotional capacities that are needed to have more people take more seriously the standpoint, reasons, and beliefs of others. The art of listening needed in a democracy is a matter of embodied habits. Without a cadre of people with certain imaginative and emotional capacities there is no hope for democracy.

Some recent deliberativists, like Robert Talisse, are moving away from rules and reasons by proposing the importance of the "deliberative vir-tues" as the intellectual habits that can "foster in the individual episte-mically responsible habits of belief."[28] Talisse, in fact, joins Hilary Putnam

and Cheryl Misak in proposing a pragmatic epistemic conception of democracy.[29] How well does this square with Dewey's view? What points of
contention are worth exploring with these nominally pragmatist theories
of democracy? Dewey would be suspicious about the separation of epistemic virtues from moral virtues; the very integrity of our lived character
forbids such separation. Thus, for Dewey, the deliberative turn must be
more than an epistemic turn. Democracy is about much more than epistemology. There is more to democratic inquiry than the exchange of reasons
and arguments by thinkers with excellent epistemic habits.

DEWEY AND THE "ONE-VERSUS-MANY" DEBATES
IN POLITICAL THEORY

A fair and productive use of Dewey today must also keep a critical eye
on how many of the debates in political theory are centered on the same
false dichotomies that he criticized in his ethics. One such debate is that
between forms of individualism and collectivism, but there is also the
one-versus-many debate that has made its way into democratic theory
around two interdependent issues: how much unity do we actually find in
moral life? And, how much unity and pluralism can one be justified in
prescribing?

Ever since John Rawls's *A Theory of Justice* it has become common to
adopt, as the starting point of democratic theory, the existence of competing visions of the good life. Many thinkers take this pluralism about the
good as a fact and as the starting point of democratic theory. As deliberativists see it, the only normative task or challenge for democratic theory is
how to bring more unity in the form of a unified conception of public
reason, or an impartial standpoint upon which we can build some consensus about legitimate reasons or rules. From the standpoint of these
pluralistic philosophers the concept of deliberation advanced by communitarians is suspect because the communitarians tend to assume a widespread moral agreement or shared moral vision about the good that does
not exist. Communitarians take that kind of unity in moral life as a fact,
but for other philosophers what needs to be taken as a fact is a radical
pluralism among conceptions of the good. From Dewey's perspective this
debate is based on serious misconceptions about moral life.

First, why is morality reduced to either a unified conception of the
good life or a homogenizing conception of right? Dewey would question
the tendency in political theory to oversimplify our moral life by sub-
suming or unifying it under one simple category. Just as in ethics, the

only difference between political theories seems to be the single, over-arching category to which their proponents believe normative issues can be reduced. Notice how Talisse's description of the contemporary political scene resembles the debates between the good, duty, and virtue-centered views in ethics that Dewey criticized. Talisse writes,

> The liberal approach involves an analysis of competing rights claims and a bracketing off of questions about the good. The communitarian ap-proach subordinates concerns about individual rights to those of the communal good. . . . The civic republican approach likewise places the good prior to the right.[30]

Second, Dewey would question the assumption that what is most fundamental to morality and the source of moral judgments is a shared moral framework. Why are moral conflicts or disagreements among peo-ple reduced to competing comprehensive visions of the good? Is moral life constituted by one or many moral conceptual schemes? Dewey would question the empirical basis of this top-down view of moral experience. Are shared conceptions of the good even part of anyone's primary moral experience, and if so, why does sharing a conception of the good entail homogeneity in moral experience? This assumes the same view of judg-ment and deliberation that Dewey criticized in his ethics. Homogeneity follows only if it is assumed that people's moral experience and judgments are determined by a derivation from some unified moral code that pro-vides the criteria of right and wrong. For Dewey, even if everyone in a society had the exact ideal conception of the good, this does not mean that there would be agreement about moral relevance and judgment in a par-ticular situation. By Dewey's lights, this is not what ideals usually do, and we should not try to employ ideals in this way.

This last top-down view of moral life is also often accompanied in political theory by what Jorge Valadez has called the "iron cage thesis." The iron cage thesis is the view that "when we try to understand a fundamen-tally different culture, we must rely exclusively on the conceptual resources of our own worldview."[31] The result of the top-down and iron cage views is the notion that the task of political theory is to have an answer to the challenge of living in a multicultural world where there is conflict caused by radically different moral standards. If one as philosopher *starts* with the fact of incommensurable moral conceptual schemes or conceptions of the good that determine specific moral judgments, then the best we can hope for is some overlapping consensus that is motivated by the practical goal of peaceful coexistence. We just need to find a way to find some common ground based on prudential reasons instead of moral ones. But this assumes that prudential reasons are inherently less controversial or more rational. This comes very close to the Hobbesian idea that the basis for tolerance is avoiding social instability or mutual destruction.[32]

Dewey presents us with an alternative view because he has a different starting point. He would question whether starting with a large global scenario of multicultural societies that are trying to deliberate is an empirical starting point or an abstraction. There are situations in which one is faced with incommensurable groups, but this does not explain why we should favor these sorts of situations in the formulation and starting point of a democratic theory. In any case, Dewey does not find democracy less of a challenge in cases where agreements can be counted on. As we have seen with Dewey, too much agreement is also one of the undesirable conditions of democracy. Why not start with these sorts of situations instead of a scenario where there is too much disagreement?

As Dewey sees it, it does not make sense to build a democratic theory on attempts to answer situations of radical moral pluralism because in most situations in life there is some measure of both agreement and disagreement. In other words, there is no reason why pluralism is the empirical fact of any present view of democracy and unity its normative side. Unity as shared experience is also an empirical, social fact and it is an important normative issue what sort of pluralism we should have once we find unity. Dewey is, of course, a pluralist, but he would be skeptical of how unity and pluralism are understood in contemporary debates. If unity means homogeneity—that is, universal agreement about moral matters—and pluralism means the incommensurability among conceptions of the good, then we seem to be caught in a false dilemma between undesirable extremes.

The normative issue of how much or what kind of unity and plurality is desirable in moral and political life is an important practical issue. But in political theory, just as in ethical theory, the problem is often understood as something that requires a once-and-for-all theoretical solution and the adoption of wholesale stances. The answer, for Dewey, is different in every situation and the never-ending democratic task (challenge) is to find a context-sensitive balance between unity and plurality even though the tensions remain.

In a previous chapter, I explained how for Dewey oppositions in ethics are usually based on choosing sides on elements that are in tension in experience. Philosophers try to find ways to undo or dissolve practical tensions. Even when they are willing to let the opposing factors co-exist, they are committed to one of the sides and are eager to set the proper limits of the opposing factor. Something similar tends to occur in political theory. Some philosophers of democracy stand for *unity,* while others stand for *plurality,* because they esteem the values associated with each, or because they are worried about the vices that can occur if they are not sufficiently affirmed and the opposing element is valorized in our society. One philosopher stands for pluralism and avoids unity because of the dangers associated with a homogeneous collectivism. Prescribing one normative view of things seems to preclude many. For instance, the commitment to substantial or thick moral values of communitarians has made them susceptible to the charge of inviting tyranny, intolerance, and oppression. On the other hand, there are thinkers committed to unity because they are concerned with the fragmentation and isolation caused by pluralism. Prescribing many entails the risk of slipping into relativism, where there are no limits on tolerance and all is permitted. Both of these concerns (and fears) are legitimate, but for Dewey they must be addressed in a particular context by a particular inquiry that finds the appropriate workable balance. Dewey believes that there is an alternative to prescribing unity as homogeneity and pluralism without limits, but it is difficult to articulate it in a way that would satisfy those caught up in this dilemma. The tension, I have argued, is a practical one, in the sense that avoiding these extremes is an inherent and crucial part of the democratic task. The balance between the one and the many is not something to be resolved by a theory. It is, rather, the challenge that one experiences when one tries to live democratically. The absolute neutrality of certain forms of liberalism, as much as the moral partiality of some communitarians, is problematic to those of us who care about democracy.

Instead of recognizing the balance between unity and pluralism as the shared practical challenge of all believers in democracy, it has become the source of theoretical debates among political theorists. Michael Sandel is concerned that his civic republicanism not be confused with the communitarians who tend to overemphasize unity (of a homogenizing type). On the other hand, Sandel is critical of Rorty and Rawls for emphasizing pluralism too much, and therefore jeopardizing the sources of identity needed in a healthy democracy. For Rorty, Sandel's view affirms identity (unity) too much. However, for radical pluralists like Chantal Mouffe, or feminists like Iris Marion Young, Rorty is not pluralistic enough.[33] Among deliberative democrats, there is a tension between those who believe the affirmation of difference should be central to public deliberation, and those who emphasize a unifying consensus as the condition or goal of deliberation.

From Dewey's standpoint these debates are wrongheaded if the aim is to settle, once and for all, which element or value of democracy is supreme. In other words, the discussion is among thinkers who, at the end of the day, believe in the same ideal. Unity and plurality, and their corresponding values, are key to democracy. Community, cooperation, identity, loyalty, and solidarity are among the things that provide unity to democracy. Individuality, difference, tolerance, and independence provide plurality to democracy. There is no pre-established harmony between these values, and whether one side should be emphasized over the other is a context-based issue. The tension between the values of democracy makes it something fragile and in need of our intelligence, but not in need of a final theoretical answer or resolution. Contemporary political theorists could better spend their energies if they would recognize the context-bound nature of their prescriptions toward either more unity or plurality. Their disagreements may be more about the present state of affairs than about the ideal. There are those who believe that the present lack of community is the problem of our democracy, whereas others believe that the problem lies elsewhere. The calls for more unity and for more plurality are integral parts of democracy, but one call in a particular situation may be more important than the other based on the conditions at that particular time.

More work needs to be done in order to fairly and fully engage Dewey's views with those of contemporary political theorists. My goal here is simply to suggest that such a dialogue is not possible, or is impoverished, if it does not confront the most basic assumptions about moral life. I claimed earlier that in trying to place Dewey in the context of the contemporary debates in ethical theory, one runs the risk of making him complicit in assumptions he sought to override. This is also true in regard to political theory. What is most promising about Dewey's political philosophy is that it proposes a way to move beyond the family quarrels between democratic theories because of a different starting point and metaphysics of ethics. Dewey's political theory may in the end prove inadequate, but unless we try to understand it from the point of view of his entire philosophy, and in particular his ethics, we may fail to consider how radical is his view in comparison to many democratic political theorists.

THIRTEEN

A Philosophical Justification of Democracy

Democracy is the faith that the process of experience is more important than any special result attained, so that special results achieved are of ultimate value only as they are used to enrich and order the ongoing process. (LW 14:229)

The Reasonableness of an Ideal

Dewey never denied the affinities of pragmatism with the democratic spirit or way of life. On the contrary, he openly asserts that "upon one thing we take our stand. We frankly accept the democratic tradition in its moral and human import" (LW 8:76). Dewey reconstructed and justified one of the most distinctive and radical visions of democracy of the 20th century.

If the only way philosophy can provide justification for our democratic aspirations is in the form of a knowledge foundation or from some historical objective standpoint, then Dewey failed as a defender of democracy. Such failure is assumed by Richard Rorty, who believes that a pragmatist must abandon, once and for all, the notion that she can provide a philosophical justification for democracy or any other particular way of life. "There is no ahistorical standpoint from which to endorse the habits of modern democracies he wishes to praise,"[1] Rorty claims, and there is no "demonstration of the 'objective' superiority of our way of life over all other alternatives."[2]

Unwillingness to accept Rorty's resolution has recently sparked an interest in reformulating Dewey's intellectual warrant for democracy. The problem with these attempts is that they often seem more eager to answer Rorty than to understand Dewey's philosophy on its own terms. It is not surprising, then, that in many of these reformulations Dewey ends up begging the question or offering an embarrassingly circular justification. According to David Fott, for example, Dewey runs into the difficulty of justifying science or the assumed historical relativism without going in circles. He finds in Dewey "an odd defense of democracy,"[3] for there is no "clear final point for his defense of democracy."[4] Fott is puzzled about the validity of Dewey's metaphysical and normative claims because he makes a common mistake among scholars: he wants to believe that at the heart of Dewey's philosophy there is some truth, proposition, or theoretical thesis from which we can derive, explain, and examine the rest of his thought. And, of course, once one has presumably identified that first thesis for Dewey, one is faced with a dogma or finds oneself unable to defend him against the charge of begging the question. Meanwhile, Dewey's remarks about doing philosophy by starting with experience and making the entire enterprise hypothetical are either ignored or reduced to the ludicrous claim that philosophy must bow to science or to its truths. Dewey did not presuppose what he set out to prove simply because he did not set out to prove anything, at least in the traditional sense of searching for premises by which anyone may be able to deductively derive a conclusion. This is a view of justification sharply at odds with Dewey's philosophy.

Even more sympathetic scholars, like Matthew Festenstein, are disappointed by the incomplete character of Dewey's justification of democracy.[5] According to him, Dewey may have an adequate answer to the skeptical threat against democracy, but it is not clear that Dewey has a response to the relativist challenge that confronts neopragmatists today. Festenstein is right only if it is assumed that any reasonable justification must answer the challenges of an imaginary radical skeptic or relativist. But this requirement for justification, like those which require an appeal to certain first axioms or an ahistorical objective standpoint, presumes a starting point of philosophical investigation that is not Dewey's.

Philosophical inquiry is invariably and inevitably enmeshed in a particular context and background (i.e., experience) so that any justification or criticism of democracy has to arise out of this context. Dewey does not think philosophy seeks knowledge of timeless truths, but neither does he think it is "a mere arbitrary expression of wish or feeling or a vague aspiration after something nobody knows what" (MW 11:46). Philosophy is the kind of inquiry that will "use current knowledge to drive home the reasonableness of its conception of life" (MW 11:46). Therefore, providing a justification of democracy cannot mean anything more than establishing the "*reasonableness* of some course of life which has been adopted from custom or instinct" (MW 11:46, my emphasis) as a response to concrete problematic situations and with whatever resources we have available at the time in lived experience.

Indeed, a basic premise of this work has been that Dewey's philosophy is an effort to establish the *reasonableness* of a certain vision about how to live. It is addressed to people in a particular place and time in history where democracy is already a live option, rather than to an imaginary skeptic or relativist. Dewey used philosophy to make his hope reasonable, which is different than seeking a foundation or a rationalization for a way of life. Philosophy "shows men that they are not fools for doing what they already want to do."[6] Pragmatism involves the preference and the choice of a way of life but this choice does not have to be based, as Rorty suggests, solely on a desire for solidarity, mere imitation, or obedience to tradition. We do not need to become ahistorical beings to make an intelligent choice; we need to constantly examine our inherited ideals in the light of present conditions and be sincere about our preferences in the sense of stating "as clearly as possible what is chosen and why it is chosen" (LW 8:78).

This contextualist view of philosophical justification is not subject to the charge of circularity because Dewey's philosophy is not a postmodern, relativist philosophy that starts with the theory that we are *in* a culture, language, or any cohesive cognitive framework. On such views justification is always circular since judgments about better and worse forms of life are just propositional assumptions of the same form of life or "language game" we are trying to validate. From Dewey's standpoint there is not much that is "post" about this sort of postmodernism. To start with the theory that there is no way to escape our ethnocentric beliefs and language is not much different than starting with the Cartesian assumption that we start trapped within our subjectivity. Douglas Browning has said this best:

> I take the so-called "linguistic turn" in recent philosophy and the lin-
> guistic and cultural relativism which has lately been spawned by certain
> so-called "Post-Modernists" to be in fact the last and dying gasp of

Modernity, Modernism, or whatever one wishes to call the subjective turn in 17th century philosophy. Deeper than foundationalism and representationalism is the Modern avowal of the irremediable enslavement of the individual to his own manner of thinking, his own ideas, wherever those ideas originated. The notion that the world which one takes himself to live in is somehow constructed intersubjectively through the medium of one's own native language or culture is only a variation upon the Cartesian theme. I cannot help but believe that Dewey's revolution was much more radical, much more thoroughgoing, simply because it rests upon a more vital shift or turn than that.[7]

To be empirical we must begin, not with theory, but where we are, with what is pre-theoretically given in the midst of our lives. We do not find ourselves in our minds, languages, beliefs, conceptual schemes, cultures, or theories. On the contrary, these are all things that are found *within* the crude and situational non-cognitive experience as it is lived. To make any of them prior to all experience is to commit what Dewey calls the philosophical fallacy.

In light of Dewey's more radical turn and his philosophy of experience, what would constitute adequate philosophical support for democracy as an ideal? What were Dewey's grounds for his faith in democracy? These are issues that cannot be discussed in isolation from Dewey's ethics and his basic assumptions about the nature of ideals, faith, and how they emerge in the context of lived experience. Recall that ideals are experienced as part of the resources (instrumentalities) operative in situations, as ends-in-view, not as final ends with antecedent existence. Because of their nature and role in experience their reasonableness can be determined in terms of (1) their adequacy to what is actually experienced, (2) their functionality, and (3) their congeniality and consistency with one's other central commitments and hopes. Let's clarify each of these grounds and how they apply to democracy.

The Empirical Grounds of Democracy

Ideals must be empirically grounded, that is, they must be adequate to experience as it is experienced. There are at least two senses in which democracy as an ideal can meet this requirement: (1) It is supported by and emerges out of actual values experienced, and (2) it is supported by how moral life in its most generic traits is experienced. These claims are based upon a certain view of how ideals or any normative standards emerge and function in experience.

It is because we experience meaningful and worthwhile experiences in a precarious and changing world that we form and rely on ideals. If all experiences were of equal worth or if there were not a need to try to secure and reproduce the best of our experiences, then ideals would not have a function. "Because of this mixture of the regular and that which cuts across stability, a good object once experienced acquires ideal quality and attracts demand and effort to itself" (LW 1:57). Ideals are experienced as imaginative projections of possibilities based on goods actually experienced. Democracy is not only based on but goes beyond the goods of associated life in the sense that it is an appreciation of its richest possibilities. These possibilities are not subjective or fictitious. In Dewey's ethics discovery and imagination, inquiry into actual conditions, and the exploration of possibilities are mutually dependent phases of inquiry about betterment. He explains this process:

> There are values, goods, actually realized upon a natural basis—the goods of human association, of art and knowledge. The idealizing imagination seizes upon the most precious things found in climacteric moments of experience and projects them. We need no external criterion and guarantee of their goodness. They are had, they exist as good, and out of them we frame our ideal ends. (LW 9:33)

Although Dewey was critical of the traditional normative ambitions of philosophy, he thought that an empirical philosophy is not limited to description; it can imaginatively propose general and hypothetical methods of participating in situations. Nevertheless, ideal proposed methods of farming, surgery, thinking, and living together are adequate to the degree that they have been informed and constructed out of an updated and comprehensive survey of actual satisfactory experiences. For instance, the pattern of inquiry presented by Dewey in his 1938 *Logic* is descriptive insofar as it is the general structure shared by different surveyed modes of thinking. Nevertheless, it is selected as exemplary for any future inquiry. It serves a normative function insofar as it provides a generic description of how we ought to think. An expert's ideal farming methods are not drawn out of the blue; rather, they come from experiencing good and bad farming. Experience provides the means to discriminate between better and worse ideals. Dewey makes the same point with respect to his inquiry into inquiry:

> We know that some methods of inquiry are better than others in just the same way in which we know that some methods of surgery, farming, road-making, navigating or what-not are better than others. It does not follow in any of these cases that the "better" methods are ideally perfect,

or that they are regulative or "normative" because of conformity to some absolute form. They are the methods which experience up to the present time shows to be the best methods available for achieving certain results, while abstraction of these methods does supply a (relative) norm or standard for further undertakings. (LW 12:108)

A philosophy of democracy is an imaginative effort to articulate in a coherent fashion the most salient traits of the most worthwhile experiences and possibilities of human interaction for the purpose of ameliorative criticism. Democracy rests on experiencing and discriminating better and worse forms of interactions in our daily life. It is precisely because meaningful and enriching relationships are hard to come by that we need to set them up as ideal and inquire into their conditions. "The problem is to extract the desirable traits of forms of community life which actually exist, and employ them to criticize undesirable features and suggest improvement" (MW 9:88–89).

Dewey insisted that this ideal must remain open to modification and improvement as new forms of communication in different contexts are experienced. Since ideals are based upon experienced goods, they can be subject to criticism and improvement based on their adequacy to these goods. For example, an ideal may assume certain goods that are no longer experienced as such or it may fail to include some important ones. In fact, our task today in reevaluating Dewey's ideal should be to ask ourselves: Are the features of democratic interactions that Dewey thought were important still experienced as positive and essential features of the best in human relationships? For instance, is it still the case that openness, tolerance, and sympathy are integral to our most enriching and meaningful communicative experiences? Things that were worth aspiring to yesterday may not be worth aspiring to today. Someone could well maintain that openness and tolerance are no longer good in most situations or that, if they are good, we should not make them part of an inclusive end-in-view. It is hard to see how one could argue for such a position, especially today when "closedness" and intolerance are so common and insidious; but as a contextualist, I must accept that someday, somewhere, openness and tolerance may well not be worth our efforts. The reasonableness of Dewey's ideal from the point of view of values experienced could also be questioned on the grounds of what he failed to include or emphasize. I have raised this criticism of Dewey in regard to trust and loyalty. A similar case could also be made in regard to responsibility, humility, curiosity, discernment, love of learning, forgiveness, and compassion. These are virtues that are usually present in the sort of interaction that Dewey envisioned as ideal, but they are underemphasized or not explicitly considered by him in his ethics.

What may seem peculiar and perhaps objectionable about this account of how ideals can emerge in philosophical inquiry is the assumption that experiencing better and worse in particular situations does not itself presuppose an antecedent ideal standard or criterion that must be made explicit. More to the point, can a philosophical defender of democracy determine what interactions are experienced as better (or valuable) without begging the question in favor of democracy? I will consider this important objection at a later point.

The Metaphysical Support for Democracy

Metaphysical support for democracy counts as empirical support when metaphysics is understood as an empirical inquiry into the most generic traits of experience as it is experienced. For Dewey, a view of democracy "not grounded in a comprehensive philosophy seems . . . only a projection of arbitrary preference" (LW 14:150). Our general view of reality must support our democratic hopes and efforts. His criticisms of traditional metaphysics and ethics were efforts to demolish a view of things that makes our faith in democracy seem unreasonable. Philosophers have for the most part, whether aware of it or not, failed to deliver philosophies that can provide intellectual warrant for democracy. Philosophers have assumed views of reality and of moral life that are not congenial to and supportive of democratic values and aspirations. Foremost among them is what Dewey called the "metaphysics of feudalism," that is, a hierarchical and fixed view of reality. This is clear in ethical theory, where the presupposed view of morality usually has a top-down structure and spirit. For instance, ethical theorists assume that among the concepts of good, duty, and virtue one of them must be primordial (i.e., that there is a set hierarchy). There is also the authoritarian belief that there is a single rule- or law-governed right thing to do in any moral situation, and that otherwise there would be anarchy. The top-down aspect of traditional ethical theory is even more evident in the shared assumption (in spite of remarkable differences) that individual acts and situations fall *under* some prior abstract or universal moral truth or code, or that one's regard for a particular individual must fall *under* some wider or higher concern (e.g., justice). This stands in sharp contrast with Dewey's radical bottom-up democratic ethical theory. As I have already argued, Dewey turned traditional ethics on its head. Each situation is both the means and end of morality. Moral reasoning and justification are not manners of working downward from rules to their application; instead, it is "working upward from concrete moral experience and decision making toward guiding moral hypotheses."[8] Even someone like Jürgen Habermas, who shares a similar communicative ideal, seems to be caught in the traditional quest for a top-down ethics in which the validation of general rules that apply to what is particular and unique is primary.[9]

If the top-down assumptions about morality and nature were only the fancy of philosophers, then Dewey's ethics is at best therapy for philosophers. But these assumptions are still part of the dominant model of morality in Western culture and, therefore, many have adopted them as their ground map (metaphysics) that provides their basic orientation in the world. Therefore, for Dewey, criticism of ethical theories that help perpetuate this erroneous view of morality is necessary, for such ethical theories undermine the spirit and hopes that Dewey considered essential to democracy. This situation is worsened by the fact that those philosophers who have explicitly tried to provide philosophical support for democracy have ended up assuming an obnoxious and dangerous type of metaphysical individualism: the notion of the isolated individual with inherent rights who is naturally self-interested. As Dewey said, when democracy "has tried to achieve a philosophy it has clothed itself in an atomistic individualism, as full of defect and inconsistencies in theory as it was charged with obnoxious consequences when an attempt was made to act upon it" (MW 11:52).

It is because Dewey conceived democracy as an aspiration about how we should relate to nature (reality) that metaphysics is an important part of its justification.[10] If, contrary to Dewey, there is in nature a set hierarchy of beings or values, and its open-ended character is an illusion, then democracy seems to recommend that we live in a way that is orthogonal to nature's dictates. But if nature is a process where new problems, risks, and the unexpected seem unavoidable, then a community and character that goes forth to meet new demands, that welcomes untried situations, and that is capable of constant readjustment is in better shape than a fixed, static one. It is because the world has certain generic traits that democracy is a reasonable way to interact in it. Dewey thought that his ethics supported democratic hopes and aspirations better than most ethical theories because it portrayed moral reality itself as open, contingent, individual, social, and irreducibly pluralistic.

In fact, Dewey's views about democracy cannot be separated from his plea that we accept a certain metaphysics, that is, that we do not turn away from or ignore the complexity, pluralism, and uncertainty of reality. Democracy is another name for a way of life that "accepts life and experience in all its uncertainty, mystery, doubt, and half-knowledge and turns that experience upon itself to deepen and intensify its own qualities" (LW 10:41). Pluralism of beliefs, religions, cultures, and social groups is increasingly an unquestionable trait of present experience. In a world where interaction is becoming unavoidable and even necessary, isolation and segregation are no longer ways to successfully cope with pluralism. We can respond to pluralism by trying to remove it, either by force, indoctrination, or by constructing a philosophical theory that explains the unfortunate pluralism as mere appearance or a result of human limitations. These responses assume that a pluralism of beliefs is merely an early stage on the way to later convergence or, perhaps, a fall from grace. For pragmatists, on the other hand, the plurality of views that are deeply believed is a positive characteristic of the human condition, rather than something to lament. For pluralism is not only the irreducible character of reality but a source of possible enrichment. Participation, communication, and sharing in a pluralistic environment can make life rich and varied in meanings. "To cooperate by giving differences a chance to show themselves because of the belief that the expression of difference is not only a right of the other persons but is a means of enriching one's own life-experience, is inherent in the democratic personal way of life" (LW 14:228).

Dewey believes that the ideals of liberty, equality, and freedom are more meaningful or congenial to the pragmatist conception of experience than to traditional metaphysics. Our liberty is more meaningful if we are participants (instead of spectators) in a universe that is a genuine field of experimentation, novelty, and constantly in the making.

> A philosophy animated, be it unconsciously or consciously, by the strivings of men to achieve democracy will construe liberty as meaning a universe in which there is real uncertainty and contingency, a world which is not all in, and never will be, a world which in some respect is incomplete and in the making, and which in these respects may be made this way or that according as men judge, prize, love and labor. (MW 11:50)

Pragmatism is a philosophy that supports the democratic ideal of equality because it rejects "the metaphysics of feudalism" (MW 11:51) that supports authoritarian ideals, while also recognizing that uniqueness and individuality are traits of experience. In a world where every existence is qualitatively unique and develops in the context of unique social circumstances, our democratic aspirations to respect the individuality of the other seems most reasonable. Dewey supports the ideal of equality by "a metaphysical mathematics of the incommensurable in which each speaks for itself and demands consideration on its own behalf" (MW 11:53). A metaphysics of democracy based on the notion of everyone having the same rights cannot elicit the same democratic respect for one another that comes from recognizing that there is something irreplaceable about each one of us in every new moment in the flow of experience.

However, individuality is not something that develops or that can be appreciated independently of association and interaction. Hence, an individualism that is not atomistic is the metaphysical basis for fraternity as an ideal of democracy.

> To say that what is specific and unique can be exhibited and become forceful or actual only in relationship with other like beings is merely, I take it, to give a metaphysical version to the fact that democracy is concerned not with freaks or geniuses or heroes or divine leaders but with associated individuals in which each by intercourse with others somehow makes the life of each more distinctive. (MW 11:53)

To be sure, democracy is not something separated from nature (the subject matter of metaphysics). It is not some sort of method or way of talking to each other by which humans can, in isolation from a valueless and chaotic world, establish some sort of order. Democracy lacks metaphysical grounding if one begins with the theory that all of our wishes, ideals, and values are nothing more than our own cultural and arbitrary (self-serving) projections imposed upon a valueless world. This dualistic picture of things is not the starting point of Dewey's ethics. For him, democracy points to values and possibilities that are experienced and have arisen in our transaction with the world. These values and possibilities are as much a part of the objective everyday world as they are ours. Democratic interaction is something we do in discourse with other humans, but we are part of nature and the context that guides the discourse is the qualitative world that we inhabit. Therefore, the ordered richness achieved by democracy is of nature and because of it.

The Functionality of Democracy

To evaluate and justify ideals requires much more than investigating their relation to how life in its actual values and generic features is experienced. For what makes them ideals is that they are in some sense beyond how things are and have been. And they are not things destined to be facts or to be fully realized. As Giovanni Sartori has said, "ideals always smack of hubris, they are always excessive. This is, as it should be, since ideals are designed to overcome resistances."[11] An ideal that is fully realizable ceases to function as an ideal. This explains why Dewey can say that democracy "is not a fact and never will be" (LW 2:328).

Ideals are experienced as ends-in-view that interact with the world and have a practical function. We could thus ask about any ideal: Is it constructive or is it counterproductive and self-defeating? Does it provide orientation, inspiration, and carry us through tough times? Does it guide action or make our individual struggles more meaningful? Does it positively provoke our imaginations in the sense of eliciting possibilities that may not be appreciated or explored otherwise? These are all important questions that would have to be considered in a full evaluation of democracy as an ideal. For now I would like to focus on one important aspect of a useful ideal according to Dewey's ethics.

A constructive ideal must assist in transforming, guiding, and inspiring but it must itself be open to improvement in light of present experience. This requires that an ideal be "sufficiently definite to be usable and sufficiently flexible to lead to its own reinterpretation as experience progresses" (LW 7:344). Dewey was aware that both excess generality and specificity in the formulation of an ideal tend to be counterproductive. He was, on the one hand, concerned that the ideal of a democratic way of life not remain an idle tool by becoming a vague abstraction. We must do better than regurgitate the political slogans associated with democracy. The ideal "must not remain vague and general. It must be translated into the concrete details of what it means in every walk of life" (LW 11:237). On the other hand, he was keenly aware that too much specificity can work against the effectiveness of an ideal. As we saw earlier, Dewey thought that ethical theory can betray its practical function if it abandons its generic character and pretends to provide specific instructions. In order to serve as an effective instrument of criticism without undermining context-sensitive reflection, democracy as an ideal must be "stated in such a way that it will apply to changed conditions of the present and the future" (LW 7:343).

This last point is relevant to evaluating an objection to Dewey that has been reconsidered by Robert Westbrook and Michael Eldridge. They find it problematic that, as Eldridge puts it, Dewey did not specify " 'in the concrete' the political means to effect the democratic ends."[12] He failed to flesh out the details of his democratic vision. But how much more thickness could be added to his ideal before it becomes counterproductive? I am suggesting that the generality and vagueness of Dewey's views about democracy are strengths not weaknesses of his position. Dewey was a committed contextualist and the lack of a more detailed vision is what allows us today to develop the specifics as they pertain to our present experience without abandoning Dewey's vision. Had he, for example, given us specific instructions about how freedom is secured in a democracy, they could have prevented us from engaging in a fresh context-sensitive inquiry into this matter today. Critics wanted to know "*what* to think" but Dewey instead would tell them "*how* to think,"[13] because the latter was more fruitful.

The lack of specific instructions in Dewey's philosophy regarding the democratic task does not mean a total lack of guidance as to what can be done to democratize experience. Let's reassess the issue of functionality in light of Dewey's ethics. Criticism and inquiry into conditions on behalf of a more democratic experience are legitimate theoretical tasks. If democracy has to do with the quality of our most immediate associations, then widespread institutional, political, or legal reforms must be tested by how they affect the quality of these relationships. If democracy is about having certain experiences, then instead of investigating rules of justice or the proper conception of human rights, philosophers and political theorists must inquire into which character traits and environmental conditions are necessary for having those experiences.

Dewey was particularly concerned with which type of education and classroom environment would provide the conditions for the development of characters that have an emotional readiness to assimilate the experience of others (e.g., openness, sympathy), and are active, flexible, critical, sensitive, and willing to cooperate in the common good. It is especially important that in a democracy each generation of children be equipped to "formulate its own beliefs and practices in light of new experiences and discoveries" (LW 11:554). Philosophy cannot set the particular conditions and means that are needed for democracy for all times and places, but it can be concerned with useful generalities such as how to inquire into them. The importance of context-sensitive reflection cannot be underestimated. In order to seek solutions in terms of concrete problems as they arise we must "surrender our faith in system and in some wholesale belief" (LW 5:119–20).

Dewey was also critical of ways to inquire into conditions and means that are not consistent with the ideal. To force individuals to be free in the name of democracy is a form of intellectual hypocrisy which leads to anti-democratic results. "The fundamental principle of democracy is that the ends of freedom and individuality for all can be attained only by means that accord with those ends" (LW 11:298). The aristocratic means of such democratic elitists as Walter Lippmann was also against the spirit and realization of democracy.[14] A democratic community cannot be created or handed down from above by a democratic elite that has a blueprint of the good life. It must rather emerge from within its voluntary associations.

The stress on immanence is consistent with the notion of a moral life that is ameliorated by its own means. In "The Ethics of Democracy" (EW 1:227–49) Dewey stresses that what really distinguishes democracy from any aristocratic ideal is the means by which all that is worth striving for is brought about. What is most objectionable about a society ruled by the few wise and good (assuming that power will not corrupt them) is that their decisions (no matter how wise) lead to benefits that are external to others in the sense that do not come from within individuals (the rest of society) working out for themselves problematic situations. Hence, it violates an important condition for ideal activity, for having the most meaningful experiences.

The defenders of aristocracy are quick to point out that the outcomes they propose are good, but for Dewey, as we have seen in his ethics, the quality of the process is more important than how good or beneficial the outcome happens to be. "Humanity cannot be content with a good which is procured from without, however high and otherwise complete that good" (EW 1:243). A society where good outcomes are given is not to be preferred to one in which these goods are the result of participation (working). It is good when others solve problems for us but it is more meaningful and enriching—it has an aesthetic quality—when we have put some of our own work or effort into the process. When we work things out for ourselves we learn, and the results of our task achieve consummatory value. Dewey offers no argument to defend this. He is just offering a hypothesis and an invitation to try it out to see whether it is a more meaningful experience. To be engaged in an activity where there is a balanced relation between means and ends, between play and work is the ideal.

It follows that the best way to help others is indirectly, by creating the conditions for them to help themselves as well as deepen and widen their relationships. This idea is easily misunderstood. But Dewey endorses it because positive freedom happens to be a condition for the enhancement of present activity (living), not because individuals are self-sufficient, must be left alone, and liberty is an absolute good.

> To foster conditions that widen the horizon of others and give them command of their own powers, so that they can find their own happiness in their own fashion, is the way of "social" action. Otherwise the prayer of a freeman would be to be left alone, and to be delivered, above all, from "reformers" and "kind" people. (MW 14:203)

This is a call for a lot of work in a society that takes democracy seriously. Leaving the individuals to themselves to whatever they want does not foster the positive freedom needed for democratic interaction. It takes great effort and communal resources to foster individuals and communities capable of working out the problems they experience for themselves.

Although we cannot export or impose democracy, we can provide or prepare the soil in which the flower of democracy may gradually emerge. There are some interesting implications and complications of this important insight. First, there is the question of who is the "we" that fosters the conditions for the emergence of democracy. Can it ever be someone from outside the community in question? Furthermore, at what point can the control over indirect conditions ruin the spontaneous emergence of what is wanted? This is especially troublesome when one aims to restore or revitalize the sort of relationships and genuine communities for which Dewey hoped. They cannot be engineered or created the way one constructs a bridge or fixes a pipe. Since community is usually associated with stability in experience it is easy to overlook the importance of contingency, novelty, and spontaneity in the creation, sustenance, and quality of a community. This becomes clear in examining the recent attempt to build gated communities. The gates, rules, and homogeneity of these communities provide the comfort of a controlled, secured, predictable, and safe environment but at the cost of sterility, boredom, and the unaesthetic. The retreat into gated communities is a flight from chance. The price for security is an environment with no surprises, where an unplanned and enriching conversation with a person unlike oneself is ruled out. Dewey, of course, would be opposed to this sort of community, but it is not clear how a more intelligent and flexible Deweyan effort to create community is not vulnerable to the same sort of problem. A Deweyan project to indirectly control the conditions for the emergence of a community may run into the problem of determining when its intervention is spoiling the needed chance and spontaneity for a community to emerge. This being said, it does not mean that the way of intelligence is to leave things alone. I can think of no solution to this difficulty except to hope that, equipped with the habits of intelligence, we will be able to determine in a particular case when we have reached that critical point where even indirect control is too much. The emergence of a genuine community is in some ways a more delicate matter than that of a flower. But just as with the flower, even if we do what is in our power we must come to terms with the fact that it many never blossom. This is all Deweyan in spirit.

Perhaps a more promising way of inquiring about conditions in the name of democracy can take the negative form of answering the question: What feature of present conditions is an obstacle to having more of the kinds of experiences associated with democracy? Just as with a flower we may decide to focus our attention on weeds. This is one way in which the ideal may serve as a tool of criticism. For example, what undermines meaningful and effective democratic public deliberation? What specific environmental conditions (economic, sociological, and political) are responsible for nurturing habits that work against the habits and spirit of democracy? What has contributed to the snobbery and aristocratic habits that continue to predominate in our society? To what extent have the habits of classifying, quantification, labeling, and ranking contributed to our numbness toward the individuality of others in our everyday experience? What in our society encourages the habit of dismissing or demonizing others instead of genuinely listening to them? What encourages dogmatism or the habit of thinking of simplistic good/evil, us/them dichotomies?

One difficulty with inquiry into the obstacles to democracy is that dualism often gets in the way. One must be careful, for example, not to assume that there are certain institutions or means that are somehow by nature intrinsically opposed to the values of democracy. The material/spiritual dualism is sometimes behind the assumption that industry and business (i.e., our economic relations) are intrinsically non-democratic or outside the realm of human values. This often has the unintended consequence of making them immune from the sort of democratic reconstruction for which Dewey hoped. "To stop with mere emotional rejection and moral condemnation of industry and trade as materialistic is to leave them in this inhuman region where they operate as the instruments of those who employ them for private ends. Exclusion of this sort is an accomplice of the forces that keep things in the saddle" (LW 5:17).

There is no realm of human experience that is immune from democratization or criticism from the point of view of democracy. If some corporations and governments are a threat to democracy we must find ways to transform them from within their everyday operations and interactions. One could argue that this is a more radical and subversive approach to the threats to democracy than merely adopting an ideological view that understands such threats as inherently evil powers that can only be subject to external control.

Technology, science, and commerce are responsible for the mobility, organization, and impersonalism that have eroded the quality of the local ties needed for a healthy democracy. But Dewey insisted that there is nothing in the nature of things that rules out that the same forces that have undermined democracy can be used to reverse their effect. "We can assert with confidence that there is nothing intrinsic in the forces which have affected uniform standardization, mobility and remote invisible relationships that is fatally obstructive to the return movement of their consequences into the local homes of mankind" (LW 2:369). There is no going back to some mythical better past. Dewey's solution was to try to turn these same forces in favor of procuring a free, diverse, but stable communal life. This is what it means to reconstruct from within our present resources and possibilities. He is, for instance, explicit about the important role that mobility and organization can play in maintaining the sort of balance that is needed. "Mobility may in the end supply the means by which the spoils of remote and indirect interaction and interdependence flow back into local life, keeping it flexible, preventing the stagnancy which has attended stability in the past, and furnishing it with the elements of a variegated and many-hued experience. Organization may cease to be taken as an end in itself. Then it will no longer be mechanical and external, hampering the free play of artistic gifts . . ." (LW 2:370).

The functionality of Dewey's philosophy of democracy could be questioned on the grounds that it is just too utopian. In other words, it is too demanding or idealistic to be taken seriously or to play any positive function. The idealistic or optimistic character of Dewey's vision in light of present conditions should be obvious. His vision was of a society in which the strength and depth of local relations (family, neighborhood, and friendships) are not a threat but supportive of the organizations and institutions we delegate to administer the indirect consequences for all social groups. He even dreamed of finding ways to extend some of the democratic qualities of the most intimate and direct relations to the wider circle of an organized society. Is there something objectionable in holding such utopian dreams and hopes?

The Utopia Objection

There are different versions of this utopia objection that must be considered.[15] On one level, it seems to be based on a misunderstanding of what an ideal is. A failure to achieve or even envision full realizability should not count against an ideal. What would be the use of an ideal if it was not utopian and beyond complete realization? But perhaps the objection is that the ideal is too idealistic, that is, too good to be taken seriously. The charge of excessive goodness can take two forms. It may be that the content of the ideal is so good and perfect that it becomes undesirable, thereby losing its intrinsic imaginative appeal as something worth aspiring to. This was the same reaction and concern expressed by James after he visited the Chautauqua community and saw "a gathering of wonderfully cooperative,

peaceful, benign, socially conscious" persons. James's account of his reaction is worth quoting here at length:

> And yet what was my own astonishment, on emerging into the dark and
> wicked world again, to catch myself quite unexpectedly and involun-
> tarily saying: "Ouf! What a relief! Now for something primordial and
> savage, even though it were as bad as an Armenian massacre, to set the
> balance straight again. This order is too tame, this culture too second-
> rate, this goodness too uninspiring . . . this city simmering in the tepid
> lakeside sun; this atrocious harmlessness of all things,—I cannot abide
> with them. Let me take my chances again in the big outside worldly
> wilderness with all its sins and sufferings . . ."[16]

Is my description of Dewey's ideal too good in this sense and therefore
susceptible to the same sort of charge? Only if one ignores what I have said
about the nature of ideals. The ideal described is not something intended
to be fully realizable or supposed to describe a comprehensive state of
affairs. Therefore, there is much that is missing in the description that is
not presented simply because it is taken for granted that it will be part of
any community. Dewey never assumes that the precarious, the uncertain,
and all the things that make our lives less than absolutely perfect—that is,
those things that are missing in the Chautauqua community—would have
to be eliminated. On the contrary, he counted on them, and I have made
that a key to my description. I have shown that conflict, tension, and risk
are an integral part of his ideal. "Balance" is understood by Dewey as
a creative but precarious tension, and not as a stable state of peaceful
harmony that we can rest on. A community that is too tame needs a dose
of danger. Fragility, contingency, struggle, and conflict are integral to a
meaningful life.

There is, however, another interpretation of the utopia objection that
any Deweyan should confront. What if the excessive goodness of an ideal
affects its practical effectiveness under present conditions? Although all
ideals are excesses, this does not mean that they can be safely maximized
beyond measure without losing their effectiveness. An excessively idealistic view of democracy can work against the democracy it is supposed to
generate. This is a danger today. The gap between our actual way of life
and Dewey's ideal is so pronounced that becoming aware of the latter may
only lead to cynicism, nihilism, and passive resignation. The point is that
sometimes when ideals become too high or idealistic relative to the present context they are nothing but obstacles to present amelioration. Pessimism is usually the result of having unreasonably high standards and
expectations about the potentialities of life and others. It is not a matter of

humility to aim or dream lower when constructing ideals, but a matter of making the ideal instrumentally effective.

This last objection raises a legitimate concern. Dewey would want his ideal to be a good means and it may be the case that Deweyans today must make the content of the democratic ideal more modest in order to increase its instrumental potency. The objection, however, is only a practical warning and does not give us a philosophical basis to evaluate the reasonableness of Dewey's ideal independently of any particular use and context. Indeed, it is difficult to assess the instrumental potency of an ideal in the abstract, independently of a particular context and of how an ideal is actually used. The threat of cynicism and passivity, for example, may be more a consequence of the bad use of the ideal than of anything related to its content. An ideal may seem reasonable in all other respects, but because it is taken as an absolute standard, it ceases to function as a possibility which provokes our imaginations and makes us nonconformist (and uncomfortable) about the present state of affairs. Those who think of democracy as a blueprint and ignore the fact that the meaning of democracy changes with time and place may be considered traitors of the ideal because they confuse the spirit with the letter of democracy. We have already seen that Dewey makes this same point regarding the use of rules in morality. Even the best moral principles can be harmful if one is not sensitive to context. Hence, even if we were to agree that Dewey's ideal has the appropriate amount of substance, detail, and appeal, it could still remain counterproductive because of the way it is employed in situations. This underscores the emphasis on the "how" of his ethics, that is, being equipped with the right habits needed to find out what democracy requires in particular situations.

The Naïveté Objection

The counterpart to the utopia objection is the charge that Dewey was naïve which affected the reasonableness of his democratic vision. This could mean that he was naïve (1) about the problems or obstacles of democracy, (2) about how bad (severe) these problems really are, or (3) about the means needed for ameliorating them. These are, of course, related. Naïveté about the means is usually a result of underestimating the problems. The most common charge against Dewey has been that his ideal seems impotent and naïve because he underestimated the extent to which conflict, power (as force and coercion), tragic irreconcilabilities, instinct, and irrationalities undermine any effort to democratize experience.[17] This claim is serious since it in effect accuses Dewey of failing to meet the requirement of adequacy to experience. In his zealousness for democracy he may have downplayed or ignored undesirable and anti-democratic forces that are intrinsic features of the human condition.

Is this charge fair? It depends on the nature of the accusation. It would not do to claim that he hoped for what is impossible, or that he expected too much out of human relationships, social institutions, and human beings because he had the wrong (and naïve) view of the nature of these things (e.g., because humans are by nature intrinsically evil or selfish). There is, for Dewey, no fixed nature of anything, certainly not of human beings. The extent to which forces plague or create limitations to what can be done in human relationships is an empirical issue because it is based on present conditions. The problem with non-empirical ways of deciding what is or is not possible (e.g., what can we expect of humans) is that it settles the issue in advance.

If, however, the charge is that Dewey did not take into account the evil and complexity that we experience today but which was not part of his situation, then this either makes no sense or it is an unreasonable expectation. But we can inquire into whether he was oblivious or blind to the ways that the anti-democratic forces operated during his time. Eldridge, for example, defends Dewey on these grounds by providing evidence that in Dewey's active involvement of the problems of his time he did not "ignore class interests" or the use of power politics.[18] There is in fact plenty of textual support to show that Dewey recognized the subtle and hidden forces that controlled public discussion.[19] He even warned future generations about how the growing forces of propaganda (control by the few) and the consumerist appetite for sensationalism are bound to prevent the possibility of democratic public discourse.[20] It is not clear to me how much more we can expect of Dewey.

The more interesting and important issue is whether our problems today are sufficiently different, and things so much worse, that Dewey's ideas and ideal seem out of touch, naïve, and inapplicable. To properly answer this question I would have to provide an empirical assessment of present conditions, something that is beyond the scope of this book. I can predict, however, that we would indeed find aspects of Dewey's view that seem naïve when compared to today's complex social conditions. For instance, given what science is today, it may be hard to have the same sort of confidence that Dewey had in its instrumentalities for moral life or in his confidence in science as the best example of communal inquiry. Given the unprecedented power of global corporations today it seems that much more is needed for positive freedom and the self-governing capacity of the public than what Dewey suggested. New technologies have made possible new ways to reduce political discourse to a sport-like spectacle where the public remains entertained but dormant. More could be said, but I fail to see how this sort of criticism constitutes a refutation of Dewey's views or a reason to dismiss their relevance. For he expected context to change, and therefore he expected that followers of his vision would reconstruct his ideas in light of present conditions, so that they do not become irrelevant, naïve, and out of touch.

The most flawed version of the naïveté charge comes from misconceptions about what Dewey hoped for and how he conceived moral life. John Patrick Diggins, for example, faults Dewey for not recognizing that democracy is full of tensions and contradictions. He claims that unlike Dewey, "Lincoln saw democracy as tragic."[21] Diggins makes the common mistake of inferring from the fact that since Dewey argued against dualisms he must have presupposed the possibility of an easygoing harmony. He says, "since Dewey denies dualism, he sees little distinction between the community and the individual. He is also unwilling to see that liberty, equality, and fraternity are value preferences and, as such, are incompatible with one another."[22] It should be clear by now that Dewey never underestimated the tensions integral to the ideal of democracy, or the difficulties and even tragic character of the decisions one must make in living by this ideal. Even if, as Richard Bernstein has recently pointed out, Dewey may have at times "relied too much on metaphors of harmony and organic unity,"[23] they must not be understood as the quest for a state without tension and conflict.

Dewey's view of moral life provides the rich and complex context or background in which we must understand his hopes for democracy. In his ethics one finds a view of moral problems, conflicts, and deliberation that should discredit most charges of naïveté. As obvious as this may be, there have been reputable Dewey scholars who have claimed that there is a lack of tragic sensibility in Dewey ethics.[24] Hilary Putnam, for example, finds Dewey's moral philosophy less satisfactory than his social philosophy because he failed to take into account the tensions and irreconcilability between human goods. James Kloppenberg thinks that because of Dewey's failure on this score we should turn to James's ethics as the basis of a democratic vision. James's sensitivity to the "tragic betrayal of some ethical ideal in every choice between irreconcilable conceptions of the good makes his variety of pragmatist political thinking perhaps better suited to our time."[25]

I would admit that Dewey, in comparison to James, often overzealously encouraged us to create instrumentalities of prediction and control. But this is just a difference of degrees, emphasis, and character. Dewey recognizes that in the paradigmatic problems of moral life there is genuine uncertainty and conflict as to the morally correct thing to do. Dewey's starting point is not a world where values are compatible and where most problems can be solved by some intellectual method. On the contrary, moral life is usually so complex and conflicting that it is no wonder we tend to flee by seeking the false security of rules or some foundation outside of lived experience. We should instead try to work with the raw resources, and trust that with perseverance and sensitivity we may find some guidance within experience. This makes Dewey faith extraordinary but not naïve.

In sum, tragic sensibility is not what is missing in Dewey's ethics. His faith in the instrumentalities of experience was tempered by an honest realization that moral life was strenuous and tragic, and that "when all is said and done, the fundamentally hazardous character of the world is not seriously modified, much less eliminated" (LW 1:45).

The charge of naïveté presents at best a danger for the democratic task. The risk of downplaying actual limitations in dealing with problems is that we may fail to rely on them in inquiry. The danger of wishful thinking is that we may stop consulting the "grain of experience," and this has consequences. Democracy is in jeopardy if people decide to ignore the actual obstacles and limitations present at any time in human relations. This is why for Dewey "choosing and acting with conscious regard to the grain of circumstance" (LW 3:105) must become habit.

But the risk in emphasizing limitations is also serious. If we convince ourselves that improving our relationships in a more democratic direction is impossible, then we have automatically precluded one of its first conditions: our faith. Because of this and because we cannot know in advance what our actual limitations will be, it seems wise to be hopeful but alert, to have faith but be critical. Naïveté today is avoided by allowing criticism to reach down to even those concealed forces that control what may seem like free public discourse. The difficulty, however, is how to do this without becoming cynical and losing faith in all dialogue and resorting to nondemocratic means. The alternative to cynicism and a primitive naïveté is the balance between faith and criticism that Dewey describes as a "cultivated naivety of eye, ear, and thought, one that can be acquired only through the discipline of severe thought" (LW 1:40).

Dewey's meliorism tries to avoid both pessimism and optimism. There is a false sense of comfort or security in these opposing views, and assent to either of them shows a failure to confront the open-ended character of life and an intellectual arrogance in claiming to know things in advance. Learning from defeat, frustration, and failure does not presuppose that there will always be a lesson or that the lessons are already there in some sense. Rather, it presupposes that we *may* learn while acknowledging that "control or power is never complete; luck or fortune, the propitious support of circumstances not foreseeable is always involved" (LW 3:105).

A different charge of naïveté can be raised against Dewey. He was not naïve about our limitations but rather about the dangers of the drive to control and ameliorate present conditions. Even if Dewey was sensitive to the tragic, his meliorism is an intellectual justification for the drive to improve that can go against certain more passive but important attitudes toward people and events. Dewey's faith in the instrumentalities of experience should have been tempered by recognition of what positive value there is to accepting things as they come. There is in life a time to ameliorate our contingent circumstances, but there is also a time to accept them, not in a grudgingly or stoical way, but in a loving way.

This is an issue that has come up in regard to technology in its seemingly endless capacity to improve our lives. In a recent article, Michael Sandel argues that what is troubling about designer children, bionic athletes, and genetic engineering is that this kind of meliorism represents "a kind of hyperagency—a Promethean aspiration to remake nature, including human nature, to serve our purposes and satisfy our desires. The problem is not the drift to mechanism but the drive to mastery. And what the drive to mastery misses and may even destroy is an appreciation of the gifted character of human powers and achievements."[26] The ethics of enhancement raises "questions about the moral status of nature, and about the proper stance of human beings toward the given world."[27]

If we can become better human beings and communities by genetic engineering, should we? Is that what Dewey's melioristic ethics implies? Is there in Dewey an acknowledgment of the attitude Sandel thinks is threatened by the new developments in technology?

Dewey has been called an instrumentalist but he was aware of the dangers of too much mastery or excessive doing.[28] I have argued that for him activity with aesthetic quality (as a balanced relation between doing and undergoing) is the paradigmatic form of activity. Beholding, savoring, accepting, and celebrating the given world does not have to be incompatible with molding, transforming, and perfecting it, even if there is a tension and risks corresponding to doing each of these things in isolation or to the extreme. The difficult balance between a transforming love and an accepting love, between molding our children and accepting their individuality, is true of all democratic relationships. The parents to be admired are not those who are willing to improve their children by whatever means and to whatever the extent. Dewey addressed these issues with respect to education. The overbearing parent is like the overbearing teacher—she does not allow for the changes that come from within the child's own transactions with circumstances. Their drive toward mastery not only has bad consequences but it is a failure to appreciate chance, novelty, individuality, and mystery. Dewey tried to point to a balance between discipline-structure and freedom in the classroom but was often misunderstood as holding an extreme view. The causes of hyper-parenting are too complex to be discussed here, but even during Dewey's time he was aware of how our education system has been affected by the pressure to succeed, compete, and produce quantifiable outcomes that characterize our society at large.

I have argued that Dewey's appreciation of uniqueness (a key to his notion of equality), valuing, and his natural piety provide a side of Dewey that is concerned with appreciating what there is for what it is, independently of our wishes or how it can be improved. It is true that in many of his writings he was mostly concerned that we be more willing to ameliorate the quality of present experience by its own resources, but this sort of encouragement is not incompatible with appreciating things for what they are, in their uniqueness, and irrespective of our wishes or outcomes for us. Even when we are able to elicit the potentialities of present experience, what actually emerges from our intervention is a source of wonder, a gift, to be embraced for what it is. The individuality of things is the basis of "the mystery of things being just what they are." This is a "mystery that is the source of all joy and sorrow, of all hope and fear, and the source of development both creative and degenerative" (LW 14:112).

The proper appreciation of the giftedness and contingency of things is, by Dewey's lights, part of a balanced attitude toward the world that falls in between two extremes. One extreme is the excessive resolve to improve and control that becomes a pride bordering on arrogance with respect to the world. The other extreme is the one that does not seem to worry Sandel. Too much of what Sandel sees threatened by the new technologies can degenerate into a passive resignation. We are so receptive and accepting of the contingent character of events that we celebrate even the evils that come to others and us without making an effort to ameliorate things. This borders on moral irresponsibility, especially when there is the technology available to ameliorate our problems. If one pole is based on an exaggerated optimism about our own powers, the other pole borders on determinism. As mentioned before, Dewey wants a humility that is accompanied with a readiness to ameliorate. This humility is a basis for democratic solidarity and the generous treatment of others.

The sort of ethics of enhancement that Sandel criticizes is a very different view than Dewey's ethics even if they both emphasize amelioration. Remember how I distinguished Dewey's view from the notion of improvement as approximation to a final end or standard of perfection. Dewey is not interested in perfection as either an ideal or as a standard. This is in no way a license to be lazy, sloppy, or unconcerned about improvement. Meliorism in Dewey is a context-relative notion (i.e., to particular problematic situations that call for improvement). He does not endorse amelioration for the sake of amelioration. The amelioration that is encouraged by his ethics is one that is grounded on problems experienced—in this sense, terms such as 'alleviating' and 're-constructing' are better than 'perfecting' or 'enhancing.' The moral agent is not someone who ameliorates as part of a general quest for perfection or even amelioration. Dewey reverses this Platonic quest. Notions of perfection are not antecedent to problematic situations; they are, at best, instruments for present amelioration whenever the context calls for amelioration. This is an important difference. The demand for improvement is not something created or projected by humans in a world that is otherwise neutral or indifferent, that is, valueless. This is a very suspicious starting point. Although Dewey would not deny the importance of having characters with the readiness to improve (as a habit or disposition), his starting point is a world that demands improvement in its problematic phases.

> Men have constructed a strange dream-world when they have supposed that without a fixed ideal of a remote good to inspire them, they have no inducement to get relief from present troubles, no desires for liberation from what oppresses and for clearing-up what confuses present action. . . . Sufficient unto the day is the evil thereof. Sufficient it is to stimulate us to remedial action. (MW 14:195)

In sum, there is in Dewey's ethics some basis to warn us about the dangers of technological enhancement as a general practice. It can erode an attitude toward the world that is part of the sort of balanced engagement that I have articulated in this book. The road toward perfectionism is the road to the sort of stability and harmony that is non-aesthetic. The contingency of our talents, fortunes, as well as of our bad circumstances are for Dewey the grounds of democratic solidarity. I said earlier that the ultimate glue in Dewey's view is a faith in experience or nature, one that is felt as the notion that "everything that's here is here, and you can just lie back on it."[29] There is an active and a more passive side to this faith. You can lie back on experience by trusting its potentialities that may be released with our intervention, but it is also important to lie back in the sense of accepting the grain of experience and affirming what it brings even if it is not in line with our wishes.

Of course, this does not answer the difficult questions. At what point does our capacity for mastery with the developments of new enhancement technology lead to the sort of unbalanced control where we have removed too much contingency, novelty, surprise, gifts, and uniqueness from our everyday lives? Dewey does not say, and given his contextualism, he would be skeptical of any philosophical attempt to fix this line a priori. Furthermore, slippery-slope-type arguments would not convince Dewey to set absolute limits to enhancement technologies; rather, he would likely eschew line drawing and assume the risks of such technologies in the name of trying to maintain a context-sensitive balance. Nevertheless, the danger is there and if it is true that today we are on the verge of too much mastery, then Deweyans today should be more resistant or watchful about the effects of technology in this regard than Dewey was.

Democracy and the Limits of Pluralism

Another way to raise the naïveté charge against Dewey would be to question the means by which conflict, force, and disagreement are to be handled. The idea that we can sit down as equals, admit everyone to the table, and have a rational discussion would seem to ignore the fact that there are people who are not willing to put their special interests aside, and that sometimes we may have to resort to force and coercion. Pragmatism, hence, would appear to be dangerously naïve because it seems too tolerant, open, generous, and inclusive. Dewey prescribes that we have a discussion with even those who may not deserve to be talked to and who may be a danger to a democratic society. How is Dewey's pragmatism any different from the "let many flowers bloom" variety that is sometimes defended?

This is, of course, a caricature of Dewey's view.[30] He was aware of the limitations of inquiry. Moreover, there is nothing in Dewey that rules out the use of force or of recognizing that there are limits to pluralism and tolerance. It is true that nowhere does he lay out rules for exclusion (i.e., as a set of necessary and sufficient conditions for excluding some views from communal inquiry), but it does not follow that there is no conceivable basis to exclude certain viewpoints in particular situations. This is the same sort of assumption that is behind the idea that if in ethical theory we cannot provide a theoretical basis to rule out someone as evil as Hitler, then there is no actual basis to do so in concrete situations and all is permitted.

Dewey did encourage us to avoid violence to settle conflicts of interest and opinion in a pluralistic society. The enemies of democracies are the enemies of inquiry and public discussion. These are not only censorship and suppression but the covert and indirect use of force. "Mankind still prefers upon the whole to rely upon force, not now exercised directly and physically as it was once, but upon covert and indirect force, rather than upon intelligence to discover and cling to what is right" (LW 7:231). But for Dewey the proper way to stand by the principles of openness and tolerance is also to stand by contextualism. The most that can be said about these principles prior to a situation is that there are good reasons to try them and to avoid the use of force, violence, and exclusion. We cannot a priori or absolutely rule out force, violence, and exclusion. But does it follow that these stand as equally warranted ways of confronting situations? Even if in a democracy we must do our best to try to consider each case on its own merits, the burden of proof is on those who do not wish to try democratic means in a specific situation. To favor democratic principles also means that in cases of doubt we should err on the side of being too tolerant than not tolerant enough.

The objection considered does, however, raise a legitimate practical concern. There are risks (or liabilities) for standing by the principles of tolerance, freedom of action, and dialogue in a democracy, but there is no reason to believe that Dewey was not aware of this. He counted on the sort of intelligent contextualism that would hopefully allow us to recognize, as we engage in particular situations, when we have reached the limits of tolerance and when it is time to use force or exclude someone. I am aware that this answer is not satisfactory for many who expect some sort of fixed criteria or rules as an adequate answer; anything less seems too lax and unstable. But from the point of view of Dewey's ethics, the habits required to be an intelligent contextualist are more stable and reliable tools to rely on (in these critical situations) than any cognitive criteria. The openness of contextualism is no comfort for those who want the security of knowing answers in advance. But from Dewey's perspective this is naïve. It is wanting or counting on what the universe cannot provide. Both absolutism and a relativism that permits anything provide a false sense of comfort.

Pessimistic views about human nature would find Dewey's views naïve because, according to them, violent warfare and the use of force seem inevitable. But for Dewey claims about inevitability are non-empirical and non-intelligent.

> Wherever the inevitable reigns intelligence cannot be used. Commitment to inevitability is always the fruit of dogma; intelligence does not pretend to know save as a result of experimentation, the opposite of

preconceived dogma. Moreover, acceptance in advance of the inevitability of violence tends to produce the use of violence in cases where peaceful methods might otherwise avail. (LW 11:55)

We must not assume defeatism in advance of actual trial. Dewey gave us many reasons why democracy seems worth trying but ultimately theoretical reasons are impotent if we do not in our own experience feel the need to ameliorate the quality of present experience. "The reasons for making the trial are not abstract or recondite. They are found in the confusion, uncertainty and conflict that mark the modern world" (LW 11:64).

Democracy and the Quality of Experience

The most important functional evaluation of an ideal is one that takes into account the particular problem from which it has arisen. After all, an ideal has a context and it is born from a particular dissatisfaction with how things are. As George Herbert Mead said, "a conception of a different world comes to us always as the result of some specific problem which involves readjustment of the world as it is."[31] Given what I have taken to be the problematic context that grounds Dewey's hopes or aspirations, the following questions are important in reevaluating democracy as an ideal: does trying to live by his view of democracy (and using it as a tool of criticism) have the power or potential to transform (improve) the quality of our interactions and present experience by its own means? Can it guide, inspire, and inform our individual struggles on this issue? That Dewey thought of democracy as the best hypothetical response to living a more qualitatively enriching social life is supported by his most straightforward and explicit remarks regarding the justification of democracy. In *Experience and Education* he said,

> is it not the reason for our preference that we believe that mutual consultation and convictions reached through persuasion, make possible a better quality of experience than can otherwise be provided on any wide scale? . . . I do not see how we can justify our preference for democracy and humanity on any other ground. (LW 13:18)

To be sure, the ideal of democracy is not a mere instrumentality to some future state of affairs where the quality of our interactions (and life) is enhanced and fulfillment is achieved. As previously noted, the aim of Dewey's ethics is a better life relative to where we are, rather than to some predetermined conception of the good life. The rewards and test of having democracy as an ideal are in the very striving and piecemeal achievement in particular situations and in light of particular problems encountered. These problems are so varied and unique that all that can be said about them is that they demand a qualitative improvement in how we interact with each other. The interaction in an oppressive working environment, the mechanical and superficial character of most dialogues, the inability of many to understand and consider in deliberations the suffering of the other, a felt lack of control over the forces that guide my conduct, the inability to learn from others and embrace the irreducible pluralism of experience, the unjust oppression of a minority, the drudgery of working with others, the capricious and arbitrary nature of our decisions, and so on are the problems of democracy. The ideal must be tested and reevaluated in light of these sorts of problems that according to Dewey characterize our contemporary social existence. There would be no point or value to democracy as an ideal in a world where we are confronted with situations in no need of qualitative improvement.

The move to justify democracy by the quality of lived present experience is consistent with a philosophy that makes experience its starting point. That which initiates inquiry and tests the validity of its results is life. This is Dewey's alternative to justifying democracy by appealing to natural rights, self-interest, or rationality. However, it is open to challenges from more traditional philosophers. How does one judge what counts as better quality? How do we determine if living by the democratic ideal tends to improve the quality of our interactions and present experience? Are we justified in believing that the democratization of our experience leads to improvement of its quality? If so, by what standards? By what criteria are we even entitled to reach any judgment that there is better and worst in interaction? If the criteria presuppose features of democratic interaction then are we not begging the question? Even Deweyan sympathizers like Sydney Hook and Robert Westbrook have found the challenge about criteria legitimate.

After quoting Dewey's claim that a democratic community is superior to other forms of association because it is "full and free," Hook raises the problem that this sort of justification of democracy will not work. "Actually this derivation of the validity of democratic society is circular, and some may even claim it is question-begging because the very choice of criteria presupposes an ideal family."[32] Hook regrets that Dewey did not devote "more pages to the problem of justification."[33] Westbrook raises the criteria challenge in a different context. "If one is willing to go this far with Dewey, a nagging question remains; that is, what criteria do we use to evaluate the success of our ends in view?"[34]

This criteria challenge is in fact one that could also be raised against my own reconstruction of Dewey. I have argued that democracy seems best or most promising from a Deweyan perspective because it has the features of the sort of interactive process in our lives that have aesthetic quality. But on what basis do we judge that events with aesthetic quality are better than those that do not have this quality? What criteria are we assuming when, for example, we hold that experiences that are fragmented or mechanical are not as meaningful and as educational as those with organic unity and diversity, and where means and ends are integrated? Can we come up with a justification of the criteria that would justify such judgments of quality without begging the question?

This objection is a good example of how important it is to understand how radical Dewey's departure is from much of traditional ethics. The objection assumes that without some ultimate (explicit or implicit) criteria there is no reasonable basis to ground value judgments. For Dewey, as we have seen, valuations are not conclusions deduced from some preconceived criteria about what is good. It is an experience that is had that certain interactions (e.g., communications) are experienced as valuable and meaningful. These experiences must be subjected to criticism and there may be plenty of disagreement among people about them. In this inquiry we may come to formulate hypotheses and rules about what is the best in human interaction, but we must begin and return to the preconceptual experiences that we have. In other words, the bottom line is that either you have the experiences that validate democracy or you do not.

The aesthetic quality and the drudgery of our everyday discussions, as well as the fact that the former is better than the latter, are judgments that can be reached without the need of some ultimate standard. This is what it means to rely on primary experience. Dewey was explicit about his starting point: "There are enormous differences of better and worse in the quality of what is social. Ideal morals begin with *the perception* of these differences" (MW 14:225, my emphasis). Some relationships are experienced as mechanical and superficial, others are experienced as optimal and deep. For Dewey, if you cannot tell the difference between one and the other, then you lack sensitivity, which is something more serious than lacking a theoretical criterion of a good relationship. Hence, when Dewey claims that democracy "makes a better quality of experience," he means that its interactions are enriching and meaningful. This claim is a hypothesis and a generalization based upon an inquiry that relies (ultimately) on judging particular experiences that have been *had,* and not on the application of some antecedent, theoretically justified criteria. To insist that Dewey must presuppose some universal standard of value is to assume that knowledge (in the form of rules or criteria) is prior to experience; this is an instance of the intellectualist fallacy.

The empirical attitude that certain interactions are better because they are experienced as such is not an appeal to intuition or to the view that it is good simply because one says so. Recall that Dewey's method is one of trusting immediate experience without closing the door to further inquiry. The need for criticism and communal inquiry about value is recurrent in a changing world where we are aware of the possible narrowness and limitations of our own experiences. What may be experienced initially as good may not be experienced that way upon further dialogue, reflection, judgment, and experience. About our most direct personal experiences, Dewey admits that they can be restricted, one-sided, and perverted but the "remedy, however, is not divorce of thought from the intimacies of the direct contacts and intercourses of life, but a supplementation of limitations and a correction of biases through acquaintance with the experience of others" (LW 6:21).

Dewey denied that there is a single universal standard or criterion of value, but he did not think that it follows that there is no basis for criticism or reasonableness, nor that one must abandon the need to provide reasons or support for our judgments. Reasons and arguments are important for reasonableness; they are arrived at in the process of critically reexamining judgments and commitments, and they play a role in further inquiry. But their mere formulation is no substitute for personal judgment based on experience. The variety of reasons presented in favor of democracy may lead others, who hold similar commitments, to test certain hypotheses and to reach similar judgments about the value and promise of democracy. You can guide but not reason someone into having the experiences that can validate democracy. And even in the best of circumstances, there is "no assurance that any one will so act as to have the experience. The horse led to water is not forced to drink" (LW 14:31). According to Dewey's denotative method, the empirical philosopher must provide arguments, but she should also guide others (through descriptions and other means) to have the experiences that may confirm their hypotheses.

Dewey's critics and sympathizers, however, continue to presuppose that Dewey's politics is grounded in Dewey's ethics because in the latter one finds the ultimate criterion of all value judgments. They presuppose that for Dewey self-realization, human fulfillment, or growth are the goods ultimately served by democracy.[35] It is hard to deny that Dewey was to some extent concerned with all of these goods, but to assume that any of them is the underlying and final telos is to fail to do justice to the radically pluralistic and contextualist view of Dewey's mature ethical thought and philosophy. There is no overriding aim to all of our moral struggles that can be used as the theoretical standard to judge all activity. The ideal of democracy is an end-in-view and, as such, it is a means. I have suggested different ways in which Dewey would want us to evaluate it as a means. But doesn't this make him a consequentialist regarding democracy and therefore bind him to some sort of criteria? Dewey does think that democracy as an ideal is a means and that it produces good results. But one can make good consequences key to evaluating action or an ideal without assuming the sort of standard assumed by consequentialists. Furthermore, Dewey found it objectionable when consequences and results are understood in terms of a future end that is remote and external to the present situation. A consequentialist might argue that democracy leads or contributes to, for example, human flourishing, the just and happy society, or the survival of our species beyond and apart from democracy itself. This assumes a dualism between means and ends, and it disregards the present as the locus of moral reconstruction.

Dewey wanted to shift the focus of democracy to the present striving or democratization of experience instead of toward future results. Democracy as an ideal is a means to present reconstruction of specific problems in a situation. Democracy is not a journey to some predefined end point, nor is it the end of the journey itself. The spirit of democracy is in the present process of adjusting democratic means and ends. Living by and with the ideal and dealing with the problems and challenges it entails for us *now* is to endorse democracy as a way of life. When the emphasis is put on the striving to be democratic, every unique contextual battle for the sake of democracy is its own reason for being, as well as a unique opportunity for celebration if won (i.e., a source of immediate enjoyment). There is no grandiose and ultimate war for the sake of which the piecemeal present battles are fought. We do (and should) carry forward the wisdom from previous battles, but there is no end in sight in the sense of a final consummation or cumulative goal that serves as the standard for all the battles. Trying to transform everyday activity to make it richer and fuller relative to concrete present problems and possibilities is what we do in democracy as a way of life. The experience of pursuing and achieving democratic ends is a means but it is valued for its own sake as the experience which it is.

Dewey was more concerned with the spirit of democracy—that is, with *how* one is engaged in democratic reconstruction—than with trying to make fixed and final normative pronouncements about democratic rules or conduct. In the ideal democratic engagement there is a balance between work and play; moreover, present activity is not taken as mere means, but neither are goals or ideals taken as mere ends. Mastery over means of execution and enthusiasm for wider aims and ideals should supplement each other. In other words, the democrat needs to adopt the "genuine interest" in an ideal typical of the artist. The ideal democrat experiences each effort on behalf of democracy in the same way that the sculptor experiences each stroke of the chisel.

> Each molding of the clay . . . is at the time the whole end in process of realization. Whatever interest or value attaches to the end attaches to each of these steps. He is as much absorbed in one as in the other. . . . A genuine interest in the ideal indicates of necessity an equal interest in all the conditions of its expression. (EW 5:128)

In sum, a consequentialist justification of Dewey's ideal of democracy is inconsistent with Dewey's philosophy, for it is central to the ideal that there should be a balanced relation between means and ends, and a concern for the quality of present processes. Insofar as the consequentialist justification of democracy would make the present striving for democracy a mere means, it is sharply at odds with the ideal of democracy as conceived by Dewey. The notion, for example, that democracy produces aesthetic satisfaction[36] or that it is a prerequisite for epistemic goals[37] seems to make democracy a mere means to a future and separate goal.

The justificatory requirements for democracy cannot be the same as those for theory. The reasonableness of an ideal way of life is to be tested in lived experience by trying to live by it. Consistency with one's beliefs and with the nature of experience is important, but this is ultimately nothing more than an intellectual warrant to try to live in a certain way. In other words, there are limitations to a philosophical investigation about better or worse ways of participating in experience. The most important one is that we can test our hypotheses only by living them. Participation can only be tested by participating. There is, then, no theoretical justification of democracy that can replace the support provided in favor of democracy by living and embodying democratic habits in our everyday interaction. That, for example, openness and tolerance usually make for a better dialogue can only be tested by adopting them in our daily interactions with others. To argue that in the end all theoretical arguments in favor of democracy pale in comparison to our attempts to try it for ourselves could not be more consistent with the very spirit of democracy.

In the last analysis, ideals are experiments. We know that the world is tolerant and fairly hospitable to our experiments. But perhaps the world does not lend itself equally to all our ideals. Of course, there are limitations to this appeal to experimentation. We cannot divest ourselves of our habits as we do with our clothes, but just because we cannot stand outside our ways of life to make side-by-side comparisons does not mean that we can never know whether we are improving or whether changes are needed in our lives. About growth or progress Dewey says, ". . . if it cannot be told by qualities belonging to the moment of transition it can never be judged" (MW 14:195).

Dewey turns the fact that we cannot stand outside of our situatedness into a positive resource, rather than a reason to abandon all objectivity. If we were to appreciate the guiding force of reflection based on a unique and pervasive quality of each problematic situation, we would find absurd the need for antecedent knowledge of the good life or some outside standpoint to know whether or not we are doing well. As Dewey said,

> there are plenty of negative elements, due to conflict, entanglement and obscurity, in most situations of life, and we do not require a revelation of some supreme perfection to inform us whether or no we are making headway in present rectification. (MW 14:195)

It is in and because of the felt intolerance and the superficial and mechanical aspects of our relations and discussions that we seek to democratize our experience. In the process of transforming these situations of conflict, entanglement, and obscurity, we need to rely on the sense of relevance and guidance found in the concrete situations where these problems are felt. We do in fact judge better from worse when guided by the same qualitative context that raises the issue, and we do this without the need for a God's-eye point of view. If Dewey's view seems like an invitation to anarchy, it is because, as opposed to most philosophies, it holds that what ultimately guides judgment cannot be articulated in terms of any sort of propositional knowledge. What can save us from nihilism in a world without foundations is qualitative, unique, and pre-conceptual.

Dewey's emphasis on primary qualitative and situated experience does not rule out the possibility of formulating general principles of democratic discourse or interaction. It may be useful in certain circumstances to lay out some rules of proper deliberation in a democracy in order to criticize present institutions. What must be avoided is overlooking the fact that these rules are only tools derived from, not prior to, having a certain quality of communication. Democracy as experience means that it arises and is ultimately justified by having certain experiences in particular situations. This is a bottom-up justification of democracy.

Have we succeeded in avoiding the charge of circularity in justification? We could play the skeptic and push the objection one more time. To test democracy by its quality in lived experience is to rely on the experimental method. But what in turn supports a reliance on experimental method? If we say that it is itself something to be tested by proceeding and guiding our lives in a certain way, then we seem to be arguing in a circle. Does not testing openness require openness? This is indeed a circle, but it is hardly a damaging or objectionable one. Being experimental about the experimental method in our lives is hardly as objectionable as assuming in a deductive justification the same conclusion we set out to prove. First, in the context of our lives this lived process of validation is never a return back to the same (or prior) place, so that perhaps a spiral, rather than a circle, is a better analogy. More importantly, it is precisely the capacity to move in a spiral motion that makes the experimental way of living attractive to Dewey. That is to say, it holds the promise of being a self-corrective process. It can be applied to itself without an appeal to an external standard to determine its direction and movement. Dewey proposed a way of approaching our problems that promises not only to ameliorate them but to ameliorate itself in the process. He was interested in the sort of moral life that can develop in its own ongoing course the standards to which further living should be submitted, as well as the experiences by which these standards must themselves be tested. Democracy is a way of life that tries and hopes for salvation from within this process. Non-democratic systems and communications do not have the built-in means to improve themselves or respond adequately to change.

We could raise one more skeptical challenge to all of this. Is Dewey warranted in hoping that we can deepen and regulate everyday experience by its own means? This is to raise a question about his underlying faith in experience. Dewey was explicit that democracy ultimately rests on faith.

Democracy and Faith in Experience

To be both empirical and to appeal to faith may seem contradictory or incoherent. In particular, how can democracy be empirically grounded when it is only an imagined possibility with much evidence against it? Granted, ideals are the sorts of thing that are supposed to be beyond evidence, but aren't we in the case of democracy going beyond what is reasonable? Why should we persist in believing in what we know, based upon the evidence, cannot be? Is it not more reasonable to abandon faith? Is not relying on faith as the basis of democracy a recognition that it lacks the reasonableness of our most rational commitments?

These questions and most of the traditional polemics about the justification of faith are sustained without questioning the assumptions either that faith is a special form of knowledge or that it is unimportant or invalid. But Dewey inherited from William James an alternative model of faith. He points out that "change from the one conception of faith to the other is indicative of a profound alteration" (LW 5:267).

James knew that it is only by presupposing the traditional epistemic conception of a believer (i.e., a detached and neutral spectator of propositions) that one can hold that faith is an auxiliary faculty, an add-on to reason (and to what is reasonable) after reason can go no further.[38] Having faith is a type of commitment, an insistence on a possibility, and a tendency to act upon it, fully aware of the risk involved in a particular context. Faith is necessary and important in all dimensions of life and not something confined to religion.

Faith is a complex and rich phenomenon where different modes of experience are brought together. And it is an active organic cooperation between the plurality of demands placed on the believer. Since we are not merely cognitive beings, says James, we represent the appeal of our believed hypothesis to be to "our *whole* nature's loyalty and not to any emaciated faculty of syllogistic proof."[39]

Hence, determining or evaluating the reasonableness of a faith in democracy is different from determining whether democracy is true or false, and different from validating a knowledge claim. There are contextual reasons relevant to this determination that go well beyond evidence or any other epistemic reasons. There is, strictly speaking, no faith in democracy in general; there are only particular faiths. Ultimately the issue of justification is a contextual one; that is, the unique context of each individual as each confronts a different set of circumstances (including evidence and needs) determines whether a particular faith is justified.

But what, then, about the question of whether Dewey was justified in his particular faith in democracy? All of the reasons presented would have to count in favor of a positive answer, but we cannot pretend here to exhaust all of the personal and non-epistemic reasons Dewey may have had to continue to have faith in democracy in spite of contrary considerations and challenges. We can say, however, that his faith was reasonable insofar as it was not uncritically adopted. As Michael Eldridge has demonstrated, Dewey's faith was "a set of enduring beliefs that ran beyond the evidence available at any given time, but that remained correctable by continued experience."[40]

The view that justification of faith is something individual and contextual does not entail that a philosophical defense of democracy is futile. A philosopher can provide support that may become part of the contextual set of reasons to be considered by an individual. In other words, the reasons Dewey gives in favor of democracy may lead others with similar commitments and circumstances to adopt a faith, or strengthen their faith, in democracy.

The different understanding of faith which is based upon a pragmatist view of experience underscores the importance and necessity of faith for democracy. James understood that the traditional conceptions of faith had been built upon the model of a passive, cognitive subject in a static universe. If the world is complete, then all the beliefs in what we want the world to be seem futile or like wishful thinking. Faith in democracy seems like believing something that is false. But if reality is in transformation—in the making—then faith is an active agency; it is not a passive certitude, but a formative factor. For often it is only by taking this kind of risk in our beliefs that we can bring about significant positive changes in the world; and "often enough our faith beforehand in an uncertified result is the only thing that makes the result come true,"[41] as James put it. In short, faith is a formative factor necessary to actualize our ideals.

Depending on their consequences, some faiths will surely be better than others, but we cannot know a priori what those consequences will be. We need to engage in "faith ventures" to find out. Sometimes we have to be explorers, open new trails, and adopt a willingness to learn from our mistakes. James and Dewey were meliorists, that is, they believed in the possibility that we can make this a better world. But they were aware that this might require a good will not only in our actions, but in our beliefs. For it might be the case that one of the first risks we need to take in order to actually make this a better world is to believe that we can.

But by basing democracy on faith, how do we avoid the risks of wishful thinking and self-deception? The answer is that we do not. These are dangers, but they should not be met by simply ruling out faith altogether or discouraging it, for there are equal, if not greater, risks involved in paralyzing our "native capacities for faith."[42] A failure to take the risk involved in having faith in democracy (and surrendering to skepticism and cynicism) is not altogether to avoid risk, but to take a different kind of risk, namely, the risk of losing those things that might depend on believing in the possibility of democracy. One of the things lost may be democracy as a way of life. Democracy requires faith for its own realization.

I claimed earlier that one of the considerations in determining the reasonableness of an ideal is how it relates to one's other central commitments and hopes. An important part of my present task has been to make explicit how Dewey's views on morality, democracy, and philosophy are part of a coherent vision. In order to engage in criticism and to learn one needs to have a clearer and more organized vision of one's commitments. Dewey thought this was a task for philosophy.

> The clearer and more organized vision of the contents of beliefs may have as an immediate outcome an enhanced sense of their worth and greater loyalty to them. But nevertheless the set of beliefs undergoes more than a sea-change in the process. (LW 6:19)

It is perhaps a mistake to ask which of Dewey's commitments and beliefs was more fundamental, for this presupposes the kind of foundational model of justification that he did not adopt. Instead, among them there was a supporting relationship in any ongoing inquiry. Dewey's philosophical investigations into each such commitment led him to continuously develop, modify, and refine the conceptions of the others. He sought a view of experience that supports his moral ideal as much as he sought a moral ideal that is congenial to his view of experience. His philosophy of experience served as a way of reinterpreting the democratic ideals and of holding that the world we live in is one in which faith in democracy is reasonable.[43] However, it is equally true that he found in democracy an affirmation of the potentialities of experience.

The ideal moral life is one that is based on and is supportive of faith in experience. Dewey could not have been more explicit that the pursuit of democracy was such a life. He claimed that, compared to other general modes of social and moral participation, it is the

> sole way of living which believes wholeheartedly in the process of experience as end and as means. . . . Democracy is belief in the ability of human experience to generate the aims and methods by which further experience will grow in ordered richness. (LW 14:229)

What is it about democracy that makes it the way of life most consistent with the pragmatist faith in experience? In social and moral matters we are accustomed to assume that amelioration and solutions must come from the top down, especially from means that are beyond or above experience. "Men have not been able to trust either the world or themselves to realize the values and qualities which are the possibilities of nature" (LW 4:240). For Dewey, this general distrust in nature is intimately tied to a distrust of those who serve as the backbone of most aristocratic ideals. Democracy's faith in the people is understood by Dewey as a faith in the potentialities and self-sufficiency of the everyday transactions of individuals if the proper conditions are provided. "Every other form of moral and social faith rest upon the idea that experience must be subjected at some point or other to some form of external control; to some 'authority' alleged to exist outside the process of experience" (LW 14:229).

For Dewey, formal and political notions of democracy are not sufficiently robust to counteract the need for some aristocratic scheme to regulate our everyday affairs. On the other hand, if democracy is understood as merely following the conversations and wishes of the people, then this seems like the abandonment of any standards. Only a robust notion of democracy that requires communal inquiry (with all that this implies) can be supportive of the faith that experience can provide the standards to which further experience may submit. Aristocracy and the need to look outside our direct qualitative world and communications for guidance will continue to appeal and flourish so long as democracy is devoid of its most promising possibilities. For Dewey, the alternative to the disillusionment with formal democratic societies where people are merely drifting, are apathetic, or are mere consumers of entertainment is more democracy; it is not the search for the guidance of a wise and benevolent dictator. Again, to take this stand requires a lot of faith in the people.

The connection between Dewey's faiths in experience and democracy is made even stronger when the latter is understood from the point of view of his ethics. Democracy fits his conception of an ideal moral life because it has in its generic features, phases, and dynamics all of the features of an intelligent and aesthetic moral life. Democratic inquiry embraces, affirms, and relies on everyday life in all of its contingency and qualitative richness to settle disagreements or to come to decisions. It so trusts the grain of experience that it tries to turn even error, conflict, incompleteness, pluralism, uncertainty, and tragedy into sources of instruction. This makes possible a moral life that can be self-educational and capable of ameliorating its problems through its own resources.

Experience cannot become educational and grow in ordered richness when our relationships are not democratic. Certain ways of interacting are cumulatively enriching and meaningful,[44] whereas others are not. It is in democratic communication that the conditions for experience to educate, enlarge, and enrich itself are maximized. These conditions consist of the predominance of the traits already mentioned: full and free communication and cooperation, generous give-and-take (reciprocity and sharing), and the exchange of experiences and ideas in an environment of sympathetic intercommunication where everyone contributes and corrects her individual limitations. The truth of this claim may be intuitively obvious to those who have had the opportunity to be part of this kind of interaction. But I think there are more general and basic assumptions that are worth disclosing behind Dewey's preference for the organic interactions that characterize a democratic way of life.

If we think of a self, a relationship, a community, or a society as wholes (constituted by transacting parts) in the context of transacting with other wholes, then this allows us to abstractly, but usefully, highlight the most general features of democratic interactions, and to highlight some of Dewey's hidden working hypotheses. In previous chapters I characterized the ideal self and community as wholes in which inclusivity, openness, diversity (distinctiveness of its parts), and flexibility coexist with fullness and intimacy of interaction. I also characterized the tension-filled nature of this coexistence in terms of centripetal and centrifugal forces, values, or tendencies. Each of these correspond to two different ways in which present experience is subject to qualitative improvement, namely, it can both deepen and widen.

The centrifugal tendencies allow a self and a community the richness of experience that comes from expansion and increased breadth. Widening the experience of children should be the result of growing up in a community or in relationships where certain virtues are encouraged. Dewey seems to be committed to the hypothesis that inclusivity and diversity as features of organic, interactive wholes are better traits than exclusivity (or "closedness") and homogeneity. In both the ideal character and the ideal community he assumes that more points of transactions and opportunities for new and diverse relations signify more opportunities for learning and releasing unknown potentialities. Expansion of horizons leads to a rich and diversified experience. On the other hand, exclusiveness, one-sidedness, homogeneity, and suppression are usually restrictions of experience. They are barriers to full development and growth that can starve the whole and its parts.

But breadth does not guarantee depth. In fact, it can be a threat if taken to an extreme. The wider and expansive self and community are not improvements in experience if there is no genuine transaction between its parts, that is, the sort of wholehearted reciprocal interaction where the parts are affected. Dewey's hypothesis is that fullness is usually better than halfhearted or superficial interaction. Interdependence and solidarity are positive traits. Where there is isolation, compartmentalization, segregation, suppression, fragmentation, and polarization there are barriers that can impoverish the lives of everyone.

The possibility of democracy is then for Dewey the possibility of *widening* and *deepening* present experience. "Every way of life that fails in its democracy limits the contacts, the exchanges, the communications, the interactions by which experience is steadied while it is also enlarged and enriched" (LW 14:229–30). The ideal is for generosity, openness, and inclusivity not to undermine fullness of interaction. The democratic community is wide and open, both vertically and horizontally, without losing its integrity. The features that provide its ability to widen experience are also responsible for its freedom and flexibility; and the ones that make depth and fullness possible contribute to its stability and order. As with any work of art there is a very delicate balance between the stable and the precarious, as well as between its centripetal and centrifugal values.

The intelligent and aesthetic characters of democracies are mutually dependent. The community most capable of learning from experience is also the one that has all the features that define aesthetic activity, which for Dewey is the most inherently meaningful type of activity in experience. The democratic way of life is able to maintain the kind of balance and rhythm in its everyday doings and undergoings that, for Dewey, characterize aesthetic experience: a balance of tensions with rhythmic variety. Ideal activity is a merging of playfulness with seriousness that allows richness and flexibility without sacrificing stability. Democracy signifies for Dewey this possibility at a social level. The democratic community is also the aesthetic community because it is constituted by relationships that are neither fixed, routine, or mechanical, nor anarchical, capricious, or arbitrary.

The democratic community falls between the extremes of a community that is disintegrated and one that is kept stable only because of some imposed external authority. In other words, it is capable of preserving its own integrity without the need of external foundations. A stability achieved through full interaction and openness and not through force or repression is required to procure its ordered richness. Since it can steer safely between complete radicalism and complete conservatism, it can rely on what is stable without falling into drudgery. But it can also be playful and welcome change without degenerating into chaos. The non-democratic ways of dealing with moral and social problems represent for Dewey a failure to use the resources and potentialities of experience. For example, in dealing with change, uncertainty, ambivalence, and pluralism, it is ineffective to deny their reality (as is often the strategies of authoritarian, dualistic, and rule-guided views). The best way to preserve order is not by trying to get rid of participation or of the diversity present in human experience.

Conclusion

Even though Dewey never wrote a single comprehensive and definitive rendition of his moral thought, he had a coherent and complex view worth reconstructing and reconsidering today. His meta-ethics (part 1), his view of moral life (part 2), and his normative ethics (part 3) mutually support one another. They are parts of Dewey's larger inquiry, namely, an investigation of the conditions and instrumentalities required to ameliorate concrete, existential, and lived experience. Dewey's theoretical inquiries in ethics had, as their problematic situation, his discontent with actual conditions, for example, extremism and the lack of meaningful moral engagement. In other words, the above three aspects of his ethics were not ends in themselves, but just different uses of philosophy as criticism, and different types of instruments to be used to liberate and improve actual moral practice.

Dewey's ethics was also a reaction to what he perceived as the failure of ethical philosophy to provide proper guidance to moral agents. Absolutist and subjectivist views of morality as well as the search for some ultimate criteria of right and wrong by much ethical theory signified for Dewey a lack of confidence in the directive powers that inhere in experience. Instead, Dewey was in search of an ethics based on the capacity of each situation to guide and rectify its own problems and challenges. This presupposes his faith in experience, a commitment that I have made explicit and that is intimately related to Dewey's philosophical methodology and to his faith in democracy.

In part 1, I set out the methodological commitments that form the basis of Dewey's reconstruction of moral theory. He puts into question the predominant theoretical starting points of philosophers in their construction of ethical theories. According to Dewey's philosophical empiricism, the proper starting point should be morality as it is experienced, that is, as it is pre-theoretically given in the midst of our lives. Although for Dewey there is no area of our experience that is exclusively or essentially moral, he designated those situations that we experience as predominantly moral as those that have the pervasive quality of demanding of the agent that she discover what she morally ought to do among conflicting moral forces or demands. This is the experiential subject matter to be studied, described, and appealed to in order to test our theoretical accounts.

Moral situations are the center of moral life. A hypothetical description of the generic traits and phases of such situations is the subject matter of Dewey's metaphysics of ethics (part 2). His account reconstructs traditional conceptions of the moral self, character, conduct, habit, moral deliberation, principles, and moral problems. Dewey also points to dimensions of moral life that tend to be overlooked and undervalued in much of modern ethical thought. Morality is a social, creative, imaginative, emotional, hypothetical, and experimental process to ameliorate present situations. Dewey's re-description of moral life was in turn the basis for his normative proposals (hypotheses) about how best to deal with moral situations (part 3).

A consequence of Dewey's empiricism is a radical contextualism that precludes moral theory from performing the functions it has traditionally performed. However, as I argued at the end of part 1, Dewey is not anti-theoretical. His empirical turn in ethics validates a legitimate descriptive function and a normative function for ethical theory. These are the two functions I explained and defended in parts 2 and 3.

Dewey does not offer a criterion for right conduct and thus challenges the traditional expectations about an ethical theory. Traditional ethical theories usually assume that the normativity or reasonableness of our specific moral judgments is solely derivative from a general standard of right conduct. For Dewey, this is backward and puts the emphasis in the wrong place. The validity of generalizations and standards depends on particular moral judgments. Judgments are individual acts about, and in, a unique qualitative context that can emerge from engaging in moral deliberation as an imaginative, qualitative, experimental, and social process. Judgments are not propositions that are the result of other propositions in an argument, located in one's mind.

Dewey advocates an approach to moral decision making that may be termed situational. He affirms that reasonable moral judgments and decisions come from intelligently exploring and assessing the situation in its qualitative uniqueness. The warrant of a judgment changes and is relative to its particular context. Instead of trying to come up with theories, rules, or criteria to solve our moral problems, Dewey claims that we should attend to the particular, the qualitative, and the unique, equipped with the best habits available. This faith in context is not a blind trust in experience; rather, it requires a balance between reflective criticism and sensitivity, what Dewey called cultivated naïveté (LW 1:40). Such cultivated naïveté can be acquired by an education that fosters the habits to be critical, and also the habits needed to listen, not just to others, but also to situations that we are in and in which we experience problems. We must take a situation seriously, letting it speak for itself, instead of trying to impose some theory or some comforting universal answer that fits all moral problems.

Dewey's ethics does not deny the importance of having, using, and carrying forward our inherited moral knowledge in the form of principles, ideals, and habits. What should be dethroned are not moral generalizations per se, but a way of using them that discourages moral sensitivity and precludes the genuine exercise of moral judgment. The most important instrumentalities for morality, the cardinal virtues, are the traits of character that can improve moral habits and, more importantly, better assist us in determining what morality requires here and now. Dewey's contextualism thus advances a view about which habits better enable a person to confront moral situations, even if it does not prescribe beforehand what to do in the moral situation. Such habits include sensitivity, conscientiousness, sympathy, and open-mindedness. These are the habits Dewey identifies as contributing to moral intelligence, which is required to become aesthetically engaged in moral reconstruction. He emphasizes that moral anarchy and chaos are not avoided by fixing moral rules, but by the proper cultivation of character. Dewey invites us to drop legalistic or absolutist models of moral conduct and to look instead to art as the paradigm of an activity that can steer between living aimlessly and living mechanically.

I hope to have undermined, once and for all, the common but mistaken notion that the ethics that grounds Dewey's politics is a type of consequentialism or an appeal to some ultimate good, such as self-realization, human flourishing, or growth. These interpretations are problematic because they are not supported by the text and are inconsistent with the pluralism and view of moral judgment of his mature ethical thought. Any consequentialist or teleological interpretation of Dewey's ethics also ignores his attempt to shift the center of gravity of morality to concrete present situations.

In moral education, Dewey proposes that the cultivation of habits is better than the formulation of, and adherence to, rules. However, this is different than claiming that moral life is centered on improving habits or on the growth of our characters.[1] Habits are our best tools, but they are not all there is to moral experience. Tools should not be mere means, but it is also important not to reify our tools. The pragmatist must be careful not to commit the version of the philosophical fallacy where what is most useful (for certain purposes) is taken as more real. The concern to refashion one's tools can in fact be distracting to what really matters to a moral agent: the reconstruction of *this* morally problematic situation. The moral agent cares to elicit the appropriate response to situations, that is, what the situation morally calls for. For Dewey, the locus of moral activity is in what is present and unique, and not on tool-building or the future. The moral end is not growth (unless we take growth to be the enhancement of meaning in the present), but it is simply the consummatory resolution of a morally problematic situation. As William Myers puts it, "the resolution of that situation may or may not result in growth—it may in fact require my death. . . . The consummation of a morally problematic situation may be tragically painful to the point of retarding my own growth."[2] The moral agent who is aesthetically engaged in present moral reconstruction has a direct personal identification with the conduct that is required of her in a situation. To attend to and try to ameliorate the moral difficulties and demands as they present themselves in a specific situation is the interest of a moral agent qua moral agent.

Dewey's ethics is a distinctive alternative that is worth considering when studying the history of ethical theory. His ethics is not a consequentialist, deontological, or a virtue ethics, but it tries to recover some key insights of these other views. This recovery is developed by a reconstruction that abandons the metaphysical and methodological assumptions that ground debates between competing views in ethical theory. The myopic character of many ethical theories is the result of their failure to be empirical. If philosophers could curb their theoretical and self-serving tendency to latch on to one aspect of moral experience and make it primary, they may be able to embrace a pluralistic and richer view of morality. To identify morals, for example, exclusively with virtue, duty, or the good is to oversimplify the moral enterprise. Such misidentification isn't merely a theoretical quibble; the practical upshot of a narrow ethics is a narrow response to broader problems.[3]

Dewey's ethics predates the emphasis on context in moral judgment that has been recently stressed by moral particularists but without the need to abandon the important role of generalities, abstractions, ideals, and principles in moral life. It is an ethics that emphasizes the individual without falling into an atomistic individualism, and it emphasizes social relationships without falling into communitarianism. Dewey tries to capture the personal character of morality without centering it on the self. Dewey's naturalistic ethics protects the dignity and autonomy of morality (as a distinctive mode of experience) without abandoning its continuity with everyday life and the subject matter of the natural sciences. Dewey is an objectivist insofar as moral values are real and capable of intelligent criticism, but he does not presuppose the absolutism and universalism that are associated with objectivism. He can be called a relativist insofar as he rejects a God's-eye view and affirms that the agent is one of the conditions of moral experience, but he does not fall into subjective or cultural relativism. In sum, Dewey's ethics defies efforts to place it within traditional pigeonholes, but this should not deter us from appreciating its originality.

Dewey thought that there are questions and problems in ethics that must be subjected to criticism, if there is to be any further advance in ethics. He thought that an inherited, but mistaken, view of moral experience shared by philosophical opponents is the only thing that keeps many discussions in ethics alive. The history of ethics is dominated by the recurrent oscillation between extreme views, each trying to compensate for what the other has failed to emphasize—for example, debates centered on character versus conduct, one versus many, individualism versus collectivism. Dewey was particularly critical of debates centered upon trying to find a theoretical solution to the dangerous extremes to which our moral life is susceptible, for example, moral anarchy and moral absolutism. The dangers perceived by these views are real, but the quest for a theoretical solution is misguided. Moral life is, at its very core, full of irreducible tensions that are conflicted, uncertain, and sometimes even tragic. For Dewey, dealing with irreducible tensions is the reality of living according to the values of democracy. There is no pre-established condition or final tension-free harmony to aim for. Those things that bring freedom, openness, and diversity to moral life are always in tension with those that bring order and stability. The quest for a theoretical and final solution to the tensions inherent in moral life and democracy is distracting (to say the least) from the practical and situation-specific challenge of living a balanced moral life. What are the limits of tolerance, freedom, and order? How much freedom should one give up to have some equality and order? These are questions that, for Dewey, are meaningful in a particular context. When these questions occur in a problematic situation, they are about the balancing of forces and cannot be properly decided without attending to the particular situation.

That Dewey had a normative view in ethics should now be clear. With the proper qualifications, he is proposing an answer to the traditional ethical issue of how to live. The moral task of ameliorating the concrete, specific, and present situations that our moral life presents us with might best be performed by the effort to participate in our moral life in an intelligent, aesthetic, and democratic way. I presented this view from the most general to a description specifying the habits, tensions, and values of the ideal character and community. I have not claimed to have provided a comprehensive list of habits or character traits. Instead, I have suggested a few virtues that Dewey neglected to emphasize, but there is a lot more work to be done in "thickening" Dewey's ideal. Nevertheless, I hope that my account is a good start, one that is thick enough to show the cohesiveness of Dewey's moral vision and the importance of his notion of balance as a relation between forces in tension. Dewey's conception of ideal activity in terms of balance is a key to his philosophy. His conception is particularly useful to understand his view of democracy.

In the last pages of this book, I explored some of the most important consequences of Dewey's ethics for his socio-political philosophy. Dewey's view of moral life provides the rich and complex background against which we must understand his hopes for democracy. Objections raised against Dewey's view of democracy are likely to be misguided if they fail to consider his view of moral life. If we want to defend Dewey today as a democratic liberal who dares to stand on some moral commitments and away from an exclusive or myopic focus on democracy as a formal procedure and electoral politics, we must consult his ethics. Dewey's ethics is also a resource to counter the contemporary stereotype of pragmatism as a philosophy without a sufficiently thick normative backbone. He never doubted that the criticism of pragmatism in ethics and politics presupposed some substantial normative moral commitments. We find in Dewey's ethics the particular virtues, relationships, and experiences that make his view of democracy substantive. Democracy was, for Dewey, part of a general moral outlook about how to engage in life and not just a mode of public deliberation.

Dewey does not provide answers, specific instructions, or a sure-fire method to resolve moral disagreement or foster democracy. Instead, he thought it was more appropriate for philosophy to prescribe in very general terms where to look and how to look for guidance. Where we look, according to Dewey, is toward the resources in those same situations that require amelioration. Among these possible resources are principles, habits, and the qualitative. Instead of prescribing what to do, philosophy should be concerned with issues that are admittedly more general and perhaps vague in comparison: how to best prepare ourselves for moral problems; how to engage ourselves and inquire in situations; how to interact with others and deal with disagreement; and how to test the reforms that are made, presumably for the sake of democracy.

Dewey focused on how to proceed because of his contextualism and because he was concerned to criticize how many individuals and communities deal with moral and social problems. For him, the non-democratic ways in which we ordinarily handle problems and interact with others only encourage non-democratic habits and a non-democratic way of life, no matter how democratic our political machinery might be. For instance, individuals or organizations are working against democracy when they make decisions and solve problems in the top-down fashion of imposing rigid rules, without listening to those closest to the relevant situation, or when they rely on a standardized approach to all problems, places, and people. The democratic task requires us to be critical of market pressure to make a profit and of new technologies if they deprive people of the autonomy and time to exercise judgment and nurture their personal relationships.

For Dewey, if we really care about democracy, then activities and environments that encourage habits that work against democracy must be criticized at all levels and in all relationships, for example, in families and in the everyday workings of a corporation. Democratic reform must be inclusive, and it is particularly important that it emerges from within the relationships that are most local, personal, spontaneous, voluntary, and direct.

Dewey's criticisms of the ordinary, but unintended, ways in which we sometimes work against democracy are a counterpart to his more positive inquiry about the optimal types of engagement and communication needed in a democracy. But even his most positive proposals were always tempered with an awareness of our limitations. Democracy cannot be exported or imposed. Neither is it something that automatically emerges by merely removing what oppresses the people, whether that is a state or the forces of propaganda. It is not under our direct control to create a more intelligent, aesthetic, and democratic way of life. Democracy and virtue cannot be taught, but we can provide the conditions for their emergence. We can only prepare the soil, and reconstruction must come from within everyday interactions. Continuous inquiry about indirect means and present conditions is the key to finding the way we can democratize experience.

In the end, what Dewey is proposing is a program for more work, a never-ending task that requires of those who have not lost their faith in democracy a commitment that is balanced with criticism, and infused with a humility that comes from the awareness of how tension-filled and precarious is that which we seek. Of all the problems of democracy, the one that strikes me as most urgent today is simply that democracy is not experienced as a task or problem. This happens when it is taken for granted, or worse, when many people have no ideal or sense of how things could be better. Without awareness that there is a crisis of democracy, there is not the felt, problematic situation that can lead to inquiry about how to ameliorate present conditions.

Finally, I have claimed that one also finds in Dewey's ethics the philosophical resources to provide an alternative justification of democracy that, while not foundational, is not problematic. What, for Dewey, is the ultimate court of appeal in ethical matters and the grounds for the pragmatist's commitment to democracy? There is no absolute authority, nor is there an Archimedean standpoint that we can take. Instead, Dewey's ultimate grounding is a historical and contextual one that he does not think is arbitrary. Dewey shares with Richard Rorty his criticism of the quest for some transcendental non-human authority, but Dewey's appeal to context is not a bald appeal to us humans, that is, our communication, consensus, tradition, discourse, or beliefs. Instead, Dewey appeals to a faith in our transactions within nature, that is, within a situation that can guide our plans, purposes, and judgments. We can look outside of the human community, discourse, or consensus for guidance and test our hypotheses without presupposing any problematic dualism. Rorty, however, continues to claim that "as Dewey saw it, whole-hearted pursuit of the democratic ideal requires us to set aside any authority save that of consensus of our fellow humans."[4]

What I provided in the last chapter was neither an ahistorical objective justification of democracy, nor the only plausible one. Instead, I presented philosophical reasons why Dewey thought the commitment to democracy was reasonable and worth trying. These reasons to commit to democracy will not convince the imaginary radical skeptic who is presupposed throughout much of philosophy. These are reasons, however, that have a chance of winning the consent of people who are already committed to certain vague and sometimes conflicting democratic values that they have inherited. They are reasons that should be of interest to people who want to ameliorate the same sort of concrete problems that troubled Dewey.

To convince someone that, through a process of democratization, our life *can* become more aesthetic and intelligent, or that we *can* both secure freedom and organization, stability and openness, or that order and stability *can* be preserved in a way of life that is also open, free, and flexible, requires more than argumentation in today's complex conditions. Philosophy cannot convert people into having a faith in democracy, but it can, through criticism, remove prejudices and obstacles that are sources of skepticism regarding the ideal. In his ethics, Dewey criticizes unquestioned assumptions about moral life that keep many from entertaining the possibility that he envisioned. For instance, what Dewey proposed seems today impossible if one assumes that only universal and absolute rules can provide order, stability, and direction to moral life. When only absolute authority will do, Dewey's appeals to virtues and to the guidance of the unique qualitative context seem like an invitation to licentiousness and moral anarchy. It is difficult to encourage someone to have a positive trust in the possibilities and instrumentalities available in a situation when they are looking outside experience for guidance, or when they assume that independent of human desire, the objective world is devoid of meaning, guidance, and values. Dewey hoped that the abandonment of traditional assumptions about moral experience would lead to more faith in the potentialities of humans within nature.

Democracy is, in the end, an experiment. With regard to democracy, what we believe and defend philosophically must be tested in the classroom, in the workplace, and everywhere there is human interaction. If I have been successful, then my elicitation and articulation of Dewey's ethics now makes his democratic ideal more amenable to testing, to further criticism, and makes it available to be used as a tool in the criticism of present practices and institutions.

NOTES

INTRODUCTION

1. Compared to this book, the three previous books devoted to Dewey's ethics, while important, are more circumspect in scope and focus. The first, James Gouinlock's *John Dewey's Philosophy of Value* (New York, N.Y.: Humanities Press, 1972), articulates Dewey's theory of value in light of his views on experience and nature. The second, Jennifer Welchman's *Dewey's Ethical Thought* (Ithaca, N.Y.: Cornell University Press, 1995), focuses on the evolution of Dewey's early ethical thought. And the third, Steven Fesmire's *John Dewey and the Moral Imagination: Pragmatism in Ethics* (Bloomington: Indiana University Press, 2003), explores Dewey's views on moral deliberation and imagination from a contemporary perspective.

2. The most common mistake is to attribute to Dewey some form of consequentialism or teleology. I argue against this interpretation throughout this book. But there have been recent efforts to classify Dewey as a virtue ethicist. See, e.g., John Teehan, "Character, Integrity and Dewey's Virtue Ethics," *Transactions of the Charles S. Peirce Society* 31, no. 4 (1995):841–63.

3. G. E. M. Anscombe, "Modern Moral Philosophy," in *Virtue Ethics*, ed. Roger Crisp and Michael Slote (New York, N.Y.: Oxford University Press, 2002), 26. Anscombe's article was originally published in *Philosophy* 33 (1958):1–19.

4. See "The Need for a Recovery of Philosophy" (MW 10:3).

5. Mark Johnson, "Cognitive Science," in *A Companion to Pragmatism*, ed. John R. Shook and Joseph Margolis (Malden, Mass.: Blackwell, 2006), 374.

6. In his first writings on morality in 1887 Dewey was an absolute idealist, but by 1908 there is almost no residuum in his ethics of his early idealism.

7. For the history of the changes in Dewey's earlier work, see the contributions of Darnell Rucker and Herbert W. Schneider in *Guide to the Works of John Dewey*, ed. Jo Ann Boydston (Carbondale, Ill.: Southern Illinois University Press, 1970), 99–130. For the changes from Dewey's early to middle period (1908), see Jennifer Welchman, *Dewey's Ethical Thought*. For the changes from Dewey's 1908 *Ethics* to his revised 1932 edition, see Abraham Edel and Elizabeth Flower's introduction to the 1932 *Ethics* (LW 7) and Abraham Edel's recent book, *Ethical Theory and Social Change: The Evolution of John Dewey's Ethics, 1908–1932* (New Brunswick, N.J.: Transaction, 2001).

8. In *Ethical Theory and Social Change,* Abraham Edel correctly argues that the most significant change between the two editions of Dewey's *Ethics* is from asserting the primacy of the good as a moral category to recognizing three independent factors in morals. Edel's main concern is the historical and biographical events that may have contributed to this shift in Dewey's thought. He also considers how changes in Dewey's theory of the self may have contributed to this. His account is perfectly compatible with mine. In this book, however, I am not concerned with the reasons why Dewey acquired a better phenomenological sensitivity to moral experience.

9. I agree with Douglas Browning that there is a shift of emphasis in Dewey's mature thought around the 1930s. His writings at this time reveal "a refreshed and more careful appreciation of the enormous complexity and subtlety of an individual's experience." Douglas Browning, letter to Larry Hickman, Director, Center for Dewey Studies, Southern Illinois University, Carbondale, August 4, 2000.

10. Dewey's early ethical writings are more psychological or self-oriented in the sense that ethical concepts are generally interpreted in terms of inner, individual processes and tensions. In Dewey's mature ethical philosophy there is more of a direct focus on a situation as the field of moral experience constituted by transactions. The moral agent is conceived of as a participant or in a network of relations in situations. The function of intelligence in moral experience is defined in terms of habits and the reconstruction of particular situations. Moral situations are characterized as requiring choice among irreconcilable demands.

11. Joseph Margolis, *Moral Philosophy after 9/11* (University Park: Pennsylvania State University Press, 2004), vii.

12. Ibid., xvi.

13. Richard Posner, *Law, Pragmatism, and Democracy* (Cambridge, Mass.: Harvard University Press, 2003), 50.

14. Jeffrey Stout, *Ethics after Babel: The Languages of Morals and Their Discontents* (Boston, Mass.: Beacon, 1988), 243–44.

15. Lee Siegel, "Cold Verities: The Chilly Ethics of American Pragmatism,"

review of *The Metaphysical Club,* by Louis Menand, *Harper's Magazine,* October 2001, 84.

16. Ibid., 88.

17. Cornel West, *Democracy Matters: Winning the Fight Against Imperialism* (New York, N.Y.: Penguin, 2004), 15.

18. Robert Westbrook, *John Dewey and American Democracy* (Ithaca, N.Y.: Cornell University Press, 1991), xvi.

19. Consequentialism is any view in ethics that bases its moral evaluations of acts solely on good consequences. Teleological ethics is a broader category that holds some ultimate end or aim as the ultimate basis of its ethical recommendations. Many secondary sources have assumed that Dewey's ethics is centered on some good conceived either as self-realization, human fulfillment, or growth. Here is some evidence:

1) Michael Slote, in "Teleological Ethics," his contribution to the *Encyclopedia of Ethics,* ed. Lawrence C. Becker (New York, N.Y.: Garland, 1992), says, "and still other forms of teleology, notably the socio-cultural self-realizationism to be found in . . . Dewey" (1238).

2) According to James Campbell, in *Understanding John Dewey* (Chicago, Ill.: Open Court Publishing, 1995), John Dewey offers "a broad consequentialism, evaluating actions by their effects 'upon the common welfare, the general well-being' [LW 7:344] and defending . . . growth as the criterion for evaluating the effects" (112).

3) Matthew Festenstein argues in *Pragmatism and Political Theory: From Dewey to Rorty* (Chicago: University of Chicago Press, 1997) that Dewey's ethics is "intended to show how the demands of morality are rooted in a certain conception of human well-being" (47).

4) Hilary Putnam, in *Renewing Philosophy* (Cambridge, Mass.: Harvard University Press, 1992), makes reference to "Dewey's consequentialism" (190).

5) In "Between Proceduralism and Teleology: An Unresolved Conflict in Dewey's Moral Theory," *Transactions of the Charles S. Peirce Society* 34, no. 3 (1998):689–711, Axel Honneth argues that Dewey's remarks about growth assume an ultimate notion of human good, that is, a "naturalistic teleology . . . incompatible with the intentions of his proceduralism" (704).

6) Andrew Altman claims, in "John Dewey and Contemporary Normative Ethics," *Metaphilosophy* 13, no. 2 (1982):149–60, that "among normative theories that are popular today, rule-utilitarianism is one of the closest to Dewey's own view" (153).

7) J. E. Tiles claims, in *Dewey* (London: Routledge, 1990), that Dewey's ethics belongs to the type of ethical theory "based upon a conception of what it is for human beings to live well and flourish in a distinctively human fashion" (212).

8) Jennifer Welchman, in *Dewey's Ethical Thought,* argues that in moral situations options for Dewey are "evaluated in terms of their potential to serve as constituents of a good life and character" (189).

9) Richard Rorty, in "Pragmatism as Anti-authoritarianism," in *A Companion To Pragmatism*, claims that "Dewey, like James, was a utilitarian" (258).

20. Hilary Putnam, *Ethics without Ontology* (Cambridge, Mass.: Harvard University Press, 2004), 10.

21. Mark Malloch Brown, quoted in Barbara Crossette, "U.N. Report Says New Democracies Falter," *New York Times*, July 24, 2002, Foreign Desk.

22. Steven Erlanger, "Why Democracy Defies the Urge to Implant It," *New York Times*, February 15, 2004, Week in Review Desk.

23. Thomas Alexander, "The Aesthetics of Reality: The Development of Dewey's Ecological Theory of Experience," in *Dewey's Logical Theory*, ed. Thomas Burke, Micah Hester, and Robert B. Talisse (Nashville, Tenn.: Vanderbilt University Press, 2002), 3.

24. For a criticism of neopragmatism from the same standpoint taken in this book, see David Hildebrand's *Beyond Realism and Antirealism* (Nashville, Tenn.: Vanderbilt University Press, 2003).

25. See the introduction to *A Companion to Pragmatism* by Joseph Margolis for a recent account of this historical interpretation of pragmatism. In my view the history of pragmatism is the history of adopting a new starting point in light of a criticism of the theoretical starting point. Charles Peirce called it "Cartesianism" because he saw it in Descartes. James detected the theoretical starting point in traditional empiricism and therefore called for a more "radical" empiricism. But once you get to Dewey, the failure to come to terms with the proper "practical" starting point is so common in philosophy that he decided to call it "the philosophical fallacy."

26. Douglas Browning, "Understanding Dewey: Starting at the Starting Point" (paper presented at the XIV Congreso Interamericano de Filosofía, Puebla, Mexico, August 19, 1999), 1.

27. See Michael Eldridge, *Transforming Experience* (Nashville, Tenn.: Vanderbilt University Press, 1998); Larry A. Hickman, *John Dewey's Pragmatic Technology* (Bloomington: Indiana University Press, 1990); Westbrook, *John Dewey and American Democracy*; and Thomas Alexander, *John Dewey's Theory of Art, Experience, and Nature* (Albany: State University of New York Press, 1987).

28. John Dewey, quoted in Max Eastman, "John Dewey," *Atlantic Monthly*, December 1941, 673.

29. Westbrook, John *Dewey and American Democracy*, p. 8.

30. This is something that Dewey himself came to stress more in his later years, and his writings from the 1930s stress this. This aspect of Dewey deserves to be stressed because it represents his own most radical shift from the canons of Western thought.

1. EXPERIENCE AS METHOD

1. See Ralph W. Sleeper, "Dewey's Metaphysical Perspective: A Note on White, Geiger, and the Problem of Obligation," *Journal of Philosophy* 57, no. 3 (1960):100–15; James Gouinlock, "Dewey's Theory of Moral Deliberation," *Ethics*

88, no. 3 (1978):218–28; and Robert L. Holmes, "The Development of John Dewey's Ethical Thought," *The Monist* 48 (1964):392–406.

2. See, e.g., Hugh LaFollette, "Pragmatic Ethics," in *The Blackwell Guide to Ethical Theory,* ed. Hugh LaFollette (Oxford, U.K.: Blackwell, 2000), 400–19; and Elizabeth Anderson, "Dewey's Moral Philosophy," in *The Stanford Encyclopedia of Philosophy,* ed. Edward N. Zalta (Spring 2005 Edition), http://plato.stanford.edu/archives/spr2005/entries/dewey-moral/ (accessed September 17, 2007).

3. It is therefore perfectly understandable why in *Human Nature and Conduct* (MW 12), a book that Dewey explicitly regarded as an introduction to social psychology, there is no reference to moral qualities. From a scientific point of view, one cannot usefully talk about moral qualities; thus, Dewey refers instead to "impulses" and "instincts."

4. Jennifer Welchman, *Dewey's Ethical Thought* (Ithaca, N.Y.: Cornell University Press, 1995), 143.

5. Ibid.

6. Ibid.

7. James Campbell, *Understanding John Dewey* (Chicago, Ill.: Open Court Publishing, 1995), 110.

8. If one tracks the historical development of Dewey's philosophy, there might be support for understanding his ethics by reference to his views on science. This is what Jennifer Welchman has accomplished in *Dewey's Ethical Thought.* But even if Dewey came to adopt an empirical view of ethics after he reexamined his own views about the nature of science, this does not mean that his views on science are the key to his ethics. My intention here is not to discredit but to supplement Welchman's work, since we are concerned about different things. She is concerned with Dewey's efforts to bring science and ethics closer together ("reconcile"), but this can be distinguished from his effort to show how to proceed in an empirical philosophical inquiry about morality. I am in this book concerned with the latter and not with the former.

9. See William T. Myers's review of *John Dewey and Moral Imagination* in the *Journal of Aesthetic Education* 39, no. 2 (2005):107–14.

10. Alasdair MacIntyre, "Moral Dilemmas," *Philosophy and Phenomenological Research* 50, Suppl. (1990):371.

11. See LW 1:40.

12. Douglas Browning, "Understanding Dewey: Starting at the Starting Point" (paper presented at the XIV Congreso Interamericano de Filosofía, Puebla, Mexico, August 19, 1999), 4.

13. This is the fallacy of taking what is eventual as given, the "conversion of eventual functions into antecedent existence" (LW 1:34).

14. Dale Jamieson, "Method and Moral Theory," in *A Companion to Ethics,* ed. Peter Singer (Oxford, U.K.: Blackwell, 1993), 477.

15. See MW 5:313.

16. James Gouinlock, *Rediscovering the Moral Life: Philosophy and Human Practice* (Buffalo, N.Y.: Prometheus Books, 1993), 267–68.

17. Douglas Browning, "Comments on David Hildebrand's 'The Neopragmatist Turn,'" *Southwest Philosophy Review* 19, no. 2 (2003):69.

18. R. M. Hare, *Moral Thinking: Its Levels, Method and Point* (Oxford, U.K.: Clarendon Press, 1981), 66.

19. Browning, "Comments on David Hildebrand's 'The Neopragmatist Turn,'" 69.

20. Michael Stocker, "The Schizophrenia of Modern Ethical Theories," *Journal of Philosophy* 73, no. 14 (1976):453–66.

21. Stocker's argument is often taken to provide a reason to abandon consequentialism and deontology in favor of virtue ethics. But, as I will later argue, virtue ethics is equally vulnerable to these problems as long as the theoretical standpoint is taken as primary.

22. See J. L. Mackie, *Ethics: Inventing Right and Wrong* (London, U.K.: Penguin, 1977).

23. See Hare, *Moral Thinking*, 79.

24. Ibid., 137.

25. Among the contemporary philosophers who favor this theoretical starting point are: James Sterba, *Three Challenges to Ethics* (New York, N.Y.: Oxford University Press, 2001); Richard B. Brandt, *A Theory of the Good and the Right* (New York, N.Y.: Oxford University Press, 1979); and David Gauthier, *Morals by Agreement* (New York, N.Y.: Oxford University Press, 1986).

26. See Gilbert Harman, *The Nature of Morality* (New York, N.Y.: Oxford University Press, 1977).

27. Hare, *Moral Thinking*, 81.

28. Ibid.

29. It is an instance of the analytic fallacy and a short step toward the fallacy of unlimited universalization. Hence, what begins as an analysis of ordinary language ends up as a theory of the good or of the meaning of "morally good" by all speakers of the language.

30. W. D. Ross, *Foundations of Ethics* (Oxford, U.K.: Clarendon Press, 1939), 1.

31. Bernard Williams, *Ethics and the Limits of Philosophy* (Cambridge, Mass.: Harvard University Press, 1985), 93.

32. See, e.g., Charles R. Pigden, "Naturalism," in *A Companion to Ethics,* ed. Peter Singer (Oxford, U.K.: Blackwell, 1993), 421–31.

33. Hilary Putnam, *Ethics without Ontology* (Cambridge, Mass.: Harvard University Press, 2004), 72, my emphasis.

34. Ibid., 106.

35. These are general concepts used, for example, by Alasdair MacIntyre in his *A Short History of Ethics* (New York, N.Y.: Macmillan, 1966).

2. MORAL THEORY AND MORAL PRACTICE

1. The term 'situation ethics' was already used by Joseph Fletcher in *Situation Ethics* (Philadelphia, Pa.: Westminster Press, 1966), but it fits Dewey's view better.

2. I am here considering the issue of abortion as a moral decision and not as

a legal issue. On the legal issue, I suppose the contextualist would be in favor of the legal arrangement that would in practice allow the necessary flexibility to be contextualist about abortion. This raises some interesting questions. Does our system of jurisprudence work against the contextualist, and toward some simple, measurable standard? China has the concept of degrees of guilt and degrees of liability whereas in the United States and the United Kingdom, guilt or liability is an either/or standard.

3. For a recent formulation of contextualism in ethics, see Mark Timmons, "Moral Justification in Context," *The Monist* 76, no. 3 (1993):360–78.

4. For an excellent account of this capacity and habits from a Deweyan ethical standpoint, see Todd Lekan, *Making Morality: Pragmatist Reconstruction in Ethical Theory* (Nashville, Tenn.: Vanderbilt University Press, 2003).

5. See MW 14:169.

6. Jonathan Dancy, *Ethics without Principles* (New York, N.Y.: Oxford University Press, 2004), 7.

7. Jonathan Dancy, "The Particularist's Progress," in *Moral Particularism*, ed. Brad Hooker and Margaret Olivia Little (New York, N.Y.: Oxford University Press, 2001), 130.

8. Ibid., 131.

9. Dancy, *Ethics without Principles*, 77.

10. Ibid., 2.

11. Jonathan Dancy, "Moral Particularism," in *The Stanford Encyclopedia of Philosophy*, ed. Edward N. Zalta (Summer 2005 Edition), http://plato.stanford.edu/archives/sum2005/entries/moral-particularism/ (assessed September 17, 2007).

12. Ibid.

13. Dancy, *Ethics without Principles*, 2.

14. Brad Hooker and Margaret Olivia Little, "Introduction," in *Moral Particularism*, vii.

15. Margaret Olivia Little, "Moral Generalities Revisited," in *Moral Particularism*, 304.

16. Testing our intuitions by comparing possible cases of "torturing children for fun" leaves out much of the contextual background that may or may not make a moral difference. Our inability to imagine one of these cases with enough contextual details so as to make it seem morally permissible may well reflect our lack of imagination and not the discovery of some self-evident truth. The common approach in ethics of testing theories by appealing to our intuitions in imaginary cases has limitations that have not been sufficiently acknowledged.

17. C. I. Lewis, "Review of *The Quest for Certainty*," *Journal of Philosophy* 27, no. 1 (1930):14–25; reprinted in *Dewey and His Critics: Essays from the Journal of Philosophy*, ed. Sidney Morgenbesser (New York, N.Y.: Journal of Philosophy, Inc., 1977), 263.

18. Ibid.

19. This is the question raised by Robert Westbrook in "Pragmatism and Democracy: Reconstructing the Logic of John Dewey's Faith," in *The Revival of*

Pragmatism: New Essays on Social Thought, Law, and Culture, ed. Morris Dickstein (Durham, N.C.: Duke University Press, 1998), 133.

20. Sidney Hook regrets that Dewey did not devote enough pages to this issue. See Sidney Hook, "Introduction," in MW 9, xi–xii.

21. Hilary Putnam, *The Collapse of the Fact/Value Dichotomy and Other Essays* (Cambridge, Mass.: Harvard University Press, 2002), 104.

22. Bernard Williams, *Ethics and the Limits of Philosophy* (Cambridge, Mass.: Harvard University Press, 1985), 17.

23. Ibid., 29.

24. Susan Wolf, "The Deflation of Moral Philosophy," review of *Ethics and the Limits of Philosophy,* by Bernard Williams, *Ethics* 97, no. 4 (1987):827.

25. Williams, *Ethics and the Limits of Philosophy,* 93.

26. Williams's deflation of theories has been received with both enthusiasm and disappointment by the philosophical community. The source of disappointment is that Williams and other contemporary skeptics do not have much to say about the direction (if any) that moral theory should take. See, e.g., Samuel Scheffler, "Morality Through Thick and Thin: A Critical Notice of *Ethics and the Limits of Philosophy,* by Bernard Williams," *The Philosophical Review* 96, no. 3 (1987):411–34.

27. Williams, *Ethics and the Limits of Philosophy,* 116.

28. William James, *The Letters of William James,* ed. Henry James (Boston, Mass.: Atlanta Monthly Press, 1920), 270.

3. THE NORMATIVE STANDPOINT OF PRAGMATISM

1. I am using the terms 'living', 'momentous', and 'forced' in the same sense that William James used them in *The Will to Believe and Other Popular Essays* (Cambridge, Mass.: Harvard University Press, 1979), 14.

2. Richard Rorty, "Solidarity or Objectivity?" in his *Objectivity, Relativism, and Truth* (New York, N.Y.: Cambridge University Press, 1991), 29, 34.

3. Ibid., 29.

4. I could have instead said that Dewey had a faith in nature or that this is what makes Dewey a naturalist. For Dewey experience is continuous with and of nature, and any claim about experience is a claim about nature. For the pragmatic view of faith assumed here, see my "William James and the Logic of Faith," *Transactions of the Charles S. Peirce Society* 28, no. 4 (1992):781–808.

4. MORALITY AS EXPERIENCE

1. J. B. Schneewind, "Modern Moral Philosophy," in *A Companion to Ethics,* ed. Peter Singer (Oxford, U.K.: Blackwell, 1993), 147.

2. Todd Lekan, *Making Morality: Pragmatist Reconstruction in Ethical Theory* (Nashville, Tenn.: Vanderbilt University Press, 2003), 30.

3. For an account of who is a naturalist in ethical theory today, see Charles R. Pigden, "Naturalism," in *A Companion to Ethics,* ed. Peter Singer (Oxford, U.K.: Blackwell, 1993), 421–31.

5. THE "WHAT" OF MORAL EXPERIENCE

1. See MW 9:172–74. This is what James referred to as the double-barreled aspect of experience. Double-barreled in that "it recognizes in its primary integrity no division between act and material, subject and object, but contains them both in an unanalyzed totality" (LW 1:18).

2. For recent skepticism about whether there can be a pre-theoretical designation of moral problems, see Alasdair MacIntyre, "Moral Dilemmas," *Philosophy and Phenomenological Research* 50, Suppl. (1990):382.

3. Dewey makes this same point, though using a different example, in "The Postulate of Immediate Empiricism" (MW 3:158–67). Contrast this, for example, with R. M. Hare, who in *Moral Thinking* claims "If I am suffering, I know that I am suffering," 92.

4. This example is from Dewey's "The Postulate of Immediate Empiricism" (MW 3:158–67).

5. This pluralism is not evident in Dewey's discussions about value in general, for example, in his "Theory of Valuation" (LW 13:189–254).

6. For more on this important aspect of Dewey's thought, see Tom Burke, *Dewey's New Logic: A Reply to Russell* (Chicago: University of Chicago Press, 1994).

7. For Dewey and cognitive science, see Mark Johnson, *Moral Imagination: Implications of Cognitive Science for Ethics* (Chicago: University of Chicago Press, 1993).

8. There are some interesting questions that I cannot address here about the nature of my own or anyone else's non-moral negative valuing of homosexual acts. Do I really find homosexual acts repugnant? Or is it that I find the thought of my engaging in such acts as repugnant? Is it really repugnance or merely an aversion to my engaging in a homosexual relationship, just as homosexuals experience an aversion to a heterosexual relationship? In any case, the important point is that none of these possibilities has anything to do with immediate *moral* disvalue.

9. See Russell Freeman, *Out of Darkness: The Story of Louis Braille* (Boston, Mass.: Houghton Mifflin Company, 1999).

10. Just as with the term 'experience', Dewey wrestled with the ambiguities and associations of value as a philosophical term. See, for example, "The Meaning of Value" (LW 2:69–77). In *The Quest for Certainty* (LW 4:207) he restricted the term 'value' to what results from valuation, perhaps hoping to avoid misunderstanding of his view for subjectivism: the identification of enjoyment with value. The same thing happened with his use of 'judgment'. In some of his writings 'judgment' was a term he used only for valuation and not valuing.

11. In his *Theory of Valuation* and *Quest for Certainty,* Dewey attacks subjective/emotive and transcendental/objective views of morality and art in one stroke.

12. Dewey claims that "to grasp this aspect of empiricism is to see what the empiricist means by objectivity" (MW 3:163).

13. For a recent article defending this Deweyan naturalism and distinguishing

it from other contemporary versions, see John Teehan, "In Defense of a Natural-ism," *Journal of Speculative Philosophy* 10, no. 2 (1996):79–91.

14. Mackie, *Ethics: Inventing Right and Wrong*, 5.

15. For example, see Gilbert Harman's *Explaining Value and Other Essays in Moral Philosophy* (New York, N.Y.: Oxford University Press, 2000).

16. Sidney Hook, *The Quest for Being* (Buffalo, N.Y.: Prometheus Books, 1961), 206.

17. Joseph Margolis, *Moral Philosophy after 9/11* (University Park: Pennsyl-vania State University Press, 2004), vii.

18. Ibid., xvi.

19. See Richard Rorty, "Putnam and the Relativist Menace," *Journal of Philos-ophy* 90, no. 9 (1993):453.

20. David Hildebrand, *Beyond Realism and Antirealism* (Nashville, Tenn.: Vanderbilt University Press, 2003), 154.

6. THE "HOW" OF MORAL EXPERIENCE

1. For Dewey on custom, see MW 14:43–60.

2. John Dewey, *Lectures on Psychological and Political Ethics, 1898*, ed. Daniel Koch (New York, N.Y.: Hafner Press, 1976), 80.

3. See LW 7:235.

4. See MW 3:20.

5. Alan Gewirth, "The Implicit Teaching of Ethics," *APA Newsletter* 90 (1990):34.

7. CHARACTER AND CONDUCT

1. Some philosophers have regarded the acts-versus-character (or doing-versus-being) debate as "perhaps the liveliest debate within recent ethical theory." Robert B. Louden, *Morality and Moral Theory* (New York, N.Y.: Oxford University Press, 1992), 27. Louden thinks this debate began in 1958 with G. E. M. Anscombe's article "Modern Moral Philosophy," in *Virtue Ethics*, ed. Roger Crisp and Michael Slote (New York, N.Y.: Oxford University Press, 2002), 24–44. Anscombe's article was originally published in *Philosophy* 33 (1958):1–19.

2. William Frankena, "A Critique of Virtue-Based Ethical Systems," in *Ethi-cal Theory*, 2nd ed., ed. Louis P. Pojman (Belmont, Calif.: Wadsworth, 1995), 336.

3. John Dewey, *Lectures on Psychological and Political Ethics, 1898*, ed. Daniel Koch (New York, N.Y.: Hafner Press, 1976), 79.

4. Ibid., 80.

5. For example, Phillip Montague defines virtue ethics as the view that "treat[s] act appraisals as explicable in terms of more basic person appraisal" in his "Virtue Ethics: A Qualified Success Story," *American Philosophical Quarterly* 29, no. 1 (1992):53.

6. See Dewey, MW 14:154–55.

7. Louden, *Morality and Moral Theory*, 29. Edmund Pincoffs has a similar

argument in *Quandaries and Virtues* (Lawrence, Kans.: University Press of Kansas, 1986).

8. Bernard Mayo, "Virtue and the Moral Life," in *Ethical Theory,* ed. Pojman, 333.

9. Bernard Williams, "A Critique of Utilitarianism," in Bernard Williams and J. J. C. Smart, *Utilitarianism: For and Against* (New York, N.Y.: Cambridge University Press, 1973), 104.

10. John Dewey, *Lectures on Ethics, 1900–1901,* ed. Donald F. Koch (Carbondale: Southern Illinois University Press, 1991), 135. Dewey once said that "the only way I can tell what I am . . . is by looking at some specific situation into which I as agent enter and then define myself in terms of the part to be played in that situation." Dewey, *Lectures on Psychological and Political Ethics,* 207.

11. Dewey, *Lectures on Psychological and Political Ethics,* 205.

12. See Dewey LW 7:289.

8. PRESENT ACTIVITY AND THE MEANING OF MORAL LIFE

1. For the metaphysical importance of the present in pragmatism, see George Herbert Mead, *The Philosophy of the Present,* ed. Arthur E. Murphy (Chicago: University of Chicago Press, 1980 [1932]), 1–31.

2. William James, *The Will to Believe and Other Popular Essays* (Cambridge, Mass.: Harvard University Press, 1979), 47.

9. CONCLUSION: THE NEED FOR A
RECOVERY OF MORAL PHILOSOPHY

1. Jen Wright, "Dewey and Dreyfus on Mature Moral Agency" (paper presented at the 2005 Society for the Advancement of American Philosophy Conference, Bakersfield, California). For recent research that seems supportive of Dewey's views on judgment and deliberation, see Jonathan Haidt, "The Emotional Dog and Its Rational Tail: A Social Intuitionist Approach to Moral Judgment," *Psychological Review* 108, no. 4 (2001):814–34; Joshua Green and Jonathan Haidt, "How (and Where) Does Moral Judgment Work?" *Trends in Cognitive Science* 6, no. 12 (2002):517–23; and Francisco Varela, *Ethical Know-How: Action, Wisdom, and Cognition* (Stanford, Calif.: Stanford University Press, 1999).

2. Dewey is explicit about how his view of situations avoids these extreme views. "The theory of experiential situations which follows directly from the biological-anthropological approach is by its very nature a via media between extreme atomistic pluralism and block universe monisms" (LW 14:28–29).

10. THE INTELLIGENT, AESTHETIC, AND DEMOCRATIC WAY OF LIFE

1. John Dewey, *Lectures on Ethics, 1900–1901,* ed. Donald F. Koch (Carbondale: Southern Illinois University Press, 1991), 331.

2. Items listed in column A are about generic traits of experience that are of utmost importance from the standpoint of work and control, while those in

column B are traits of experience from the standpoint of play, immediate enjoyment, and consummation. One could also argue that A and B can be identified, respectively, with the Enlightenment and romantic modernity.

3. In his early lectures Dewey claimed that "the more subjects we took up the more we would be convinced that they show up everywhere and that they show themselves in a practical, working opposition to each other," *Lectures on Ethics, 1900–1901,* 331.

4. It is an instance of what Dewey called the "fallacy of selective emphasis." For Dewey the above oppositions do not place us in an ontological either/or dilemma; rather, opposing generic traits of experience are all equally real.

5. Dewey, *Lectures on Ethics, 1900–1901,* 329, my emphasis.

6. Ibid.

7. Ibid.

8. The extent to which Dewey's notion of balance is similar to Aristotle's notion of the mean depends on one's interpretation of Aristotle. There are recent neo-Aristotelian views that, insofar as they entertain a particular and context-relative notion of a mean and the interdependence of the virtues, are similar to Dewey's view. See, e.g., Martha Nussbaum, *Poetic Justice* (Boston, Mass.: Beacon, 1995); and Barry Schwartz and Kenneth E. Sharpe, "Practical Wisdom: Aristotle Meets Positive Psychology," *Journal of Happiness Studies* 7, no. 3 (2006):377–95. Differences between Dewey and these neo-Aristotelians may be worth further inquiry.

9. Dewey can hold that the biological is the "roots of the esthetic in experience" (LW 10:20) without committing himself to a reduction of one to the other because of the "postulate of continuity" and "emergence." Dewey shared these postulates with George Herbert Mead; see LW 12:30.

10. Dewey, *Lectures on Ethics, 1900–1901,* 342.

11. Alan Ryan, *John Dewey and the High Tide of American Liberalism* (New York, N.Y.: W. W. Norton, 1995), 329.

11. THE IDEAL MORAL SELF

1. For more criticism of epistemology from a Deweyan perspective, see my "Open-mindedness and Courage: Complementary Virtues of Pragmatism," *Transactions of the Charles S. Peirce Society* 32, no. 2 (1996):316–35.

2. See MW 9:366 and LW 8:136.

3. In the 1908 *Ethics* (MW 5:376) Dewey takes conscientiousness as a more inclusive virtue that includes sensitivity and thoughtfulness. There is no inconsistency between this and the classification that I have adopted from his 1932 *Ethics* (LW 7), for all genuine and actual conscientiousness includes sensitivity.

4. For Dewey's notion of responsibility, see LW 7:31–33, 44–46.

5. Usually sympathy means a shared compassion or agreement. See Diana T. Meyers, "Moral Reflection: Beyond Impartial Reason," *Hypatia* 8, no. 3 (1993):21–47; and Nel Noddings, *Caring: A Feminine Approach to Ethics and Moral Education* (Berkeley, Calif.: University of California Press, 1984).

6. George Herbert Mead, *Mind, Self and Society: From the Standpoint of a*

Social Behaviorist, ed. Charles W. Morris (Chicago: University of Chicago Press, 1934), 299. The importance and influence of Mead on Dewey's ethical thought has been largely underappreciated.

7. See my "Dewey and Feminism: The Affective and Relationships in Dewey's Ethics," *Hypatia* 8, no. 2 (1993):78–95.

8. James Hayden Tufts, "The Moral Life and the Construction of Values and Standards," in his *Creative Intelligence: Essays in the Pragmatic Attitude* (New York, N.Y.: Henry Holt and Company, 1917), 389.

9. Ibid., 395.

10. See LW 17:338.

11. In fact, he provides an ethics that can be of value to the feminist postmodern transformation of ethics; on this, see my "Dewey and Feminism." In 1930 Dewey pointed out that present moral notions "are almost exclusively male constructions" and predicted that "the growing freedom of women can hardly have any other outcome than the production of more realistic and more humane morals" (LW 5:276).

12. This same view of character is already implicit in William James's 1881 public lecture "Reflex, Action and Theism," in his *The Will to Believe and Other Popular Essays* (Cambridge, Mass.: Harvard University Press, 1979), 90–113.

13. Love is the "higher power of interest" (EW 3:305).

14. See EW 5:126 where he first makes this distinction.

15. The exceptions to this are contemporary feminists in ethics. On this, see Virginia Held, "Feminist Transformations of Moral Theory," *Philosophy and Phenomenological Research* 50, Suppl. (1990):321–44.

16. John Dewey, *Lectures on Psychological and Political Ethics, 1898,* ed. Daniel Koch (New York, N.Y.: Hafner Press, 1976), 214.

17. Ibid.

18. Ibid., 213.

19. Ibid.

12. DEMOCRACY AS THE IDEAL MORAL COMMUNITY

1. Remarks made in 1929 by Dewey at the celebration of his 70th birthday. See George Dykhuizen, *The Life and Mind of John Dewey* (Carbondale: Southern Illinois University Press, 1973), 233.

2. For the historical origin of the distinction between negative and positive freedom, see Robert Westbrook, *John Dewey and American Democracy* (Ithaca, N.Y.: Cornell University Press, 1991), 37–45.

3. Ronald K. L. Collins and David M. Skover, *The Death of Discourse* (Boulder, Colo.: Westview, 1996), 6.

4. Cornel West, *Democracy Matters: Winning the Fight Against Imperialism* (New York, N.Y.: Penguin, 2004), 7.

5. John Katz, "A Birth of a Digital Nation," *Wired Magazine,* April 1997 (my emphasis), http://www.wired.com/wired/archive/5.04/netizen_pr.html (accessed September 17, 2007).

6. William James, "On a Certain Blindness of Human Beings," in his *Talks to Teachers on Psychology: And to Students on Some of Life's Ideals* (New York, N.Y.: Henry Holt and Company, 1899), 264.

7. See Andrew Light and Eric Katz, eds., *Environmental Pragmatism* (New York, N.Y.: Routledge, 1996).

8. James Gouinlock, *Rediscovering the Moral Life: Philosophy and Human Practice* (Buffalo, N.Y.: Prometheus Books, 1993), 55–56.

9. Seymour Martin Lipset and Gabriel Salman Lenz, "Corruption, Culture, and Markets," in *Culture Matters: How Values Shape Human Progress,* ed. Lawrence E. Harrison and Samuel P. Huntington (New York, N.Y.: Basic Books, 2000), 112–25.

10. Joseph H. Kupfer, *Experience as Art* (Albany: State University of New York Press, 1983), 30.

11. See, e.g., James Campbell's descriptions of democracy in terms of "cooperative intelligence" in his *Understanding John Dewey* (Chicago: Open Court Publishing, 1995), 200–12.

12. For a wonderful explanation of this difference, see chapters 3 and 4 of Kupfer, *Experience as Art.*

13. George Herbert Mead, *Mind, Self and Society: From the Standpoint of a Social Behaviorist,* ed. Charles W. Morris (Chicago: University of Chicago Press, 1934), 325.

14. See my "Dewey's Philosophical Approach to Racial Prejudice," *Social Theory and Practice* 22, no. 1 (1996):47–66.

15. For a pragmatist interpretation of rights, see Beth Singer's *Pragmatism, Rights, and Democracy* (New York, N.Y.: Fordham University Press, 1999).

16. This is clear in *How We Think* (LW 8) where Dewey describes inquiry in terms of the habits that are operative in this process.

17. For more on this contemporary debate, see Daniel M. Savage's *John Dewey's Liberalism: Individual, Community, and Self-Development* (Carbondale: Southern Illinois University Press, 2002).

18. This is a concept that was very important to Martin Luther King, Jr. In his famous "Letter from Birmingham Jail," he wrote, "I must confess that I am not afraid of 'tension.' I have earnestly opposed violent tension, but there is a type of constructive, nonviolent tension which is necessary for growth." Martin Luther King, Jr., "Letter from Birmingham Jail," in his *Why We Can't Wait* (New York, N.Y.: Signet Classic, 2000), 64–84. See also Martin Luther King, Jr., *Where Do We Go From Here: Chaos or Community?* (Boston, Mass.: Beacon, 1967).

19. William James, *The Will to Believe and Other Popular Essays* (Cambridge, Mass.: Harvard University Press, 1979), 232.

20. John Patrick Diggins, "Pragmatism and Its Limits," in *The Revival of Pragmatism,* ed. Morris Dickstein (Durham, N.C.: Duke University Press, 1998), 207–208.

21. See the Public Agenda website at: http://publicagenda.org/. For further discussion of democracy and the problem of power relations, see Alison Kadlec

and Will Friedman, "Deliberative Democracy and the Problem of Power," *Journal of Public Deliberation* 3, no. 1 (2007):article 8, http://services.bepress.com/jpd/vol3/iss1/art8 (accessed September 17, 2007); and, for a defense of Dewey's democratic vision from radical democratic theorists who claim that extant democratic deliberation is blind to power relations and ill-prepared to combat such relations, see Alison Kadlec's *Dewey's Critical Pragmatism* (Lanham, Md.: Lexington Books, 2007).

22. Westbrook, *John Dewey and American Democracy,* 166.

23. From liner notes by Brad Mehldau in his music CD *Elegiac Cycles* (Warner Brothers, 1999).

24. John Dryzek claims that "an emphasis on deliberation is not entirely new. Antecedents can be found in . . . theorists of the early twentieth century such as John Dewey," John S. Dryzek, *Deliberative Democracy and Beyond* (New York, N.Y.: Oxford University Press, 2000), 2. Richard Posner also considers Dewey a deliberative democrat; see his *Law, Pragmatism, and Democracy* (Cambridge, Mass.: Harvard University Press, 2003), 50.

25. See Iris Marion Young, "Communication and the Other: Beyond Deliberative Democracy," in *Democracy and Difference: Contesting the Boundaries of the Political,* ed. Seyla Benhabib (Princeton, N.J.: Princeton University Press, 1996), 120–36.

26. Frank Cunningham, *Theories of Democracy: A Critical Introduction* (New York, N.Y.: Routledge, 2001), 180.

27. This is at least one most common understanding of Habermas. See Cunningham, *Theories of Democracy,* 176.

28. Robert B. Talisse, *Democracy after Liberalism: Pragmatism and Deliberative Politics* (New York, N.Y.: Routledge, 2005), 314.

29. Hilary Putnam, "A Reconsideration of Deweyan Democracy," in *Pragmatism in Law and Society,* ed. Michael Brint (Boulder, Colo.: Westview, 1991); and Cheryl Misak, *Truth, Politics, and Morality: Pragmatism and Deliberation* (New York, N.Y.: Routledge, 2000).

30. Tallisse, *Democracy after Liberalism,* 62.

31. Jorge Valadez, *Deliberative Democracy, Political Legitimacy, and Self-Determination in Multicultural Societies* (Boulder, Colo.: Westview, 2001), 89.

32. According to Andrew G. Fiala, Dewey, Rawls, and other pragmatists share the same view about tolerance: "Toleration is a pragmatic response to the practical need to coexist with others who have different conceptions of the good." Andrew G. Fiala, "Toleration and Pragmatism," *Journal of Speculative Philosophy* 16, no. 2 (2002):103. Needless to say, I disagree with Fiala.

33. For Rorty's view on Sandel, see his "A Defense of Minimalist Liberalism," in *Debating Democracy's Discontent: Essays on American Politics, Law, and Public Philosophy,* ed. Anita L. Allen and Milton Regan (New York, N.Y.: Oxford University Press, 1999), 117–25. Chantal Mouffe criticizes liberals, like Rorty, for not being pluralistic enough in her "Democracy, Power and the 'Political,'" in *Democracy and Difference,* ed. Benhabib, 245–56.

13. A PHILOSOPHICAL JUSTIFICATION OF DEMOCRACY

1. Richard Rorty, "Solidarity or Objectivity?" in *Post-Analytic Philosophy*, ed. John Rajchman and Cornel West (New York, N.Y.: Columbia University Press, 1985), 12.

2. Ibid., 16.

3. David Fott, *John Dewey: America's Philosopher of Democracy* (Lanham, Md.: Rowman & Littlefield, 1998), 82.

4. Ibid.

5. Matthew Festenstein, for example, argues in his *Pragmatism and Political Theory: From Dewey to Rorty* (Chicago: University of Chicago Press, 1997) that Dewey offers a plausible, but incomplete, philosophical justification for his normative ethical and political theory.

6. This is a quote from Justice Oliver Wendell Holmes, Jr., that Dewey uses in LW 1:313.

7. Doug Browning, "Remarks on Rorty's criticism of Dewey's Metaphysics" (unpublished paper, May 1990).

8. Rogene A. Buchholz and Sandra B. Rosenthal, *Business Ethics: The Pragmatic Path Beyond Principles to Process* (Upper Saddle River, N.J.: Prentice Hall, 1997), 63.

9. For more about comparing Dewey with Habermas's discourse ethics, see Matthew Festenstein, *Pragmatism and Political Theory*, 146–61; and Scott R. Bartlett, "Discursive Democracy and a Democratic Way of Life," in *Perspectives on Habermas*, ed. Lewis Edwin Hahn (Chicago, Ill.: Open Court Publishing, 2000), 367–86.

10. Recall that, for Dewey, nature (i.e., reality) is not something apart, outside, or behind experience.

11. Giovanni Sartori, *The Theory of Democracy Revisited* (Chatham, N.J.: Chatham House, 1987), 69.

12. Michael Eldridge, *Transforming Experience* (Nashville, Tenn.: Vanderbilt University Press, 1998), 83. Eldridge traces the history of this objection to Dewey (see pp. 70–84). Eldridge defends Dewey against Walter Lippmann, John Herman Randall, Jr., and Robert Westbrook by providing some Deweyan guidelines that could be part of a "Deweyan manual to political action" (113). My defense of Dewey consists, instead, in raising doubts about what is assumed by the objection.

13. This way of expressing the objection is Alan Ryan's. See Alan Ryan, "Pragmatism Rides Again," review of *The Promise of Pragmatism*, by John P. Diggins, *The New York Review of Books*, February 16, 1995, 33.

14. For more on the Dewey-Lippmann debate, see Robert Westbrook, *John Dewey and American Democracy* (Ithaca, N.Y.: Cornell University Press, 1991), 293–300.

15. For a recent book on this issue from a pragmatic standpoint, see Erin McKenna, *The Task of Utopia* (Lanham, Md.: Rowman & Littlefield, 2002).

16. William James, "What Makes a Life Significant," in his *Talks to Teachers on*

Psychology: And to Students on Some of Life's Ideals (New York, N.Y.: Henry Holt and Company, 1899), 270.

17. Reinhold Niebuhr was the most persistent critic of Dewey on the issue of naïveté. For the history of this criticism of Dewey, see Westbrook, *John Dewey and American Democracy,* 523–36; and Eldridge, *Transforming Experience,* 52–62.

18. Eldridge, *Transforming Experience,* 54.

19. For instance, in *The Public and its Problems,* Dewey says, "As long as interests of pecuniary profit are powerful, and a public has not located and identified itself, those who have this interest will have an unresisted motive for tampering with the spring of political action in all that affects them" (LW 2:348).

20. He was aware of "the influence of private interests in procuring suppression, secrecy and misrepresentation," and of "the triviality and 'sensational' quality of so much of what passes as news" (LW 2:347).

21. John Patrick Diggins, "Pragmatism and Its Limits," in *The Revival of Pragmatism: New Essays on Social Thought, Law, and Culture,* ed. Morris Dickstein (Durham, N.C.: Duke University Press, 1998), 213.

22. Ibid., 212.

23. Richard J. Bernstein, "Community in the Pragmatic Tradition," in *The Revival of Pragmatism,* ed. Dickstein, 149.

24. See Raymond D. Boisvert, "The Nemesis of Necessity: Tragedy's Challenge to Deweyan Pragmatism," in *Dewey Reconfigured: Essays on Deweyan Pragmatism,* ed. Casey Haskins and David I. Seiple (Albany: State University of New York Press, 1999), 151–68; James T. Kloppenberg, "Pragmatism: An Old Name for Some New Ways of Thinking?" in *The Revival of Pragmatism,* ed. Dickstein, 83–127; Westbrook, *John Dewey and American Democracy,* 163, 416–17; and Hilary Putnam, "Reconsideration of Deweyan Democracy," in *Renewing Philosophy* (Cambridge, Mass.: Harvard University Press, 1992), 190–99.

25. Kloppenberg, "Pragmatism: An Old Name for Some New Ways of Thinking?" 114.

26. Michael Sandel, "The Case Against Perfection," *Atlantic Monthly,* April 2004, 54.

27. Ibid., 51.

28. See LW 10:54.

29. John Dewey, quoted in Max Eastman, "John Dewey," *Atlantic Monthly,* December 1941, 673.

30. As Michael Eldridge has argued in *Transforming Experience,* there is more to inquiry than having a rational discussion; see pp. 24–42.

31. George Herbert Mead, *Selected Writings,* ed. Andrew J. Reck (Chicago: University of Chicago Press, 1964), 5.

32. Sidney Hook, "Introduction," in MW 9, xi–xii.

33. Ibid.

34. Robert Westbrook, "Pragmatism and Democracy: Reconstructing the Logic of John Dewey's Faith," in *The Revival of Pragmatism: New Essays on Social*

Thought, Law, and Culture, ed. Morris Dickstein (Durham, N.C.: Duke University Press, 1998), 133.

35. For textual support of this claim, see endnote #19 in this book's introduction.

36. This seems to be Richard Shusterman's view in his "Putnam and Cavell on the Ethics of Democracy," *Political Theory* 25, no. 2 (1997):193–214.

37. This is the view of Hilary Putnam in "A Reconsideration of Deweyan Democracy," *Renewing Philosophy,* 180–200.

38. See my "William James and the Logic of Faith," *Transactions of the Charles S. Peirce Society* 28, no. 4 (1992):781–808.

39. William James, *The Meaning of Truth* (Cambridge, Mass.: Harvard University Press, 1975), 139.

40. Eldridge, *Transforming Experience,* 145.

41. William James, *The Will to Believe and Other Popular Essays* (Cambridge, Mass.: Harvard University Press, 1979), 53.

42. Ibid., 7.

43. Dewey's metaphysics, as Westbrook correctly suggests, is a metaphysics that supports democracy; it is a "metaphysics for the common man." Westbrook, *John Dewey and American Democracy,* 361.

44. James Gouinlock argues this same point eloquently in "The Moral Value of a Philosophic Education," *Teaching Philosophy* 3, no. 1 (1979):37–50.

CONCLUSION

1. Dewey's views on moral education and his moral philosophy are closely intertwined and perhaps inseparable. Nevertheless, these are different inquiries initiated by a different problem. We must not confuse the standpoint of an educator concerned to provide the best tools or prepare others for moral life with the standpoint of a philosopher concerned with ethics as an inquiry of morality as it is experienced. Interpretations of Dewey that take his emphasis on growth and the cultivation of our characters as central to his ethics sometimes confuse these two standpoints.

2. William T. Myers, review of *John Dewey and Moral Imagination,* by Steven Fesmire, *Journal of Aesthetic Education* 39, no. 2 (2005):113.

3. I owe this way of articulating this point to Steven Fesmire.

4. Richard Rorty, "Pragmatism as Anti-authoritarianism," in *A Companion To Pragmatism,* ed. John R. Shook and Joseph Margolis (Malden, Mass.: Blackwell, 2006), 257.

BIBLIOGRAPHY

Alexander, Thomas. 1987. *John Dewey's Theory of Art, Experience, and Nature.* Albany: State University of New York Press.

——. 2002. "The Aesthetics of Reality: The Development of Dewey's Ecological Theory of Experience." In *Dewey's Logical Theory,* ed. Thomas Burke, Micah Hester, and Robert B. Talisse, 3–26. Nashville, Tenn.: Vanderbilt University Press.

Altman, Andrew. 1982. "John Dewey and Contemporary Normative Ethics." *Metaphilosophy* 13:149–160.

Anderson, Elizabeth. 2005. "Dewey's Moral Philosophy." In *The Stanford Encyclopedia of Philosophy,* ed. Edward N. Zalta. Spring 2005 Edition, http:// plato.stanford.edu/archives/spr2005/entries/dewey-moral/ (accessed September 17, 2007).

Anscombe, G. E. M. 2002. "Modern Moral Philosophy." In *Virtue Ethics,* ed. Roger Crisp and Michael Slote, 24–44. Oxford, U.K.: Oxford University Press.

Barber, Benjamin. 1984. *Strong Democracy.* Berkeley: University of California Press.

Bartlett, Scott R. 2000. "Discursive Democracy and a Democratic Way of Life." In *Perspectives on Habermas,* ed. Lewis Edwin Hahn, 367–386. Chicago: Open Court Publishing.

Bohman, James. 2000. *Public Deliberation: Pluralism, Complexity, and Democracy.* Cambridge, Mass.: MIT Press.

Boisvert, Raymond D. 1999. "The Nemesis of Necessity: Tragedy's Challenge to Deweyan Pragmatism." In *Dewey Reconfigured: Essays on Deweyan Pragmatism,* ed. Casey Haskins and David I. Seiple, 151–168. Albany: State University of New York Press.

Brandt, Richard B. 1979. *A Theory of the Good and the Right.* New York: Oxford University Press.

Browning, Douglas. 1990. "Remarks on Rorty's Criticism of Dewey's Metaphysics." Unpublished paper.

———. 1992. *Ontology and the Practical Stance.* University Park: Penn State University Press.

———. 1999. "Understanding Dewey: Starting at the Starting Point." Paper presented at the XIV Congreso Interamericano de Filosofía, Puebla, Mexico, August 19.

———. 2003. "Comments on David Hildebrand's 'The Neopragmatist Turn.'" *Southwest Philosophy Review* 19:67–69.

Buchholz, Rogene A., and Sandra B. Rosenthal. 1997. *Business Ethics: The Pragmatic Path Beyond Principles to Process.* Upper Saddle River, N.J.: Prentice Hall.

Burke, Tom. 1994. *Dewey's New Logic: A Reply to Russell.* Chicago: University of Chicago Press.

Campbell, James. 1995. *Understanding John Dewey.* Chicago: Open Court Publishing.

Collins, Ronald K. L., and David M. Skover. 1996. *The Death of Discourse.* Boulder, Colo.: Westview.

Crossette, Barbara. 2002. "U.N. Report Says New Democracies Falter." *New York Times,* July 24, 2002, Foreign Desk.

Dancy, Jonathan. 2001. "The Particularist's Progress." In *Moral Particularism,* ed. Brad Hooker and Margaret Olivia Little, 130–156. New York: Oxford University Press.

———. 2004. *Ethics without Principles.* New York: Oxford University Press.

———. 2005. "Moral Particularism." In *The Stanford Encyclopedia of Philosophy,* ed. Edward N. Zalta, http://plato.stanford.edu/archives/sum2005/entries/moral-particularism/ (accessed September 17, 2007).

Dewey, John. 1976. *Lectures on Psychological and Political Ethics, 1898.* Ed. Daniel Koch. New York: Hafner Press.

———. 1969–1972. *The Early Works of John Dewey, 1882–1898.* 5 vols. Ed. Jo Ann Boydston. Carbondale: Southern Illinois University Press.

———. 1976–1988. *The Middle Works of John Dewey, 1899–1924.* 14 vols. Ed. Jo Ann Boydston. Carbondale: Southern Illinois University Press.

———. 1981–1991. *The Later Works of John Dewey, 1925–1953.* 17 vols. Ed. Jo Ann Boydston. Carbondale: Southern Illinois University Press.

———. 1991. *Lectures on Ethics 1900–1901.* Ed. Donald F. Koch. Carbondale: Southern Illinois University Press.

Diggins, John Patrick. 1998. "Pragmatism and Its Limits." In *The Revival of Pragmatism,* ed. Morris Dickstein, 207–234. Durham, N.C.: Duke University Press.

Drysek, John S. 2000. *Deliberative Democracy and Beyond.* New York: Oxford University Press.

Dykhuizen, George. 1973. *The Life and Mind of John Dewey.* Carbondale: Southern Illinois University Press.

Eastman, Max. 1941. "John Dewey." *Atlantic Monthly,* December.

Edel, Abraham. 2001. *Ethical Theory and Social Change: The Evolution of John Dewey's Ethics, 1908–1932.* New Brunswick, N.J.: Transaction.

Eldridge, Michael. 1998. *Transforming Experience.* Nashville, Tenn.: Vanderbilt University Press.

Erlanger, Steven. 2004. "Why Democracy Defies the Urge to Implant It." *New York Times,* February 15, 2004, Week in Review Desk.

Fesmire, Steven. 2003. *John Dewey and the Moral Imagination: Pragmatism in Ethics.* Bloomington: Indiana University Press.

Festenstein, Matthew. 1997. *Pragmatism and Political Theory: From Dewey to Rorty.* Chicago: University of Chicago Press.

Fiala, Andrew G. 2002. "Toleration and Pragmatism." *Journal of Speculative Philosophy* 16:103–116.

Fletcher, Joseph. 1966. *Situation Ethics.* Philadelphia: Westminster Press.

Fott, David. 1998. *John Dewey: America's Philosopher of Democracy.* New York: Rowman & Littlefield.

Frankena, William. 1995. "A Critique of Virtue-Based Ethical Systems." In *Ethical Theory,* 2nd ed., ed. Louis P. Pojman, 334–345. Belmont, Wash.: Wadsworth.

Freeman, Russell. 1999. *Out of Darkness: The Story of Louis Braille.* Boston: Houghton Mifflin.

Gauthier, David.1986. *Morals by Agreement.* New York: Oxford University Press.

Gewirth, Alan. 1990. "The Implicit Teaching of Ethics." *APA Newsletter* 90:34–37.

Gouinlock, James. 1972. *John Dewey's Philosophy of Value.* New York: Humanities Press.

———. 1978. "Dewey's Theory of Moral Deliberation." *Ethics* 88:218–228.

———. 1979. "The Moral Value of a Philosophic Education." *Teaching Philosophy* 3:37–50.

———. 1993. *Rediscovering the Moral Life: Philosophy and Human Practice.* Buffalo, N.Y.: Prometheus Books.

Green, Joshua, and Jonathan Haidt. 2002. "How (and Where) Does Moral Judgment Work?" *Trends in Cognitive Science* 6:517–523.

Haidt, Jonathan. 2001. "The Emotional Dog and Its Rational Tail: A Social Intuitionist Approach to Moral Judgment." *Psychological Review* 108:814–834.

Hare, R. M. 1981. *Moral Thinking: Its Levels, Method and Point.* Oxford: Clarendon Press.

Harman, Gilbert. 1977. *The Nature of Morality.* New York: Oxford University Press.

———. 2000. *Explaining Value and Other Essays in Moral Philosophy.* New York: Oxford University Press.

Hickman, Larry A. 1990. *John Dewey's Pragmatic Technology.* Bloomington: Indiana University Press.

Hildebrand, David. 2003. *Beyond Realism and Antirealism.* Nashville, Tenn.: Vanderbilt University Press.

Holmes, Robert L. 1964. "The Development of John Dewey's Ethical Thought." *The Monist* 48:392–406.

Honneth, Axel. 1998. "Between Proceduralism and Teleology: An Unresolved Conflict in Dewey's Moral Theory." *Transactions of the Charles S. Peirce Society* 34:689–709.

Hooker, Brad, and Margaret Olivia Little. 2001. "Introduction." In *Moral Particularism,* ed. Brad Hooker and Margaret Olivia Little, vii–xi. New York: Oxford University Press.

Hook, Sidney. 1961. *The Quest for Being.* Buffalo, N.Y.: Prometheus Books.

James, William. 1899. *Talks to Teachers on Psychology: And to Students on Some of Life's Ideals.* New York: Henry Holt and Company.

———. 1920. *The Letters of William James.* Ed. Henry James. Boston: Atlanta Monthly Press.

———. 1975. *The Meaning of Truth.* Cambridge, Mass.: Harvard University Press.

———. 1979. *The Will to Believe and Other Popular Essays.* Cambridge, Mass.: Harvard University Press.

Jamieson, Dale. 1993. "Method and Moral Theory." In *A Companion to Ethics,* ed. Peter Singer, 476–490. Oxford: Blackwell.

Johnson, Mark. 1993. *Moral Imagination: Implications of Cognitive Science for Ethics.* Chicago: University of Chicago Press.

Kadlec, Alison. 2007. *Dewey's Critical Pragmatism.* Lanham, Md.: Lexington Books.

———, and Will Friedman. 2007. "Deliberative Democracy and the Problem of Power." *Journal of Public Deliberation* 3:article 8, http://services.bepress.com/jpd/vol3/iss1/art8 (accessed September 17, 2007).

Katz, John. 1997. "A Birth of a Digital Nation." *Wired Magazine,* April, http://www.wired.com/wired/archive/5.04/netizen_pr.html (accessed September 17, 2007).

King, Martin Luther, Jr. 1967. *Where Do We Go From Here: Chaos or Community?* Boston: Beacon.

———. 2000. "Letter from Birmingham Jail." In his *Why We Can't Wait,* 64–84. New York: Signet Classic.

Kloppenberg, James T. 1998. "Pragmatism: An Old Name for Some New Ways of Thinking?" In *The Revival of Pragmatism,* ed. Morris Dickstein, 83–127. Durham, N.C.: Duke University Press.

Kupfer, Joseph. 1983. *Experience as Art.* Albany: State University of New York Press.

LaFollette, Hugh. 2000. "Pragmatic Ethics." In *The Blackwell Guide to Ethical Theory,* ed. Hugh LaFollette, 400–419. Oxford: Blackwell.

Lekan, Todd. 2003. *Making Morality: Pragmatist Reconstruction in Ethical Theory.* Nashville, Tenn.: Vanderbilt University Press.

Lewis, Clarence I. 1930. "Review of *The Quest for Certainty.*" *Journal of Philosophy* 27:14–25. Reprinted in *Dewey and His Critics,* ed. Sidney Morgenbesser. New York: Journal of Philosophy, Inc., 1977.

Light, Andrew, and Eric Katz, eds. 1996. *Environmental Pragmatism.* New York: Routledge.

Lindsey, Brink. 2001. *Against the Dead Hand: The Uncertain Struggle for Global Capitalism.* New York: John Wiley & Sons.

Lipset, Seymour M., and Gabriel S. Lenz. 2000. "Corruption, Culture, and Markets." In *Culture Matters: How Values Shape Human Progress,* ed. Lawrence E. Harrison and Samuel P. Huntington, 112–125. New York: Basic Books.

Louden, Robert B. 1992. *Morality and Moral Theory.* New York: Oxford University Press.

MacIntyre, Alasdair. 1966. *A Short History of Ethics.* New York: Macmillan.

———. 1990. "Moral Dilemmas." *Philosophy and Phenomenological Research* 50:367–382.

Mackie, J. L. 1977. *Ethics: Inventing Right and Wrong.* London: Penguin.

Margolis, Joseph. 2004. *Moral Philosophy after 9/11.* University Park: Penn State University Press.

———. 2006. "Introduction." In *A Companion to Pragmatism,* ed. John R. Shook and Joseph Margolis, 1–10. Malden: Blackwell.

Mayo, Bernard. 1995. "Virtue and the Moral Life." In *Ethical Theory,* 2nd ed., ed. Louis P. Pojman, 331–333. Belmont, Wash.: Wadsworth.

McKenna, Erin. 2002. *The Task of Utopia.* Lanham, Md.: Rowman & Littlefield.

Mead, George Herbert. 1934. *Mind, Self and Society: From the Standpoint of a Social Behaviorist.* Ed. Charles W. Morris. Chicago: University of Chicago Press.

———. 1964. *Selected Writings.* Ed. Andrew J. Reck. Chicago: University of Chicago Press.

———. 1980. *The Philosophy of the Present.* Ed. Arthur E. Murphy. Chicago: University of Chicago Press.

Mehldau, Brad. 1999. Liner notes in his compact disc recording *Elegiac Cycles.* New York: Warner Brothers.

Meyers, Diana. 1993. "Moral Reflection: Beyond Impartiality and Reason." *Hypatia* 8:21–47.

Misak, Cheryl. 2000. *Truth, Politics, and Morality: Pragmatism and Deliberation.* New York: Routledge.

Montague, Phillip. 1992. "Virtue Ethics: A Qualified Success Story." *American Philosophical Quarterly* 29:53–61.

Mouffe, Chantal. 1996. "Democracy, Power and the 'Political.'" In *Democracy and Difference: Contesting the Boundaries of the Political,* ed. Seyla Benhabib, 245–256. Princeton, N.J.: Princeton University Press.

Myers, William T. 2005. Review of *John Dewey and Moral Imagination. Journal of Aesthetic Education* 39:107–113.

Noddings, Nel. 1984. *Caring: A Feminine Approach to Ethics and Moral Education.* Berkeley: University of California Press.

Pappas, Gregory. 1992. "William James and the Logic of Faith." *Transactions of the Charles S. Peirce Society* 28:781–808.

——. 1993. "Dewey and Feminism: The Affective and Relationships in Dewey's Ethics." *Hypatia* 8:88–95.

——. 1996. "Dewey's Philosophical Approach to Racial Prejudice." *Social Theory and Practice* 22:47–66.

——. 1996. "Open-mindedness and Courage: Complementary Virtues of Pragmatism." *Transactions of the Charles S. Peirce Society* 32:316–335.

Pigden, Charles R. "Naturalism." In *A Companion to Ethics,* ed. Peter Singer, 421–431. Oxford: Blackwell.

Pincoffs, Edmund L. 1986. *Quandaries and Virtues.* Lawrence: University Press of Kansas.

Posner, Richard. 2003. *Law, Pragmatism, and Democracy.* Cambridge, Mass.: Harvard University Press.

Putnam, Hilary. 1991."A Reconsideration of Deweyan Democracy." In *Pragmatism in Law and Society,* ed. Michael Brint, 217–246. Boulder, Colo.: Westview.

——. 1992. *Renewing Philosophy.* Cambridge, Mass.: Harvard University Press.

——. 2002. *The Collapse of the Fact/Value Dichotomy and Other Essays.* Cambridge, Mass.: Harvard University Press.

——. 2004. *Ethics without Ontology.* Cambridge, Mass.: Harvard University Press.

Rorty, Richard. 1985. "Solidarity or Objectivity?" In *Post-Analytic Philosophy,* ed. John Rajchman and Cornel West, 3–19. New York: Columbia University Press.

——. 1990. *Objectivity, Relativism, and Truth.* New York: Cambridge University Press.

——. 1993. "Putnam and the Relativist Menace." *Journal of Philosophy* 90:443–461.

——. 1999. "A Defense of Minimalist Liberalism." In *Debating Democracy's Discontent: Essays on American Politics, Law, and Public Philosophy,* ed. Anita L. Allen and Milton Regan, 117–125. New York: Oxford University Press.

——. 2006. "Pragmatism as Anti-authoritarianism." In *A Companion to Pragmatism,* ed. John R. Shook and Joseph Margolis, 257–266. Malden, Mass.: Blackwell.

Ross, W. D. 1939. *Foundations of Ethics.* Oxford: Clarendon Press.

Rucker, Darnell, and Herbert W. Schneider. 1970. "Dewey's Ethics." In *Guide to the Works of John Dewey,* ed. Jo Ann Boydston, 99–130. Carbondale: Southern Illinois University Press.

Ryan, Alan. 1995. *John Dewey and the High Tide of American Liberalism.* New York: W. W. Norton & Company.

——. 1995. "Pragmatism Rides Again." *The New York Review of Books,* February 16.

Sandel, Michael. 2004. "The Case Against Perfection." *Atlantic Monthly,* April.

Sartori, Giovanni. 1987. *The Theory of Democracy Revisited.* Chatham, N.J.: Chatham House.

Savage, Daniel M. 2002. *John Dewey's Liberalism: Individual, Community, and Self-Development*. Carbondale: Southern Illinois University Press.

Scheffler, Samuel. 1987. "Morality Through Thick and Thin: A Critical Notice of *Ethics and the Limits of Philosophy*, by Bernard Williams." *The Philosophical Review* 96:411–434.

Schneewind, J. B. "Modern Moral Philosophy." In *A Companion to Ethics*, ed. Peter Singer, 147–157. Oxford: Blackwell.

Sen, Amartya. 1999. "A Decade of Human Development." Paper presented at The First Global Forum On Human Development, United Nations, New York, July.

Shusterman, Richard. 1997. "Putnam and Cavell on the Ethics of Democracy." *Political Theory* 25:193–214.

Siegel, Lee. 2001. "Cold Verities: The Chilly Ethics of American Pragmatism." Review of *The Metaphysical Club*, by Louis Menand. *Harper's Magazine*, October.

Singer, Beth. 1999. *Pragmatism, Rights, and Democracy*. New York: Fordham University Press.

Sleeper, Ralph W. 1960. "Dewey's Metaphysical Perspective: A Note on White, Geiger, and the Problem of Obligation." *Journal of Philosophy* 57:100–115.

Slote, Michael. 1992. "Teleological Ethics." In *Encyclopedia of Ethics*, ed. Lawrence C. Becker, 1235–1238. New York: Garland.

Sterba, James. 2001. *Three Challenges to Ethics*. New York: Oxford University Press.

Stocker, Michael. 1976. "The Schizophrenia of Modern Ethical Theories." *Journal of Philosophy* 73:453–466.

Stout, Jeffrey. 1988. *Ethics after Babel: The Languages of Morals and their Discontents*. Boston: Beacon.

Talisse, Robert B. 2005. *Democracy after Liberalism*. New York: Routledge.

Teehan, John. 1995. "Character, Integrity and Dewey's Virtue Ethics." *Transactions of the Charles S. Peirce Society* 31:841–863.

———. 1996. "In Defense of a Naturalism." *Journal of Speculative Philosophy* 10:79–89.

Tiles, J. E. 1990. *Dewey*. New York: Routledge.

Timmons, Mark. 1993. "Moral Justification in Context." *The Monist* 76:360–378.

Valadez, Jorge. 2001. *Deliberative Democracy, Political Legitimacy, and Self-Determination in Multicultural Societies*. Boulder, Colo.: Westview.

Varela, Francisco. 1999. *Ethical Know-How: Action, Wisdom, and Cognition*. Stanford, Calif.: Stanford University Press.

Welchman, Jennifer. 1995. *Dewey's Ethical Thought*. Ithaca, N.Y.: Cornell University Press.

Westbrook, Robert. 1991. *John Dewey and American Democracy*. Ithaca, N.Y.: Cornell University Press.

———. 1998. "Pragmatism and Democracy: Reconstructing the Logic of John Dewey's Faith." In *The Revival of Pragmatism: New Essays on Social Thought, Law, and Culture*, ed. Morris Dickstein, 128–140. Durham, N.C.: Duke University Press.

———. 2005. *Democratic Hope: Pragmatism and the Politics of Truth.* Ithaca, N.Y.: Cornell University Press.

West, Cornel. 2004. *Democracy Matters: Winning the Fight Against Imperialism.* New York: Penguin.

Williams, Bernard. 1985. *Ethics and the Limits of Philosophy.* Cambridge, Mass.: Harvard University Press.

Williams, Bernard, and J. J. C. Smart. 1973. *Utilitarianism: For and Against.* New York: Cambridge University Press.

Wolf, Susan. 1987. "The Deflation of Moral Philosophy." Review of *Ethics and the Limits of Philosophy,* by Bernard Williams. *Ethics* 97:821–833.

Wright, Jen. 2005. "Dewey and Dreyfus on Mature Moral Agency." Paper presented at the 2005 Society for the Advancement of American Philosophy Conference, Bakersfield, California.

Young, Iris Marion. 1996. "Communication and the Other: Beyond Deliberative Democracy." In *Democracy and Difference: Contesting the Boundaries of the Political,* ed. Seyla Benhabib, 120–135. Princeton, N.J.: Princeton University Press.

INDEX

absolutism, 7, 10, 12, 48, 56–57, 77, 118, 157, 170–71, 188, 254, 285, 304

act-centered ethics, 129–41, 144, 156, 318n1:7. *See also* being; doing

Alexander, Thomas, 11, 12

alienation, 140–41

Altman, Andrew, 311n19

altruism, 35, 211–15. *See also* egoism

analysis, 26, 49, 60, 96–97, 103

analytic fallacy, 26, 314n29

anarchy, 10, 56, 70, 188, 266, 292, 302, 304, 308

Anscombe, G. E. M., 2

Archimedean standpoint, 61, 71–72, 74, 76, 117, 307. *See also* God's-eye point of view

aristocracy, 246, 272, 297

Aristotle, 4, 69, 194, 320n8

Art as Experience (Dewey), 8, 173

art, 82, 83, 86, 101, 109, 113, 118, 143–44, 167, 178–79, 211–12, 230, 234, 264, 291, 302;

and balance, 173–75, 177, 182, 238, 299; music, 241, 250; and science, 8, 12, 116

authority: divine, 38; external, 75, 166, 308

balance, 172–77, 179–84, 205, 210, 220, 247–49, 276, 305

being, 140; and doing, 129, 134–36, 196, 213

beliefs, 22, 40, 90, 120, 123, 166, 191, 268

Bernstein, Richard, 279

bottom-up theory, 266, 292. *See also* top-down theory

Braille, Louis, 109

Brown, Mark Malloch, 10

Browning, Douglas, 11, 24, 33, 34, 262, 310n9

Buddhism, 150

Campbell, James, 19, 311n19

censorship, 222, 285

certainty, 50, 76, 134, 167

change, 53, 56, 73, 117, 169, 177, 191, 220, 248; openness to, 245–46

Gregory Fernando Pappas is Associate Professor of Philosophy at Texas A&M University. He is the author of numerous articles on the philosophy of William James and John Dewey. He has been the recipient of a Ford Foundation Postdoctoral Fellowship as well as the William James and the Latin American Thought prizes by the American Philosophical Association.